THE
ITALIAN AMERICAN EXPERIENCE
IN NEW HAVEN

SUNY series in Italian/American Culture

Fred L. Gardaphe, editor

ANTHONY V. RICCIO

The Italian American Experience in New Haven

FOREWORD BY MARY ANN McDONALD CAROLAN
AFTERWORD BY PHILIP LANGDON

STATE UNIVERSITY OF NEW YORK PRESS

Published by

STATE UNIVERSITY OF NEW YORK PRESS
Albany

© 2006 State University of New York

For information, address
State University of New York Press,
194 Washington Avenue, Suite 305, Albany, NY 12210 - 2384

Production and book design, Laurie Searl
Marketing, Fran Keneston

Library of Congress Cataloging-in-Publication Data
Riccio, Anthony V.
  The Italian American experience in New Haven : images and oral histories /
Anthony V. Riccio ; foreword by Mary Ann McDonald Carolan ; afterword by
Philip Langdon.
      p.   cm. — (SUNY series in Italian/American culture)
  Includes bibliographical references and index.
  ISBN-10: 0 - 7914 - 6773 - 2 (alk. paper)
  1. Italian Americans—Connecticut—New Haven—History—20th century.
  2. Immigrants—Connecticut—New Haven—History—20th century.
  3. New Haven (Conn.)—Emigration and immigration—History—20th century.
  I. Title. II. Series.
  F104.N691875 2006
  974.6'800451—dc22   2005024369

  ISBN-13: 978 - 0 - 7914 - 6773 - 2 (alk. paper)

10 9 8 7 6 5 4 3 2 1

To the memory of

my father, Joseph Riccio,

and my sister-in-law, Julie.

CONTENTS

FOREWORD

The concept of ethnic identity is of great interest today in America, the land built by immigrants. All Americans are hyphenated. To be American means to have one foot here and one foot in another country. The story of each immigrant population resonates with us regardless of our country of origin. We all remember some portion of the stories our parents and grandparents related about the family's arrival in America and the struggle to assimilate.

The Italian American Experience in New Haven examines the lives and experiences of individual immigrants with a reverence for each life, each person's contribution to the welfare of one community. Each portrait tells a part of the story of the Italian American community in New Haven while shedding light on the experience of all Americans. Anthony Riccio's insightful essays and his subjects' compelling oral histories trace the Italian American experience from its origins in Italy beginning in the late 1800s. This volume describes, both in words and images, the physical, emotional, and spiritual sensibilities of the Italian immigrant. These stories, like the photographs that accompany them, are a fundamental part of our individual and collective experience as a nation.

Italians left their country in droves and faced the daunting and often perilous journey from poor, agricultural regions where they experienced dire economic conditions, social unrest, disillusionment with the political reforms of the Italian unification movement (*Il Risorgimento*), and an ancient and well-founded distrust of authority. The desperate masses came mostly from the illiterate lower classes of southern Italy. They had little to lose as they headed westward toward what promised to be a brighter future in America. The transatlantic crossing, for most Italians, was uncomfortable and unsanitary in steerage class, which provided little light or fresh air, rancid food, and cramped quarters. After landing in New York and successfully passing through government immigration controls, the immigrant began the American leg of the journey. The subjects in this book headed to New Haven, where their relatives and countrymen (*paesani*), as well as the promise of factory work, beckoned.

Assimilation into the American way of life was difficult for Italian immigrants. They confronted prejudices based upon the perceived "invasion" of southern

European immigrants willing to work for low wages, difficulties communicating in English, health epidemics, political injustices, and unsanitary and dangerous working conditions. These injustices were difficult to confront, for Italians harbored a deep distrust of state institutions, including schools. Most immigrants overcame these obstacles, but others found the challenges too daunting and returned to Italy, some richer and some just as poor as they were when they left. The Depression, coupled with legislation limiting the number of immigrants allowed into this country, slowed the tide of immigration in the 1930s.

Celebrations shared with community members offset the hardships faced by Italian Americans in New Haven. Feasts in honor of patron saints supported neighborhood churches and mutual aid societies while offering entertainment and food to all comers. Italian immigrants established mutual aid societies, just like the ones they knew in Italy, to provide unemployment and death benefits to members and their families facing financial hardships. These clubs, which provided social and recreational outlets for men and women, were places where news from Italy was disseminated. Italians expressed themselves through the arts as well; leading sculptors, painters, and decorative artists left their mark on America's monuments while singers such as New Haven native Giuseppina Pane delighted Italian and non-Italian audiences alike with renditions of traditional Neapolitan songs.

Food has always played a critical role in Italian American culture: certain foods are central to the celebration of traditions and holidays. Italians in New Haven continued their habit of shopping in markets devoted only to meats or produce or other specialty foods, all essential to both daily meals and "feasts" (feste) or special occasions. The table in Italian American homes revealed regional differences, as traditional recipes connected the immigrant, in a sensual manner, to his homeland. Where there was food, there was talk: the table was the locus of storytelling as well as eating. Gatherings of extended families produced their own oral histories, which were then passed down from one generation to the next. These traditions flourished, and they continue to flourish today. Family meals embody a reverence for the past and for those people, our grandparents, who mediate the past and our sense of who we are and where we have come from.

In New Haven, Italians congregated in several geographically diverse neighborhoods—the Annex, Wooster Square, the Hill, Forbes Avenue, Fair Haven, and Legion Avenue. In some of the neighborhoods, and especially in the Hill, tensions between northern and southern Italian immigrants were reminiscent of the geographical divide in Italy. Whereas some of the neighborhoods were marked by strife between the newly arrived Italian immigrants and the established residents of Anglo-Saxon, Irish, Polish, and Lithuanian origins, Legion Avenue, the first stop for many immigrants in New Haven, was truly a melting pot. Residents of diverse backgrounds—Italian, Jewish, Irish, African American, Greek, Ukrainian, Polish—lived together, worked together, and supported one another. The Oak Street Connector Project, developed to direct traffic to the center of New Haven, necessitated the razing of this ethnically diverse, yet harmonious, neighborhood. Richard Lee, Mayor of New Haven, capitalized on the city's strategic position at the intersection of Interstates 91 and 95 by proposing major highway and building projects. Wholesale urban renewal and highway expansion resulted in New Haven's designation as the "Model City" in the 1960s, as well as the destruction of many of the city's Italian American neighborhoods. Tragically, what was lost to urban renewal—the vibrant essence of life in Italian American and other ethnic neighborhoods—has not found an authoritative voice until recently. Observers of the New Haven scene have begun to focus on the inauguration of the Model City era as a time of loss as well as gain, and to tell the story of the people whose lives were so deeply affected by this sweeping reform.

Mayor Richard Lee's 1957 campaign promise to ameliorate the deplorable conditions in tenement buildings along Legion Avenue recalls a similar pledge in Italian history. Shortly after the unification of Italy, Minister of the Interior Agostino Depretis called for the demolition of the slums of Naples to address the cholera epidemic caused by overcrowded conditions. A response to Depretis's chilling assertion that "*Bisogna sventrare Napoli*" ("We must gut Naples") appeared in Matilde Serao's *Il ventre di Napoli* (*The Belly of Naples*), published in 1884. Serao argued against carving up her beloved Naples in favor of rebuilding the city, claiming that the government official did not really know the city. In this short work, Serao addressed Depretis directly, telling him that neither he nor his army of bureaucrats had any idea how much meat the Neapolitans ate, how much wine they drank, how important the weekly lottery was to their lives, how money lending was organized in the city, or how religious shrines were constructed. In effect, Serao accused the minister of attempting to eviscerate a living being whose vitality, and humanity, he failed to appreciate. Over one hundred years ago, Matilde Serao told the unofficial, personal story of a city, Naples. Now Anthony Riccio tells the story of New Haven, through the words and pictures of Italian Americans, many of whom came to this city from areas surrounding Naples at the turn of the century.

The Italian American Experience in New Haven tells personal stories, related in the subjects' own words, sometimes in their native dialect, of everyday life. When taken together, these first-person accounts and the accompanying photographs weave a tapestry of life that is far richer than any official history of the city. The neighborhoods may have been *sventrati,* or gutted, but the people's stories and images remain. By allowing his subjects to tell their stories in their own words, Anthony Riccio captures the essence of the Italian American experience in the city of New Haven over the course of the twentieth century. Instead of focusing on one authorial voice, this book proffers a multitude of voices that represents the diversity of Italian American life. Personal recollections are not usually elevated to the discourse of official history, but this volume is different. Anthony Riccio allows each of these individuals to tell the unique and universal story of the struggle to become an American, while remaining Italian, through the beautiful simplicity of the spoken word. We are invited to feast at their tables and look through their family photo albums. This volume is a uniquely warm and insightful contribution to both the scholarship on and experience of Italian Americans, and indeed of all Americans. In his previous collection of oral histories, *Portrait of an Italian American Neighborhood,* Anthony Riccio painted a portrait of Italian American life in Boston's North End before the neighborhood lost its characteristic flavor to the

Big Dig and gentrification. In *The Italian American Experience in New Haven,* he has preserved the story of an entire community of immigrants before memories of it vanish. As we read the words and see the pictures of those ordinary people, we are grateful for Anthony Riccio's important contribution to the history of the city of New Haven.

Mary Ann McDonald Carolan
Fairfield University

ACKNOWLEDGMENTS

In June 1998, I received a phone call from Neil Proto, a guy from the old neighborhood who had seen my book on the Italians of the North End of Boston. Neil was excited about the idea of creating a similar type of book in New Haven, and he gave me a substantial financial donation to get the project started, saying, "Anthony, you better hurry up before all the old Italians are gone." Ever since, Neil has been my good friend and benefactor, encouraging my efforts during the project's nine-year journey to publication. Neil spearheaded a fundraising drive with a mutual friend, Chuck Mascola, to offset the considerable production costs of this ambitious work. After Chuck and Neil's letter writing campaign, and their two generous donations, members of the New Haven community gave their support with financial contributions that made this book possible: Diane and Eugene Avino, Mary S. Brockett, Frank Carofano, Harry DeBenedet, Joe and Ida Ginnetti, Chuck and Marcella Mascola, Edward Morrone, Neil Proto, Richard Proto, Anthony and Maryanne Santacroce, William Savo, Mark and Dorothy Spatuzzi, the members of the Santa Maria Maddalena Society, and the members of the New Haven County Police Order of Centurions.

Because of the many contributions to this project by so many Italian Americans and the wonderful support of their families and friends, it is my sincere belief that this book belongs to the people of the greater New Haven Italian American community more than to me. Through their generosity and goodwill, the storytellers of New Haven welcomed me warmly into their homes, granted me access to their old letters, work documents, family album photographs, and graciously shared the gifts of their precious life stories. In their unique Italian American village idiom, these unassuming verbal artists created their own people's history. It has been an honor to record each of these stories, a deeply enriching experience to witness and preserve this history of a people who possessed great inner strength, loved life and their families, worked hard, sacrificed, and overcame.

I am indebted to the New Haven storytellers who openly shared their life experiences for this book. I owe my deepest gratitude to Nick Aiello, Mary Altieri, Joe Amarone, Pasquale Amarone, Anthony Anastasio, Pasquale Apuzzo, Pasquale Argento, Theresa Argento, Larry Baldelli, Pasquale Barone, Joseph Bergami,

Louise Bombace, Amelia Buonocore, John Calamo, Frances Calzetta, Eugene Calzetta, Frank Carrano, Rose Caprio, Mike Caprio, Carlo Catania, Emiddio Cavaliere, Silvio Cavaliere, Rose Cimmino, Aldo Clini, Gino Clini, Viola Clini, Julia Coiro, Ettore Coiro, Antonette Coppola, Concetta Criscuolo, Angelina Criscuolo, Andrea Colavolpe, Antonio Colavolpe, Tom Consiglio, Joseph Criscuolo, Rosina Ginnetti Cusick, Luisa DeLauro, Giuannine DeMaio, Frank DePonte, Alfred DiBenedetto, Josie DeBenedet, Rose Del Pizzo, Mel DiLieto, Joseph Dogolo, Rose Donaruma, John Donaruma, Rose Durso, Anthony Esposito, Attilio Fasano, Anna Fasano, Jennie Fazzone, Anthony Fiondella, Rosemarie Foglia, Terese Gabucci, Anna Gambardella, Salvatore Garibaldi, Lawrence Gherardi, Rose Gherardi, Mary Giangregorio, Al Ginnetti, John Ginnetti, Mary Ginnetti, Orlando Ginnetti, Concezio Giuletti, Dominic Giuletti, Rose Marie Guarino, Louis Guarino, Al Jones, Betty Jones, Louis Landino, Diane Landino, Bart Laurello, Josie Pane Lawrence, Ralph Marcarelli, Joseph Marchionni, Mary Marino, Anna Marino, Charlie Mascola, Clorinda "Schoolgirl" Mongillo, John Mongillo, Edward Morrone, Ron Mortali, John and Mary Nappi, Alfred Nargi, Fred Nuzzo, Rose Nuzzo, Maria Oddo, Louise Orefice, Joseph Panicali, Rene Pantani, Lucy Pastore, Mary Pesce, Eleanor Raccio, Dominic Randi, Jenny Randi, Lena Riccio, Joseph Riccio, Anna Rosati, William Rossi, Annette Ruocco, Gennaro Ruocco, Anthony Sacco, Salvatore Salemme, Antonette Salemme, Nina Pane Sanseverino, Rose Sansone, Anthony Santacroce, Mary Santacroce, Maryanne Santacroce, Bill Savo, Rose Savo, Joseph Scarpellino, Antoinette Sicignano, Joe Simone, Raffie Strianese, Nick Sorvillo, Sabatino and Giovannina Troiano, Renee Vanacore, Anthony Vanacore, Pina Vatore, Annamaria Poma-Swank, Nick Vitagliano, Marie Vitagliano, Tony Vitolo and Bill Zampa.

When word of the book project began to spread through the Italian American grapevine, people from the neighborhoods turned into photo archeologists on my behalf, sifting through family albums and public and private archives, uncovering rare, never-before-seen images of the city and slice-of-life photographs from family albums, which appear in this book. The rich collection of photographs in this book would not have been possible without the help of Jerry Acquarulo, Bobby and Millie Antonetti, Justin Appi, Peter Buonome, Mike and Laurel Caprio, William Carey of the Greater New Haven Labor History Association, Congresswoman Rosa DeLauro, Andy DePalma, Harry DeBenedet, Lisa DiBenedetto, Debbie Elkin, Karen Gilvarg of the City of New Haven, Antonia Ginnetti Arena, Chrissie Gorman, Dr. Barry Herman and Marvin Bargar of the New Haven Jewish Historical Archives, Ken Innocenzi, Patricia Klindienst, Antonette Mangler, Chuck Mascola, Frank Mentone, James Midolo, Anna Mongillo, John Mongillo Jr., Sandra Piontek, Jennie Randi, Anthony and Dottie Russo, and Mark and Dorothy Spatuzzi.

Other important contributors who arranged oral history interviews with their parents, aunts, uncles, grandparents, and elderly friends were Diane Avino, Al Carfora, Tom and Rosemary Calamo, Laurel and Mike Caprio, Robert and Bridget Carlo, Dennis Clini, Patricia Gianotti, Antonia Ginnetti Arena, Mary Hendricksen, Luke Lucchetti, Louis Matteo, Lou Nargi, Adeline Normand, Michael

Nuzzo, Robert Orefice, Andrew Proto, Mike and Kim Rogers, Louise Simeone, Joe Simone, Gino and Nancy Troiano, Maria Vitagliano, and Joe and Sandra Vitale.

I am also indebted to Frank Annunziato for his research and articles on the history of the labor movement in New Haven's needle trades. His work provided critical documentation and historical information that prevent, as he told me, "losing the details of our history." I want to thank Ed Flynn, a veteran firefighter and official historian of the New Haven fire department, who had the foresight to save original documents from the Franklin Street Fire and graciously shared them with me. I also want to thank my friend Phil Langdon, a gifted author of many books, for writing the epilogue and providing his advice at many points during the writing of this book. I want to thank my friend, Professor Mary Ann Carolan of Fairfield University, who wrote the foreword of this book and was always there to support my efforts these last nine years. I also want to thank my friend and author Professor Raeleen Mautner for generously sharing her important research on Italian discrimination. During his stays in New Haven, another good friend, Professor Francesco Sirugo of the University of Rome, helped decipher the calligraphy of the old letters presented in this book, unlocking their syntax and interpreting their meaning. My colleagues at Yale's Sterling Memorial Library—Matthew Glickman of Access Services, Natalia Sciarini and Kevin Pacelli of the Microtext Department, Michael Frost of the Manuscripts and Archives Department, Abraham Parrish of the Map Collection Department, Joseph Szaszfai of the Audio Visual Department, Susan Klein of the Preservation Department, and my sister Joanna Gorman—were all extremely helpful in countless ways during the researching and writing of this book and deserve my sincerest thanks. I would like to thank Dean Stephen Lassonde for his sincere interest in bringing this book to light and his love for all things Italian. His review of the manuscript and his expert advice added a special dimension to the book. Many thanks to Professor Douglas Rae for supporting my efforts to document this untold history of the local community. I especially want to thank James Peltz, Laurie Searl, Susan Petrie, and Fran Keneston for their monumental efforts to design and produce this book—they were all a pleasure to work with. My wife Bunny and daughter Annalisa deserve my deep appreciation for patiently enduring the many times I disappeared from sight during the past nine years to work on this book project.

During the long journey to publication, I was often asked by many of the storytellers and their families who wanted to know when the book would finally be finished. One episode stands out in my mind. Going to the novena one day, I noticed an elderly woman sitting in the congregation who I had interviewed six years earlier when she was 88 years old, in 1999. When the service ended, she waited for me in the vestibule and, amidst the crowd of exiting churchgoers, called out to me: "Hey, Anthony, when are you gonna finish that book? How much more time you think I got left over here? I'm 94 years old!" My only regret is that some of the storytellers did not live long enough to see the stories and photographs in print they so graciously contributed to this project. It is my hope that I have given their legacies the dignity they deserve.

PREFACE

This book began with a journey back to my Italian roots on a summer day in the late 1950s. My relatives—uncles, aunts, cousins and grandparents—lived on the same street in the Annex, one of New Haven's old working-class neighborhoods. It was an area of modest, well-kept homes on tree-lined streets, a place where the constant hum of the local American Steel and Wire mill could be heard in the well-tended backyard gardens of Italian immigrants. I was a young boy and I remember taking my grandmother's hand for our daily walk around the block for ice cream at Tony Stomboli's grocery store. But this day we took a different route, to Grampa Morrone's next door garden and the gently-curving footpath that divided the flower patches from the vegetable plots. We walked past rows of tall multicolored gladiolas standing at attention to our left and along neat rows of tomatoes, peppers, and eggplants on our right. We passed Grampa Morrone's little grove of prized pear and peach trees in the distance. As the path straightened I sensed Gramma's urgency, and her pace quickened. The tightened clasp of her warm hand in mine transmitted concern. We reached the end of Grampa's yard, by the green clapboard tool shed where his pet rabbit, Chee-Chee, lived among the hoes, rakes, and shovels. Skipping on a narrow, crudely-constructed wooden ramp over the ditch, we entered Mr. Gallucci's backyard and walked under his trellised, Gothic-shaped grape arbor, the large clusters of plump, fragrant black grapes shielding us from the strong sun.

Mr. Gallucci, dark-skinned from long hours under the sun tending his vegetable garden and dressed in wide green pants and Italian-style undershirt, looked up to greet my grandmother, "Buon iuorno, signora Riccio!" She nodded, waved to him, and continued straight toward the cool shaded area of Mr. Gallucci's ancient chestnut tree, down the driveway leading to Farren Avenue and Josie Mirando's house. Josie was waiting on the porch, motioning to us with open arms. The two small women exchanged pleasantries in Italian and hugged. Josie, ruddy and round-faced with short blonde hair and dressed in a well-worn plaid apron with oversized thigh pockets, led us through the house to her large kitchen, where the two sat across from each other at a white porcelain table with curving chrome legs. The noon rays of summer sunlight streaming through tall Victorian windows reflected off Josie's polished linoleum floor, bathing their wizened faces in a golden glow. Sitting at Gramma's side, I sensed a drama about to unfold.

Gramma had an uncharacteristic look of seriousness etched into her dark olive face, her coal black eyes intense. She reached inside her black dress and pulled out an envelope with odd-looking stamps. A letter had just arrived from Gramma's hometown in southern Italy, and Josie was the only person she knew who could read Italian. Solemnly, she handed it to Josie who carefully adjusted the steel-rimmed glasses resting on the tip of her nose. Time seemed to stand still. Gramma awaited her cue to begin a ritual they had performed many times before, each woman knowing her part. She paused, cleared her throat for the right pitch, and began reading. I sat stunned as Josie, who never raised her voice, suddenly turned into a polished orator, speaking a foreign tongue I could not understand. I watched Gramma lean toward Josie as she became more animated with each sentence in Italian, the news from home gaining in importance with every word. At one point, Gramma grabbed Josie's raised arm in midsentence to stop the flow of words and ask a question. Josie answered her in reassuring tones and slowly read the sentence over and over until the expression on my grandmother's face gradually changed from worry to a smile of satisfaction. Apparently, the news from home was good, though I was not certain. The reading ended, Josie calmly removed her glasses, folded them carefully, and the two smiled briefly at each other. As they concluded their "sacra conversazione," a sense of peace drifted over the kitchen in a moment of arrested silence. She thanked Josie for reading and we left for ice cream at Tony's.

What seemed dramatic to me was in fact nothing more than an old world ritual between two Italian women, "una visita," in which news from the village in the old country was discussed in the home. In this "visita," I had my first exposure to southern Italian culture, the language of my ancestors, and a code of behavior transplanted to New Haven. Having discovered my grandmother's other identity, her Italian side, I wanted to learn more. As time went by, I asked her questions. "So Gram, when you left Italy to come to America, weren't you scared because you didn't know how to speak English? What did it feel like the day you said goodbye to your family? How come you left, Gram? Why did so many of your friends come to New Haven with you? Italy has the greatest art and music in the world, right, Gram? So why would you leave all that?" With typical southern Italian stoicism, she answered all my questions in broken English, "Becausa, I no like," or with peasant shrugs that initiated my lifelong quest to know more about where she came from and the world she had left behind.

Forty years after "la visita," I began an oral history project, conducting interviews with elderly Italian Americans from six neighborhoods of New Haven—the Annex, Legion Avenue, Fair Haven, the Hill, Wooster Square, and Forbes Avenue—to answer those questions. These tape-recorded interviews, sometimes in English, at other times in Italian, took place in their homes, in social clubs, in nursing homes, or in their place of business. Having no thesis in mind, I began with simple, open-ended questions like "Where did your parents come from?" or "What was your first job?" The storytellers, at liberty to talk about experiences close to their hearts, revealed many unexplored sides of New Haven's history.

Speaking in blue-collar patois sprinkled with Italian phrases, many described the rhythm of daily life and the pulse of the streets in New Haven's vibrant old ethnic neighborhoods. In simple yet eloquent narratives, they chronicled the unreported downside of urban renewal in the late 1950s, when the fabric of New Haven's neighborhoods was torn apart and people were forced to leave. Oftentimes, a son or daughter listening to our conversation was surprised to hear stories about New Haven that had never been told. My grandmother and her paesani had taken part in the greatest exodus from any country in modern history. Eighty percent of her compatriots were poor farmers, with little formal education, "giornalieri," or "bracianti," unskilled laborers who could no longer live off the land. Many settled in urban industrial cities like New Haven, where the prospect of steady work represented a marked improvement from the hard life they had left behind. They came from southern towns like Pacheco and Trapani in Sicily; Girifalco in Calabria; from Cerreto Sannita, Sarno, Amalfi, Acerno, San Carlo, Gioia Sannitica, and Castellammare di Stabia in the Campania region; from Conversano in Puglie; from Fano and Barchi in Le Marche and San Valentino in Abruzzi of centrally-located regions; and from Cordenons and Schio in Veneto and Ciocarro and Grezzano di Badoglia in Piedmont of the northern regions.

By the 1920s, the Italians had surpassed the Irish and the Jews as the biggest ethnic group in New Haven. At the New Haven railroad station, newly-arrived Marchegiani were met by sponsors who took them to construction jobs the next day. Italians from Atrani and Amalfi disembarked at their final destination at nearby Sargent's wharf in New Haven harbor where the expression "O boat si ferma a Sargent's," or "The boat stops at Sargent's," was coined, meaning the immigrant's first stop in the new world was at the Sargent's plant, where gritty, labor-intensive jobs as boiler stokers, metal pressers, brass finishers, meat grinder assemblers, and packers awaited.

During the peak period of Italian immigration in the United States, from 1900 to 1920, New Haven was a bustling manufacturing town whose eight hundred firms produced and exported goods all over the world. Italian men and women joined the production lines in labor-hungry factories like Sargent Manufacturing Company, A. C. Gilbert, and L. Candee Rubber. After a few years, some returned home with enough money to buy land. Many, like my grandmother, left families in Italy, never to return. Some lost their lives to the Spanish flu epidemic. A few flourished, quietly shedding their old world provincialism to become American businessmen and entrepreneurs. Still others, mostly men, were fortunate enough to go to college, the most ambitious of them becoming well-known doctors, notable lawyers, and respected community leaders. Most immigrant women and their American-born daughters had few career choices and toiled in deplorable sweatshops. A number lost their lives in the tragic Franklin Street Fire.

In an interview I conducted for this book with an elderly couple shortly before they died, I asked to look through the family album. They handed it to me, and after I carefully leafed through pages containing snippets of their lives in black and white photographs affixed to tattered black pages with little silver corners, I was startled when, as I turned the final page, they asked if I would please take their old family album home. They wanted me to keep it. I refused their offer, politely telling them it belonged more to them than to me. The elderly woman sighed and said, "Anthony, if you don't take this album home with you, the kids will eventually throw it out when we're gone. What do they care about the past?"

But Italian Americans are interested in learning about their heritage. For many, the connection is to an ancient peasant culture with roots running deep in Italian soil, an earthy people of humble lineage who expressed themselves mainly in the spoken rather than written word. Because the Italian American oral tradition—that body of fables, proverbs, and life experience stories by which a family knows its past—is rarely recorded but kept in memory, the legacy fades as generations pass on. Old World customs and rituals lose their original meaning; traditions slip away. Few immigrants who made the arduous transatlantic journey to America survive to pass their stories on to grandchildren. The second generation who lived through the Depression and World War II is fading quickly. Their third-generation children, many with college educations and professional careers, have assimilated into the American mainstream. But many third- and fourth-generation Italian Americans regret losing the language and traditions of their grandparents. Long after old familial voices have been silenced by the passage of time, many turn to researching family trees, sometimes traveling to ancestral birthplaces in Italy in search of their roots. Some write family histories for future generations with captioned photographs of grandparents and elders of the family. Others visit "Little Italies" like Boston's North End for a nostalgic return to the old neighborhood recalled from youth, where upscale Italian restaurants now proliferate and original Italians have long since passed on. Competing with the interest in learning more about Italian heritage and the search for ethnic identity is the movie industry that for decades has consistently showcased Italian Americans as subintelligent gangster types like the Sopranos, who have become the latest in a long line of stereotypes, reinforcing the negative image of Italian Americans as mobsters and wise guys. For the new generation of impressionable moviegoers going to see *Shark Tales,* Stephen Spielberg casts his animated mobster sharks with Italian surnames. With little written history or cultural preservation resources to counteract the steady barrage of gangster images in the media, or educational programs to highlight the notable contributions Italian Americans have made in many fields, some accept the decades-old depiction of themselves as wise guys and mobsters.

It is my hope that this book, with family album photographs illustrating daily life in New Haven, with my portraits of the storytellers, and with stories transcribed exactly as they were told, will invite all Americans to gain a deeper understanding of Italian Americans. It is also my hope that future generations will reexamine this collection of oral histories and photographs, reinterpreting its meaning as time passes, so that it never dies. A few years before he died, my father spoke to me words that could well have expressed the wishes of his generation and generations that preceded him: "Anthony, if I die and you don't remember me, then I'm dead; if I die and you remember me, then I'm alive—so don't forget me."

Life in Italy

For centuries, Italy has been a land situated at the crossroads of contending cultural influences, including the effects of numerous foreign invasions. The fusing of foreign blood with that of native inhabitants began during prehistoric landings of people from east and west and continued with Greek colonizers who established cities from Naples to Sicily in the seventh century B.C. and who named the south of what is now Italy "Magna Grecia." From the north, Germanic tribes used ancient roads and Alpine mountain passes to push into upper regions that still bear their names; the word for Italy's Le Marche region comes from a monetary word for German currency, "the mark." From the south, Arabs based in northern Africa conquered Sicily in the ninth century. The Sicilian town of Marsala still bears its Arabic name, "the harbor of Allah." A German-Norman king, Emperor Frederick II, governed the region of Apulia in the thirteenth century. Young boys in the streets of Naples are still called "guaglióne," Neapolitan for young lad, a word that arrived from France in the fourteenth century when French Angevins ruled the city.

By 1860, Italy resembled a collection of foreign-controlled regions rather than a country. The Kingdom of Lombardy-Veneto was part of the Austrian empire, which also ruled the duchy of Tuscany including Parma, Massa, Lucca, Piacenza, and Modena. A king of the House of Savoy ruled Piedmont and Sardinia while the middle region, the Papal States, fell under the jurisdiction of the Pope. The Spanish Bourbons ruled the Kingdom of the Two Sicilies, a territory extending from below Rome to Sicily, the "Mezzogiorno," a land that produced 80 percent of the Italians who came to the United States. When north and south joined in 1861, Italian society still retained remnants of its anachronistic system of lord and serf, which had evolved into wealthy "galantuomini," the land-owning gentry of the old feudal aristocracy and capitalists, and "braccianti" and "contadini," poor field workers and farmers.

In his book *The Man Farthest Down*, Booker T. Washington, who visited the sulphur mines and farms of Sicily in 1910, compared the southern Italian peasant to poor Blacks in the American South: "The Negro is not the man farthest down. The condition of the colored farmer in the most backward parts of the Southern States in America, even where he has the least education and the least encouragement, is incomparably better than the condition and opportunities of the agricultural population of Sicily." For the majority of southern Italians of the lower classes in the late-nineteenth century, life was an endless cycle of grinding "miseria," a "stato d'animo," a psychological state conditioned by centuries of political oppression, economic hardship, and social alienation. Southern villages were squalid, backward places whose people lived in a closed society with little interaction with other parts of Italy. Only 2.5 percent of the population understood the Italian language and most people spoke regional dialects that were unintelligible in other parts of Italy. Formal education was reserved for a privileged few.

Giuseppe Garibaldi's famous March of the Thousand in 1860 culminated in the defeat of the hated Bourbons and in the union of north and south into one state. Italy was declared a nation under King Victor Emmanuel. Shortly after the declaration, the Piedmontese prime minister, Marquis Massimo D'Azeglio said cynically, "We have made Italy, we have yet to make Italians." The country's euphoria over its new status faded quickly. "United Italy" imposed higher prices, high taxes, and introduced conscription. Northern industrialists, misunderstanding the south, imposed heavy taxes on the peasantry to promote the north's industry. Mules, considered the trucks of poor farmers, were taxed, while cows and horses of wealthy landowners were not. In the view of poor southerners, Italy's political leaders squandered the chance to provide equity for its poorer citizens. Armed insurrections against the northern occupation of the south by southern "briganti" led to bloody reprisals and mass executions by the army of the newly formed Piedmont-based government. The failure of the Risorgimento led to the greatest migration of any country in world history. At the port of Naples, Italians leaving on ships for America expressed their disenchantment with Italy. As they boarded, they were heard saying, "Put your shovels down and let someone else pick them up."

"Born in the Haystacks of Le Marche"

Josie DeBenedet spoke at her kitchen table on June 6, 1999. She proudly pointed to the tiled walls of her kitchen that had been installed by her late husband, Odorico, a highly-skilled Venetian craftsman.

Like my father said, he was the oldest of sixteen children—my adopted father—he was the first one. So the mother was pregnant and he was born on July 6, 1874. The hay at that time was ripe, you had to pick it and take in the hay before it would rain. If it rained then the hay would be spoiled. And his mother started labor pains. So he was born in the haystack. Then the mother wrapped him up in a blanket and somebody brought him home. And she continued working—the poor woman—to hurry up to get the hay in. On a Saturday night they used to go dancing. They would never wear shoes. And they would all meet in the town of Fano, they called it La Via Croce, the street of the big cross, and that's where everybody would meet. And they would take off their shoes before the dance and then coming home they would put their shoes on over there because they were always barefooted. And they would just

JOSIE DEBENEDET
in her kitchen,
North Haven, 1998

A. Riccio

go dancing together and then come back and sing going home. They wore those big clog shoes, they call them "i zoccoli," those big clog shoes they wear now too, they never get out of style, those big heavy things.

66LIFE ON A FARM IN FANO99

Renee Vanacore and her husband Anthony spoke on their back porch on November 20, 1999. They were married without a ceremony during World War II on a fifteen day pass.

My mother grew up on a farm. I remember the house. There was all corn in back of us. From my mother's house to my grandmother was quite a distance. And over my grandmother's house, alongside there was a bridge and water. That water I used to

ALBEROBELLO, ITALY, 1975

A. Riccio

drink, it was so clear, it's not like over here. And my mother had a goat for the milk, rabbit to kill for food, chickens. I don't know where the hell the market was, the store. And downstairs she had hay with all the animals to stay in the wintertime and we had our rooms upstairs. The animals used to help to heat the place in the wintertime. We had a fireplace to keep the animals from freezing because we used to get cold weather. I never used to go anyplace. In back of us was a little hill and the people had corn and lettuce and tomatoes. We used to get everything; she used to go up the hill and go and get the stuff. We ate; we didn't starve. It was a good life.

"THE CAT CHOKER FISH"

Nick Vitagliano spoke at the kitchen table of his Branford home with his wife Mary and daughter Maria on June 2, 2000. He recalled his father witnessing the 1908 earthquake recovery in Messina, Sicily.

As a boy, he [my father] says, "Ca ci sta sempre una miseria," There is always misery here. He said you couldn't get away from it. It was inbred. Even the dust in the street would give you misery, you couldn't escape. He said he just wanted to make a change and go away somewhere where he would have nothing to do with this country [Italy]. He never wanted to go back and he meant it. When his days were numbered I said, "Pa, why don't you go to Italy and visit?" But he didn't want to go back because he had bad memories of Italy. My father came here because he was sick and tired of "I Borboni," the Bourbons. My father used to say, "Chilli Borboni, mala gente, si rubavano tutte cose," Those Bourbons are bad people, they steal everything from you. My wife's father knew first hand, the Bourbons. He was fisherman. He used to go out with the little boat and then he used to return. When he used to return, best fish, he used to clean them up and send them out. The Bourbons would walk along the shore and take all the fish for themselves. They used to leave the little ones, my grandmother used to call them "li affocagàtte," the cat chokers. Those little fishes, they were so bony that even the cat would choke on it! They were the scrap; you know what I mean? My grandmother on my mother's side, oh she was a tough one, she used to stand up to these people but she couldn't do too much about it, she was too little. They ran the country; I don't know how such terrible people can take hold of power. Where they lived in Castelmare di Stabia, they used build ships. They used to have to get permission from the captain to go in the "cantiere," the shipyard, with the boat because not too many people went in there to fish. So there was always fish in there. " 'O Borbon," the Bourbons, used to keep them out of there but they used to get in. You had to be nice to the people who owned "'o cantiere" so that you could go in the area where the shipbuilding was taking place. And it was accommodating for the fishermen because there was always a box or traps to fish off the grounds where they were building the ships. My mother and her friends used to run through the ruins of Pompeii and she used to have fun. She used to say, "Oh, nuie fuievano sempre cuando uscievano la polizia di Borboni, perche erano mala gente," Oh, when the Bourbon police used to come out, we used to run away because they were such bad people.

CHILDREN AT PLAY IN AN ALLEY, ROME, 1975

A. Riccio

❝THEY WERE BAD PEOPLE❞

Anna Fasano spoke Italian at her kitchen table with her husband Attilio
where they were processing tomatoes for winter canning on August 8, 1998.

A ninety-year-old woman named Irena from my village in Castellabate used to tell
me stories [in the 1930s] that she remembered when she was a child under the rule
of the Bourbons. The Bourbon leaders were in complete control; everything was in

their hands. They were the law. They used to say that when someone in the village got married, they had the wedding ceremony and the party afterward. At night the husband had to bring the new wife to the Bourbons. The Bourbons slept with her that first night; they did whatever they wanted with her, and the next day they would hand her back to the husband. And if she was a "disonorata," dishonorable, and not a virgin, this meant she was dishonorable in the eyes of the Bourbons and they would kill her. They thought having sex with someone who wasn't a virgin would bring them dishonor. How many bad things the Bourbons did! They would rob everything, kill people. They were bad people.

(translated from Italian)

❝THEY EXCHANGED PICTURES❞

Rosemarie Foglia spoke in a conference room next to her office at City Hall on June 28, 1999.

We were one of the few northern Italian families on this side of town, which was on Greene Street [Wooster Square]. As a matter of fact I don't know of any other northern Italian family in that immediate area. My mother and father were from Provincia di Asti and my father came from Grezzano di Badoglia and my mother came from a neighboring town, Ciocarro, an area between Milan and Torino. My father came here because he was the third child in his family and my grandmother believed in the oldest child running the entire family. So my eldest uncle would actually put his younger brothers to work and then he would allocate the allowance and my father just couldn't really deal with this because he would be doled out x amount of lira per week and was told what to do and how to do it. And my father could not really handle the idea that his older brother was handling all of the money and very frugal in his style. And also my father came to this country because he had been engaged to marry a young woman from his town but her father developed tuberculosis and my grandparents would not allow my father to marry her because obviously in those days the feeling was that tuberculosis was hereditary. So my father did not marry the woman that he had really been involved with for years and to this day I have a silk letter folder that this woman had sent letters to my father and then eventually sent this letter folder where the letters could be kept in.

My mother lived in a neighboring town and my father's sister had the adjacent farm. And my mother had been involved with a young man also from that town but he too was the second child, which meant that my mother would have to move into what was their family estate. Now that was all well and good, however once the war started and all the men went into the service, my mother ended up running what was her farm and hiring and firing and just running it. And my grandfather was quite sick at the time and could see the handwriting on the wall because by the time my mother's fiancé returned from the service my mother was in control of almost everything. And I'm inclined to say my mother had a bossy streak and my grandfather realized this would never do, that my mother would have to my marry this fiancé and then go into this household and be second. And my father just saw problems. So my grandfather forbade my mother to marry this young man and my paternal grandparents forbade my father to marry the young lady that he was involved with. My father had been here for a few years and worked around the clock in an attempt to save money and make money because his goal was to have his fiancée come to this country and when they had enough they would go back. Now my father first came to New Haven, but ended up working in New York on Bleecker Street, horse and buggy delivering wine because they delivered wine on Bleecker Street, the same as a milk delivery. A bottle of wine was delivered every day and he delivered wine to Bleecker Street all to the Italian people. Now remember you're talking about tenement houses so no one could make their own wine, they didn't have the facilities, they didn't have the basements, they didn't have the dark cellars, they didn't have anything. So my father ended up working for someone that made wine and he would deliver it horse and buggy like we know milk deliveries.

But the years were going by and obviously my father's fiancée in Italy realized that she would probably never come to this country and my father would not disobey his parents. So my aunt who was a neighbor of my mother's talked to my maternal grandfather and said, "Look my brother is in the United States alone, you're trying to break up this romance, we should try and set them up." So this is how it happened. My mother was twenty and my father was thirty, which was a very acceptable thing in those days. And my father started writing to my mother and eventually asked for her hand in marriage through my grandfather in Italy. They never met. They exchanged pictures. And they all said yes but now my maternal grandfather could not have my mother come here alone and they had a gentleman that was like the town politician that lived in Manchester, Connecticut and was a banker as a matter of fact. And this is key because it affected their entire life. And my grandfather said my mother could come to this country when this gentleman went back to Italy and he would be my mother's guardian to accompany her to the United States. Well that happened in January of the following year. So my mother came here at twenty accompanied by this elderly "cavaliere," gentleman, which was a very recognized thing in Italy. Cavaliere Bosco and his wife went to Manchester and my father went from New Haven to Manchester and met my mother and they were married two weeks later. And their marriage lasted till death. And they celebrated their fiftieth anniversary and it was a fine marriage. But the thing was my mother and father saved and were very frugal and all because their goal was to return to Italy and buy a farm and make their home there. And my father entrusted all his money with this cavaliere and this cavaliere would bring the money back to Italy and my father had probably at that point something like fifteen thousand dollars in American money, which had been sent to Italy. The banks failed and my mother and father lost all of their money in Italy when all the banks failed. I guess because of the war and the dollar, the banks failed, not here but there, and my father lost the money that he had worked around the clock for.

" He Never Wanted to Go Back "

Mary Santacroce was ninety-seven at the time of her interview in her kitchen on December 21, 1999. She recalled having given birth to all her children at home.

My father never had any inclination to go back. He said that life was too hard there because living in Atrani he had to go up to the bigger cities to work. So he was away from home like for weeks at a time in what would be the same as a Stop and Shop warehouse, that's where he worked up north. And he'd be away from his family even for sometimes a month at a time and then would come home with whatever money he earned. And that's why when they came here, he never once had an inclination to go back. He said he was happy here. Because my husband used to work hard in Italy and he used to go work out of Atrani and he used to send the money home because the father was dead and he had two young sisters at home.

The Journey to America: Life on the Ships

At the turn of the twentieth century burgeoning manufacturing firms and expanding railroad companies in the United States looked toward Europe for new sources of cheap labor. On the other side of the Atlantic, millions of Italians found themselves trapped in a static system of economic stagnation and political oppression that forced them to leave. Italians followed the same trans-Atlantic pattern of earlier waves of Scandinavian, Irish, and German immigrants who had been recruited during the mid-nineteenth century to work in mines, factories, and on building railroads. With the prospect of steady employment and guaranteed working contracts from John Bradford Sargent's agents, southern Italians of the Campania region left for labor jobs at Sargent Manufacturing Company in New Haven.

For many Italians, the momentous decision to make the long voyage meant leaving familiar pastoral settings and seasonal rhythms of farming for living by the factory whistle in sooty industrialized cities. Italians of the lower classes were unaccustomed to life beyond the horizons of their villages and clung to the contadino's austerity, often expressed in the adage "una vita di pane e cipolla," which meant living a simple life of eating bread and onions. The majority of Italians who left ancestral villages for New Haven—unskilled field laborers, poor tenant farmers, fishermen, shepherds, bakers, shoemakers, barbers, proprietors of small stores, and carpenters from the southern regions—shared the same sense of inferiority and apprehension in the new world from centuries of living under foreign oppression and grinding poverty.

For generations, the conservative ways of the Italian contadino was stated in a simple yet powerful proverb, "Non si cambia la via vecchia per la via nuova, sa quello che tiene, no sa quello che trova," or never change the old road for the new one because one knows what one has, but never knows what one will find. But with tearful farewells to childhood friends and loved ones, many young fathers left families and "la via vecchia" with intentions of returning home quickly with enough American-made money to buy land or to start a small business. Families seldom migrated together and young married women were left to raise small children with little finances or resources. Many husbands departed promising to send money for wives and children to follow soon after; some found new wives in America and were never heard from again, leaving their young Italian brides "vedove bianche," or white widows. In the south, families without a head of household in some areas reached almost one in three.[1]

Few who decided to leave could have imagined the hardships awaiting them along the journey to America. In the early days of emigration the trip began by walking long distances or riding mules to the busy port of Naples, where vendors sold "American clothes" to those who wanted to conceal their Italian identity. In the confusion of the busy port, thieves posed as baggage handlers offering to carry luggage on board ships and were never seen again. To increase profits, greedy travel agents sometimes sent families to ports ahead of departure times requiring longer stays in hotels. Ships went from port to port in prey of passengers with unreliable timetables for arrival in New York. By 1890, improvements in steamship technology reduced the time to reach American shores from six weeks to seven days and steamship companies expanded their fleets with larger ships to accommodate the mass exodus of Italians leaving for America.

Life on trans-Atlantic ships was an unrelenting and torturous ordeal. The poor who could only afford steerage class were crammed below water level into closed quarters with other families, seldom seeing the light of day. In dank and dark living conditions deep below with few sanitary facilities or ventilation, cholera and typhus quickly spread and seasickness could last the entire trip. Arriving at New York, entire boatloads of sick passengers endured the heartbreak of being sent back to Italy; in one case over a hundred Europeans died before reaching New York.[2] In 1891, Adolfo Rossi, a young adventurer from Lendinara in the Veneto region, sailed aboard the "Canada" to New York and later wrote "Un Italiano in America," which chronicled daily life on board and exposed the undocumented dangers of unregulated trans-Atlantic travel. Rossi described the trauma and heartbreak of immigrants upon discovering an entire "peculio," or life savings, which had been sewn into a belt or secret pocket before leaving Italy, had been stolen while the unsuspecting victim slept. More ominous than robberies were unsolved murders mysteriously committed under the cover of darkness on the high seas, with victims furtively thrown overboard amidst the splashing sounds of the passing waves. When the missing passenger was reported the next morning by hysterical family members, the captain entered "death by suicide" into the ship's log without further investigation. Few on board believed any passenger who endured the long trip with the hope of finding a better life in America would have suddenly chosen such a death.

As boatloads of beleaguered and bewildered Italian immigrants disembarked at Ellis Island, wealthy Americans of the Gilded Age, writers, and intellectuals were setting sail in the opposite direction, to Florence, Venice, and Rome, and to ancient Greek and Roman archeological sites of the south. Inspired by the grandeur and beauty of Italian art, music, literature, and history, Americans traveled extensively throughout Italy pursuing Italian high culture, of which arriving immigrants of the lower social classes had little knowledge or experience. Adelina DeCusati, who left Amalfi for New Haven and endured a month-long ordeal in steerage, expressed the feelings of her fellow immigrants, telling her children she would go back to Italy "Cuando fanno'o ponte di sacìccia, tanno che vaco all 'Italia,'" "when they make a bridge out of sausage, that's when I'll go back to Italy."

"CONDITIONS ON BOARD IN 1890"

Salvatore "Gary" Garibaldi spoke at the Santa Maria Maddalena Society on Wooster Street on April 10, 2000. He was the president of Wooster Street Business Association.

My mother-in-law came in the 1890s. She told me the trip was very long and boring; sanitary facilities were cruel. Just think of a ship loaded with maybe two, three hundred people on it and ships in those days didn't have toilets and sanitary things. And she would say how people from the first day they got on the ship never changed their clothes because they were scared that the ship might sink. And there was a lot of ill rest among the people on that ship. And the food was unbelievable; everybody ate the same food, cooked the same way. And you had to wait a half-hour to three-quarters of an hour to get in line to get fed. And most of the time on the ship they would stay upstairs, up on the deck to get the fresh air because of the foul air in the below deck compartments.

"COMING OVER IN 1899"

Pat Barone spoke from the living room of his West Haven home on May 5, 1999.

My father came from San Lorenzello, province of Benevento. He came from the farm country. His father had come to the United States before him. My father and his mother were living alone back in Italy while his father, my grandfather, was here. When his father came back to Italy, he wanted to come back to America again. But my father said, "No, you stay here with your wife and I'm going to go." When my father left Italy he was only fifteen years old and he left all by himself. He had no relatives; he had nobody here. He came alone and he came here green as the day was long. I could remember my father telling me it was thirty-five days to come from Italy. They would go five miles ahead one day and four miles back the next day on the boat. They had very poor transportation in them days; it isn't like today. My father said they were all in the bottom of the boat there and who was getting sick and who was crying. He said when they reached New York they didn't know what to make of it. And of course they got into Ellis Island. He met up with some other Italian and he was coming to New Haven so he asked my father where he was going. My father said, "I don't know, I'm just going to America." So he came here, he got off the boat, and the man that was picking up this fella in New York told him to come on down here. Because years ago they used to look for people coming from the old country. Because most of the houses, in order to make a living, a lot of them had rooms they used to rent, they used to call them the boarding houses. And my father started to rent a room with him. He used to tell me how tough it was here when he first came. Didn't know anybody; couldn't speak. He didn't have an uncle or an aunt or anybody to guide him or anybody to help him in any way.

"She Thought She Was in Italy"

Antonette Sicignano spoke from her kitchen on Wooster Street on August 30, 1999. She said when her mother ate figs she thought she was back in Italy.

I think it took my mother a couple of weeks, a long time. She said, "You know how they used to have it then?" They used to have bunks, maybe four or five up. And you had the ladder to go up there. My mother—I don't know how old she was, four or five. She said the lady on the top had kids. They got sick and they were throwing up. If my mother ever looked over she would have got it on her head or something. She said one night, because in Italy they used to come and serenade you and all that, she was sleeping in the bunk. She said she heard the music. She said she thought she was in Italy. And she hit her foot near there and her head. Then she realized; she looked down from the bunk. Somebody was playing maybe downstairs in the big room that was there. And she used to go talk to all the elderly women and they used tell her things, you know, what happened. My mother always used to listen to older people, all the time. She used to say, "I used to go always to the older people."

"But I Sold All My Furniture"

Amelia Buonocore spoke from the living room of her elderly complex with her daughter Carmel on September 11, 1999. She said her father used to take her to the Bijou Theatre in New Haven to see silent movies even though he could not read the captions.

We left in December 1908, and my boat took eleven days. My mother, Matteo, Jennie, Florence, and me. My father was already here. We were supposed to be here before that but something happened in old country and the boat that was going to take us here couldn't make it. It had to take the people that were sick—they had something went wrong over there that they had pick up a lot of people and bring them to hospitals. We had to stay three days in Naples because that boat couldn't make it. My mother said, "I got to leave, I sold all my furniture, I've got no place to go." So the agent said, "Well, there's a boat from Germany coming by here but you have to pay more money if you want to go on that boat." So my mother said, "Yeah." So in three days we got that boat. There was a lot of people, people from Germany. We were on the second floor. They had different levels—we were on the top level. It wasn't that good because you had to climb up and go down. That boat, instead of eleven days, it made it in nine days—made it sooner—so we got here at the same time with the German boat, the Star or some name like that.

AMELIA BUONOCORE
In her living room,
Bella Vista elderly complex,
Fair Haven, 1999

A. Riccio

"THE BOAT ALMOST TIPPED OVER"

John Nappi spoke from the kitchen of his East Haven home on July 6, 1999.
He recalled Yale professors having their suits hand made and shoes repaired
on Wooster Street.

My sister Carmel, my sister Rose. and my brother—God rest his soul, he would
have been ninety-five. They were all on the ship, they came together. And you
know how they used to travel in those days, you just dumped them in a hole and
that was it. My mother told me they caught the worst storm ever. They didn't think
they were going to make it. That ship was bouncing around in the Atlantic like a
ball. She said everybody was praying because they didn't think they were going to
make it, that when they saw the Statue of Liberty they all ran to one side. They

were praying and the boat almost tipped over. She said the people were so happy that the captain had to make an announcement to tell them to balance the ship because they all ran to one side when they saw the Statue of Liberty.

"THEY WERE GOING TO THROW GENNARO OVERBOARD"

Anna Rosati spoke at the kitchen table of her daughter Louise's home on May 7, 2000.

It was nice on the boat. We used to have a good time. They used to serve you, put tables out. Beautiful! We were in the second class but the better second class. We were on top. The other class was more lower. It was nice on the boat. I liked it, yeah. What you do all day? You get up late, they ring the bell, you dress up, you go

CARLO CATANIA AND
MOTHER PAOLINA
Aboard the "Conte di Savoia,"
August 12, 1936
Catania family album

and get your breakfast, whatever they give you. Then you go back in your cabin, you take a shower, you dress up, you go upstairs. Walk around the boat, you meet this one and you talk, and a lot a ladies from New York, a lot of those old ladies they'd make you laugh, you know, and the day goes by. It was nice on the boat. We went in November to Italy, the waves were high. My brother Gennaro, he was a little boy, got dysentery on the boat and my mother said if he didn't get better they were going to throw him over. It was nice, though. When you're young, you don't think nothing [of it], right?

"SAILORS SAUCE"

Tony Sacco spoke at a table in his Wooster Street restaurant, Tony and Lucille's, on May 19, 2000.

My grandfather was a sailor; he was always on the water. He came from the village of Amalfi. Now, as my father told me, those days were very, very tough. Most men went to work on the boats. He went to either Naples or Genoa, one of those ports, and he got a job. He was fifteen years old. And they put him on board as a wood boy. A wood boy is you carry the wood for the boiler. In those days they had just converted from the sail to steam. So they used to go to Naples and make short trips to Argentina, back and forth, then from Argentina to America. Then the way he tells me the story that when they came to America they hit a storm in Virginia and they hit a rock and a lot of them ended up on the lighthouse there. I don't know how many they took out of the sea but they wound up in the Norfolk Virginia Hospital. And that's how he came to America, by accident. I don't think he could afford to come here, he had no money. It was totally by accident and almost by death. So he winds up in the hospital and the hospital likes him—my father tells me they loved him—he works around the hospital, he was frostbitten and they took care of him well. And then they found out he had some relatives in New Haven, Andrea Sacco. And that's how it all comes together. My father used to say to me, "I'll make you some marinara sauce" [like your grandfather made on the boat]. I'd say, What's marinara sauce? He'd say, "Well, how do you think they named it marinara sauce? The sailors [marinaio]. In those days what did they have on the boat? They could only bring macaroni, garlic, salt pork, anything dry, tomatoes, "e mangiava marinara" [and they used to eat marinara]. Sailor sauce. They used to make a fast sailors sauce in the pan and capers, whatever, anything that was dry. And that's what they call sailors sauce. It started over when somebody put mushrooms in the marinara sauce. My father says, "Where did you ever hear of mushrooms?" [in marinara sauce]. I said, "Well, that's the American way." He said, "They never put mushrooms in the marinara sauce, was never done." It's oil, garlic, capers, basil, tomatoes, olives, dry olives, anything that they could bring aboard and lasted—in other words; it doesn't have to have refrigeration. That's why they ate all that stuff. Anything that was cured and dried. Simple. You get the water from the sea, put the macaroni in, nu' poco 'e pomodoro [a little tomato] in the frying pan with a little oil, garlic, capers, if they want to put in some alècchia [anchovy] in there, they throw a little alècchia in there and that's it. Five minute sauce. Today it's a big deal.

"But I Didn't Come in through New York"

Frances Calzetta and her brother Eugene spoke in the living room of their Forbes Avenue home on October 10, 1998.

In the Italian embassy in New York in 1988, they were honoring my father because he was the oldest man there. The Scalabrini Order of priests, as an arm of the Pope, were the ones that came to America to make the Italian people comfortable in their new environment, make sure they didn't lose their roots. And it was their hundredth anniversary. So it was a big celebration day. At the plaza in New York, and so we're at the luncheon and they're going into the history of the immigration people. And father Joe is up there and he's the one who dealt with Congress on immigration. And first he says, "And we have somebody among us who was there [at Ellis Island] and we'd like to honor at this lunch the oldest person who is here today. Because he's the one who went through this. Will Mister Carmen Calzetta please stand up?" My father is absolutely stunned. I said, Dad, stand up. They're saying, "You were great, blah, blah." Now another portion of the day was to go over to the Italian embassy, meet the Italian ambassador and father Joe, it would be great to give dad the personification of the Italian male who came to this country, worked hard, didn't want to become a millionaire, wanted a better life, raised a good family, family life, tradition, become an American, be an American citizen. We're at the embassy and it's the year of the Statue of Liberty. They asked him at the microphones, "How did you feel when you saw the Statue of Liberty?" And my father revealed something none of us ever knew. "Oh! I didn't come into New York; I came in through Boston!" He had come in on a French ship [laughing] and the ship left Naples but went to Boston. So then they had to take a different . . . They said, "Well, what was the first thing you did when you hit land?" He said, "I bought a hot dog." They asked, "Well how was the boat ride?" A lot will tell how terrible this boat ride is across the Atlantic. He said, "I thought it was great! The weather was beautiful." He came over in September; I mean what better weather do you want across the Atlantic than in September so he spent most of his day above board. And when I took him to see the ship Constitution in Boston, we go in it, he says, "Hey, this is just the kind of ship I came over on."

"Twenty-three Days On The Water"

Rose Savo spoke at her kitchen table in her Annex home on July 28, 2000.

I remember that [boat trip] so distinctly. I was five years old when I came here. I was on the boat. I had a younger sister, she was two years younger and my sister was Carmel. I remember we had little capes and I think it was the captain of the boat—

he took a liking to us—he used give us chocolate bars. And how he loved Carmel, she was a pretty little girl anyway—how he loved my sister! He used to hug and kiss her. We came on December 12th, 1912. We came on a wing and a prayer. The boat even lost communications, what do they call it, the Marconi wasn't working. They couldn't even ask for help. We had a rough time. We were on the water for twenty-three days, yeah. I remember the boat, the "Ancona." The sailors were beautiful. They loved my sister and I, they used to give us chocolate bars, they were northern Italians and you could hardly understand them—their dialect was different. I remember, too, three or four sailors used to get together and they used to sing in their own [dialect]—they used to harmonize so beautiful, beautiful. I remember that boat trip. And the noise! Hey Ma, che è? [Hey Ma, what is it?] My mother used to say, "Chilli song'i pisci" [The fish are making all that noise]. They used to get caught under the boat and that was the noise. It wasn't; she was just telling us that. I don't know how we got here. There was three decks, three floors—down the basement, the first floor and further up. We were in the middle. And I remember another thing—the cots where you slept. There was a porthole. So I remember one day sticking my foot out that porthole—all of sudden it dawned on me. I said, Oh my god! I pulled my foot in—maybe I shouldn't, a fish will go by and chew my foot off. I pulled it in a hurry!

3 A New Life in New Haven

Since the early-nineteenth century, New Haven had been a city where European immigrants gained their first foothold in the New World. Irish immigrants arrived en masse in the 1820s to help build the Farmington Canal, followed by Germans in the 1850s. The late-twentieth century brought new additions to the city's growing foreign population with influxes of Lithuanians, Poles, Armenians, Greeks, Ukrainians, Scandinavians, and Russian Jews. African Americans arrived from the South in the 1920s, Puerto Ricans in the 1930s.[3] The earliest known Italian to arrive in New Haven in the nineteenth century was Luigi Roberti, who established a boarding school for women in 1849. In 1861, The Registry of Birth at City Hall recorded the name of Gianetto Corso, a joiner, at 23 Chestnut Street.[4] The emigration of the Roberti and Corso families to New Haven presaged the atmosphere of prejudice Italians would experience at the end of the century and later when they represented the largest ethnic group in the city. As early as the 1850s, Italians avoided publicity for fear of reprisals and even rioting in some New England states by members of the "Know Nothing" party whose intense nativism fomented hatred of foreigners who supplied cheap labor. Connecticut's own governor, William T. Minor, was a member of the "Know Nothing" party from 1855 to 1858.

Italian immigration into the city gradually began to increase after the 1870s when ex-sailors from Genoa established themselves in New Haven, followed by skilled tradesmen and northern "prominenti." By 1900, over 5,000 Italians represented the first wave of Italian immigration to the city. Between 1890 and 1920 the city doubled in population, from 81,298 to 162,537, and as Irish immigration waned, the second wave of Italians, according to some estimates, reached as high as 60,000.[5] The growing numbers of olive-skinned, dark haired Italians dressed in "foggia secolare," or provincial outfits, who spoke in strange tongues and expressed themselves with unfamiliar mannerisms and gestures, ate odd foods and worshipped saints with special healing powers, bore the brunt of hatred and distrust for all of New Haven's immigrants. In 1890, *The New Haven Register*'s editor, Everett G. Hill, wrote *A Modern History of New Haven* where he commented that the substantial growth of the Italian population in the city from the 1880 census revealed "a warning of Italian invasion which, has in the years since disturbed a good many citizens too much." In 1901, the *Yale Courant* published a poem written by a Yale student Sidney Dean where Italians in garish dress who lit candles to the saints were blamed for the loss of the aristocratic way of life of the wealthy Wooster Square neighborhood:

The old white church in Wooster Square
Where Godly people met and prayed—
Dear Souls! They worship Mary there,
Italian mother, man and maid
In gaudy Southern scarf's arrayed;
The horrid candles smolder where
The Godly people met and prayed.
Alas! The fall of Wooster Square!

Morty Miller, New Haven:
The Italian Community, undergraduate senior thesis,
Department of History, Yale University, 1969, p. 65

Warnings by native-born crusaders against Italian immigrants they considered as an inferior race reached the national level. Madison Grant's *The Passing of the Great Race*, published in 1917, sounded the alarm across the country that Southern and Eastern Europeans were "mongrelizing good American stock." After ex-president Teddy Roosevelt gave a speech in 1915 where he stated, "There is no room in this country for hyphenated Americans," President Wilson went a step further in a speech stating, "Hyphenated Americans . . . have poured the poison of disloyalty into the very arteries of our national life." In a highly charged atmosphere of nativism on the local and national level, the Italians, whose strong work ethic had been welcomed at first by American industrialists like John Bradford Sargent, who personally recruited and sponsored their Atlantic passage to cities like New Haven, suddenly became suspect and viewed as un-American because of their willingness to accept low wages as "cheap labor" in exchange for steady work.[6]

Despite unwelcoming voices from some sectors of the host culture, New Haven's Italian immigrants quietly persevered with the same inner strength they had developed for centuries in Italy as subjects of the landowning class that held them in contempt. Turning inward to the strength of family, they followed in the footsteps of preceding Irish immigrants to three arrival neighborhoods: Oak Street, The Hill, and Wooster Square. To the newly-arrived Italian who could not speak English, understood little of American norms of behavior, and had to master technical jobs in the workplace, New Haven must have seemed worlds away from the isolated country villages left behind. Prior to the urban experience in America, most had little social interaction with anyone beyond the boundaries of their small towns. But in the many shared spaces of the industrial city—on busy factory floors, sandlot ball fields, in schools, churches, in multistory tenement houses, on streets, and in neighborhood stores—Italians interacted with other ethnicities for the first time. Some returned to Italy when the first snows fell; others left believing that the traditional ways of the rural towns with their old world sense of "quotidianita"—

the timeless rituals of everyday village life—were better than the modern ways of the American city. A number of unskilled laborers who found themselves without financial security in poor paying jobs moved away in search of better jobs. But the longer immigrants stayed in New Haven, the more they tended to stay permanently and assimilate into mainstream America. Compared to the limited social mobility and severe economic stagnation Italians had experienced in Italy's rigid class system where no social ladder existed, New Haven abounded with opportunities. Factory jobs provided weekly paychecks and afforded families a sense of economic stability unheard of in southern Italy. For some immigrants, the once inconceivable dream of owning a home in Italy became a reality in New Haven. In the '20s and earlier, Italians obtained loans to buy homes from a number of sources. Family members pooled enough money together to help each other acquire homes. Informal corporations comprised of groups of men with enough capital, known as "le cooperative," sprang up all over the city offering loans with minimal interest to compatriots. Established fishermen lent money to their poorer fishermen friends to buy homes in the Annex; barbers and fruit and vegetable peddlers gave loans to locals from the neighborhood without signed contracts and simple handshakes; the Santa Maria Maddalena and Sant Andrea Society gave interest-free loans to society families with an agreement that if the family "came into money" at a later time, a donation would be made to the society. The Pallotti Andretta & Co. bank in the Wooster Square neighborhood gave loans on a handshake rather than signatures or bank notes. Both parties abided by the honor system; the lending officer always charged minimal interest even to the most unsophisticated, non-English speaking arrival; for borrowers, repayment was regarded as a question of family honor. By the '30s, thirty-seven percent of Italians owned homes, surpassing twenty-seven percent of the native born homeowners of the city.[7]

In this land of opportunity, steady work in a host of factories and manufacturing firms gave immigrants the option to break with family "mestiere," or trades passed down from father to son in the old country: fish peddlers became bakers, grapevine trimmers became landscapers, and shepherds apprenticed as stonecutters. Many unskilled young men entered the ranks of New Haven's four major semiskilled trades and apprenticed as masons, barbers, carpenters, and shoemakers. In this booming industrial town of the '20s and '30s, Italians opened small businesses in neighborhoods across the city: Domenico Fodaro from Girifalco in Calabria opened Domenic's Shoe Repair in Fair Haven, Salvatore Savo from Amalfi, a barbershop on the corner of Chestnut and Wooster Street who charged ten cents for a haircut, Luigi LaViola from Conversano in Puglia opened LaViola's Nursery on Forbes Avenue, and Antonio Esposito from Atrani opened Esposito's Italian American Grocery on the corner of Forbes and Fulton Street where customers as far away as Bridgeport stopped for his freshly-prepared lunches, paying more for tolls than the sandwich.

New Haven's school system was one of the best in the country and offered the promise of brighter futures for American-born children. Higher education and the chance for professional careers were now a possibility. Sargent offered a four-year scholarship to Yale for its employees. In Italian enclaves around the city, Italian newspapers "La Stella d'Italia" and "Il Corriere del Connecticut" were available at Italian-owned newsstands and a recently-returned paesano often provided the latest news from home at the local club or society. Italian importing companies brought Italian delicacies to every major shopping district in the city. Famous Italian opera singers made guest appearances at New Haven "spettacoli" to sold-out audiences. Italian-speaking clergy said Sunday mass to the faithful in Italian at Saint Michael's or Saint Anthony's.

In 1921, Antonio Cannelli, a printer by trade, self-published a history of New Haven for the large Italian-speaking community, "La Colonia Italiana di New Haven, Connecticut." Illustrated with portraits of successful Italians who had assimilated into the American way of life and prospered in professional careers, Cannelli highlighted their many contributions in the fields of medicine, business, engineering, politics, music, and art. Cannelli recognized the long-term social and economic opportunities available in New Haven that were unimaginable in Italy. Paying homage to the city for the opportunities given his countrymen, Cannelli described New Haven as "this beautiful city of Connecticut that we love dearly, where we spend so much of lives, where our children are born and are educated, and where so many dreams can come true or fade away."

"THEY CAME TO THE LAND OF OPPORTUNITY"

John Nappi spoke in his kitchen at his East Haven home on July 6, 1999. He spoke with the enthusiasm and energy of someone half his age.

Ninety-nine percent of them went to work for Sargent. When anybody came here and they were an immigrant, they couldn't speak English, they had no education. So Sargent used to go down to New York, sign them up because then there were no work laws. They'd come right here and they'd go right to work at Sargent. They would go down there and meet them at the boat; they would sign them up. Then you had to have somebody to sponsor you to be in this country. If you didn't have a job they could give you a hard time but the majority of them over there they came down, they signed them up and they told them they'd have a job for them and they'd go to work right at Sargent. And that's why ninety-nine percent of the people from this area worked in Sargent. Paul Russo was one of the educated people who came from Italy to this country and he either sponsored or he got in touch with the big manufacturing companies here in New England, not only in New Haven. And they used to write to Italy or have partners in Italy and send so many immigrants from Italy to the New Haven area. And he in turn would go to Sargent and they would say yeah, we need so many workers, and he would take them and bring them to work. But there was a little p.c. in it for him too. I mean they didn't do it out of the kindness of their heart. He got them a foothold, started in the city. It's just amazing how somebody would help somebody—even though he was benefiting by it—but at least they came to the land of opportunity. My father started there at fourteen years old in 1903. He was a polisher and a buffer, the worst job you could have for your lungs. They didn't have any exhaust fans to suck out all that dust. When you polish it, it's a sanding wheel; you take all the rough spots off. After you get all the rough spots off, then you polish it with the buffing wheel, like a soft cloth wheel, and it brings it up to the high luster and that's what his job was. That's what he died from—occupational lung disease. The conditions were miserable—no ventilation. Maybe thirty, forty, fifty polishers in one line with buffing machines in front of them with no vents. Piecework, all day long. He'd come home and when he'd blow his nose, he'd have the mask on for his glasses, you'd see all that red polish and buffing and when he spit . . .

"PRINCES AND PAUPERS"

Ralph Marcarelli spoke in the living room of his home on Wooster Square on May 28, 2000.

I would describe it as catch-as-catch-can when they first got here in terms of the skills that they brought over, the ability to put those skills into action. People did whatever they could do. It was harder for the "better" families among them than it was for the others. Because part of the class structure in Italy demanded that people behave in a certain way according to their origins and according to their state in life. Obviously if you were among the great numbers of the peasants or the day laborers or whatever, you did whatever you had to do and that was quite normal. If you were beyond that and above that it was a social stigma in Italy to reduce yourself as it were to the kind of labor that you would not be seen ever doing there in terms of the public cognition of your status there. And I think that some families made it and broke that and others did not. Among the "better" families in terms of social recognition in Italy I think there were probably initially fewer professionals than there were coming out of the poor families. Because the poor families would do whatever had to be done—pushcart in hand or whatever else under the sun—people simply did whatever they had to do and set up in whatever form of enterprise they could in order to make a buck. That's what it came down to—and they survived. The better families had a much more difficult time because they could not be seen doing certain things. There were social imperatives. If for example you had lost your money in Italy—heaven knows how many generations of it—which by the way meant that you could probably not go to the university to be educated because there were not funds. Then if you had to support yourself you looked to do what a gentleman could do. That happened in the case of my father's family. They were a noted family; they were, among other things, generals, judges, what in essence is the Attorney General of the Kingdom of the Two Sicilies. Giuseppe Marcarelli was Ministro di Grazie e Giustizia del Regno. My great-grandfather, Giulio Marcarelli was a "doppia laurea"; he was both a doctor and pharmacist. My great-grandfather had begun the military career, which was always an option for those families. Somebody went into the army; somebody went in to the navy. Great-grandpa went into the navy and by his thirties he was already a captain. And

PARENTE FAMILY PORTRAIT
Flaviano Parente, standing,
taken in Castel Venere,
Benevento, 1882

Calzetta family album

that was in fact among the better Italian families, the naval career was always a so-cially accepted kind of thing. But in any event when all hell broke loose for what-ever the reason, my grandfather and great uncle were left without funds and with-out possibilities. And I remember my grandfather telling me that they had to find work that gentlemen could do. And as such what they found was an apprenticeship to the better artists. And as young fellows they would go to the various homes and churches and so on for purposes of decorating walls and ceilings with murals of every sort and variety. Clearly, when they came to this country they couldn't do that because people didn't do that, short of having done some work in the churches. They did marvelous works in our house, a pity that it could have not been preserved because there wasn't a room in the house that wasn't filled with hand-decorated walls and ceilings. It was a beautiful thing to behold. The bedrooms were all trellises of flowers and ivy, done in a formal way; living room and dining rooms were murals of marvelous Italian scenes, all hand painted. What they had to do finally was to become painters and decorators in the sense that we understand what a painter and decorator is—they were the best in the business, there was no question about that. But again you see they were compelled to find work that gentlemen could do. And again this was a question of personal honor. It's what you did; it was what society demanded. The irony of that situation, however, was that others from simpler class who were not so constrained just did anything that came about to make the buck and very often they progressed materially faster than the families who had been wealthy because of those social constraints. There was another element in the faster progression of the lower classes. And that a cultural grasp, the difference in cultural grasp, the difference therefore in what today would be called "values." Attitudes among them. My grandfather said to me one day, "We've known what it means to eat 'bistecca' [steak] every day and we've known what it is to eat 'pane e cipolla' [bread and onions] and we're always the same." So there was a question of noblesse oblige, there was a question among the more educated and cultured families obviously of the real grasp of the culture and a modus vivendi which reflected the grasp of that culture which was not hidebound toward the acquisition of material things. Because those things were somehow taken for granted because they had been possessed for so long that they didn't seem to be the kind of things over which you salivated. Certainly never the kind of things over which you salivated and broke every value that you had been raised with in order to attain. Whereas so many people who came here really had been so dreadfully poor. There never would have been that opportunity in Italy for people of the so-called working and under classes to achieve, of a profession or a breaking out of the class structure. Once they got here, no holds barred; there were no longer any strictures so they could do whatever—and that was a marvelous opportunity, God knows, in New Haven.

"Garlic"

You had that tremendous animosity among the Irish. To the degree that the vehemence of it had a largely economic measure to it. You'd find it among the working class of the poor Irish to a far greater degree than those who had become affirmed so called "lace curtained." It was attenuated there so that its expression would not be quite as immediate or quite as vulgar. But it was still there; it was certainly there among the WASPs. My grandfather, who was a great gentleman, was working on a home on Saint Ronen Street—the owner was a gentlemanly individual. I'm telling you the story to illustrate the subtlety of the discrimination, of the manifestation of the discrimination as you got into the upper classes, the more well-heeled. My grandfather would bring his lunch every day. And one day—and I knew that in terms of an individual, certainly in terms of craft—that the guy had immense esteem for grandpa because they had founded the painting company and there was scarcely a house in that area they had not decorated. And grandpa was there and the guy said something about, "You people eat garlic all the time. You know, the garlic eaters." My grandfather said nothing. And not long thereafter he brought his lunch and my grandmother had baked an Italian cream cake. And my grandfather was eating it and the owner—who was an industrialist in New Haven said, "What's that Mister Marcarelli?" So he tells him and he said, "Would you care for a piece?" And he said, "Yes." And he began to eat it and to wax profusely, "This is absolutely delicious, this is wonderful. What did your wife make it with?" And my grandfather said, "Garlic."

"You Can't Come into Town"

Anthony Anastasio spoke at the kitchen table of his Aunt Rosie's home in Fair Haven on August 15, 1998.

My father-in-law, Louie Sansone, with his mother and father, horse and wagon, coming over the dirt road, which is now Route 1, were stopped at Lake Saltonstall, which is the town line. Three town fathers, three Yankees, they stopped them, "You can't come into town." "Why not?" they asked. "Well, uh, you don't have a place to live." They went all the way to see Paul Russo, a half a day's trip back to Paul Russo, and he got him a menial job in the M.I.F shop, the big foundry there. Now they come back out a second time, stopped again at the town line—they didn't want them in there. "Well, I got a job." They said, "Well, uh, you don't have a place to live." Paul Russo found them a shack sitting in the swamp. Now they had a place to live. Come back out, they had a place to live such as it was, they had a job such as it was. The third time out, they stopped them and said, "Well, uh, you can't come in, you got no money." The old guy reached into his pocket like that and he said, "Is that enough money?" So they had to let him in. They were the first Italians in Branford. When my mother-in-law went to school and they played ring-around-the-rose in the schoolyard the other girls wouldn't hold her hand because she was Italian.

"Taking Care of the Brothers"

Salvatore "Gary" Garibaldi spoke at the Santa Maria Maddalena club on Wooster Street on April 12, 2000.

The movement in the late 1800s was that America had gold in its streets. And they lived in poor neighborhoods and communities; there's no question about it. And those who came before them wrote back to their loved ones stating how they were making a go of it and very happy that they came here because of the different style of living. They looked forward to prosperity, a job, which in their country they had no chance to advance. If your father in Italy was a barber, your grandfather was a barber, his great-grandfather . . . that was a tradition that was kept within the family. So when they came to America it was a different lifestyle. The unfortunate part of it was that when the came to America they had two, three strikes against them. They had a language barrier; they were not professional people or skilled or semiskilled trade workers. Young in age but with the hope and prayer that they wanted to advance themselves in life. And they saw no future if they stayed at home. My mother-in-law from Amalfi had two brothers, Bartholomew and Frank Amendola, who came to America in 1897. They went to work at Sargent. Naturally, they sent letters home saying how they were doing good, and the mother felt that they needed somebody to take care of them. So she called upon her daughter Theresa to go to America and take care of her brothers. But just think of the courage and determination of that woman, of that young girl! Going to a country—unknown—language barrier, no trade, nothing. Because in those days women were not considered to be in the work force. And to think that you're going to leave you mother and father and brothers and sisters that are there—and God only knows if you'll see them again. Because remember in those days it wasn't easy to travel. You travel by ship and that took maybe anywhere from four to six weeks to get to America in the 1890s. And then you had to go through Ellis Island, being on that ship and the ships had poor sanitary and health conditions, like a slave ship. They put as many as they could on. Then on the way they were told that they were going to go through an examination and if the people on Ellis Island found them to be sick they would be returned home. Naturally, when she did arrive and was examined she was found fit. Her brothers were there waiting for her and took her home.

"I'll Go to America"

Amelia Buonocore was ninety-seven at the time of our interview in her living room of her elderly apartment at Bella Vista on September 11, 1999.

My mother and father had a piece of land in Vettica Minori—they were farmers. My father had land on one side; my mother had land on the other side. When they got married, their parents gave it to them. But they couldn't put it together. By the time they go and split it that land wouldn't be worth too much. So they rented it. And now renting it and being four, five, six kids, they couldn't manage no more. They used to have the guys working for them. They used to sell the potatoes and different things and that's how they used to make their living. We had two cows; we used to sell the milk. I was six, I remember. So that's how my father said, "I'll go to America. People go over to America—they got nothing—they go over there, they make some money, come over here and buy land." He said, "I'll go to America, I'll get some money, we come over here and we'll get a bigger place." So he came here by himself. He said he made a promise within a year he'd go back to the old country or my mother would come over here. So he made a promise with my mother. It didn't work. Sperry and Barnes wasn't working. That time they were having a new president and there was no work. He only made enough to make his board in 1908. Because he was a farmer he knew how to pickle, he used to pickle things, hands in the water all the time. So the year went by. And the words he didn't know how to write, so somebody used to write for him. Instead of writing what he wanted to say they used to write something different. And my mother used to say, "That's not my husband's talking. Something is wrong someplace." Within a year, there was no change and she came over here—my father didn't even know it. So she picked up, she didn't tell anybody. She sold the cow, whatever she had, the furniture and everything and she came over here.

“THERE WAS NO CHOICE”

Ralph Marcarelli spoke in the living room of his Wooster Square home, pausing and reflecting from time to time during our interview on May 28, 2000.

As far as who came to New Haven what you had was a transplanting of the cross-section of the society of the particular area involved. The area involved was overwhelming that of the south. The immigration more or less reflected the class culture of Italy of the former Kingdom of the Two Sicilies. Other people like the Marchegiani in New Haven from Le Marche suffered the same pangs of loss being from the Papal States area; there were some Piedmontese but not many. I think that probably all of them came as a direct or indirect result of the unification of Italy and the economic problems that the unification caused. What you really had was the conjoining of hitherto independent states with essentially their own economy, their own laws, their own modus vivendi. You had a certain small number of noble families, of upper-middle class families, of middle class families and then this enormous number of what turned out ultimately the poor, which of course was the great motivating factor in getting them over here. The poor being anyone from tradesmen down to day laborers who simply could not find bread in Italy any longer given the economic destruction that was wrought when the House of Savoia took over. Certainly, whatever its problems may have been, the Kingdom of the Two Sicilies still managed to provide for its inhabitants and in many ways better than other places. We know here that there are members from particular towns in this country now greater than the numbers still left in those particular towns so it is a very serious emigration. Is it true that the numbers of the nobility and the upper class were few in contrast to the overwhelming numbers of people? Yes. But it's also true that was the variation in Italy. They came here because everyone suffered in one way or another. There were literally princely families in New Haven, very literally. The Capecelatros were the Dukes of Morrone, for example. Princes all over the place. Were there many? No, there weren't many. But were they enough to be counted? Yes, they certainly were. They came for the very same reason because they too had lost their lands and their holdings. And they too were no longer able in the various economic shifts that occurred there. All you needed was a cataclysm of this nature in so many cases along with whatever may have been idiosyncratic hardships in any given family—that I can't answer too broadly. But there's no doubt about the fact that this country was viewed then as the land of opportunity—not in the mythological sense but in the sense that they simply had no other choice. When you stop to think of the fact that when the migration started it was a pretty safe bet that those who left Italy realized they were leaving Italy never to return again, never to see their families, never to see their friends. Imagine the impelling need to leave and come here. Of course they weren't coming here—again a part of the myth—coming here for personal freedom, for politics—nothing of the sort. I've stood on the shores of Amalfi, Capri, Ravello, Sorrento on the Amalfi coast and elsewhere in Italy, seen scenes of enormous, compelling beauty. As to bring to my mind immediately, why would anyone ever leave this place to come to New Haven or any similar number of places? Of course the obvious answer is because they had to—because there really was no choice.

"Now Is My Chance to Marry Him"

Antonette Sicignano spoke in her kitchen on Wooster Street on August 5, 1999.

My mother had a fight with her father in Italy. Now in Italy they were talking from the balcony to downstairs and my mother was talking to her boyfriend. He whistled. He called her; he wanted to talk to her. She met this boyfriend. She talked to him from the balcony and my grandfather gave her a beating for talking to anybody. She [my mother] came out but she was mad because his [boyfriend's] mother didn't like her. But then he said to her, "I'm going away but I'll come back, I'm going to marry you." She said, "No, I don't think so." And while he was gone his mother was talking about her and everything. So when he came back he said to her, "I want to marry you." She said, "No, your mother don't like me." He said, "You don't marry me, I'm going join the army—my mother ain't gonna see me anymore." So she said, "I can't help it, your mother don't like me."

My mother knew my father in Amalfi, but he went away to London. When he came to New Haven they used to have men boarders. That's how they used to live, the ladies. They used to wash their clothes, they used to cook. They used to call them boarders. And so he knew my mother's aunt. He said, "Is your niece married yet?" So she said, "No she's not married yet." He said, "I want to write her a note, is it all right if I write her a note? Could I send for her? I want to see if she comes to America, I'll marry her." Because he knew my mother. So that's what happened. When she had a fight with her father, she said, "I'm going away to America." "Why?" he said. "Well, because you hit me. This fella wants to marry me." And she went.

Then my father sent for her, she got the letter. She said, "Now is my chance to go to America and marry him." She [already] knew my father though. But she had a nice man [that she left] in Italy; she used to say he had red hair, a nice looking fella. She said when he came here from Italy he knew my father and he wanted to see my father. He came to my mother's house. My mother looked at him. He saw the kids, I forgot how many she had. He said, "Those should have been my kids." So she said, "Well you can get married." He said, "No, I wouldn't get married." He wouldn't. He really loved her.

"LEAVE QUICKLY, THERE'S GOING TO BE WAR"

Anna Fasano spoke from her kitchen in Fair Haven on August 15, 1998. Her husband Attilio was in the backyard roasting coffee beans with an old-fashioned hand-turned roaster Italians called "abbrustulaturo."

Italy in the 1930s there was the very rich and the very poor. The poor worked in the countryside. Where we lived, Castellabate, in the province of Salerno, where the Amalfi coast begins and winds up to Sorrento, is all sea sides and all very beautiful. Where we lived there were no factories, there was nothing. We just lived off the

ANNA AND ATTILIO FASANO
In kitchen,
Lombard Street,
Fair Haven, 1998

A. Riccio

land we worked. We were too far deep in the south from the north and there was nothing we could do about it. There was nothing. The bathrooms were outside. The rich people in the country owned everything like today, but they never had what we have here in America, never. But if you went into the cities, especially in the north, beginning in Rome and going up, it was just like America. There was no difference; there was industry, everything, because everyone worked. And that's why everyone from the south went to the north in search of work, to Switzerland, to France, to Milan, Florence, and Genoa. On Christmas and Easter the husbands used to return to Castellabate, to the families they had left behind and after fifteen days they would go back to work. It was not easy; life was tough for everyone. I remember Mussolini when we were in under the fascists. I can't say anything good or bad about Mussolini. But he did some good for us. In 1932, Mussolini sent schools huge boxes full of toys and sport items, children's games like "i cerchi," rings you threw, with two sticks you threw them and then you went and retrieved them. He sent pencils, books to read. In the back of each one was written, and they were in every house: "He who curses or goes against God, says no to the homeland. —Benito Mussolini." Then he made a law that said all the children of Castellabate, all the children in Italy had to go to school. If they didn't, they threw their parents in jail. They arrested a lot of parents on the farms because the fathers were thick-headed, saying, "I work and my children have to work too." Mussolini said, "No, you are a swine and your children shouldn't grow up to be swine." And everyone had to go to school. My mother's cousin, his name was Alfredo Uglietti, worked in the office of Benito Mussolini—it was Mussolini, him and another person from Castellabate. They were all journalists and they worked with Mussolini. And he told my mother, "Get out of here right away, there's going to be a big war but don't say a word or they'll kill you." He already knew there was going to be a war. I was fifteen when I left in 1934.

(translated from Italian)

"Don't Let Her Go With Nobody"

Concetta Criscuolo spoke in her living room at her East Haven home on January 31, 1999.

I was in Italy with my grandmother because my mother—her husband died and I was a little girl, I must have been two years old. So she left her mother—my grandmother—and she came here and she says, "I'll make some money." And she used to send money to her and me to take care of me. So she took care of me all that time. In the meantime my mother got married again over here. People used to tell her, "You're too young to be . . . why don't you get married?" So I was in Italy. And my grandmother used to take care of me so my mother used to send money for her and me. She wanted me to come here but my grandmother never wanted to come. So she got married again, she got that boy. She used to send money for her and me because she had her son with her—she wouldn't come back to Italy. My grandmother wouldn't send me [to America] with strangers—they weren't strangers, they were our paesanis [friends from the same town]. So she used to say to her, "If you want your daughter you got to come and get her yourself—I won't send her with anybody." So finally she came to Italy and she brought that boy with her. And she was there about a year. Then my stepfather wrote, "If you don't come here I won't send you no more money, you got to come back over here because after all, he wanted her here. She came back to America—my grandmother wouldn't come. My grandmother came to Palermo on the ship and I remember as if it was today, I was crying that I didn't want to come, I didn't want to leave her. So finally we got here and in New York down the ship my stepfather was there waiting. We saw the Statue of Liberty—I didn't know, I said "Oooh!" My mother said, "Look, look, we're in America now." I remember that, it was big high thing in the water. My mother bought bananas when we got off the boat. She said, "Eat that, it's good." That was the first time I had bananas, I never saw them. I spit it out, I didn't like the banana. We ate a lot of those, the ones where the skin pinches, it's a fruit, you peel it and you eat the fruit, the "ficorini." My grandmother used to pick them from the tree and grow them up the attic and keep them all winter, we used to eat them, gradually, every day, every other day. That was the fruit. The figs—the big figs—she used to pick off the tree. We took the train. So we came here and we lived here in New Haven. But in the meantime on the ship—the "Princess Serena"—she got sick. She got sick so they used to give you this soup, they used to bring the soup and instead of eating the soup myself I used to give it to my mother. My life, the way it went, I used to take care of her. I knew just what to do. She came here, she got double pneumonia, they rushed her to the hospital and she died. In the meantime she had her sister here and she was married. And she said to her sister in the hospital, "I know I'm going to die—you take care of my daughter—don't you give my daughter to nobody." And my aunt and uncle really took care of me as if I was their own daughter. And I stayed with her till I got married on January 15, 1920. My uncle gave me away.

❝Stop Signs and Corn❞

Anna Fasano spoke while we sipped "cafe nero" or espresso, in the kitchen of her Fair Haven home, along with her sister Irena and husband Attilio on August 15, 2000.

The first thing that impressed me when I came to America was, "Oh, Mamma, look there, 'Stoppa.'" I said, "Dad, who is this Stoppa, what does it mean?" My father said, "Oh no, that's stop, it means the cars have to stop." Oh Papa, I said, "Stoppa." And then I used to hear, "Corne, corne! What are these corne?" In Italy 'le corne' are like this, [second and fifth finger thrust to ward off evil], which means someone is cheating on a spouse. But what are these 'corne' here? I found out they meant corn, the corn that grows on the stalks. I said to myself, even in America they have the 'corne.'

"I Wasn't a Foreigner"

Anna Rosati spoke at her daughter Louise's home in the Annex on May 7, 2000.

We lived in Italy. My father wanted to go to Italy, sold the house, he had a dairy. He sold the whole business. And we went. He was a merchant; he came back and forth five times. Italy is nice, we lived in Salerno, like here in Lighthouse [annex]. By the time we came back, we were older. I was fourteen, fifteen. Then, when we got to New York, they wouldn't let us out. Because my mother had three children born in Italy, they wouldn't let us out. They said, "The Americans get off, but not the Italians." So we stayed three or four days in that place, on Ellis Island. Madonna! Come erano brutte chille gente! [Mother Mary! How awful those people were!]. The police womans, they thought like we were crooks or what. Madonna! Terrible, those Irish police womans. They used to holler. First of all, we didn't know much of the language. When we came back from Italy, we didn't know the English, we forgot our English, we went to school over there but we talked the good Italian. How could we talk to them, chilli dei paesi? [those people from the country]. No, and then we didn't talk no dialects, you couldn't understand. There's a thousand dialects. There was some from Italy, there was the better class. Then there was other class, those other ladies, I dunno, they didn't dress right. You know, in dei paesi scordati all'Italia [in the remote, forgotten towns in Italy] how they dress. They were all contadini [farmers]. They used to dirty on the floor, they didn't know they had to go to toilet. Oh Madonna! It looked terrible. You know the American people were tough on the poor people coming in. At night, six o'clock we had to go to bed. Big room with everybody else. There were a lotta Italian people from different parts of Italy, too. They didn't understand nothing. Madonna! How you gonna stay in the bed? Every night they used to give you a piece a soap so before you went to bed, you had to get washed. Then six o'clock in the morning we were up! What we had to do in that big hall all day long? It was like a prison. We had to stay in there all day long, once in a while they used to let us out for a half hour, get some air, then you had to come in. Then three o'clock in the afternoon they used to give us a glass of milk. So the men, they wouldn't give it to the men, so they used to make us take it, we used to give it them. Madonna! The Americani, they're no good, the Irish. All the Jews near the wailing wall. The Jews stood there near the wall with a book, a-du-du, a-du-du, all day long. They prayed by the wall all day long. I don't know che facevano [what they were doing]. It was fun though. You know why? Because we were young. The only thing, we no like to go to bed so early and get up so early. Che erammo a fa at six o'clock in that hall? [What was there to do at six o'clock in the morning in that hall?]. Eh, like us, when you're young, you don't think so much, yeah. After five days they had a make like a talk [hearing] if we could get off in New York and they said the Americans could get off but not the others, the mother and father, they go back. Who was gonna take them? She [my sister] was a baby, the other two were small, the twins. And so the Americans could get off and "Youse go back." My father [who was not a citizen] says, "No, or everybody, or we all go back." We were happy if we went back. È vero! [really]. So finally we got off because we were more Americans born over here, me, my sister Mary, Esther, we were six or seven. I wasn't a foreigner because I was born here, we hadda go through like the other people went through. My mother had three born in Italy, because we coulda got off right away, my mother had six, seven children born here. I was born in North Haven, the others were born on Chapel Street.

Becoming American Citizens

For Italian immigrants, the act of becoming an American citizen signified their official participation in the entitlement to rights and provisions under the law. But for many Italian-born raised in the countryside and hinterland of rural Italy, citizenship did not mean the sudden abandonment of traditional beliefs or changes in the old ways of Italian life. Most had little experience with public education in Italy and the language barrier in the early days of immigration posed a daunting obstacle for many who applied for American citizenship. Many who were getting along in New Haven's neighborhoods where only Italian dialects were spoken chose to remain noncitizens, never bothering to learn English. Those who passed citizenship examinations by answering questions from the examiner often relied on American-born children or close friends to stand by their side.

New Haven's Italians relied on an informal network of bilingual advocates in every neighborhood of the city, civic-minded men like Anthony Paolillo, Salvatore "Gary" Garibaldi, and Cataldo Massa who assisted immigrants from their wards in the process of obtaining American citizenship. Middle-aged men and women with little or no formal education had to learn to write their names for the first time; in some cases the applicant had to write names of various presidents under the watchful eye of the examiner. Some enrolled in evening classes to learn English in the same schools their American-born children attended during the day. In grammar school classrooms they tried writing English by reciting simple nursery rhyme sentences. Grown men and women who had never held a pen in their hands practiced writing their names over and over, filling the lined pages of personal notebooks in scrawled, unsteady script, "My name is Vincenzo. I live on 163 Fairmont Avenue."

In 1917, Congress passed a mandatory literacy test into law as a way to curtail Italian immigration. In 1924, the National Origins Act imposed quotas, drastically reducing the number of Italian immigrants into the country. After the war in the 1940s, with anti-immigration tensions relaxed, citizenship proceedings in New Haven were more a formality for Italian immigrants than a serious test of literacy or loyalty to the country. Oftentimes the appointed advocate, usually a friend of the family, filled out the application forms, located and verified birth records, and sometimes acted as "precura," or power of attorney. On the day of the hearing, the advocate sometimes answered questions on behalf of the non-English speaking person before the examiner. Questions about the applicant's work record were answered with, "Oh, he is a hard working man." Examiners often asked the applicant the number of children in the family. And finally, when the question why citizenship should be granted was asked, the answer was always, "We should be proud of him or her because he or she loves America." Neighborhood advocates who appeared at citizenship hearings with new applicants eventually gained the trust of the court examiners who recognized them as credible witnesses, which made the process smoother for the next Italian applicant.

"AMERICA! AMERICA!"

Salvatore "Gary" Garibaldi spoke at the Santa Maria Maddalena Society on Wooster Street on April 12, 2000.

Annuziàtìna Consiglio called upon me and said she'd like to become a citizen. Naturally in those days [early 1950s] you had to fill out citizenship papers and I did that for her. I asked her the questions, I wrote them out and filled it out. I told her that the day would come when they would call upon her to be interviewed and that she needed a witness and that I'd be more than happy to be that witness. She was with her husband, the owner of the Big Apple restaurant. She was very happy to think that I would go all through those extremes to help her become an American citizen. So I took her to the federal office where you submit your papers and she was admitted and sworn in to become a citizen. When I told her to raise her hand, she wasn't that fluent in English, I said, 'Nunziàtine, alza a mano, cuando 'o giudice dice, 'Nunziàtine, raise your hand when the judge speaks. And she said, "Si, si signore Garibaldi," Yes, yes, Mister Garibaldi. Full of respect. Well, she was not the only one there, there were other aliens of different nationalities and they also had a helping hand, someone there as their witness to help them do the same thing that I was doing on behalf of 'Nunziàtine. Well, when they raised their hand and the judge swore them in he told them, "God bless America and I am sure that you will all fulfill your obligation to become great citizens of our country because of your volunteering to become American citizens and therefore my clerk will give not only a pamphlet with the song 'Star Spangled Banner,' but I'm also going to give each and every one of you an American flag as a gift." Well, she was looking at me and then the young woman clerk, when she handed her the American flag, she turned around and she said to that young woman in Italian, "May God bless you and God bless America . . . America! [Voice rising] America! [shouting] America!" Now she was going into saying America about six or seven times that it caused people around her to look at her and because of the way she was yelling that the judge turned around [yelling happily] "We're all American!" Because now she had everybody saying "America." And naturally her husband and her son were with her and they sat in the rear. And when we got through the son said to me, "Gary, has to

SALVATORE "GARY" GARIBALDI
At the Santa Maria Maddalena Society,
Wooster Street, 1999

A. Riccio

be my mother to act like that." I said, I'll tell you why—that was one of her proudest moments in America, that she wanted to become an American citizen. And the day came where she saw that she was sworn in as a citizen of this great country and fortunately the only way she expressed herself was when she started yelling, [laughing] "America! America!"

"Trick Questions"

John Ginnetti was ninety-three at the time of our interview. He spoke at the kitchen table with his wife Mary, son John, and brothers Al and Orlando on August 21, 1999.

My father tried to become a citizen three times. They used to have trick questions in those days [1900s]. So the last time he went before the examiner, "Who's the president of the United States?" He told him at the time who was the mayor of New Haven. And he answered all the questions accurately. Then the last question was: "How many stars are there on a quarter or a half dollar?" They had stars imprinted on those coins. So my father didn't know. The examiner said, "Well, go back to school." My father said, "You go back—that's your business," and he walked out. And at the time who was being examined was the former mayor's father, Mister Celentano. He came up. The same thing. "How many stars on the quarter?" Mister Celentano said, "I don't know. Do you know how many oranges are in a crate?" The examiner said, "No." He said, "That's my business—I know. How many stars? That's your business. You know." And it turned out that his son became the mayor years later. It's ironic. But my father never passed and never became a citizen. He didn't want to go back. Now here's my father, a plain hard working citizen, never been in trouble, and he was denied a citizenship. And you get a lot of these people that are citizens that are felons, that are crooks and everything else. They did away with that [trick questions] eventually I understand.

"The Pigeons"

Bill Savo spoke from his kitchen at his home in the Annex on July 28, 2000.

My grandfather went up for his citizenship papers. He's sweating bullets. And so the judge is trying to get straight answers for all his questions. So finally he said, "Well, I'll give him an easy one. So he asked my grandfather, "What flies above City Hall here?" My grandfather said, "The pigeons." The judge said, "O.K., you're right." And he gave it to him. He should have said the flag. He said the pigeons. He was right.

"I Keese the Flag"

Nina Pane Sanseverino spoke from her kitchen with her sister Josie on Bishop Street on July 30, 1999.

When my grandmother—Antonette Pastore—got her citizenship they said to her, "If you saw the American flag on the ground all torn up and everything what would you do Mrs. Pastore? She said, "A me? Me?" And she immediately turned

COLUMBUS SCHOOL
Eighth grade graduation ceremony at Waterside Park
Sargent factory in background, 1938

Midolo family album

on the tears. She said [sing-song voice], "Si! I see the American flag, I pick it up a, I sew it, I wash it, I fold it and I put it closer to my heart. And I keese it, I keese it." They said, "Granted."

"WE'LL MAKE YOU AN AMERICAN CITIZEN"

Rose Savo spoke in the kitchen of her brother John Nappi's home in East Haven on June 23, 2000. Her brother John was the son referred to in this story.

She went to school to study for her citizenship so I went with her. When my mother went for her citizenship papers she was a little scared. She was sweating bullets. But she knew what she was talking about. So the judge called her, "Misses Nappi! What can I do for you?" So the judge asked her different questions. So now she waited and waited. So anyway, then she got up—she was nervous. She says in half Italian and half in English, "Signore giudice [mister judge], I gone to school a long a time—I learn a nu-ting [voice rising]. Just like that. Fee you wanna give a to me, thank you, fee you no wan a give a to me"—instead of saying if, she said "fee"—"you no wanna give a to me, thank you just a same." So the judge comes over, puts his arm around her. "Yeah, Misses Nappi, I'm gonna give it to you." Then, you know, she got encouraged, she says, [drawing her breath] "Signore giudice, [voice rising] Mister Judge, eh, my son, he fight in do Pacifica [in the Pacific] five a years—and now he's a sick boy—you're not doin' me any favors!" My brother had a big write up because he volunteered as the G.I. guinea pig for the malaria [experiments] during the war. So she told him, "My son, he's a sick boy, he fight in do pacifico [in the Pacific], five a years, five a years!" The judge said, "I give it to you mamma, I give it you." And she said, "He's not doing me any favors." Oh, he was so nice that judge. He felt bad. "Your brother is sick?" I said, Yeah, he's got malaria—he gets terrible attacks. He was a hospital in New Zealand I don't know how many months. There wasn't enough blankets to put on him.

"I NO LIKE A MISS FINECHELLE"

John Nappi spoke at the kitchen table of his East Haven home on July 28, 2000.

Her name was Miss Finnegan. She was the teacher, I remember her, she used to be a school teacher. I tell you, you know the [Wicked] Witch in the Wizard of Oz? She looked just like her, pointed nose and everything. The old man used to go to the class. So he used to come home, he used to say, "Miss Finechelle, I no like." He used to call her "Finechelle," he didn't like her. You know something? On account of her he never went to get his citizenship papers, I swear to god, he didn't like her. So she asked, "How come your father told my sister, how come he doesn't come no more?" Well, he couldn't tell them that he didn't like her, so he didn't go, that's it. Maybe the way she acted I guess. I don't know why. He was easy to get along with. Maybe her attitude, he just didn't like her. They taught them who was the president of the United States, how many states in the union, how many stripes in the flag, all about the pledge of allegiance you had to learn, things like that. I remember when I was going to the Dante School; they had a stage show. All the old people, they had a play about the Constitution, about the flag and all that. And they dressed these old Italian ladies—it was a joke—like they did the pilgrims. And they had to recite in English and they had to march. You want to hear them when they tried to speak half-English, half-Italian; they tried to put on the show. You would have laughed. But they did it.

5 *Going to School*

In 1877, the Italian government passed a law making school attendance compulsory for children between ages six and seven. The law was ignored by officials in the south who funneled heavy tax revenues imposed on the peasantry to fund the superior northern school system. Italy had the poorest school attendance among countries in Europe. Schools in the south were often poorly constructed, lacked heat, and were unsanitary.[8] After the government supplied initial funding for building schools, the burden fell on town administrations to run and maintain them. Overtaxed southern municipalities had little money to pay teachers who were often untrained and ill-equipped to teach children. Books and study aids were almost nonexistent. For many poor families struggling to survive, the inability to meet clothing requirements meant a child could not attend school. Poor farming families' dependence on extra young hands in the fields for survival outweighed the need for school. Children of aristocratic families were encouraged to continue their schooling while daughters and sons of the poor were ridiculed by teachers for attending. By 1871, the illiteracy rate in the south reached ninety percent. Few learned formal Italian, which was taught in schools as a foreign language. Most people continued speaking dialects, restricting their ability to read rarely-found newspapers or any forms of literature. Many relied on the spoken word of literates—town officials, doctors, and lawyers—or hearsay for their information. To poor southerners, those who were educated and spoke Italian were looked upon with disdain as wealthy landowners, corrupt politicians, or northern tax collectors who exploited them in a feudal system of lord and serf.

Many Italian immigrants retained the old world distrust of education when their American-born children began attending New Haven schools. For some Italians, sending a child to school posed a threat to parental authority and eliminated a wage-earning son or daughter who could compensate for the meager earnings of a working father or brother. As a new world institution where attendance was mandatory, Italian parents believed that modern "American ways" fostered in schools would corrupt their children to think of themselves as future adults with progressive ideas that collided with conservative Italian values and beliefs.[9] To Italian-born immigrants, family relationships, respect for parental authority, and the importance of home superceded any values imposed by outside institutions.

In classrooms of the Dante, Columbus, and Woodward schools, where Italian children observed the mannerisms of genteel Irish and Yankee school teachers, they were taught that the old world ways and the language spoken by their parents were considered "foreign" and thus "un-American." Teachers changed the names of their Italian students from Generosa to Jennie; surnames like San Giovanni to Saint John. As school children became increasingly Americanized, stark contrasts between the modern, urban lifestyle learned in schools and rural Italian folkways of immigrant parents caused tensions at home and often boiled over into heated arguments between the less-assimilated first-generation parents and more-assimilated second-generation children who began to disparage their Italian heritage. In the eyes of many American-born children, the folkish lifestyles of Italian-born parents became a source of shame, their native language that of "cafoni," or boorish peasants, their old-fashioned way of life and customs that of outdated "greenhorns." When a son or daughter challenged a parent with the often-repeated slogan heard in school, "America is the greatest country in the world," how could a mother or father respond?

The cultural divide between first and second generation Italians and the assimilation of American values by second-generation children over the ways of their parents reverberated through later generations of New Haven's Italian Americans. Today, many third- and fourth-generation Italian Americans in search of their cultural roots regret their loss of heritage, especially the ability to understand and speak the language of their Italian-born ancestors.

"THE FIVE-DOLLAR GOLD PIECE"

Joseph Riccio spoke in the kitchen of his home in the Annex on June 26, 1999. He attended the Woodward School in the Annex during the 1920s.

We felt almost as ashamed as intimidated [in the 1920s]. At school after Thanksgiving particularly I remember for the fourth, the fifth, the sixth, the seventh grade. When we went back to school we had to tell what we had for Thanksgiving—I remember in the fourth grade—they always used to say dessert. And I said, Gee, they don't even know how to spell desert. Honest to God. What's dessert? We didn't know what dessert was. We had cookies, all the pastries; we had "le zeppole" with honey and sugar on them all that stuff. That was not our dessert; it was our goodies. It wasn't till about the fifth grade that I had the nerve to say, Well what did you have for dessert? [Student] "Pumpkin pie." How come? [Student] "Well pumpkin pie goes with Thanksgiving dinner you know." I said, Oh, dessert. You learned these things. They intimidated you because they were so much more ahead of us in the going-ons in this country. We were ashamed of [being] Italian. They came to school dressed, all dressed up nice. We came with clean clothes but never nothing fancy like those people wore. The Carlsons, the Griswolds, they came the girls all primped up, all dressed up, the guys all white shirts and everything. And the Italian guys like us, we came with clean clothes—always cleaned and pressed—but we looked like slobs compared to them. You felt intimidated. It wasn't until you started being the first one in arithmetic in the fifth, the sixth, the seventh, and the eighth grade that you got a little confidence in yourself. Every time we used to have a test I used to finish, I would look around. Nobody was finished and I used to put the pencil down. And one day Miss Hines came by and she said, "Joseph, what are you doing?" I said, I'm all through. So she said, "Well, bring it up." So I brought it up. She said, "What are you ashamed of?" I hated to be the first one—you're showing off, you know. After that I wanted to be the first one all the time. And I was good with arithmetic. We spoke Italian before we spoke English; we had to learn the English language. You know what I mean? Yeah. So we were intimidated and it wasn't until we started growing up. When I graduated from grammar school, Mrs. "Paloma" [butterfly] Vanacore who was a friend of my mother came across the street because we were having the graduation exercise and she had to come and see. She said to my mother, [in Italian] "What did you give you son for a graduation gift?" My mother said, [incredulous voice] "What do you mean? I got to give him a present for graduation?" She said, "Oh yeah, you have to give him something, it don't look nice—everybody gets something." So she said, "Here, I got something." So she gave her a five-dollar gold piece. My mother takes the five-dollar gold piece. She said to me, "I want get it back, though—Paloma let me take it." So my mother gave me a five-dollar gold piece just for the graduation exercise, to show that I got a present for graduating from grammar school. She didn't give it to me; I showed it to the kids at school just for that afternoon. The kids asked, "What did you get?" I showed them—Here, I got a five-dollar gold piece. They said, "Oh boy, Riccio got a five-dollar gold piece!" I didn't know what the hell a five-dollar gold piece was—what did a five-dollar gold piece mean to me? I put it in my pocket and I gave it back to her, that's all. I knew it wasn't mine. My mother said, "Don't lose it." Everybody got something. We didn't know. We were children of peasants; people who came from the earth. They came here, work, work, work. They instilled in us, "Vai a scuola e nun fa 'o ciùccio come ama fatta nuie," Go to school so you won't have to work like jackasses like we did. That's it.

"CINDERELLA"

Mary Marino spoke from her living room on Warren Street in the Wooster Square neighborhood on August 24, 1999.

I was thirteen years old when I graduated and I wanted to go to school. I got sent home by the teachers that my grades were good and they thought it was a shame that I had to waste my education. But in those days [early '20s], they weren't fussy. My mother said, "You're crazy, you got to help me." I went to Boardman Trade school because I begged her. So she said to me, "No, Tu ai ì a faticà, Mamma ci serve i soldi." [No, you have to work, mother needs the money]. So I went to

MARY MARINO
In her living room,
Warren Street,
Wooster Square, 1999

A. Riccio

Boardman Trade. They told you how far away from the table you got to get. And I was a little pale. Because I know why. So I came, she said to me, "See, 'o piglia, ti ha fatt ianca, ianca a bella mamma. Ti aiuta a scuola? Chilla faccia ianca, ianca, bella mamma." [See how pale your face got from going to school? Oh what a pale face.] She [meaning I] was very pale but when she [I] went to work she [I] wasn't pale. So I worked in the house, helped in our grocery store. That's how we fed the eight kids. So then after they sent down a man from the education. And he said, "You know your daughter has got to go to school." My mother said, "What school? I need her for me." Meanwhile she and my sister got sick with typhoid fever. They said that everybody had to get out of the house—we couldn't stay in the same house. We had to take all the scarves off the bureaus. They had to boil meat and drink the juice. The nurse used to come every day. The doctor came three times a day. My mother didn't believe the doctor. In those days, [laughing] you put oil on anything you had. Everything we used to have, my mother used to say, "Miette l'olio caldo, Put warm oil on it." They say that's a healing thing. You know what? I was suffering from something and I told the doctor nothing works. He said, "What are you doing now?" I said, "I put olive oil." But they left Cinderella home [laughing]. They didn't give a damn if I got the goddamned typhoid [laughing heartily]! They had a label on the door: "Do not enter." And they left me, the sucker, the Cinderella. And I had to do housework, try to take care of the store. Then after that she got better. Thank the Lord.

"Let Tony Go to School"

Anthony Vanacore spoke on his back porch with his wife Renee at his North Haven home on November 20, 1999.

A lot of Italian people were compassionate; that was one of the traits that helped them to survive. They took care of each other; your troubles were my troubles, see? That's why we survived, I'm sure. Like you now. I don't know what your background is but you must be educated right? College? In my time, college was impossible. You were lucky if you could go to school. Because you had to go out and support the family. I remember my brother John used to fix cars in a rented garage on Wooster Street and my brother Andrew quit—he was going to high school—and it was my turn to high school from grammar school. He dropped out of high school so I could go to high school. And he got a job to help support the family. I never forgot that. And my father didn't want to . . . He said, "No, stay in school." My brother said, "No, I want Tony to get an education—I don't need it. I can get along on my own." See, so that's what he done. He quit high school so that I could go to school. I graduated from Hillhouse in 1930. So they survived, sent their kids to school. That's why you got to be very proud of your heritage, very proud. Because whatever they had and whatever they got came from the sweat of their ancestors, see?

"She Made Us Proud"

Joseph Riccio spoke from his kitchen table at his home in the Annex on June 26, 1999.

Misses Katherine Vandervelden was a wonderful teacher at the Woodward School [in the '20s]. She made you feel that it was the best school in the city because of you. The district here, the Granniss Corner, the 32nd ward, the Annex, was the best place because you helped make it that way. Your home was the best home on the block because you made it that way. You felt it; we took pride. Every year they used to have a school week and we used to have a marching fife and drum school band. We always won first prize. Allan Rockwell [chuckling] used to be the baton guy.

"GOING TO SCHOOL, GOING TO WORK"

Annette Ruocco spoke from her kitchen at her home in the Annex.

I went to Columbus school and I went to the sixth, the seventh, and the eighth grade. And they used to have divisions in those days, three levels for each grade. And thank God I was always in the higher division, even though I didn't have too much time studying. I don't know how I got my work in because when we came home from school we would stop at Buonocore's dress shop. And we would get work to bring home, a dozen, a dozen and a half, or two of skirts to hem or to put the snaps on them or buttons. And once I got home I would be helping my mother sewing at night and earning a few extra dollars because in those days they didn't have unions. They were allowed to give you a bundle of work, bring it home and give you a few pennies a dozen, maybe twenty-five, fifty cents. My mother at the end of the week would earn maybe a five dollar bill—that was a lot of money. My mother had to do that dozen and the next morning when my brother and I went back to school we would drop them off. And the following day we'd stop in again and if they had work that to be handmade, you know hems and snaps—they didn't have machines to put on buttons or overcasts to make a hem. You did that all by hand. And if they had it you'd get another dozen so by the end of the week she'd earn a few dollars.

When I graduated from grammar school we had a beautiful graduation ceremony. On the day I graduated because my birthday is June 22nd. I was lucky because I couldn't get out of there because I wasn't fourteen. I would have felt terrible if I weren't able to graduate. That happened to a lot of kids. And what was sad in those days. If you weren't up with your marks they would put you in a room, they called that the "opportunity room." And you learned maybe to cook if you were in domestic work or if you were somebody that could take up being a carpenter, they did carpentry work. And then when they were of age to go to work they came out of there and never graduated. Whereas I was lucky, I went to the eighth grade. I don't think my parents had intentions of taking me out but anyway they didn't have to. I graduated on June 22nd, my birthday and that's when I was fourteen. I had signed up to go to Commercial High School because if you went in for business you went to Commercial. So I signed up because I had very good marks in the eighth grade and I graduated right on my fourteenth birthday. So that summer I started working at Insler's turning belts and getting very little money. They were paying maybe fifteen cents an hour. You'd make four, five dollars at the end of the week, if you even earned that much. I never went back to [Commercial] because I started earning those few dollars and that meant a lot. And the Italian father, he didn't think that it was that important that you . . . as long as I could read, I could write, I could cook, I could sew, or I made a good wife, see? I taught my mother recipes because I could read the recipe in English so we'd make the bread. My father marveled at that. Then I went to night school for typing and I took up Italian. He didn't like me going out at night. Then you're disrupting the family because if he came home at six and I had to be on my way to Commercial; they didn't like that. So I never went to high school. Since I was the oldest one in the family and I had to start working. If you were, say, third or fourth in line their families, they're the one to go to high school and on to college. I never got into a dress shop because the dress shops were all families—one brought a sister, the aunt brought in a niece, but I didn't have anybody like that to take me in.

"How Beautiful They Looked"

Antonette Sicignano spoke from her kitchen on Wooster Street on August 30, 1999. She spoke wistfully about her lost dream of dressing up in white and graduating from grammar school.

I didn't go to graduation. I was only thirteen years old, now I'm eighty-eight. What a difference! My mother used to do like this. Because we were a lot, my father was a sick man with bad asthma; he died when he was in his fifties. If one daughter wanted to get married, the other one's going to be thirteen, fourteen years old. She used to say "You can't go to school, you got find a job." My sister got married that September. I found a job. I had to go to work in the shirt shop; that's how I started working in the shirt shop. But I didn't graduate; I wanted to graduate. Because there was going to be a room, just for all the girls. They had no boys; they had all girls. And I went to see the graduation the year before, the ones that graduated. I loved it. They were all in white for graduation with all big flowers. How beautiful they looked. And I sat there watching them and I said next year I'll be up there on the stage. We had a stage at Greene Street school. But I never went. No, I couldn't. School closed in June; the week after I went to work. And I had to go take a test, everything you learned in school, the president and all that. And if you passed it, you would get your ticket there, the working papers and you could go to work. You had to show that at work. That was our time. What are you gonna do? My mother had fourteen children. She was a strong woman my mother, very, very strong. She was small, chunky. We were ten girls and four boys. We didn't think nothing of it. We had to go to work. My father was sick. I used to work because I loved my father, he was such a good man. He loved us all. We used to get up during the night and try to fan him. My mother used to say, "Put his hands in hot water, he can breathe better." Now they got oxygen and all that. We used to call the doctor and he used to come at two o'clock in the morning to give him morphine. He used to shake all up and then he used to go to sleep.

"In Loco Parentis"

Frank DePonte, a retired school teacher, spoke in the living room of his old friend Joseph Riccio's home in the Annex on November 21, 1999.

I can't think of anybody who didn't or couldn't compute. And we had kids sitting next to us, some of them just came off the boat, didn't speak English. They'd sit

COLUMBUS SCHOOL GRADUATION,
with girls dressed in white,
Greene Street, Wooster Square, 1934

Nappi family album

you next to somebody who just came from Italy. They didn't have special classes, you stuck him next to somebody else and you interpreted for them and maybe in a couple years he would speak better than you. They didn't have those programs; they couldn't afford them. We were taught by people—in those days you could be a teacher with a two-year normal school degree. And they were all women, most of them unmarried, most of them Irish or Jewish. But everybody knew how to read and write. You never went to school and got hit and went and told your parents. You had to be a nut. You'd get another beating. They had in those days and they may still have it today, the teacher was "in loco parentis." It's a state law. In other words when you were in school, your teacher was your parent. And if they hit you, it was like a parent hitting you. So you can't sue your parents. First of all if they hit you, you realize you were absolutely wrong. There was no way you could be right and the teacher could be wrong. I don't care what happened. So you didn't go home because you knew they were never going to take your part, they were going to take the teacher's part and get a beating again. So you kept your mouth shut. And then if you did something wrong—and in those days wrong was relative—and you had to bring your parent in, this is really an embarrassment, I mean you can't control your own kid? He doesn't know respect for the teacher? What kind of a parent are you? They were embarrassed because they would have to come. A lot of them didn't speak English and they were embarrassed about that. The teacher could tell them anything, they didn't understand. Their only out was, "That's your teacher—whatever she says is right." You could have forty-two witnesses that the teacher was wrong, but you were wrong. That was a completely different style of schooling. And the boys used to go in one entrance and the girls in another; never the twain shall meet. When the war came I couldn't think of anybody who was turned—they may have relaxed the restrictions—but I can't think of anybody who was ever turned down because they were illiterate. We have all these problems now; I can't understand it. We know so much more, you have to have so many degrees before you can even begin to teach and half of them can't get out of school who can read and write. We didn't go on to college because that was out of our reach, really. It wasn't even something that was in our imagination, very, very few people went.

"You Know How to Write Your Name—That's Enough"

Rose Savo spoke from her kitchen at her home in the Annex on July 28, 2000.

My mother never sent me to school, whatever little bit I know I learned myself. I used to love to read. My mother never went to school. She used to say, "It isn't important for a girl to go to school, a boy has to go to school, not the girls." I never was in school. And one day I threw it up to my mother, I says,"Mi ha fatto venire na' dumbell, non mi ha mandato manco a scuola," You made a dumb bell out of me, you didn't even send me school. She said, "Manc' i cani, che eva scuola, tu," It shouldn't happen not even to a dog, that you went to school. I knew too much already. But I was already too far behind in school because I was never there. I was like a little ol' lady—that's all I did, housework. I couldn't reach the washtub. She made a nice little box and I used to stand on the box and wash the clothes, yeah. So when I was fourteen my mother said, "Tu sai legge, sai scrivere 'o nòmme tùjo—a basta!" You know how to read, you know how to write your name—that's enough! My mother had her own beliefs and she stuck to it.

6

The Spanish Flu Epidemic in New Haven

The Spanish Flu killed more Americans than World War I, World War II, the Korean War, and the Vietnam War combined, with the estimated loss of life at over a half million victims.[10] Striking every continent, it killed millions within a year, more than any famine, war, or infection in recorded history. In *Epidemic and Peace, 1918*, Alfred W. Crosby Jr. described the first alarm in September 1918 when hundreds of robust young soldiers at Fort Devens, Massachusetts, preparing to leave for the battlefields of France, were suddenly overcome with flu-like symptoms. The sneezing, aching legs, and fever pointed to a familiar sickness—the grippe or flu—requiring bed rest. As bedridden soldiers began turning tints of blue, their lungs were filling up with a thin, bloody fluid causing mysterious deaths within forty-eight hours. Doctor William Welch, the nation's foremost pathologist assigned to Fort Devens, could not produce any antibiotics or medical techniques to help stem the speeding tide of death. While doctors stood by helpless, courageous nurses, themselves stricken by the flu from attending to the sick, kept soldiers alive with warm food and blankets and old-fashioned tender loving care until the flu passed.

Theories about the cause of the flu abounded. Some health experts thought the flu had its antecedent in the Black Plague in fourteenth-century Florence, transmitted by breathing in close quarters. Others believed the disease emanated from the battlefields of France, where soldiers fought alongside rotting bodies and lived in filthy conditions. Some health experts pointed to the extreme amount of mustard gas and explosives detonated during the war. In San Francisco, full-page newspaper advertisements petitioning all citizens to wear masks turned the city into a surreal masquerade of white masks and laws were enacted with penalties for those failing to cover their faces. One doctor in an industrial area of New Jersey expressed his inability to isolate Italian patients due to anywhere from four to twelve family members hovering over the sick person, oblivious to the seriousness of the contagion.[11] In Philadelphia, which had the highest mortality rate of any large city, the flu struck 1,500 more women with mothers born in Italy and other European countries. Almost a quarter of American Indians on reservations were stricken and nine percent died at a rate four times that of large cities.

Many of New Haven's Italian Americans had first-hand experience with large-scale epidemics and natural disasters in Italy. Cholera outbreaks, malaria, and other plagues that swept through southern Italy were well-known throughout the south. The eruptions of 1905 in Calabria and Basilicata killed hundreds of people. In 1906, Vesuvius and Etna in 1910 destroyed entire towns, killing thousands of people. But the magnitude and speed of death caused by the Spanish Flu that scythed through urban centers in the United States overshadowed earlier experiences the immigrants had with disasters in Italy. "Little Italies" that had sprung up in virtually every major American city suffered some of the highest rates of death in the United States.[12] Between the years 1915 and 1919, thousands died from the ravages of the Spanish Flu in New Haven.[13] In a corner of Saint Lawrence cemetery, land was set aside for the many victims who died so suddenly that they had to be buried quickly in mass graves. With no proven antibiotics developed that could successfully treat the flu, a pharmacist in the Annex neighborhood experimented with his homemade concoction of mixed patent drugs to combat the symptoms his local customers reported. Healthy Italian American children were sent to school wearing garlands of garlic around their necks to ward off the flu. Newspaper advertisements in the New Haven area appeared with phony elixirs and pills guaranteeing miracle cures. Doctors prescribed daily shots of whiskey to some of their patients. For many years afterward, Italians often recalled the names of lost friends and family members who died during the Spanish Flu pandemic in New Haven, referring to them as "the ones who died from 'a Spagnola.'"

"I Had to Put Her Shoes On"

Giuannine DeMaio, ninety-seven, spoke by the pool at her granddaughter Laurel's home in North Branford on July 1, 1999. When she won a shooting contest at a local feast during World War I, the men said "Hey Uncle Sam can use you! You could win the war by yourself!"

You know, when that came out, I had a girl friend, she was two days older than me. But I was always a little skinny thing. But she was chubby, not fat, but strong and everything. And I always used to lay her down, you know wrestle her down. Even though I was skinny I was stronger than her. Everybody used to say, "Gee, you're skinny," but anyway, one day we were going to work. So she says to me, "You know Jen, I don't feel too good." So I said, well, what made you come to work today? Because we used to have to walk it. She says, "I dunno." I said, Well if you don't feel good, go [home] when go you in. She went in, "I don't feel good." In three days she was dead. Her name was Anna Danteo. She was only, maybe fifteen years old. Everybody on the street had that sickness but this girl was the only one that died at the time. I could remember it like it was the other day. Her and I were like sisters. So when I came home from work the mother sent for me. She says, "Jenny, you know, we believe in the best friend has to put the shoes to the dead girl." Can you imagine? They waited for me to come home from work to put her shoes on, when she was laid in the coffin. Because I was her best friend. And when I picked her up I can still picture, it was like a stone and I put the shoe on. I remember that.

"THEY WERE DYING SO FAST"

Joe and Lena Riccio spoke from their kitchen in their Annex home on July 22, 1999.

Somewhere between 1917 and 1918 we lived in Fair Haven and across the street from our house the Washington Coal and Ice Company had a hearse and carriage that they attended funerals with. And our cousin Frank Russo—had to be about seven or eight years old—had died with the influenza. And we went to see him. We went to first in the carriage, a closed carriage just like a stagecoach that you see on television, horse and coach. I'll never forget it was the first wake I ever went to and I was surprised to see this little boy laid out all in white with confetti and pennies and nickels and dimes in there. The casket was opened. The wake was in the house. I was stunned because it was the first wake I ever saw. I was impressed; little white casket, the kid dressed in white. My friend's mother died of the influenza and she was buried in a common grave at the cemetery. It took them a long time to find her. There was a big field that was all one common grave. That whole area was filled with influenza people that died. They just dug a ditch and kept putting them in one after another. Where were they going to put them? They were dying so fast. They have little markers now; people went over and traced them. My friend traced where his mother was. They [parents] were talking about somebody, "Chill' è mòrte da influenza," That one died from the influenza. And they used to name different people that they knew.

"HIS PRESCRIPTIONS KEPT PEOPLE ALIVE"

Ninety-nine year old Anthony Fiondella spoke in the living room of his East Haven home on December 5, 1998. He apprenticed as a pharmacist and later bought the Granniss Corner Pharmacy.

When that deadly flu was around, and that was around 1918, it killed a lot of people. Doctor Conte used to take fifty cents because the people didn't have any money. The doctors had it hard in those days. They'd visit with you, have coffee, play cards with you. Today they don't want to bother with you hardly. Doctor Boardman had a good record. Not as many of his patients died as other doctors. I don't know why. His prescriptions kept people alive; he had better formulas maybe. He lost fewer patients of any doctor I knew around. Now the doctors just order what the companies tell them about. We were putting up prescriptions till two or three o'clock in the morning, one after another. We didn't get anything—what did you get, seventy-five cents for a prescription those days? The doctor's formula, whatever he wrote the prescriptions in those days had eight or ten ingredients to be

PHARMACIST ANTHONY FIONDELLA
Standing on Granniss corner by
the Granniss Corner Pharmacy, 1964

Fiondella family album

mixed. It wouldn't be just aspirin or something. They're not even heard of today, some of the ingredients but some are still used today in the drugs. In those days, we made all our medicine from the crude drug. Then the Eli Lilly Company, which was a big laboratory in those days, came out with fluid extracts and powdered extracts saved us that first tough step of using the mortar to make a powder of it. It was a lot of work to get the drug started first. We didn't have to do that anymore. We would just take a little of their extract and make the same thing we would make with our own extract. Lilly saved the day with their fluid and powdered extracts because they extracted the drug that we wanted. All we had to do was take some of their extract to make what we wanted. That was in 1915. Why? Is that a long time ago [smiling]?

"They Put Them in the Basement"

Ninety-seven year old Amelia Buonocore spoke with sadness in her living room on September 11, 1999, as she recalled the Spanish Flu.

A lot of people were dying and the undertakers couldn't take care of them. They used to put them down the basement because they couldn't take care of them, there were so many. And my sister Jennie got sick too that time, but she got better. But that lasted quite a while so when things got over then they started taking them out and burying them one by one. I was just a kid, I just went to work.

"A Ticket on the Door"

Mary Altieri spoke as she cooked supper for herself in the kitchen of her Fair Haven home on January 13, 1999.

I remember 1918 because my sister Lucy was born. We didn't have it. Houses used to be quarantined—you couldn't get in. They would put a ticket at the door and you couldn't get in. When my brother had the diphtheria, we had a ticket near the door. Nobody could come and see my mother. Everything was contagious. And yet, all that disease years ago, nobody in my family got it. The boy got it from school, whatever, but then the rest of us didn't get it.

"Dad Sold Her Body to Yale"

Josephine DeBenedet, eighty-four, spoke at her kitchen table in her North Haven home on September 10, 1999. She recalled the birth dates of her twelve grandchildren, saying, "Of course I have to remember them, I gotta give them a present, don't I?"

The Spanish Influenza, they called it "a Spagnola." The people were dying like hotcakes. My mother died in the Spanish Flu. I was only four years old, but I remember everybody being sick and then my mother, she passed away because she didn't have any money and my dad never worked. She used to wash clothes for people, try to earn something for us to eat but we didn't have much to eat. And the story they told me was the few dollars she had she gave it to my dad to go and buy the medication but instead he went to the saloon. I don't think there was much medication. And I remember the day my mom died because my older brother— he was twelve—he took me by the hand and he said to me, "Sis, come over here because they're going to take mamma away." I always remember them taking her, they had her in a straw casket, like a basket. It isn't like now, they put you on a stretcher. At that time, this was in 1918; I saw the basket go away. My brother and I, when we got older, we wanted to look for her grave so we could go and visit her. And we went to all the cemeteries. Nobody knew. Then one day we went up to Saint Lawrence Cemetery and we went in the office and they told me and my brother that at that time that Yale was interested in bodies for autopsies to see, to study, and my dad had sold her body to Yale. So we couldn't look for my mother. I said, what, well, what they do after, the bones they throw all in one place, I don't know where Yale did.

"A Vow to Our Lady of Pompeii"

Luisa DeLauro spoke at her kitchen table in the Wooster Square neighborhood on August 9, 1998.

My father died in 1918. I had the [Spanish] Flu with my father, both of us had the flu. I was his pet, I was always in his arms. So the flu was contagious so we both had the flu. He died from it, I survived. In three days, in three days. There were no antibiotics in those days. Nothing. I got through it. My mother made a vow that if I survived that she would dress me in red—she had a lot of faith in Our Lady of Pompeii and she was dressed in red—and she made this vow that she would go begging from door to door. And she did. Imagine my mother, big businesswoman, begging from door to door. They used to give her twenty-five cents, fifty cents. And then she would take me with her, it was like begging, from door to door. A lot of people didn't make it. People were dying in the streets. People would drop dead in the street.

"Drink A Glass of Whiskey"

Louise Orefice spoke about the Spanish Flu in matter-of-fact tones from the living room of her Annex home.

I remember it because my mother was pregnant and my grandfather was kind a nervous because he was afraid she would get the flu. So he went to the doctor, there used to be a doctor on the street, way down Wooster Street, and he was always drunk. But he went to the doctors and he told the doctor about my mother. So he says, "Tell her to drink a glass of whiskey every day." I don't know where that came in [laughing]. So that's what my mother did. And she got away with it, my grandfather got away, none of them got sick. Yet across the street there was a man in one of the families on Wooster Street where they lived, he passed away. A lot of people passed away in those days. Saint Raphael's, I remember was like a house, it was a small place way back then.

"My Mother's Death from the Spanish Flu"

Giuannine DeMaio spoke by the pool at her granddaughter Laurel Caprio's home in North Branford on July 1, 1999. She recalled picking dandelions on the estate of the Kendall family in the Forbes Avenue neighborhood.

So my mother used to go in every house and cook. She used to cook soup and bring it to them, here and there. I'd say, "Ma, don't go in that house because you're gonna get sick." But she didn't believe it. You know the Italians, they don't believe you get "mischia," when you "mischia" that means you won't get the germs, the illness. So now she used to go and make the beds for them, take care of them and everything and I used to get so mad because she used to go when I wasn't around, when I was workin' you know. She used to help everybody. But our house was the only one that never got it. The year after, my mother is pregnant. My mother got it. I didn't get it. My father didn't get it but two of my brothers got it. But they lived through it. My mother was sick in bed. Now they were delivering coal to my house—we had coal stove not furnace, coal. So my father had to order the coal. My mother was sick in bed. So now the coal man delivers the coal with horse and wagon and he can't come in because it was the month of March when she died. He can't come in, there's a lot of snow. And he wants to dump the coal on the corner, he wants to dump the coal. So I was workin' so my aunt lived next door, she said to my mother, instead of goin' and tell the guy, "Hey, whataya doin?" She goes in and tells my mother, my mother was sick in bed, "Julietta, the guy's gonna drop your coal over there." "What, what is he crazy?" She puts on a blanket or something, walks barefooted to the corner with that nightgown on, and the guy sees her. He says, "Oh my God, what I did!" He says, "No, no go back to bed, go back to bed, I'll bring it." You know they used to have a chute in the window and the coal used to come down the cellars, they used to put it. So now when he saw my mother with the nightgown on he figures she's sick, so he's gonna deliver the coal. Why didn't he do it before? So my mother caught a worse cold. So when I come at night, I didn't know none of this story—I was working. When I come at night somebody says, "Your mother went to the hospital." I says, for what? She sick? So my father and I went to see her and they said she had Spanish Influenza. She was eight months pregnant. She was a whole month in the hospital, she didn't like the food, she didn't know how to talk English. It was around Easter and Palm Sunday I went to go see her and she was saying, "Palm Sunday and I'm in bed over

PASQUALE LUCIBELLO
Victim of the flu

Piontek family album

here." And then the next day, she gets her baby. They called us up, but the baby was born dead, it was a girl. So when we heard it, they called us up, my father and I—we used to go up every day—so we went there and my mother was crying and crying. I says, "Ma, what are you cryin' for, you got seven kids home, what are you cryin' for?" "Oh she was so pretty, they were hittin' her and everything but. . . ." So at night I said to my father, I'm gonna come again tonight, because I had to go to work. He had to go to work, too. So we were goin' up the stairs. Down the stairs comes my mother's brother, sister, and they were crying. And I says, What's the matter? "Your mother just died, she died." Even the doctors were surprised that she died. From Spanish Influenza, that's what she had.

7

Justice Denied: The Execution of Sacco and Vanzetti

In 1927, Nicola Sacco and Bartolomeo Vanzetti were convicted of murdering a paymaster and his guard in South Braintree, Massachusetts. Their seven-year imprisonment, trial, and execution remains one of the most controversial and unsettling cases in American legal history. On the day of their execution at the Charlestown State Prison an eyewitness described the howls of protest emitted by the crowd when the prison lights dimmed as two electrical charges surged through their bodies. It was an unanswered cry for justice that echoes to this day.

The Sacco and Vanzetti case in the 1920s coincided with a period of anti-Italian immigrant sentiment and antiradical paranoia in the United States. The Red Scare, fears of Russian Bolshevik world dominance, concerns that the European economy might crumble in the aftermath of World War I, and bombings by radicals at a New York City post office and at the home of Attorney General Palmer in Washington added to the heightened sense of anxiety throughout the country. In 1917, President Wilson enacted the Sedition Act and the Espionage Act, granting Attorney General Palmer unlimited powers to unleash his infamous "Palmer Raids." Armed agents stormed homes of Italian immigrants without warning, prisoners were detained without counsel, and innocent Italians were deported to Italy. In West Virginia, Colorado, and Louisiana, Italians were lynched by angry mobs of vigilantes.* Organized labor was also targeted with dozens of its members crammed into federal prisons.

Nicola Sacco and Bartolomeo Vanzetti were not ordinary Italian immigrants. Their progressive ideas of humane conditions for workers, of the recognition of human dignity in the individual, and the right to speak out against injustice and to organize and educate workers, collided with the nativist view held by many Americans that treated foreigners with suspicion and worker rights activists with disdain. The presiding judge, Webster Thayer, a self-proclaimed immigrant-hater, charged the two with "consciousness of guilt" after they witheld information about their

---

* As early as 1891, eleven Italian immigrants had been lynched by a mob of citizens in New Orleans after they were found innocent of the murder of the police chief. This was the largest single lynching of any ethnic or racial group in American history. See Richard Gambino, *Vendetta* (Richard Gambino and Guernica Editions, Inc.), 1998. Preface, ix.

political beliefs and affiliations during police interrogation. He was reportedly overheard saying, "Did you see what I did with those anarchist bastards the other day?" Throughout the trial and appeals, eyewitness testimonies in support of the defendants were struck from the record, while eyewitnesses who identified Sacco and Vanzetti at the scene were coerced by the district attorney to give false statements later confessed to perjury under oath. The gun used in the shooting was proven not to have been Sacco's. Despite contradictory evidence introduced during appeals that would have proved their innocence, Judge Thayer refused their inclusion in the proceedings and convicted the two of "consciousness of guilt." News of Judge Thayer's decision set off worker-led demonstrations in major American and European cities who rallied in support of Sacco and Vanzetti. Fearing reprisals, the government sent the military and police to guard courthouses, banks, railroads, and the homes of influential families.

Despite the injustice of their seven-year imprisonment, both men remained committed to worker causes to the end, writing eloquent letters of encouragement to friends and family.[14] The execution of Sacco and Vanzetti in 1927 stunned common people around the world who viewed the United States as a beacon of justice. Throughout the United States, Italian Americans believed the two were innocent and considered them unlucky victims caught in the same unjust legal system they had experienced in Italy. The execution of Sacco and Vanzetti dealt assimilating Italian American communities a bitter psychological blow and damaged relations between Italians and other ethnicities across the country. Many Italians internalized their collective anger and grief, remaining silent about the case for fear of being labeled radical or anti-American. A young schoolgirl in New Haven, Luisa DeLauro, who was eager to show her teacher her scrapbook of the trial, had it confiscated by an aunt who feared reprisals. As an antidote to the harm inflicted on Italian identity, Italians all over the country kept the memory of Sacco and Vanzetti alive in private conversations, reciting their names followed with the words "ingiusto" and "innocenti," or unjust and innocent.

The controversy over the fairness of the Sacco and Vanzetti case has continued since their execution in 1927. It is still considered one of the most disturbing cases of the miscarriage of justice in American judicial history. The specter of Sacco and Vanzetti still looms whenever poor defendants receive incompetent legal representation at trials, whenever the accused are held in prisons without counsel, or whenever DNA evidence disproves the guilty verdict of an innocent defendant wrongfully put to death.

"THEY FELT IT WAS A TRAVESTY OF JUSTICE"

William Rossi spoke at a picnic table during the Oak Street Reunion gathering on August 27, 2000.

Well, that was during the time of the witch hunts—the "Red Herring." A time of witch hunts and these guys were union people, labor people. And they had a very

Newspaper headings
from around the world

good following, they were in the North End of Boston if I remember correctly, am I right? They had a very good following and people listened to them. And so, evidently, they were in the way of the politicians both locally and nationally. So Sacco and Vanzetti had to be moved out of the way. My neighborhood—Legion Avenue—was very upset. The Italian people in New Haven were very upset over it. They felt it was a travesty of justice. That's the way they felt at the time. Whether it was absolutely so or not I can't swear to it but we all have our own private feelings about things. I heard much conversation about it throughout the neighborhood and you know in those days people used to sit on the front porches, used to gather on the corners and talk on hot summer nights—not in a loitering fashion—but in a neighborly fashion. See, there's a difference. And they used to complain about . . . they didn't like what happened to Sacco and Vanzetti.

"WHAT WAS PASSED DOWN TO ME"

Ralph Marcarelli spoke from his living room in the Wooster Square neighborhood on May 31, 2000.

One would hear of it from time to time. I can remember—not verbatim—but I can remember about my mother talking about the terrible injustice done to these two innocent men who were killed because they were Italian. I can remember my grandfather of course talking about the same thing. It would come up in the context of injustices or in the context of the animosity against Italians in this country, in the context of the very fallible and untrustworthy system of justice in this country. The Italians had a notorious distrust historically for government. There was nothing this government did to change that notion. There was cognition, you see, and a general belief that in fact they were innocent. And they weren't killed as innocent men like maybe any other innocent man might be executed. They were executed because they were Italian. That was the concept among Americans and of course it was very true as far as I'm concerned to this day. Neil Proto has written about that and he's been terribly concerned with that whole phenomenon and he sees it as maybe the primary cause of the second-class feeling among the Italians; their sense that they were a denigrated people. Quite legitimate, really. It had a dreadful effect on the Italian population at large. What the feeling of frustration must have been I can only imagine.

"NO, IT HAS TO BE PROVED FIRST"

Rose Sansone spoke at the kitchen table of her Fair Haven home on August 2, 1999. She made espresso for us, creating her own version of cappuccino by adding scoops of vanilla ice cream into our large cups.

We had a piano, we were the first ones on Clay Street to have a piano; we were the first ones to have a telephone. We had the song, a roll for the piano, of Sacco and Vanzetti and I remember the case and they were talking about it. And I can still pic-

JOE. ESTHER. NUNZIATA. AND VIOLET NATALE
(cook, unidentified) Reading "Sacco and Vanzetti" headlines
at 81 Bay Avenue, Atlantic Highlands, New Jersey

Natale family album

ture when they were electrocuted, when the kids come down the street [shouting],
"Extra! Extra! Sacco and Vanzetti was electrocuted, extra, extra!" I still remember
when they used to do that because we didn't have radio to bring the news and every
time something used to happen these kids used to come the street hollering,
"Extra! Extra!" With all the newspapers so the people could buy the paper and read
all about it. I remember the case and I saw the movie. Everybody at that time was
saying that they were innocent, the poor Italians were innocent. But other people
were saying, "No, no, no, they're not innocent, they did it." Because I had Irish people next door to me that lived on Clay Street. They were saying, "Oh no, no, you
Italian people, you all say that they were innocent." And they were saying they were

guilty because they were all Irish. I think we were about the second Italian family that lived on Clay Street [in Fair Haven]. And all the Irish people next door were always contradicting us, telling us because we were Italian, we favored them too. But they went to death anyway. So we didn't have no argument, but still they always used to say that we were wrong. And then when they did [execute them], they said "See, see we told you that they were guilty and you didn't believe it." So that's how I remember Sacco and Vanzetti. When they [Irish neighbors] heard about it, they used to read about it in the paper and they used to say, "See, you people are going for Sacco and Vanzetti but they are guilty." And we used to say, "No they're not, it has to be proved first, they never done it, they never done it." But all the while, they electrocuted them. We only got the news in the paper. My mother and father didn't say a word; [they] couldn't read or write in English. We got along good; we had some good neighbors. That's the only dispute we had was over the Sacco and Vanzetti trial but otherwise we got along good with them.

"THEY HAD A SONG ABOUT THEM"

Josie DeBenedet spoke on June 6, 1999 in the kitchen of her North Haven home.

I remember it. I still see the picture in the newspaper of the two Italian men. And they were innocent, they were innocent, Sacco and Vanzetti. Matter of fact, I used to have the record that they made, "Sacco and Vanzetti: Innocenti." I don't know who made it but we had a record on our victrola of Sacco and Vanzetti, that they killed the innocent people and all that. I don't remember how it went but I know we bought it and they sang a song that two honest men . . . my mother and father felt bad, too, especially when they found out. It ain't like now that we have television; we didn't even have a radio, nothing. And then they didn't know how to read and write. I taught my mother how to write her name to get her citizenship; my father, I always had to make a cross and I used to put his mark and my name under. They never had any schooling in Italy.

"WE THOUGHT SOMETHING BIG WAS GOING TO HAPPEN"

Pat Barone spoke from his living room in West Haven on May 5, 1999.

I went to Yale and listened to that trial. I remember when they shut everything down—schools down, all the businesses, everything. They thought that something real big was really going to happen. I still don't think those guys were guilty. They thought that something was going to happen. They thought that people were going to get involved in it. I still, from my point of view, don't think that they—they might have been around or involved—but I don't think they committed the murder. Today, with the way the courts are today, those guys would have gotten a better trial. But again, they were Italians.

"We Saw Them in Pictures in Italy"

Anna Fasano spoke at her kitchen table at her home in Fair Haven on August 15, 1998.

I remember when I was very young, my father always sent the American newspapers to us in Castellabate. In those days there was "Il Progresso Italiano" from New York. And my father always used to get this newspaper. And I remember when my father used to send these newspapers to my mother [in Italy], she used to put them on the table and we used to look at the pictures. We saw these two Italians that they said had killed someone in Boston. They said, "We are innocent, we never did anything like that." But someone else said, "We saw these two do it." And now and then my mother used to tell us what was happening.

(translated from Italian)

"Yale University and the Sacco and Vanzetti Trial"

Nick Vitagliano spoke at his kitchen table in his Branford home on June 2, 2000.

I don't remember it [the trial] but of it very clearly. They were anarchists because they didn't believe in the government. Now that's when they should have stayed in Italy and get the Bourbons out a there! It was a mistake, they came over here, now they didn't like this party here, and they didn't like this system here. At least this system was free. I mean they were open, they could do anything they wanted. They were falsely accused, what are you gonna do? My father said, "That's a big mistake, they should never have done that because they were innocent people." Somebody reported that they wanted to kill the president. And people believed it. This [their innocence] was proven in court, too, because I was in a moot court in Yale University. When an attorney is gonna graduate from Yale University, he's got a show his proficiency in the court, right? So they have a fake [trial] and they always pick the Sacco and Vanzetti trial. They always do. They always will. They'll probably do it again now. My brother Sal, he had a nice big mustache, my older brother. We knew all these trial lawyers or [lawyers] to be because they used to come into our cleaning business, they were customers of ours on Broadway, we used to run the Blue Jay Cleaners. Now they asked him, "Hey, Sal, want to help us out, we're gonna have moot court and you look just like Sacco and Vanzetti with your mustache. You don't mind, do you?" Sal says, "I'll do it, why not, I'll see what this is all about." So I went to the trial. And I heard the whole thing right from scratch, they were arguing, "You made a mistake, you know, these innocent people" and everything else. And when the trial was over they were convicted and everything, you know what I mean? Oh, the whole court was in an uproar because what a mistake they would have made. It was published in the paper, my brother's picture was in the paper. Oh it was a nice thing to see. And I know all about that trial so very vividly in my mind because they reenacted the whole thing.

8

Letters to Loved Ones

Old Letters provide intimate glimpses into the daily lives of those who left for America and loved ones who stayed behind. Although letters were often grammatically imperfect and sprinkled with words in Neapolitan dialect spelled phonetically, they were nevertheless eloquent in expression and complex in thought. Assunta Nappi, an immigrant woman living on Wooster Street in New Haven whose son John was fighting in the Pacific, wrote a relative in Italy in late August, 1945, with a wish that "la tempesta," the war, would end soon. Two days later her wish came true when the atomic bomb was dropped on Japan, catapulting the world into the atomic age. A letter written in 1949 from the town of Acerno in the Campania region of Italy's south to a relative in New Haven mentions his gratitude for the bumper crop of chestnuts that season. Chestnuts, unlike their poorer American cousins, were harvested in winter around Christmas and used to make "dolci," or holiday desserts known as "la castagnata," in the form of cookies, puddings, or cakes. Contadini setting off for the fields carried packs of roasted chestnuts to snack on while working, eating them continuously through the day.

In New Haven, illiterate parents dictated messages to their bilingual children who wrote letters in Italian to loved ones waiting to hear news of the family in America. Before and after World War II, Italian American families sent parcels of salami, cheese, bundles of clothes, and gallons of olive oil to needy relatives in Italy. Women constructed large packages with remnants of cloth feedbags stitched together with heavy string. A piece of cardboard was then cut and carefully stitched to the large, dice-cube shaped package with the address written in crayon. When much-awaited return letters arrived with news of the village, children read them carefully to anxious parents who hung on to every word. Sometimes a trusted "cummara," a word meaning godmother but widened in New Haven to mean a close friend from the same village, was asked to compose letters. In the early days of immigration, the padroni charged illiterate clients a small fee to write letters but were eventually replaced by community advocates who wrote and read letters free of charge.

Napoli 18 Maggio 1926

Carissimo figlio

Apprendo con mio sommo dolore i
tuoi dispiaceri, per la perdita della
tua bambina, però devi rassegnarti
al volere di Dio, perchè tutto ciò che
nel Mondo si verifica, è il suo
volere, non senza una ragione,
solamente conosciuta da Lui, che
opera; a noi ci sembra male nel
senso materiale, a Dio sembra
bene dal lato spirituale, perchè
l'uomo fu creato per il Cielo, e
non già per la terra, perchè questa
è una perenne valle di lagrime
per tutti, questo è il fine, per cui fu
creato il Mondo e il genere umano.
Perciò non essendo la terra, la patria
dell'uomo, ma sibbene il Cielo, quanto
più presto si parte di qui, meno soffre,
e si può certo salvare quando è piccolo,
e non già quando cresce, col passare
degli anni nelle cose terrene, per
dannarsi in eterno, perchè la
salvazione dell'anima dell'uomo, è
molto difficile, perciò Dio sa quello
che fa, per nostro bene, e non

devi tanto affliggerti, perchè la bambina è nel Cielo al cospetto di Dio, è prega per te e noi tutti.

Ti scrissi, che io fui chiamato per la poliza, che repostammo alla Posta, e ci feci conoscere il tuo indirizzo, e non mi hai scritto, se fosti o no chiamato, dal Console Italiano.

Ti scrissi di tua sorella, e non l'hai nemmeno ora nominata, nè salutata, e forse l'hai dimenticata, per la disgrazia sofferta, essa però ti saluta, e si addolora delle tue sventure.

Io ho avuto due paralisi, una quattro anni fa, non potetti parlare un mese, e mezza vita indurita come legno, ma io agiva con energia, e aveva più fame; e senza ricorrere ai medici o stare a letto, stetti buono dopo un mese. In seguito due anni fa, ebbi un'altra paralisi facciale, la bocca storta, e l'occhio destro aperto, da non poterlo più chiudere; e senza ricorrere ai medici, me sono ristabilito da solo, senza medici e medicine; vedi che Dio non parla, opera, e fa quello che vuole, in Cielo e in terra; perciò pensa a ritornare subito, che oggi l'America è per ogni dove, quando si lavora. Io vecchio a 73 anni, infermo, con ernia, costretto a lavorare per vivere, e dopo aver lavorato soffro la fame. Fui incaricato dallo Scultore Parisio, a formare un Monumento, che impiegai 4 mesi. In acconto lire 400. Il lavoro ascende a lire 5200. Il Parisio si impossessò delle forme, e chiuse lo studio senza avermi dato il resto di lire 4800, quindi sto in causa, per avergli fatto querela di truffa, e perciò ora sto senza lavoro, e senza denaro. Saluto tua moglie, un bacio ai bambini e abbracciandoti, vi mando la Santa Benedizione, e prego Iddio che vi dia salute e provvidenza secondo i vostri bisogni lo Sdelusa...

Letters to loved ones played a critical role in New Haven's immigration history. In the late 1880s and '90s, the stream of "American letters" to Italy were anticipated by relatives who were anxious to know how a recently-departed family member was faring in the new world. Letters often masked the hardscrabble conditions and economic hardships the first immigrants faced in New Haven, and the actual degree of financial success achieved in the new job was sometimes exaggerated. But the encouraging tone of American letters eventually convinced even the most reluctant family members in the old country to venture to New Haven. When word reached Italy that L. Candee Rubber Company, the railroad, and Sargent Manufacturing Company were offering the prospect of steady work to Italians, it sparked a second wave of immigration that included young and old family members who had stayed behind. From 1900 to 1910, Italians arrived in record numbers, soon surpassing all other ethnic groups in the city. One immigrant, Francesco Celantano, was persuaded to emigrate by American letters and he joined his brothers Vincent and Joseph in the pushcart business. His son William C. Celantano became the first Italian mayor of the city in 1945.

Acerno, April 15, 1913

My Dearest Daughter,

I am answering your letter and we are comforted to know that everyone in the family is enjoying good health. From the state of things here I can tell you that we are all fine thank God. Daughter, you are upset because you cannot send me anything. Daughter, I don't need anything because your brothers are here who are taking care of me and I have everything I need. I only miss the rest in sleep because I suffer [missing word]. As you know I cannot lie down to rest sometimes and I would like to die quickly rather than suffer like this, God wills this for me and I console myself knowing that my children are well and that Serafino has learned how to write. I want him to always write me in his own hand. I want you to know that your brother Giovanni wrote to me and that they are all doing well, your brother Giuseppe wrote me and they are well too. Your sister-in-law Angela Maria wrote me and is fine and she wants to hear from you if you want to write her, this is her address: Mrs. Alfonsina Cuozzo, Calle Solta e Schima, Marco pa Republica Tucuman, Argentina.

I send you all warm regards to everyone in the family as does your sister Rose, your brother Antonio and his family and I, as mother, send you a holy blessing to everyone. And I sign, forever, your faithful mother,

Cuozzo, Maria

Write back with good news soon.

Naples, May 18, 1926

Dearest Son,

It is with my greatest sorrow that I was informed about the loss of your child, but you have to surrender yourself to the will of God because everything that happens in the

STEFANO TIDDEI
Father, letter writer

Caprio family album

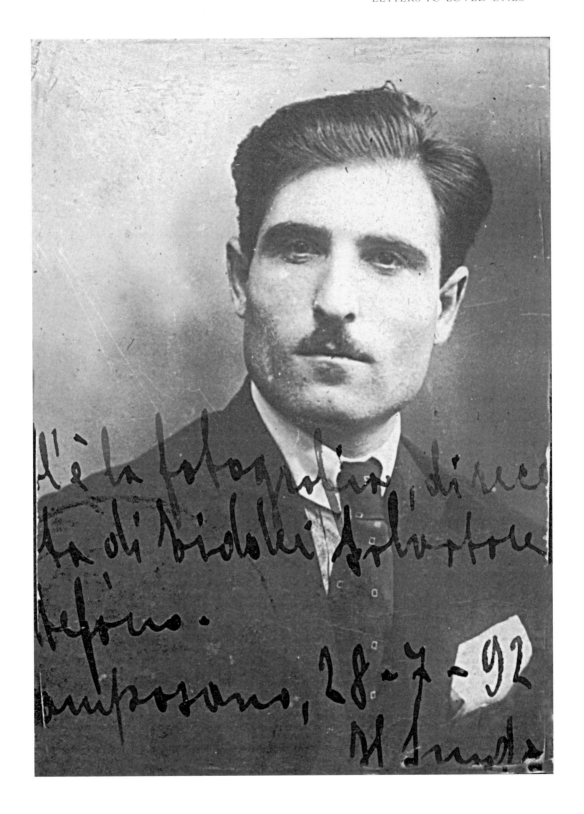

SALVATORE TIDDEI
Son, letter receiver

Caprio family album

ROSINA TIDDEI
Deceased daughter

Caprio family album

world comes from the will of God for a reason only He knows and operates; it seems terrible to us in the material sense, but to God on a spiritual side it seems good because man was born for paradise and not for the this earth, because life is a perpetual valley of tears for us and this is the purpose of the creation of the world and the human race. For that reason, not being of the earth, man's real home is heaven and the sooner we leave this world, the less we will suffer, and it is certain that the young are redeemed but not those older who with the passing years get involved in earthly things that eternally damns his soul to Hell. Because the salvation of man's soul is very difficult. That is why God knows what He does is for our own good and you should not despair because the little girl is in heaven before the Lord and prays for you and all of us.

I wrote to you because I was called about the insurance policy we deposited at the post office bank and we gave the clerk your address but you haven't written back to me to let me know if you were notified by the Italian Consulate about the policy. I wrote to you about your sister and you haven't even written to her nor have you greeted her and maybe you have forgotten her because of your sorrowful misfortune, but she sends her regards and mourns your tragedy.

I had two strokes, one four years ago and I couldn't speak for a month and paralyzed from the waist down like a piece of wood, but I overcame it with energy and I got my appetite back and without going to the doctors or having to stay in bed, I was well after a month. Following that, two years ago, I had another facial seizure that left me with a crooked mouth and my right eye wide open which I couldn't close any more. Without going back to the doctors I got healthy again without medicine or doctors; see how God does not speak and works in his own way, in heaven and on earth; so why don't you think of coming back home soon because America today is no different than everywhere else when one is working. I am an old man of seventy-three years and sick with a hernia, still compelled to work to live. And even having worked I am still not doing all that well. I was commissioned by the sculptor Parisio to make the base for a monument that I worked on for four months. He gave me 400 lire and the work is worth 5,200 lire. He took the base and closed his studio without paying me the additional 4,800 lire and I am therefore suing him and having him arrested for cheating and that's why I am without work or money. Regards to your wife, a kiss to the children and hugging you I send you all a holy blessing and pray that God will give you health, watch over you and attend to your needs.

Stefano Tiddei

August 3, 1945 New Haven

My Dear Nephew,

I am answering your letter right away. You can't imagine how badly my heart feels to hear about your suffering but even more is my unhappiness that I cannot immediately help you with the things you need because we cannot directly mail you any packages. We can only send packages destined to places like Naples, Rome or Milan, etc. If you have a friend or someone you trust in Naples I can send you whatever you need. In fact I sent two packages to my husband's sister Catherine in Naples and it has been two months and I haven't heard anything yet and I hope it has arrived.

Dear nephew, as I write this letter I am also writing to your brother. He tells me he is well and I am happy about that, but he wants to come back home and he will suffer like you all have but at least he will have food to eat and drink and clothes to wear. Anyway, here in America we want for nothing and I hope I explain myself to cousin Nilo that I did write to Macalato, my Aunt Felicia's son. This war has been the ruin of the world and I too have a son who has been in the service for a year and a half in Japan. I have not seen him for three years and we are always thinking of him. I hope this other "tempesta" with Japan ends quickly and that way the world will be at peace. Well what you wanted to say in your letter about the provisions and prices was cut out by the authorities and we couldn't make out anything. I say to do like I told you; you can send whatever you want; if not, it is my fault. I wanted to send something to your brother, the prisoner of war, through the Red Cross. I have nothing else to say only that the letter you receive sends greetings to your mother. I'll stop here sending you our dearest wishes and kisses from me and my husband and from all my children, with kisses to my brother as well.

From your aunt and uncle,

Gaetano and Assunta Nappi
86 Wooster Street
New Haven, Conn

Naples, October 23, 1949

Dearest Brother,

Yesterday I returned to Acerno with my first two oldest sons, Carmine and Agostino. At Acerno Angela Maria stayed behind with my son Mario to oversee the chestnut harvest. Your dearest letter arrived in Acerno and I hope my last letter I sent to you got there. [lost line] The environment is generally very civilized and follows the progress of civilization. We even have a beautiful movie theatre and also a soccer team, naturally we have a sports field and every Sunday the youngsters have a good time there. The chestnut harvest represents the wealth of the town and thank God this year it is going well. I will return to Acerno at the end of this month. I am going with the family to fulfill the sacred duty for our dear departed ones. Spreading flowers on their tombs, lighting a candle and praying to the Good Jesus who welcomes their souls into Paradise, only in that way we do our share of duty to them. Have our compatriots with Giovanni Vestuti arrived all right? How are they? I ask you to give them my warm regards. Regards to your wife and your children and regard also from my children. A kiss to you,

Your brother Stanislao

Write back to me in Acerno

New Haven, May 2, 1951

To my dearest grandson Giuseppe Jeremia,

I received your letter and I am very happy that you are doing well and I will tell you

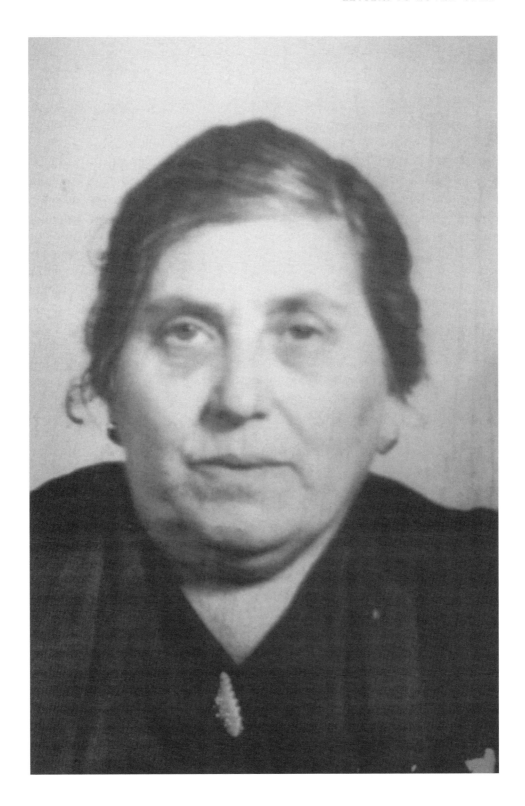

ASSUNTA NAPPI
Wooster Street

Nappi family album

*how I am doing and everyone else. We are all doing very well, I go to your house every
Saturday because I don't work anymore on Sunday, I want to rest. We are fixing up so
many things in the house. I taught your father how to be a bricklayer and how to lay
sidewalks. I taught him how to do everything well. Mornings we get up early and
begin working until it gets dark because I only have time to work around the house on
Saturday and Sunday. When you come back you will find so many things done
beautifully that weren't done and you'll going to be very happy to see what we have
done. Thanks so, so much for the birthday wishes that you sent for my birthday. I hope
you can read this letter and I suggest that you learn how to read and write Italian.
With the pen I leave you but never with my heart. Your mother and your father and
the family send their regards and I salute you with a true heart.*

Your grandfather,
John Simoni

I advise that you stay away from the women because they are the ruin of youth.
I salute you again,
John Simoni

❝Letter Writers and Community Advocates❞

Salvatore "Gary" Garibaldi spoke over supper at Tony and Lucille's restaurant on Wooster Street on May 17, 2000

Letters are going back [to Italy] that they are making successes of themselves in
this country. The tone was optimistic. My mother-in-law didn't read or write Italian; she had no education. So as far as writing she had to depend on someone in
the community that they could go to and say, "Look, I'd like to write to my mother
and father in Amalfi." And they would extend the courtesy and they would write
the letter. So much so that the person who did that for her would also see to it that
it was mailed because she didn't know where to go to get a stamp or what stamps
was necessary. So he was actually a person that she had to rely on for communication between her family in Amalfi and her two brothers and herself. In those it
took about two, three weeks because they went by ship. And by the time the person
received it, by the time they answered, there would be a period of time from anywhere from four to six weeks. And then when she did receive the letter she was able
to read it to a certain degree but again she had to call on her friend and more or less
digest the letter much more efficiently than she would pick it out to be. Then she
would ask him if he would be kind enough to make an answer to that letter. And
that continued for years. Later on, around 1914, there was a gentleman by the name
of Anthony Paolillo. His family came here at the turn of the century and they lived
on the corner of Collis and Wallace Streets. He knew how to read and write and
became a well-known fellow in the neighborhood. And he would be called upon

practically every day and night to help his people from Italy and he would write letters for them. Anthony Paolillo was a great, respected gentleman in this community and very loyal to his neighbors and to his family friends until the day he died. He got into helping his people in the community and the reason was because his parents told him to do it because they were very friendly with the people around them and people needed help—help when they received notices or letters, they were not aware because they didn't know how to read English. He loved to do it; and he did it with his whole heart with no motive of any remuneration or gifts. He just loved to do that and he prided himself in doing that. So much so he ran for alderman of the tenth ward and he served the community for more than twenty years. Today we would call him a social worker. Naturally in those days, the early Italian immigrants didn't have the knowledge of city affairs, what to do, what not to do. They would get excited if they got a letter.

" WRITING TO MY GRANDFATHER "

Rose Durso spoke at the Annex home of her friends, Joseph and Lena Riccio on February 1, 1998. She and Lena had just finished making Italian cookies in Lena's kitchen.

I graduated from eighth grade with an honor diploma I got. Then my uncle would come—my uncle was a very intelligent man—he had a big printing establishment on Grand Avenue, enormous. Compared to us, he made a dollar. He would come up with the Italian books on a Sunday; the opera books and I learned from opera and all that. And he'd open the book and he'd say to me, "Sit down and read out of this book." And I had to read, out a book, in Italian. I wish I had it now. Then he said, "Now that you've learned the Italian and you know what it means, write to grandfather in Italy." Which I did, and my grandfather read all the letters—he could read them fluently—he wrote back to me and he wanted to know. And I wrote it's your granddaughter that's writing these letters. On Sundays I would write and my uncle would be there in back of me, over my shoulder, seeing if I had made any mistakes in Italian. Then he brought books of different Italian songs and I learned all those songs. I used to sing at my father's club when he had weddings next door on Main Street [Annex], the small Melebus club. And I'd go in there—I had a lot a nerve as a kid I had a lot a nerve and I'd sing. And all the people would clap, tutti canzioni Italian'—beautiful Italian songs. And I would carry out my voice. And the men—they had a men's club, "Eh, che bella voce che tiene chella figlióla!" What a beautiful voice that child has! I never got any money for it but we entertained. It was great. Weddings would come and they wanted someone to entertain. I just jump up there and sing. I would never do it now, I wouldn't have the courage, but when you're innocent and you're young, you do it. "Le Donne a Sorrento," "Guitara Romana," "Diciette cel a Vuie." Then he [grandfather] died and that stopped. But now, if I gotta remember the letters precisely and the spelling, it's years ago. I spoke Italian at home. But it was the fine Italian that my uncle told me, it wasn't like us, "'o store, vai in mezz' 'o street," the store, go in the middle of the street, it was "la strada." The street, the fine Italian, but who could remember it now, I wish I could.

9   *Fables and Proverbs*

Italian immigrants brought few books to New Haven in their wooden steamer trunks and suitcases. No personal diaries or journals survive to tell us what the early immigrants experienced in their first days in New Haven or what their first impressions of their new adopted country were. Autobiographies took the form of recalled life stories rather than written accounts. Italian immigrants carried handed-down ancestral experiences, family histories, and folk tales in collective memory, transmitting them through the spoken rather than the written word. Throughout the centuries, the rich Italian oral tradition incorporated other cultural influences. As early as the seventh century B.C., Greek colonists who occupied Magna Grecia in southern Italy brought myths and legends of the gods, which were later absorbed by the Romans into pagan deities. These gods reappeared as earthly church saints with supernatural powers whose stories were kept alive by common people in legends passed down through generations. Every villager in the south knew legends of patron saints of their towns and their miraculous powers to protect the faithful from foreign invaders, earthquakes, and epidemics. The story of Saint Andrew and his miraculous powers as the patron saint of Amafi was well-known by many Amalfitani immigrants who settled in New Haven's Wooster Square neighborhood.

"THE MIRACLE OF SAINT ANDREW"

Told by Grazia Minichino to her seven grandchildren. The story originated
from Amalfi in the Campania region and was told by Theresa Argento.

Saint Andrew has two celebrations. The first is in November 30th, which is his name day, the one on June 27th for the miracle. The story that was passed down to us from our grandparents tells us that his bones are buried in the crypt downstairs in the cathedral of Saint Andrew in Amalfi and the back part of his head is encased in a crystal decanter with all gold, with his gray hair in a pony tail and the front of his skull is in Saint Peter's. The Turks, because Saint Andrew preached in Balkans and Greece and Turkey, and the Turks revered Saint Andrew so much that they were coming in to the shores of Amalfi to take his remains and bring it back to Turkey. And they came with the pirate called Barbarossa, which is in all the history books. And they prayed to Saint Andrew because they didn't want to lose his remains. There was an elderly man on the beach of Amalfi and he was whittling a stick. And every shaving that came off that stick fell into the Mediterranean Sea and each shaving formed a tempest and the tempest drowned all the Turkish vessels. And that's how the body of Saint Andrew still is in Amalfi and that's why they have the summer celebration, the miracle of Saint Andrew.

In the small villages throughout the Mezzogiorno, Italian families often gathered around the warmth of the hearth for "Racconti del Focolare," where people entertained each other by storytelling. Stories of devils appearing as earthly men to local townspeople and tales of ancient treasures buried beneath hilltop medieval castles nearby kept children at the edge of their seat. Others were wisdom tales with animals personifying humans who illustrated time-tested truths and everyday lessons. The tradition continued in New Haven on Sundays and holidays when Italian families gathered around dinner tables where epic conversations took place amidst sumptuous home-cooked meals prepared by the women of the house. When an elder or another respected family member was asked for advice, the response was often sprinkled with an allegorical story or a proverb that pointed in the direction of correct action according to the southern code of morality. Central to their ancient culture, New Haven's Italians abided by a strict code of family loyalty, a deeply-rooted tradition of unquestioned respect for parental authority and elders within the family. Children, regardless of age, were expected to care for the aged at home until the end. Two allegorical stories of the old father and son who climb to the summit of a mountain illustrate the consequences of breaking with traditional ways by not respecting an aging parent.

"WHAT YOU DO TO ME WILL HAPPEN TO YOU"

Told by Cristoforo and Theresa Proto in Neapolitan dialect to their thirteen children. The story originates in Atrani in the Campania region and was told by Rose Sansone.

This father used to live with his son and his wife. And the wife couldn't stand the father-in-law no more. And she said to the son, "You got to get rid of your father. A muglièra ha ditto vicino 'o marìto, tu aive a fare 'na cosa con 'o pàte tùjo che 'i non lo voglio chiù."

The son said to the father, "Dad, let's go up to the mountain. 'O figlio a ditto vicino 'o pàte, Pa, mo jiame 'ncòppa a montagna. Hanno saliuto 'ncoppa a montagna, hanno venuto n' ppòco 'o figlio ha ditto, Pa, è buon che ti meno vàscio per cà?" They went up a bit and the son asked, "Pop, is it all right if I throw you down from here?" "Eh, [father sighing] come dici tu," Whatever you say, son. All right, jiame chiù assàja, All right, let's go up further. Hanno aiuto chiù assàja, they climbed up further. They went up further and the son asked, "Pa, are we all right over here?" "Eh, come dici tu," Whatever you say son. The son said, "Eh jiame chiù assàja," Let's go up higher. "Eh, Pa. . . ." The father interrupted the son, "Eh, ha ditto 'o pàte, come fai a me, ti venne pur a te," Son, whatever you do to me now will someday happen to you. The son said, "Oh, Padre mi, jiame cchine a casa!" Oh my father, let's go back home.

❝ THE OLD FATHER AND THE SON ❞

Told by Vincenzo and Cesarina Riccio in Neapolitan dialect to their two sons, Joseph and Anthony. The story originates from the town of Alvignano in the Campania region and was told by Joseph Riccio.

A temp' antica, facevano 'o cunto, cuando arrivavano 'o na' punto che si faceva viécchio che non si puoteva sta' accúorto sulo. Una in da famiglia, 'o chiù avanzato, era sempemàie a toccato a che portava 'o padre 'ncòppa na' montagna. Steva a nu vicchiariéllo che è arrivato 'o tempo sùjo che 'o primo figlio è toccato a portare 'o pàte 'o posto per murì' 'ncòppa 'na montagna. Camminendo 'ncòppa a montagna, e arrivavano a nu' punto che iettàva 'o padre da' ncòppa a montagna. Camminendo, camminendo, prima che arrivavano a nu punto 'o figlio si è stancato—'o viaggio era lungo—e voleva arrepusà' a nu ppòco e a na' prèta, si è asettàto. 'O padre si è settato insieme pure isso a nu' prèta e guardando 'o figlio, ha ditto, "Figlio mi! Chesta è la stessa prèta cuando ho portato 'o padre mio a 'o posto per murì." 'O figlio è pensato a nu' ppòco e pensava. "Madonna mi, cuando mi faccio viécchio pure i' mio figlio mi porta pure a me per murì." È pensato a nu' ppòco e ha ditto, "Papa, jiame cchine a casa, cuando 'o Buon' Dio ti chiama, tanno è 'o tiempo che spartimmo."

In the old days, when an elder reached the point where he couldn't take care of himself any longer, it was the responsibility of the oldest of the family to bring the father up to a mountain. There was a little old man whose time had come and his oldest son took him to the mountain to die. They walked and walked on their way to the place where the father would be thrown to his death. At one point on the way the son became tired and sat on a rock. The father sat beside the son and said, "This is the same rock my father sat on when I took him to be thrown from the mountain." The son thought it over a moment and said, "Madonna! When I get old my son is going to do the same thing to me." Then he said to his father, "Come on Dad; let's go home, when the Good Lord calls you, that's when we'll part."

The story of the people of San Carlo illustrates the unrelenting tax burdens imposed by the new northern-based Piedmont government that caused the collective suffering of millions of the poor who lived a threadbare existence throughout the south. The symbolic revolt by the townspeople against tax officials represents the victory of the Italian underclass over generations of injustice and exploitation. In another short parody, four hundred years of repressed hatred of the Spanish Bourbons was distilled into a comic mime portraying the occupiers as hapless simpletons who blind themselves by making the sign of the cross and accidentally killing themselves after taking a laxative.

"THE TAXATION OF SAN CARLO"

Told by Carmine Calzetta to his four children. The story originated in the town of San Carlo of the Campania region and was told by Frances Calzetta.

Overlooking the beautiful grassy plains and the Mediterranean Sea, San Carlo, near Sessa Aurunca, is the high point of the Sessana mountain range between Rome and Naples. In the 1860s, San Carlo was an agrarian society. This was the era of Garibaldi's expedition of ten thousand, which brought territorial unity of the south with the new unity of the Italian nation. But the new state ignored the south. King Victor Emmanuel II supported the indiscriminate application of the administrative, judicial, and fiscal structures of the old Piedmont, which was now unified with the new Italian state. This created a divide between Italy's more economically developed northern and central regions, and the southern region, the Mezzogiorno. In addition, Pope Pius IX, angry at the loss of Rome and the Papal States, forbade Catholics to take part in the politics of the kingdom. Against this backdrop, millions of southern Italians migrated to the Americas. With Unification, the city of Sessa was given taxation powers over the lovely hill towns of the region. King Emmanuel II authorized taxes based on Piedmont structures. These taxes became an outrageous burden on the people. Especially notorious was the milling tax on wheat. Stefano Calzetta and his friends in San Carlo frequently protested to Sessa officials about the tax burdens, but they turned a deaf ear. Stefano and his San Carlo friends met and decided to attack City Hall. They marched with pitchforks in hand to Sessa. They stormed City Hall, overturned files, and so frightened the officials that they ran away as fast as their legs could take them. A pitchfork is a mighty powerful weapon when it is staring you in the face. One official foolishly hid himself in a storage box, which the men threw down the stairs. When the box popped open the official was dead. Their tax point made, the men returned home. The next day the police came to San Carlo and arrested the men. No due process. No trial. The sentence was three weeks in jail. When the police came to Stefano's home he told them, "Aspettate un momento," Wait just a moment as he went for the socks he was knitting so he could finish them in jail. Although punished by the Sessa government, the people of San Carlo won the day. Sessa levied no further taxes on San Carlo.

"Spanish Jokes"

Told by Antonia and Antonio Morrone in Neapolitan dialect to their eight children. The story originates from the town of Cescheto in the Campania region and was told by Edward Morrone.

The Italians used to tell Spanish jokes much like the Americans told Polish jokes. They used to be the brunt of their humor. They used to joke about Spaniards [Bourbon viceroys who ruled Naples]. And they used to talk about: "'O sai 'o fatt' dell' 'o Espagnol'?" Si aiuta a fa a cróce, e si è cecato. Did you hear the one about the Spaniard? He was making the sign of the cross and blinded himself. And they'd say, "Sai 'o fatt di 'o Espagnol'? Sentiva a nu' pòco malata, ha pigliata 'na purga, e mòrte," Did you hear about the Spaniard? He wasn't feeling too well, so he took a laxative and died.

The allegorical story of the wily fool of Rome who dared criticize the king's grandiose public art project is a fable rich in symbolism. The fool's common sense and keen eye for detail represents the collective wisdom of the lower classes who were looked down upon as subintelligent by the ruling class, illustrating that those who rule are not necessarily the wisest. In another tale, an old man representing the archetypal peasant living in tune with nature teaches a king the importance of eating healthy meals. In the humble peasant's simple way, he shows the king that good health and longevity are worth more than wealth or earthly power.

"The King and the Statue"

Told by Assunta Nappi in Neapolitan dialect to her six children. The story originated in Sarno of the Campania region and was told by John Nappi.

In Rome, they built a bronze statue of the king on horseback. Now, when they were supposed to unveil it, people from all over the world went. It was the unveiling by one of the greatest sculptors who did the job. People from all over all said they saw it, they took pictures—it was beautiful. Now there was a guy, he used to be, in other words, the city boob, he said, "That thing is beautiful but there's something wrong." He used to talk to himself and walk around. They used to feed him. So the carabinieri, the police, said to him, "Hey, keep quiet, you're going to get in trouble." Everybody, they all looked at it, they said it was beautiful. He kept on saying, "Oh no, there's something wrong with that piece." They wouldn't believe him. So he says, "You know, if the king finds out you're going to get in trouble." Anyway, the King Umberto found out. So they sent for him. He goes and sees the king. The king said, "You say there's something wrong with the statue?" He says, "Yes." The king said, "Show me." He goes out with the king, "See over here on the side, it got the stirrup where you put your foot—on the other side they left one out!" There was something wrong with the statue. On one side it didn't have the stirrup, where you put your foot in it, and he noticed it out of the thousands of people.

"Umberto and the King"

Told by Assunta Nappi in Neapolitan dialect to her six children. The story originated in Sarno of the Campania region and was told by John Nappi.

Another guy, his name was Umberto; he had an audience with the king. The king wanted to know why he lived so long. He had a ruddy complexion in his eighties, healthy. He even had all his teeth; he was in good shape. So he sent for the old man to see how the old man is the way he is, what he eats or what he does. So now, when you go, you're supposed to bow this way to the king, but he came in backwards, in other words with his ass first. The guy told him, "Hey, you're going in the wrong way." He said back, "What's the difference, this is the way I go in, so I'll turn around when I get to see him." So anyway the king gets to see him. So he says, "Look, you're going to dine with us." And then everything from soup to nuts. So he wouldn't eat nothing. So the king says, "How come you're not eating?" You know he wasn't a rich man, he was a poor guy. The king said, "What do you want to have?" He said, "I'll tell you what I want to have. Give me a piece of bread; bring me a piece of steak, an onion and a glass of wine. I don't want fresh bread. I want day-old bread." Well he ate that, he didn't have none of the dessert, they had all fancy dessert. The king said, "How come you only ate that?" The old man said, "I want to show you something. Get me a vat that's air tight, I'll show you. Now everything you ate put it in that jar. Then I'll put everything I ate in this jar. Open it up tomorrow, all right?" So the next day, the king is curious. They opened up the jar with the food he ate; there were all maggots. What the old man ate, it was the same what he ate, clear with none of the junk, the cream and all that. He meant to say, "See, that's why, I eat all stuff that's good for me—you people are mixing cream, you mix this and you mix all that—it's no good for you. That's why I am what I am."

Following the time-honored principle of the "religione della famiglia," families worked and struggled together for the common good. In the rural Italian countryside where many young hands were needed to help large farming families eke out a living tending the land, children often competed for the love of their parents. A mother's response to her children was simple and from the heart.

"The Five Fingers"

Told by Cristoforo and Theresa Proto in Neapolitan dialect to his thirteen children. The story originates in Atrani in the Campania region and was told by Rose Sansone.

Then he [my father] used to tell us the story about the five fingers. 'O figlio faceva vicino a mamma, "Hey, ma, tu vo' bene chiù chill' altro figlio chiù buona di me." 'A mamma ha ditto, "I tenga cinque dite, non son' tutto lo stesso, ma voglio bene a tutte 'e cinque. Accussì ti voglio dice pur' a te, come voglio a chill' ti voglio bene pur' a te."

A son went to his mother and said, "You love your other children more than me." His mother said, "Just like I have five fingers, and none are the same, yet I love all five of them. So like that I'm telling you: The way I love them is the same way I love you."

Old proverbs conveyed the timeless ways of the peasant rooted in the collective experience and wisdom of the past. Proverbs were based on southern Italian moral principles and righteous behavior, which often reverberated with meaning and could be applied to everyday problems. The most often heard of these proverbs was "Fa buon' e scurdá , fa male e pensá," Do good [actions] and forget, do bad and think about it, an Eastern-sounding adage that held all individuals accountable to a higher power for their actions, a cosmic warning that wrongful actions eventually bring their own punishment. Children were warned against wrongful actions that could bring dishonor to the family name with the saying, "Cammina con una faccia pulita," Always walk with a clean face. The importance of keeping friends of good moral character was expressed with "Chi cammina con lo zopp' a capo d'anno, esce zoppa e cecato," He who walks with the crippled one, at the end of the year, finds himself both crippled and blind. Italians firmly believed in the virtue of family honor and keeping the family name in good standing in the community.* In 1931, the Wickersham Commission on Law Observance and Enforcement reported in its Survey on Crime and Foreign Born that "in proportion to their respective numbers, the foreign-born commit considerably fewer crimes than the native-born." In the Italian version of "all that glitters is not gold," the aphorism for not being fooled by surface appearances or face value was "Cuando 'o diavolo t'accurezzà, l'anima va trovando," or when the devil hugs you, he's looking for your soul. To combat jealous people and ruthless competition of the outside world, parents warned children, "Nesciùna ti dice che lavàta 'a faccia che pare chiù bella di me," No one is going to tell you to wash your face, that you look better than me. Italian parenthood, and the long-term commitment to support children from youth to maturity, was summed up in the rhythmic proverb:

> Figli piccerilli,
> Guàji piccerilli.
> Figli gruoss'.
> Guàji gruoss'.
> Figli 'nzurati,
> Guàji doppiati.

---

* Giovanni Verga's masterpiece of "verismo," or realism, "I Malavoglia," provides a literary example of the almost religious importance placed on family honor among the peasantry in the poor Sicilian fishing village of Aci-Trezza. The protagonist, Master 'Ntoni, struggles heroically against the man-made and natural forces for the sake of family name. See also "The House by the Medlar Tree" in English.

Little children,
Little troubles.
Big children,
Big troubles.
Married children,
Double troubles.

Life's disappointments had been common experiences for the Italian under-class and were expressed in sayings with ironic twists of fate, "'A Madonna manda i biscuot' a chi non tiene 'e denti," Mother Mary sends biscuits to those with no teeth and, "O cane muozzèco sempamàie 'o chiù stracciata," The dog always bites the most ragged one. The bitterness of generations of the poor who suffered eco-nomic and social injustice while the rich lived in luxury was summed up in "'O sazio non capisce 'o iuórno," The well-fed do not understand the hungry. Patience, one of Italian contadino's greatest virtues applied in the face of uncontrollable natural and man-made forces, was captured in a rhyme of a peasant woman who went out to search for wood.

A muglièra,
Va pe' legna,
Esce a mattina,
E vinne alla sera.

The wife
went out to find some wood,
She left in the early morning,
and came back late at night.

Earthly masters of the poor—wealthy landowners, government officials, and edu-cational professionals of the upper classes—expected their lowly brethren to abide by a centuries-old custom of showing respect for authority by outward displays of humility and subservience, even in the face of insults and arrogance. Poor farmers often kissed the hand of the lord, greeting him with a request for his blessing. "Vossia, mi benedica," or "Bless me, your honor." The Italian version of holding one's tongue in the presence of the powerful, was expressed in the proverb,

Tuòsseco in canna,
Miéle in bocca.

Poison in the body,
Honey in the mouth.

At the turn of the century, millions of contadini in the Mezzogiorno were the working poor of Italy trapped in the feudalistic "mezzadria," or class system of lord and serf that relegated "giornatori," or day laborers, and "mezzadri," or sharecroppers, to a life of bare subsistence. A small percentage of these farmers were "affituari," or renters, who held short-term leases on the land and hired helpers; in turn they paid a yearly sum to the "gabelotto," or middleman, who ruthlessly managed the land for the small class of wealthy landowners, the "latifondisti" and "galantuomini." The landowner's armed "campieri" and "mazzieri" kept order on the lord's property and held farmers in a perpetual state of dependence. Farming methods remained crude and the failure to rotate crops exhausted the soil. Farmers often competed for the privilege of working the land. As agriculture decreased and the land produced less, rents increased on the poor who could barely feed their large families. In 1905, an average field hand in Basilicata, Calabria, and Sicily earned between thirty and thirty-six cents for a ten-hour day.[15]

In the early days of immigration, northern Italians went to California to start farms. Southern Italians, seeing advertisements at Ellis Island for farm states, continued the migration to far-flung states where they began successful farming communities in Missouri, Texas, Alabama, Arkansas, Maryland, and Virginia. In 1904, Louisiana's white supremacists welcomed them in the interest of replacing African-American field workers with Italians. For many contadini who escaped the Mezzogiorno's oppressive class system, New Haven offered a transition from the archaic working conditions and hardscrabble existence of the Italian countryside to the urban environment of an industrialized city. For some, the exchange of "la zappa," or the hoe, for the polish and buff machine of the factory was considered a blessing. New Haven's undeveloped land around the outskirts of town offered Italians an opportunity Italy could not: the chance to buy their own farmland. With savings from steady factory jobs or the railroad, farmers purchased land and started small truck farms in Woodbridge, North Haven, and Branford that grew into large productive businesses. Farmers brought crops to the market in the Hill where horse and wagon and pushcart peddlers began their daily routes through the neighborhoods selling fresh fruit and vegetables. Some peddlers became store proprietors of Italian import and dry goods stores around the city. Some, like Antonio Pepe, who worked at

Sargent and became an importer of Italian foods, evolved into a wholesale dealer and president of a private bank. In the Annex, parcels of open land owned by old established Yankee families—the Grannisses, Townsends, Woodwards, Burrells, and Kendalls—were sometimes bought or rented by Italians who converted them into vegetable gardens for family use, turkey farms, and commercial truck farms. In scenes reminiscent of daily life in farmlands of the Italian countryside, women who tended the crops at Caprio's farm in the Annex walked with bushels of vegetables on their heads to their homes in the Burwell Street neighborhood. Factory hands living in the city escaped the summer heat to the open acres of rural East Haven and the Annex where they lived in shanty huts and tended vegetable gardens on small plots of undeveloped land. The Troiano family lived in a clapboard farmhouse in Fair Haven, marking the passing seasons by planting and harvesting times rather than their children's school calendars. Whenever a great deal of manual labor was needed to do a job, Italians in New Haven referred to the old farming expression, "Eh, va a zappa," which meant to work and sweat, like a field hand in the old country.

"Italian Farmers"

Pat Barone spoke in the living room of his West Haven home on May 5, 1999.

All up in through Woodbridge, up in North Branford, North Haven was all farms over there. These guys used to come in six, seven, and eight o'clock at night down to Silver Street [the farmers market in the Hill], near South Orange Street there with the horse and wagons. They'd come and they'd have a little lantern on the side of the wagon—some used to come down nine, ten o'clock—because they used to pick the vegetables and by the time they got them in boxes, in bushels, load it on the wagon. They would be there all night long. They'd sleep right there in the wagon. And they'd leave maybe five or six o'clock in the morning, after all the business places would come down and bought all the wares and took it back to their stores. Most of these farmers, I would say, ninety percent were Italian. And hard workers. And they used to have these wagons and they would even sell you a half a bushel of something. Like, say you come down you had a whole bushel of lettuce. You only figured you could sell a half a bushel in your store, say, "I only want a half." They'd sell you whatever you want. I knew a lot of them farmers. A lot of them have gotten rid of their farms and are still living in Woodbridge, but they sold all the land for redevelopment.

"They Wanted To Move To the Country"

Anthony Fiondella spoke in the living room of his East Haven home on December 11, 1998. He lived to be 101 years old.

My father was very good at trimming grapevines. In those days people had grape arbors in the backyard, where they sat under it every day in the summertime in the shade of the grapevines. That's what he did in the wintertime. Different people would have him come and he'd trim and tie up the vines for the next season. You had to know how to do it. How much did he get? Probably a dollar or two for each job. In back of Burrell Street the Burrell family owned all that property. And some Irishman bought the land from Burrell and developed it into building lots and sold them to the people from Wooster and Wallace Street, down that way, to buy the lots. They were mostly Italian; they wanted to move out into the country. Everybody wanted to live in the country in those days. They wanted to have their own little garden and down on Wooster Street you couldn't plant a garden. Every weekend my father acted as an interpreter and after he sold some of the lots for this Irishman that owned the property—I think his name was Dailey—weekends my father would be there either as an interpreter and I guess he sold some of the lots and got a commission. So that's how made a few dollars to support the family.

❝THERE'S A BEAR IN THE YARD❞

Annette Ruocco spoke at the kitchen table of her Annex home on November 17, 1998. She came from a fishing family in Atrani on the Amalfitano coast.

We lived on Chestnut Street, twenty-one dollars a month with electricity. My husband Rocky [Anthony Ruocco] was convinced—because he came from the Annex and now we were living in the city—because his father wanted me to live in his house. He used to say, "Aye, l'aria la 'ncòppa è cchiù fine," the air up there is better. The Annex was like the country; there was country air [laughing]. Well, maybe it was true, who knows? We moved to Burrell Street [in the Annex] in 1945. There were all lots back there where they farmed. I was so ignorant about animals and things like that. The first winter I look out my window [voice rising] and there was—I thought it was a bear. Hey, Tony, come here! I said, Look at the bear in the yard! He said, "It's a pig." I [laughing] had never seen a black pig. I thought a pig was always a tan color, light, brown and tan. But we had pigs up the hill. And once in a while they strayed down. Every Sunday morning there were these guys from Granniss corner played bocce in the road and had beer from Zi' Antonio's, Uncle Anthony's. There was always that will to get to Burrell Street.

❝CICÒREA AND HIS LOT❞

Joseph Riccio spoke at his kitchen table from his home in the Annex on April 16, 2000.

In the New Haven area, in the suburbs, a lot of the Italian people had little lots and they would work on them during the summer. A lot of the men used to work in the shops in town and then on Saturday and Sunday they'd be up at their lot. They had a little shanty built, just a shed. And if they had to they'd sink a well sometimes to give them running water and [they had] an outhouse. And they lived there for the weekend and built a little farm. A lot of them lived off it, you know, they'd bring the stuff home and canned tomatoes and everything. It was prevalent through the East Haven, Foxon areas—a lot of people their little lots. It was something that they brought back from Italy, you know, from the earth. Then later on, as things got better, they built homes on them. Mr. Funaro was one of the guys and he had a bunch of kids, nine or ten children, and he used to come on his lot from East Street in New Haven—a lot of times he used to walk. One I remember closely was this guy they used to call "cicòrea," dandelion, I don't know where they got the name from, that's the only way we knew him. He used to go there every weekend, used to stay nights too. He lived in that shack. And he used to have a piece of land on Milton Street before it was road—it was just a path, which was all mud in the summer time, the fall and winter.

66 WE WORKED ON SUNDAYS TOO 99

Sabatino "Sam" Troiano spoke at the dining room table with his wife Giovannina, "Jennie" and son Gino at his North Branford home on May 27, 2000. He recounted the old-timers who made wine "squeezing grapes so hard you could roll it down the street."

My father came over when he was sixteen years old from Italy, from Santa Maria di Capua Vetere. He came to the United States because in Italy his father had a restaurant and they worked seven days a week. And he heard in the United States they never worked on Sundays. So he comes, he was sixteen years old, he got enough money together to come over to the United States and when he got off the boat they picked him up, his uncles [the Perrotti's] from Woodbridge. He got up in the morning—he's workin' on the farm. Sunday comes. He lay in bed, you know. And pretty quick the uncle comes to the door and knocks on the door and says, "What are you doin' in bed?" He said, "Well, today's Sunday. We don't work." He says, "On the farm we work seven days a week." Well, my father said he used to go into the horse stable and he'd cry because he didn't have enough money to go back, and he worked on the farm till he was about twenty-three, twenty-four years old. Then he got a job at Bartolini's quarry in Woodbridge. At those time [1925] Woodbridge flats they used to call it, there was about eight or nine, maybe ten farmers in the Woodbridge flats, all Italians. There was Luciani, there was the Perrotti brothers, there was DeLucia. Of course one of the Perrotti's sons, the oldest one, he had a farm there too.

66 LIFE ON A FARM IN NEW HAVEN 99

Then he moved to where Bella Vista is today. There was an old salt box house there, a big old salt box house. As far back as I can remember they had the oil lamps in the ceiling and he used to light them at night. We had no electricity, no bathrooms, no heat whatsoever. When we were kids we used to go to bed at night and

TROIANO BROTHERS ON THE FARM. LEFT TO RIGHT:
GINO, SABATINO, PASQUALE, AND GAETANO,
1930s (site of the present day Bella Vista complex, Fair Haven)

Troiano family album

wake up in the morning, steam would be coming out your mouth because it was
so cold. We had a lot a blankets on the bed but we had just one little oil stove in
the kitchen. My father rented from Dailey. Dailey had a big pig farm, they used to
collect the garbage in New Haven. They had about eight or ten garbage wagons
and teams of horses and they'd bring it back and they used to feed these pigs back
there behind Bella Vista, to the Municipal Golf Course with this garbage. Then

they'd clean all this garbage, it would be all manure and everything and bring it to the farm that we were farmin'. My father was rentin' from them. We rented the farm from them. Twenty-five dollars a month. And they'd spread it all over, you know, and then we'd plow it up. And we used to raise some great vegetables on it, I mean I remember lettuce heads used to be that big [cupping hands], that stuff was really powerful stuff. And we used to use their horses. They had about twelve, fourteen teams of horses—they had no trucks. All the garbage was picked up by the garbage wagons with horses. We used to ride to school with them. We knew all the guys; we'd ride to school [laughing] on the garbage wagon. In the wintertime they'd plow the snow with a wooden snowplow, a v plow. They used to plow the snow with the garbage wagon, they used to plow the city streets so the garbage wagons could get out with a big v plow made out a wood.

The four of us were born in the house—no hospital—we were all born in the house. The doctor used to come to the house—ten or fifteen dollars he used to get or something like that. Yeah. My mother, she'd work on the farm, especially in the summertime. We lived on sandwiches in the summer mostly because we didn't have that much time. She was pickin' beans one day, string beans. She went into the house and had my sister. And two days after she was out on the farm workin' again. And when we, as soon as we could hold a hoe in our hand, we'd be out there. We had no education at all and as soon as we got to be sixteen, got yanked out of school because we had to work on the farm. You know, when we went to school we had to learn the English language. My father and mother always talked to us in Italian. We all stood back in the first grade. No kindergarten. Back then, no such thing as a kindergarten. So we had to learn the English language and that's why we were so far behind. The other kids, they were all smarter than we were, I mean they knew how to talk. I never knew how to play baseball till I was about fourteen, fifteen years old. I didn't know what it was all about. We never could play with any of the kids. Cuz' my father was, he was really an old-time, rough Italian. Boy, we had to work. It was twenty-five, thirty acres; everything was plowed by hand with a twelve, maybe fourteen-inch plow, with a team of horses. To plow an acre probably takes you a good half a day. You walk in back of the plow, yeah. And then cultivating. I remember I used to ride the horse sometimes and keep him in line between the rows of vegetables. I remember he ran away from me once, I almost got killed that time. I fell off and the cultivator teeth missed me by that much, it would a ripped me apart! Then that was the end of ridin' the horse anymore, my father wouldn't let us get on the horses no more. We used Dailey's team of horses, couple a team of horses. All plowin', the harrowin' was all done with a team of horses. And we all did it. We got twelve, thirteen years old we used to work the horses. One horse would walk to the end of the furrow and the other horse would be on the top of the furrow and right to the end. And of course we used the same horses all the time so more or less they knew what to do, and they knew just how to go. In fact, we had one horse, "Carbonella" [little dark one] they used to call him, and that horse, you didn't have to drive him, you used to cultivate with him, and he'd go so slow, you know, so you could do a real good job. And he'd get to the end of the row, he'd turn around by himself, go back down the other row. He was a good horse, yeah.

"The Farming Seasons in New Haven"

It used to start in February. We used to get the horse manure, pile it up, and it used to get real hot, it get so hot you'd burn your hand if you put it in, you used to get blisters on it. We'd take it and put it in the hotbeds, big long hotbeds. They were about two feet deep, you know, about six feet wide. We'd put it in about ten inches and pack it down real tight and put about four inches of dirt on top and put seeds on top there and in three days the heat from that manure make the plants all come up—lettuce, cabbage, tomatoes, broccoli. Then we'd have to weed the things and then after that when they got so big we'd take and transplant them into the greenhouses to get em' bigger. And that's what you did in the winter, you worked all winter and if you weren't doin' that you're spreading manure by hand out with a fork. Back then, you know, we used to seed in the end of March; the weather isn't like it is now. When the spring broke it got warm back then. Over here for cryin' out loud, in May it's still cold! It was different. From the transplanting, when we weren't doing that, we'd be spreadin' manure. We never had no time off. And even during the summer when we were harvesting we'd work like heck and my father's friends used to come and help us work on the farm. Maybe we got a half a day off on Sunday afternoon. Homework? If we tried to do our homework, my father'd break the book over our heads. I mean it. You didn't do no homework. You come home from school, you go out and work. You come in the house, you eat and you got to bed. Back then you know there was no TV. I remember the latest we stayed up was to listen to the Lone Ranger. It used to come on at 7:30, it was on for a half-hour, we'd listen to that and then [go to bed]. Television, I don't think they ever heard of the thing.

Now in April you get all your plants out. We all worked together. Now we get out in this lettuce field and you hoe the whole field of lettuce, all by hand. We never had a tractor until 1944 was the first tractor we bought. By April, then you start pickin' your winter crops, like broccoli rabe, and winter-over spinach, you plant that in the fall and you pick it in the spring. By then, that'll be your first crop and you start getting a little money. Then at the end of May and June, we start pickin' lettuce and then you run over into your tomatoes and your eggplants. We used to raise a lot a eggplants because it was good land for eggplants. Those darn things were so darn big.

We used to go down to the New Haven market on Hill Street in New Haven. Back then I'd say [there were] at least one hundred farmers in New Haven market from the area—Hamden, Woodbridge. And today there's only about three farmers left in the whole area, that's all that's left. Oh, the market. We were little kids then, we used to go on Saturdays and help my father sell, you know. Everything was ten cents, twenty-five cents. The only time you made some money is if you got some really early tomatoes. I mean you probably got a coupla dollars, three dollars a basket. Oh my God, that was big money, yeah. We had no money but we lived better. We had our own cows; we made our own butter and cheese. My mother made her own bread, we had chickens, we had the eggs, we raised and my father killed four pigs a year. And then my mother, she'd have the cellar full of all kind a can goods— peaches and pears and everything. We never had to leave the house if we didn't want to in the wintertime. Because we had everything, even the vegetables. We used to make these ditches in the ground and put celery in there and fenùc- chio[fennel], put them in, then make a pyramid out of savoy cabbage with the roots up in the air and you'd have cabbage all winter long.

"CHRISTMAS ON THE FARM"

We didn't have the luxuries like today, forget it. Toys? We never got. I remember one time, one time Santa Claus came. I dunno, my father must a run into some money somewhere. We got a little kiddie car, one toy apiece. And that's the only time, I remember, we ever got a toy. It was supposed to be Santa Claus but we didn't know; we were still small. We never got no toys. Like if ever got anything, it would be a brand new hoe [laughing]. Or a little, we used to call 'em "the hook," they used to be shaped like a C, with a handle on it [scythe]. Oh, on my hands and knees, you'd be on your hands and knees for days and weeks, we had to weed it, thin out the lettuce, it's all done with those hooks, the front part would be sharp, and you'd weed around.

"I MADE A DOLLAR A WEEK ON THE FARM IN 1913"

Giuannine DeMaio spoke by the pool of her granddaughter's North Bran- ford home on July 11, 1999. In 2003, the State of Connecticut declared De- cember as "Jennie DeMaio" month.

When I was ten years old there was farm land in the Annex [where Brown Place is today] and there was a road, you walked down the road, and as far as your eye could see—nothing but flat land. And then came the water [Long Island Sound], the water came up to this land, but long. So the farmers, they used to rent pieces and they used to plant it and then with the horse and wagon they used to go the market and sell the stuff. So I fell in love with workin' on a farm. Ten years old I used to get a dollar a week. In the morning till six or seven at night. Five days, sometimes six days for the dollar. But them days a dollar was . . . I was born in 1903, so it was 1913. I wanted to work there, I really did. So my mother used to brag, "My daughter makes a dollar a week," to her sisters. And then she'd say, you know my daughter makes a dollar a week, and right away, the daughter, "I want to go to work with her, too." After two hours work, "The hell with this, you work." And I stayed in the sun without a hat, with no cream, never had that stuff, I never tanned, I dunno. I never minded the heat because I was so used to it. And when I went to school in Septem- ber, I used to run home, change, and run down the [DiCaprio] farm and work. I used to plant. I used to hoe. When the stuff was ready I used to pick. Then we used to fix the tomatoes, you know, nice big tomatoes, fix them in the baskets and then I used to load em' up on the wagon. If it was raining and you were plantin', let's

TROIANO FAMILY TABLE

Troiano family album

hurry up and finish plantin' so we don't have to water. We used to get soaking wet. I never minded. There was another kid, Johnny Fiondella, he used to work there when I was kid, once in a while, not long. He worked a little while with me—nobody worked long. I was the only one who worked for years. I used to love it, I really worked; I really loved to work. I couldn't wait to come back to work right after school in the afternoon.

This here happened before the Tweed airport opened up. Now it was during the First World War when all this happened. The airplane—see he had to land—

and there was a fence and on the other side there was runway. One plane used to go by. And the plane would land and they would try bombs because the thing was nothing but a piece of land. They'd drop bombs to see how they were workin'. Real bombs. They used to drop the real bombs and they'd come down. Now, one time we were hoein' peppers, pretty soon the plane came up and dropped a bomb. You know, I never wore stockings in them days—cuz you were working in the land, old shoes and everything—all my legs over here, you know when you hit something and it makes a hole, all the little bits of pebbles hit all my legs—the pebbles hit my legs—from the bomb that they threw. The airplane went across. So the next thing you know, the two guys—the plane came back again—two well-dressed guys from the Army, you know uniforms, they wanted to see if they killed anybody or damaged anything. They were scared, they wanted to know if anybody got hurt. And we said no we didn't get hurt, but I got a bunch of pebbles all over my legs. So the guy says to me, "Do you wanna go for an airplane ride?" So I said to him, Who's gonna go with us? "Only you and I." Oh no, I ain't goin' with you—you go by yourself—I was only a kid, maybe eleven that time twelve or something like that. And they went and talked to Tony [the landowner]—I know he must a got a lot a money because it made a big hole like that on his farm, in the peppers. I dunno how it didn't hit any of us. So now he come back on the path [runway] where they [planes] used to go down. They only had one plane could go down, they had only one path, one runway, no Tweed airport in them days. So they used to test the bombs. The war [World War I] was goin' on then, I was eleven or twelve.

"On Being the Oldest Daughter"

Rose Durso spoke in the living room of Lena and Joe Riccio's home in the Annex on February 1, 1998.

My father had a horse and wagon and before Christmas he would put us on the horse and wagon, "Guaglióne, young boy, come on, I got a buy you the suit." Once every year we'd get a suit and a coat—the coat didn't last forever, so he'd put us on the horse and wagon—cold, bitter days—it had a hood, it was a covered wagon. So we get in there all bundled up with clothes and everything in the back and he'd stop at Perlemutters on Grand Avenue—that was the famous store for all the Italians, a dollar a week, a dollar down. We'd stop there, my father would go in, and Mister Perlemutter would say, "Hello, Nick." [My father] "Allo Mista Perl-a-mutter, you good?" [Mr. Perlemutter] "Yeah, me good." My father would say, "Wan a suit forda boy eh coat forda girl." Okay, the broken English that's okay. "All right, Nick, anything you want here, just let the kids try it on." He'd pick out a coat and my brother—always knickers, gray knickers with the gray jacket. And before we even went in the store my brother would start crying. So I'd say to him, "What's the matter, Paulie?" [Paulie] "Now I know that when I go in that store pop is gonna buy me the blue suit like he does every year and I don't want it." So I said, "Well I'll get a beatin' if I answer Papa." Paulie said, "I don't want it. Well tell [Papa] him." I said, "He'd beat me up. Well then shut up and take the suit." We go in there, the poor kid ends up with the blue, the knickers the strap and the jacket with the pleats. So my father would say, "How much a you want?" And Mister Perlemutter would mention a price. "No goot!" My father would grab me, my brother and my mother. "Jiame chine" [Let's go]. We'd go out, bang! The door—pow! Bang the door, that was all right. "Nick, come back, all right, come on, let's make a deal, let's make a deal." We go in again. [Papa] "How much a you want?" [Perlemutter] "Well, all right, I'll take two dollars off." [Papa] "No goot!" Run out again, back in the wagon. Mister Perlemutter would get so disgusted, he wanted to close up or something, so, "All right, Nick, come on, all right, I'll give another three dollars off." [Papa] "All right, attsa goot, now it's a goot." He would even get in the wagon, he'd say to my mother, "See, aggiu ditt' [See how I spoke up], if I argued with the guy, I would get the price." He didn't realize that Mister Perlemutter still made money on him, okay? And we'd go home and my father would cry for weeks over that suit and me with the coat. And that was it. Once a year we'd go there. And then we'd go across the street to Kleigers for shoes, the only shoe store on the avenue. The same thing, "How much a you want?" "Well, the shoes are . . ." "No goot" [laughing]. In and out, in and out a that door till finally he thinks that he fooled the guy, he doesn't know the guy still made money on him. He had to earn a living the man, you know. And that was our life.

"CARRYING THE VEGETABLES HOME IN THE ANNEX"

Lena Riccio spoke in the living room of her Annex home on February 1, 1998.

Bushels, with vegetables. She [my mother Antonia] used to come up all the way down the Annex field. She used to work on the farm, walk all the way down where we lived [Oakley Street] with a bushel on her head. She used to make a tourniquet with the handkerchief, roll it up, make it round, stick the bushel on her head, she used to walk all the way from there down to the house with vegetables in it at night. That bushel never moved.

"BRINGING MOM TO A FARM"

Rose Durso spoke in the living room at Joseph and Lena Riccio's Annex home on February 2, 1998.

My father came from Amalfi, Italy in 1911. Then, when he went back he met my mother, they fell in love, and he came here to make some money at Sargent's, where he was treated rotten. He went back, he married my mother and he brought her here. When he brought her here there was no apartment available, nothing. So he had to bring her in a tenement house with ten families on Wooster Street and live in with one of my aunts. And she had children and we had a family and we

ROSE DURSO
On the Caprio farm,
Main Street, Annex, 1929

Durso family album

slept three in one bed, the kids. My mother came from Minori, Italy. My mother
was ill with anemia among other things. So my father, struggling with a little
money, goes to the doctor. He took her to the doctor and the doctor said, "Where
does your wife come from?" So my father said, "From Italy, from a small village."
So he said, "Was it country, was it rural?" So my father said yes. He said, "Well,
you better take your wife and bring her to the same environment that she had in
Italy." So my father saved a little money and he bought that farm. At that time, in
those days, you could buy for a little money, very little money. So he bought the
farm and went in my mother said, "Addo mi è portat'?" Where did you bring me?
The pumping water, the boards with spaces that big on the floor, bedrooms that
the water by the walls was coming down. Water, dampness, condensation on the
walls, my mother said, "I' mi muóre cchiù amprèssa" [I'm going to die faster here].

But, he fixed it, he worked hard till two or three o'clock in the morning. He made a home out of it. And she got better, she got strong. And she worked hard. Planting everything so we'd have our stuff for the winter, our foods, all our provisions. And that was my life. And us kids enjoyed it because that was the only life that we knew. Nothing else. In the fall, go make a bushel of potatoes, dig it up before you go to school, my brother and I. Dig the potatoes—digging with our feet, with our nails, with little shovels, digging the potatoes—my mother had to cook the potatoes and all—put the rest down the cellar and then we would go to school. Another day it was pick up the apples. Another day was picking up the pears, always something was going, all the time. That was our life. I took care of all the other little ones. Like my mother would go out on the farm, pick up things, and I'd be by the stove cooking. See, that's where I learned to cook too. It was six acres of land, it extended all the way to the back of Huntington Avenue [in the Annex]. And my father would plant a nice percentage of it, anything you could think of—onions, garlic, the radishes, escarole, cabbage, you name it, it was there—pumpkins and everything. And we stored for the winter, see, we stored for the winter. My mother, till three o'clock in the morning, the jars of peaches and pears, put em' down the cellar—that's what we had, peaches and pears—peaches and pears, [singsong, rhythmic voice] pears and peaches [laughing]! That's how it was, you know, that's how we had a live. The beans—dry the beans off a vine, pick 'em in their shell, the pinto, the brown kidney beans, let them dry out, and then shell them and put them in different containers and put em' away. See, which was interesting too. When Christmas came there was nothing in the stocking [laughing], tangerines, figs, prunes, and oranges—those were our gifts. But we were happy kids because we knew no other way of life. And we were happy. And until the day that I got out a my mother's house, I never suffered hardship. My father made sure that we didn't—he had no money—sure, we were deprived of things, but not that we had hardship—we had food, we stored it, we canned it. A big barn where we kept our horse, our animals. A chicken coop, all that. Clean the barn. The swallows would come in and out on the second floor of the barn and we'd try to catch them. We'd jump on the hay—and we'd get beat up to a pulp, "You jump on the hay and the horse won't eat it up because it's all matted up," and we kept doin' it and doin' it but then we grew up and everybody went their own way and then of course my mother died and we came into this era.

11

Working Life Experiences

By the time the first wave of Italian immigrants began to arrive in the 1880s, New Haven had already been transformed from a mercantile trading city into a bustling manufacturing center whose mammoth factory buildings stretched the length and width of several blocks. Roland Osterweis's *Three Centuries of New Haven: 1638–1938,* described the momentous change in the physical character and pace of the city: "In place of the peaceful farmhouse and the slow tempo of isolated living appeared the large factory, the hurrying crowds of workmen, and the solid rows of city dwellings."[16] New Haven's version of Gilded Age optimism and economic expansion was fueled by the demand for cheap labor from abroad. Between 1890 and 1910, 1,900,000 southern Italians came to American shores: seventy-seven percent were unskilled from the lower economic class, fifteen percent were in skilled occupations and less than half of one percent were classified as professionals.[17]

New Haven's factory and railroad owners quickly recognized the eagerness and productivity of unskilled Italian workers who had recently been farmers, shepherds, fishermen, or laborers in Italy. The unskilled day laborer, who earned twenty-five cents a day in Italy, found backbreaking work in the 1880s on the railroad digging roadbeds, laying track beds, and building overpasses. By 1908, the railroad had 10,000 Italians on its payroll earning the unimaginable wage of $1.20 a day. As early as the late 1870s, Italians were hired by Yankee owners in the shoe and rubber industry when surnames Riccitelli, Villani, and Gaudio began to appear on weekly payrolls of L. Candee Rubber Company. Surnames of Mongillo, Conti, and Mendillo began to appear on the payroll of the New Haven Wire Company. The New Haven Clock Company, the world's largest clock factory in 1920, employed Marescas and Gagliardis among its 2,000 workers in the late 1880s. By 1881, Oliver Winchester's factory, the Winchester Repeating Arms, was one of the largest producers of gun cartridges in the United States and surnames Russo, Guerra, and Lupoli were listed. Nine corset firms, employing over 3,000 mostly Jewish and Italian women, made New Haven the largest corset-producing city in the United States. The largest of these factories was pioneered by Isaac Strouse and Max Adler. Hundreds of Italians worked at the National Folding Box Company, the world's largest paper box factory, and at A. C. Gilbert Company, which produced toys for children and household goods.

In 1890, a few skilled workers who had apprenticed in Italy where they received technical and vocational training and ranked relatively high in the Italian social scale, found occupational opportunities in their trades and opened businesses in New Haven as tailors, barbers, carpenters, and shoemakers. Artisans, "mestiere girovaghi," who traveled from town to town in Italy producing metal and leather items and repairing clocks, found work in New Haven's trades and factories. Skilled dressmakers and tailors who cut and fit clothes for customers in Italy opened tailor shops. Colorful "venditori ambulanti," or street vendors, who were peddlers, tinkers, and cobblers confined to towns and sold household utensils, mended pots, eggs, milk, fruits, and rags in Italian villages, found new clientele in the teeming streets and beehive tenement houses of New Haven's neighborhoods. Former small shopkeepers of herbs and old clothes, locksmiths, horseshoers, and tobacconists began small retail businesses on the corners and on the main thoroughfares of the neighborhoods. By the late 1890s, Italians had opened fifteen retail and wholesale grocery stores specializing in imported Italian products. By the '20s, skilled artisans, the highest position attainable by a peasant in Italy, gradually began to secure positions in New Haven's occupational hierarchy. Between 1890 and 1900, painters named Conforti and Colangelo appeared on the city directory; a musician named Maestro Rizzo opened a vocal studio in 1882, and Francis Coiro opened an artisan studio in Fair Haven where he and his staff designed and built stage sets for theatre companies in New York. In 1892, Sylvester Poli, an immigrant from Tuscany who became one of the most successful businessmen in the city, chose a name for his newly-built movie house that captured the spirit and optimism of the times, the Poli Wonderful Land Theatre.

❝WORKING AT A.C. GILBERT❞

Rose Sansone was the youngest of thirteen children of parents from Atrani.
She spoke at the kitchen table in her Fair Haven home on August 8, 1998.

After I got married I worked at A.C. Gilbert at night from three to eleven for eighteen years, from 1948. I worked every kind of a machine you wanted, all the men's jobs I worked. I worked the drill presses, I worked the power pressers, I worked every kind of press you want to have. We worked piecework. There were no men working on those kind of jobs, they were all women. They didn't hire men for those kinds of jobs. I don't know why. Because we were stupid. All we made was twelve dollars a day. After twelve dollars a day you couldn't work. If you made more than twelve dollars a day, they would cut the price on the job, cut the jobs because you were making too much money. So we were making twelve dollars a day and then ten percent for working nights we were making thirteen dollars and twenty cents — that was big pay. And that was a heavy job. I used to pick up boxes with fan bases and drill through cast iron and then tap the cast iron jobs. Then I used to work the

A. C. GILBERT FACTORY
Giordana Diamontini holding egg beaters at center
Fair Haven, 1920s

Diamontini album

multi-head drills with eight thin drills to put the holes on the trim where they put the little wires all around the kid's big trains. I worked the big power presses with the things on your arms that throws your arms over. Everything was piecework. If you didn't make it, you got eighty cents an hour. I used to stand up eight hours a day. And I never brought lunch while I worked—all I brought was an apple. At 6:30 everybody would sit down and have lunch. I would bring just an apple and buy a cup of coffee. That was it. And I never lost a pound. And not only that, when I used to get through working that I used to make my twelve dollars, I used to go helping the other girls that didn't make their twelve dollars. I was the best one in the machine department. They graded you with a report card. We had to go to, they called it training; you had to stay three weeks on every different machine and every different job. And at the end then you would graduate. If you didn't do good then they wouldn't hire you. And they gave me a diploma. They said, "With this diploma you can go anywhere in the United States and get a job." I said, "Yeah, with this and ten cents" [laughing].

The men were our supervisors; they trained all the women who worked on machines. No union but the supervisors treated us very good. When it was your birthday old man Gilbert [the owner] himself would come around, give you a card, shake your hand and say, "Happy birthday." For Christmas he would have a Christmas party for the employees with all the kids. They all got a gift and they had a nice Christmas party right in the shop itself over there. You could buy your HO and big trains there.

"You Making Any Money?"

Rose Sansone spoke at the kitchen table of her Fair Haven home on August 8, 1998. Her spirited response to A. C. Gilbert illustrated the intersection of the Italian American working class and New Haven's wealthy Yankee captains of industry.

Every Thursday night, the old man Gilbert would come around and say to you, "Are you making money?" You would say to him, "Well, yeah, I'm making my day's pay." But if you didn't make your day's pay he would want to know why you weren't making a day's pay. I was working on the bases of the fan. At that time there they were cast iron—not like now. You had to put them in a big jig. You had to drill the hole, then you had to ream it and then you had to tap them. Then you had to push the thing around. You couldn't make money; nobody could make money on that job. Because the one that timed us wouldn't give us a better price on it. Oh yeah, you get timed on a job. The timekeeper comes with the time clock, see how long it takes you to do a piece and that's how they give you a price, that's how you get piecework. The time study man come around and they time you, from the beginning you pick up the piece till the piece is done and you put it in the box. Well, they time you. Then at the end they come up with a price. Say, well you got two dollars for a hundred, all right? So now you got to make six hundred of those a day to

* (COMPLETED ON THE JOB TRAINING)
NAME: SANSONE, ROSE   413076   MACHINE   MISC. BENCH & MACHINE OPERATOR

> On this page you see an actual co-workers' card. Note that skills are listed and graded. On top of page six you see the reverse side of card. This side deals primarily with the history of conveyor skills.

SKILL GROUP	GOOD	POOR	EXCELL	SKILL GROUP	GOOD	POOR	EXCELL	SKILL GROUP	GOOD	POOR	EXCELL
1 ASSEM HAND				C MULT WET				C SCRAPE HAND			
2 ASSEM CONV				D ELECT DRILL				D SCRAPE MACH			
3 ASSEM ACT CAB				20 FILLER CHEM				32 METALLIZER			
4 AUTO TAPPER				A LABLER				33 METAL SAW			
5 BODINE ASS'T				B TIGHTENER				34 MILLER HAND			
6 BUFFER "A"				21 FILLER PARTS				A AUTO			
A BUFFER "B"				22 FOLD MACH OPER				35 MOLD PLASTIC			
B BUFFER "C"				23 FOUR SLICE				A BRIK			
C AUTO				A RING FORM				B WOOD			
7 BROACHER				B MULTI				36 PACK CONV			
8 BALANCE ARM				C CUTOFF				A GOVT			
A BLADE				24 GLUE LABEL				B SHIP CART			
9 COLLATER				A LENS				C TRACK			
10 CUTTER CORD				B TANK ENDS				37 PAINT SPRAY "A"			
11 CUTTER CORNER				C VELOUR				A PAINT SPRAY "B"			
A LABLES				D WINDOWS				B PAINT SPRAY "C"			
B SCORER				25 GRINDER CENTER				C AUTO			
C SLITTER				A CRUSH				D DIP HAND			
D STITCHER				B GEAR				E DIP OVEN			
E STRIPPER				C HOBBER				F PASCHE			
F QUAD				26 HEADER				G STRIPPER			
G WRAPPER				A KNURLER				38 PART WASH			
12 CUTTER GLASS				B THREADER				A CHIPS			
A BENDER				27 INSPECT DEPT.				B OIL			
13 CUTTER TOOTH				A GATE BREAKER				39 PEXTO ROLL			
14 DECALER				B TESTER				40 PICK TIE			
15 DEGREASER				28 KICK PRESS			X	41 PLATEN PRESS			
A BONDERIZER				A ARBOR				A FILLING			
A RONCI				B TRIM FOOT				B HOT STAMP			
C STRIPPER				29 KINGSBURY				C MARKEM			
16 DIAL COUPLER				30 LATHE HAND				42 PLATE AUTO			
17 DIAL WHEEL				A BENCH				A AUTO CONV			
18 DIE CAST HAND				B CONTOUR BORE				I BLACK MAGIC			
A DIE CAST AUTO				C DEBURR				C BLACK NICKEL			
A ROTOR CASTER				D DIAMOND				D BRASS			
19 DRILL PRESS DRY			X	31 LEAD CONNECT				E CHROME			

SKILL GROUP	GOOD	POOR	EXCELL	SKILL GROUP	GOOD	POOR	EXCELL	SKILL GROUP	GOOD	POOR	EXCELL
H STILL				A EYELET				A MACH			
43 POLISHER LENS				B HI SPEED				58 TAPER MACH			
44 POWER PRESS				C SPINNER	X			59 TRACK DIAL			
A AIR				49 SANDER BELT				A CUTOFF			
B ASSEMBLY				A GRINDER				B PINNER			
C AUTO				B FILER HAND				C RADIUS ROLL			
D BRAKE				50 SC MACH AUTO				60 TRIMMER CUP			
E DOUBLE ACT				51 SLICER				61 TUMBLER			
F H. & W.				52 SLITTER STEEL				62 VACUUM FORM			
G HYDRAULIC			X	A HELPER				63 WINDER ARM			
H PEARLESS				53 SOLDERER IRON				A MULT ARM			
I PIERCE				A BRAZE				B GANG			
J SHEAR				B DIP				C LEVEL			
K SINTER				C ELECTRIC				D MULT COIL			
L TRIM				D ELECTRONIC PART				E SPRING			
45 POWER SAW				E GUN							
A AIR CLAMP				F INDUCTION							
B BAND				54 SPINNER							
C HINGE				55 SPOTWELDER							
D NOTCH				A BUTT							
46 RACKER				B MULTIPLE							

ROSE SANSONE'S WORK REPORT CARD

From A. C. Gilbert

Sansone family album

make your twelve dollars. Well you couldn't make six hundred a day because the job was too heavy and you couldn't do it. So, he [Mr. Gilbert] came around one night and he said to me, "Are you making money on this job?" I was working and he got all dirty because it was cast iron. I said, "To tell you the truth Mister Gilbert, I'm not making day rate." He said, "What do you mean you're not making day rate?" I said, Well, no matter how hard you work you can't make your day's pay. "Well how about the girls on days?" Because I was working nights. So he went and check her time. She wasn't making it either. So he got a hold of the time study man, he said, "Why aren't these girls making money?" He said, "Well, I timed them, from here to there, and they're supposed to be making money." Mister Gilbert said, "Did you time them on the weight that they're pushing around?" He said, "No." Mister Gilbert said, "Oh, well, then you change it." He changed it and we all made money after that. But if you didn't talk up you never got nowhere.

"THEY CALLED THEM 'TIME STUDY MEN'"

When they would come around to time you, right, and they'd say, "Okay, now you start here." You take the piece and he watches you. You pick up the piece. You put it in the jig. You close the jig. And you drill it, right? Then from there you take the jig and you push over here while he times you how long it takes you from here to here. Then he takes how long it takes you to drill, then you got to ream the hole. It takes all the burr out of the hole that you drill. Then you got to take the piece out of this jig, put it in this other jig, you got to turn it around and put it in this other jig. Then you got to tap it so you could get the screws in, where they put the screws in underneath. When you got to take it from there, you got to blow it out and then you got to put it in the box. And all we could put in the box is probably seven or eight pieces. Then you got to start all over again. So they time you from here to the end when it goes in the box. They don't time you for how much it weighs. They only time you how long it takes you to go from one place to another—that's how they time you. Now when you're working on a machine, say

ROSE SANSONE'S CONFIRMATION
WITH BROTHER MATTHEW PROTO
Saint Donato's Church,
Fair Haven, 1923

Sansone family album

you're working on a kick press. It's a little machine and you have little pieces you have to put in and then you have to kick it. Then you got to take it out, and you kick and kick all day long. Then they had the dial machine. And they time you from the minute you put how many pieces you put on the dial machine—it goes all around, all around—that's how they time. And that's how they come up with a price, see? Fifty cents a hundred, it all depends how fast they go, too. Like the dial machine; that goes fast, all you do is put them on and they fall off, all they do is just put on, put on, put on. It goes all around and that's how they time you. They call those time study men. And our time study man was named Mike Criscuolo; he was Italian but he was terrible. He was the worst time-study man you want—he wasn't for the workers at all.

"THEY NEEDED MANPOWER"

Salvatore "Gary" Garibaldi spoke at Tony and Lucille's restaurant on Wooster Street on May 17, 2000.

It would be like word of mouth. Like Sargent's needed some manpower, A. C. Gilbert needed manpower. Well, they would ask the fellas, "You know anybody who wants to work?" "Oh yeah, my cousin, my brother." The other would say, "My sister." It all depended what kind of production or what product they were making. Like A. C. Gilbert would be more or less hiring a greater ratio of women because they were making toys. Sargent's would be more or less rough and ready—men who were needed in the foundries, making locks. So that's the way manpower was hired. You never made an application; they didn't know what an application was. It was all done by word of mouth. So as soon as you heard any inter-party—some people were a little nosy—they would pick up a word from the bookkeeper that they needed more manpower. She wouldn't say nothing to the person working next to her because she figured she had the advantage of talking to the guy before she becomes aware of it, to get her sister in. That's how they operated. If I knew they needed manpower next week I wouldn't tell my fellow worker next to me but I would get around one of the foremen—the floor worker—and say, hey, I hear there's going . . . He'd say, "Yeah, keep quiet, who do you want?" I'll get my sister. He'd say, "All right, keep quiet until they make the announcement." Well now that job is already sewed up for my sister.

"WORKING ON THE RAILROAD"

In 1892, my father got a job in the Cedar Hill yards digging ditches and laying tracks. But because he went to school—he was a child in an orphanage asylum—he knew how to read and write English. His boss was named Cornelius Shugrue because in those days most of the men and the women of Irish descent were in those jobs as bosses, as executive officers. And the poor early immigrant—regardless of what nationality he was—was subject to their fancy whims. They were not the boss or anything—they were the workers. Cornelius was called "Connie"; he was a great man about six feet tall, about two hundred pounds. So Connie turned to my father and said, "Philip, you take care of your paisans [countrymen] and tell them what to do because I cannot relate to them in Italian." So my father said, "All right, I'll do that." So after a month or so my father is working laying down tracks along with his paisans. But making the same money. So after a couple of months my father went up to Connie and said, "Connie, I want to tell you something. I'm working like them, I'm telling them what to do and I'm getting the same pay. Well I'm not going to do that anymore—you tell them what to do." So Connie said, "Don't get excited Philip, I'll think about it." Two days later he said to my father, "You are now a straw boss." In those days straw boss meant assistant foreman. Now he got a big raise, [laughing] he got ten cents more an hour. Of course that was a lot of money in those days. They used to break their backs. Everything was manual; they didn't have the kind of equipment that you have today. If you had to move track there would be about six, seven guys pick up a track piece maybe ten feet long. It wasn't like a rig. Sometimes you'd find rock and they didn't use dynamite in those days. And you'd be with a pick and bang and bang. State Street was all barren land and so now as they were laying down the track in a line when they got to here they caught rock. Well they can't just go this way so they used to break it—my father used to say, backbreaking. And they laid that track under weather conditions—hot, cold. They worked, say in March, and lay track until it got cold in October. They had a water boy working there. A water boy would be like a young kid who just got a job. And his job was to get pails of water and give it to the men working. And they used to scoop out of the same pail, the same scoop and drink from it. In those days if he made eleven or twelve dollars a week, that was big money. But look how the industrial people used our parents as slave workers.

"THE AGENTS"

Here in New Haven at that time [1900s] we had a few outstanding Italian men who emigrated from Italy. Like the honorable Paul Russo who came from Sorrento. He was a professional in Italy as a lawyer. When he migrated to New Haven he could not practice law because he was not a citizen. But he became a leader in the community and a strong leader for the welfare, betterment, and growth of his so called paesani's [countrymen]. So he opened up a grocery store on the corner of Chapel and Wooster Place and there he held court. From then on, anyone who wanted to know anything about Italy or to write to their loved ones, they went to his grocery store. And naturally he would write for them but for a little charge. He became so well known with the officials of the industrial plants in the Wooster Square area; he became like an agent for them. They would call him up and say, "Mister Russo we can use thirty-five, forty men in our operation of our plant." You have to remember at the turn of the century the industrial age was revolutionary, overnight. So he would have friends in Amalfi or Atrani or any of the little towns, and [his agents] would say to them, "Whoever wants to come to New Haven . . . the cost of trip will be paid by the Forbes Sargent Company." So naturally they would register with the agent working with Paul Russo in Amalfi or Atrani. Naturally I'm sure there was a financial stipend for him [the agent] to sign up young boys and girls to come to America. And there was a big movement at that time—everybody wanted to come. But you also had this not only in this Wooster Square area, you also had that in the Hill section. Sabato Capasso was also an agent and took care of the factories like Seamless Rubber Company, different corset shops, dress shops, and shirt factories in the Hill section; they were organizing and growing. What happened is that he would write to his people and it seemed that he would write more or less to the Marchegiano people [from the Le Marche region in central Italy]. Because geographically, where they came from, I could tell you where they worked. If your father was a mason he must have come from Marche territory because they were skilled and semiskilled masons. Now remember we're in a revolutionary period of the industrial age in New Haven; every company needed manpower. You have to look back and imagine how he had to say it to encourage or induce men to come from those small towns to America knowing that they were going to have a job in their field. I'm looking back at the early 1920s. Yale University is going to construct and build seven or eight colleges. And if you notice it those Yale colleges today outside two or three that were built later on, were all built during the mid-'20s to the mid-'30s, those residential colleges. And they were all built by the men who came from those towns, Marchegianis. These people were stone masons and they were skilled operators and they were wanted; when they came here they knew they were going to be masons. The Yale dormitories had fireplaces in the rooms. Well, naturally the fireplaces were all one style. These men who were working there had such pride that they deviated away from the architectural plans of the fireplaces. In other words, Giovanni did his, what he thought should be a fireplace. And unknown to anyone, in the fireplace he would sculpt an image of his child that he left in Italy. Well now, Pasquale would look and say, "Ha, I can do better than you." So he made his fireplace. And that's why all those fireplaces are not all alike as according to the blueprint. Well, naturally when the contracting people went in there and looked and that's how they found out there was a competition among the workers competing, "I can do better than you." And they always put something in that fireplace of the town or family they came from. Notice above the doors, what do you see? Figurines of court people, judges. And the gargoyles around the Yale Law School—you'll see a policeman, a judge. They did that to dress the building up. Where did they get that idea? From their towns or cities in Italy that did that. I'm not saying they deviated from the plans of the architect—they put in what they thought would make that building that much more accepted to the general public or to get acknowledgment of what that building is. The architects couldn't believe it; they let them do whatever they wanted.

"To Save Ten Cents"

Mary Ginnetti, her brother-in-law Orlando Ginnetti, and her husband John spoke with her daughter Antonia Arena listening at their kitchen table in the Annex on August 28, 1999.

My grandfather was living on East Street and they had the blizzard in 1888. They couldn't get out of the house. They dug a tunnel across the street where there was a grocery store and they were able to buy groceries. My father got a job in Sargent's working on locks or something. He moved his family from near the shop from East Haven so he wouldn't have to pay five cents for the trolley—to save ten cents a day. So that's how we moved to New Haven, to Hamilton Street. Ten cents a day you could buy a loaf of bread or a quart of milk in those days. For ten cents they used to buy a bag of bananas. The carts used to come around and all the ones that were starting to go bad, he would put them in a bag and sell them for ten cents a bag. So my father would bring them home with five kids so we could eat.

"Walking to West Virginia"

My father was born in 1888. They came from Italy in 1907 and they all lived together as a group down around East Street [Wooster Square]. And then there was no work. They came here to work because there was no work in Italy. They came to work and they heard about the railroad. So then they decided to go down. They heard there were jobs because they were building the railroad. So in 1888, my grandfather, Dominic Palmeri, and eleven men from New Haven went to West Virginia. But when they got there, they weren't hired. The railroad work had been finished. This was one of the depressions that we went through. They got on the train and there was no work and there was no money. Nobody would have them come near their door. People wouldn't even let them in, no. They would shut their doors when they saw them. Well you see a group of men walking, you're going to let them in? They'd see a gang of men, you know. They were afraid. It was during harvest time and there was one lone apple up on the tree, the rest must have been picked. One man climbed up and got it and started eating and everybody said, "Save me a bite, save me a bite." Because every time they approached a farmhouse for a handout the doors would close. It took them a month to get [walk] back home. My father always told the story. A lot of times we used to kid him, "Oh, come on Pop." So my uncle—my mother's brother verified it, he said "Oh yeah, it's true." We couldn't see all those men walking down for work and coming back.

"You Couldn't Get a Job"

Pat Barone spoke in the living room of his West Haven home on May 5,
1999.

My sister graduated from Hillhouse High School. The Water Company, The
United Illuminating Company and the Gas Company used to give three top students in the class a job. When it came to my sister graduating—she was one of the
top three in her class—she didn't get the job because her name was Barone. Italian
people couldn't get a job. Italian people couldn't go be a fireman. Italian people
couldn't go be a policeman. Italians in them days swept the street with a broom for
the city to make a living. Italian people went and dig ditches by hand to make a living. Italian people when the snow was on the ground—they went to the city to
work a day—at that time they used to clean all the center of the city—we used to
have two feet, three feet of snow at that time. They used to give you a shovel. You
went out and you shoveled the snow up into the truck for eight hours in the cold
and everything. And you brought the shovel back and they gave your day's pay.

"I Went Through Yale"

Orlando Ginnetti spoke at the kitchen table of his sister Mary's home in the
Annex on August 28, 1999.

In the '30s I delivered telegrams for Western Union. You had to buy your own bicycle, two dollars a week. I never paid cash [chuckling], I paid time payments
there. They used to get twelve cents to deliver a telegram all the way out to the
Hamden Town hall. That's why when people ask me if I went to school, sure I
went right through Yale—I went to every school and every building in Yale—I
knew them all. I went to medical school, law school—you name it and I went
through it—with telegrams. They used to say, "What did you do today?" I'd say, "I
went through Yale." [laughing]

"Working Life at Sargent"

John "Johnny Blake" Calamo, with his son Tom, spoke at the kitchen table
in his apartment complex for seniors on December 29, 1998. He got his
nickname, "Johnny Blake," from hitch hiking rides on the back of Blakeslee
trucks.

My mother was from Atrani; my father was from Amalfi. I started working there
in 1922 at fifteen. My first job was as a finisher helper. The hardware—the lock
parts—we used to finish the iron lock parts, we used to have to dip and put it in

muriatic acid, cold water, cyanide, cold water, and then hot water. I used to work on the wheel, the brass wire bushes. I liked it over there because I lived right around the neighborhood there, no problem. I started to work there and I became, after years, top man on the job—this was the later years. In 1926, Sargent's got an order from Sears and Roebucks for six million dollars. In those days six million dollars was six million dollars. And we were getting a bonus—the pieceworkers. If we made four dollars a day, piecework, we got four dollars and eighty-four cents. We got twenty-one cents an hour for bonus. Come the depression a lot of the people were laid off but I worked, you understand. And during the depression I was making piecework, thirty-three cents an hour [laughing]. We were working five and a half days a week. Why they kept me on, because I worked. I done my work and they knew, they knew it. And not only one job. And at the time they had a casket hardware department. Now when I got through on my job at 3:30, I used to go down there and work till eight o'clock. Before I got on to the job on casket hardware, the handles around them, I use to hit my finger with the hammer so many times. So one of the fellas in the department—he saw me—he showed me how to do it. And I got on to it and I was doing good, I was making piecework, too. I didn't make the lock parts, I finished the lock parts—I was a finisher on the locks. Then later in years, during the Second World War, my job folded up and I went down to the machine room. Now when I started on machines I started on a drill press. Then different machines. So I was working on a lathe [laughing] and I was making good. But you couldn't put what you made in, you know what I mean, on the job because if you made the money they would cut the job. At that time, what were they allowing you? When I went down to the machine room I was making about seventy-five cents an hour. And I got onto the jobs, you know, and I was ahead all the time. So they put me from one job to another. There was a job that the men down there were working on, they had three gauges for one hole and they weren't doing it right. So the foreman told the set up man—he was a friend of mine too, I played football with him—he showed me, I was working. Every once in a while the head foreman would come around, pick up the work, put the gauges in. When I finished that job the foremen used to tell the set up man what jobs to give me because he could rely on me on doing good work. As we went along during the war there was a precision job. Now on the precision job, it was a good job. The day people got hungry. It paid eleven dollars and something a hundred pieces. So what happened. They cut the job to three dollars and eighty cents a hundred. I'm working nights, 3:30 to 12:00 and when I went in they told me about it, I got a hold of the steward. I said, "Look, this job—I ain't gonna make no money and I don't want to do it. You know that was a big drop from eleven to three! So the steward went into the foreman and he talked to the foreman—boo-bang—I got the job up to six dollars a hundred, okay? Now we had three automatic milling machines with micrometers on them. On the micrometers on the machines I used to set it once. I used to put one piece through, take it off and gauge it and set the micrometer. I wouldn't touch it all night. Because if you fool around with something like that you're going to run into trouble. If the work is coming good—I used to gauge the pieces after they were done and everything—they were good—and that's it. I'd go in at 3:30, I started working. I worked two machines; one machine fast [laughing], the other machine slow, because when the fast machine finished I could change the piece and give the other one by the time it stopped. And I used to make 212 pieces a day. No more. I used to clean that machine off; we used go in and play cards. And we had gauges I could have made more, I was done at half-past nine; I used to quit. I wouldn't do nothing till twelve o'clock. That was piecework; that's all I did—212 pieces, I quit—because they didn't want to pay me more. Because we had an inspector, the next morning he used to gauge every one of them. So my set-up man come over to me, he says to me, "You know, you done all bad work last night." I said, "Oh, that's okay, I got paid for them." He said, "No," he smiled, he was laughing, he said, "The inspector goes through your work in about fifteen, twenty minutes because all of them was good. They all gauged right, you know?" So from there I went on to another machine—lathe—I was making different things, automatic lathe, too. And I had a woman on another lathe, a smaller lathe and the foreman said to me, "You watch her." The machinist, the days after, they come to me and said, "How come the night woman does better work than the day woman?" I said, I don't know. I knew because I used to set her machine up before she started to work. I used to get the piece. The gauge wouldn't fit. She said, "The gauge don't fit." I said, It's okay, put it on. So she kept working. So maybe an hour or two later I would get the piece, I would get the gauge. "The gauge fits," she said. I knew why [laughing]. When it's hot it expands, understand? But I never told nobody that. No way. I wouldn't tell them nothing. What I learned, I learned myself. And they all gauged right. I said, "I don't know—she works on it—that's it." I wouldn't tell them nothing. No way. And anytime I learned anything on my own I never told nobody because they'll always try to give you the business.

During the war I was a supervisor for bomb shackles, I used to make those. A bomb shackle is a shackle that holds up the thousand pound bomb. We had an inspector from the Navy. And before I went on the job 2,300 of them were rejected by the Navy. So I went on the job and the inspector used to show me letters from Philadelphia—that's where they went—my work was over ninety percent accurate. But I wasn't making no money; I was a supervisor with fifteen girls and one fella working for me and I was doing more work than they did because I used to have to inspect them myself—you couldn't trust anybody. The women were good; they done their work and when they finished they'd come to me and say, "Hey, we ain't got no more work." I said to the girls, "Look, the door is over there—watch who comes in—if you see somebody, you pick it up, take it apart and put it together again, the shackle. They were heavy and I had to put them on an electric place—for the release. Sometimes the springs weren't strong enough—I used to repair them too. I used to take the old springs out and put another spring in, put her through—it was all right. The spring—if it didn't release them [the bombs] the spring is weak and it won't release them. And if it doesn't release the bomb is no good to the plane because they can't land. Oh yeah.

"Shining the Shoes"

Joseph "Babe" Dogolo spoke at the kitchen table of his East Haven home on September 15, 1999.

We were shoeshine boys in the '30s. We sold newspapers in the snow, the rain. We shined shoes in the cold, cold weather on the corner of Chapel and High Street where the Waldorf Hotel was. Cold, cold winters. Yale was playing Dartmouth in football. Cold, cold, we were ready to come home. Our hands were frozen, me my brother and my three other friends were ready to go home down to Wooster Street. So here comes this big Dartmouth student with the cigar in his mouth, tobacco out a here. He took all the papers; he bought all the papers from the guys. So he said to us [voice growling], "Give me a shine you guinea bastards." Our folks always said, "No matter what anybody says, zitt' con a bocca, never say a word, don't say nothing." He had shoes about that big, he had! So we shined his shoes and when we got through he said, [gruff voice] "I ain't got no change you guinea sonafabitches, you guinea bastards." He was half drunk because they were happy that Dartmouth beat Yale. My brother said, "Well, give me the twenty dollars, I'll go around the corner and change it." He said, "You know what you got a do?" We said, "What?" He said, "Leave your shine box over here as a deposit." So we all walked away. When we got about twenty feet away from him we said, "Hey you big Irish sonofabitch, take the shoeshine box and stick it up in your ass." You know how much for the box? About sixty cents and we took the twenty dollars and we ran all the way home. My mother and father said, "Ha fatto buon"[You did good]. Because they always said, "Don't say nothing, but as long as he called you this and called you that, when he gave you the twenty dollars, there's your shine box we left him as a deposit."

"Working at Candee Rubber in 1916"

Amelia Buonocore spoke in the living room of her apartment complex for the elderly on September 11, 1999.

So I was fourteen years old and I went to work. I went to work in 1916 for three dollars a week, forty-eight hours in a shirt shop on Brewery Street. They used to make shirtwaists at that time. And silk blouses made of georgette, royal and all silk materials. Georgette was a very sheer fabric. They gave me the job going up and down between two floors, if they needed something, a piece of cuff, they would send me downstairs. The tailors and cutters were downstairs and I'd go and get it and bring it upstairs. They needed something else, I'd go up again. Then they put me on trimming the inside of shirts. I worked there for about a year and then I heard that the stocking shop was hiring for five dollars a week. I had to turn stockings inside out. Then they put me to inspecting the stockings.

Then in 1916, I heard the rubber shop was making a dollar a day at Candee's. That wasn't candies! The first two weeks you get five dollars while you learn. After that you go piecework. If you make more and you get through early, you get more—the next day the forelady gives you more. If you can't make it, you're slow, you don't get any more so you don't make it. If I was fast enough I made more. They don't expect you to make forty pairs but if you're good enough to make it, all right. But you can't leave anything over for the next day, you got to finish everything this same day. The other shoes you get less because they were harder to make or they were heavier to carry. I was making rubbers for children up to six, seven, eight, ten, twelve, maybe thirteen years old. You get the wooden form and fit ten on one side and ten on the top, make ten pair of shoes. Then you fix the lining—you put the rubber, the cement and you stick them, first the lining, then another piece, and then another piece and then a piece for the heel. Then at the end you put the soles on, you put the cement, then you put the soles on. There used to be sheets of rubber in big plastic books and I used to get the sheets of rubber—they were already cut and shaped and everything—get them, put them over the mold and then you seam it in the back. They had different people coming around. If you needed different rubbers or you were short on something, you order and they had to go downstairs and put the order in and bring it to you. They had a man to come over when you were through, take those shoes and put them in the cart and you get a new rack and you put the new rack over there and you put some more shoes. I used to make forty, fifty pairs a day when I got good. I used to make twenty, twenty-two dollars a week. And that was good pay for my mother. And summertime I got two weeks vacation. But I wanted to work [during my vacation] on the sewing machine at Lesnow's in 1918 because everybody said my clothes smelled of rubber. The rubber I didn't smell it because I was used to it. People come near and they smell the rubber—that's why they didn't want to work in that place because it smelled of rubber. But what was I going to do? That's where I made a dollar. I said, I'll go to work on the sewing machine, maybe I'll change my clothes. He put me on starching the collars. How much? Five dollars a week. I worked for a week during my vacation—I wouldn't work there for five dollars a week. I asked him to put me on the machine, he said, "When I get a chance when I get an empty machine." Hey, I knew he was kidding me—he just wanted to keep me there for five dollars a week on that job. So I went back to L. Candee, used to make my twenty dollars a week. Sometimes if I got finished early in the afternoon with the other girls, we used to go six o'clock in the morning, we used to work, we used to make our work, and then in the afternoon we'd get out early and a few times we went the Hyperion theatre. We used to get everything ready the day before to get out early. My mother never wanted me to go to the show—I never went to the show with my mother. Any place I went my mother had to come—I couldn't go no place. That was it, that was my life. I went out with my husband; my mother came. I didn't go out with my husband. My mother walked with my husband and I walked with my sister.

❝Working at Sperry and Barnes**❞**

John Nappi spoke at the kitchen table of his East Haven home on July 3, 1999.

And when I went to see my father in the slaughterhouse in the '20s—I used to bring him lunch once in a while at Sperry and Barnes—the animals wouldn't work like that, the way they worked. They had Polish, Ukranians, Czechoslovakians, Italians working in the slaughterhouse. Some went to Saint Kasmir's; they were Yugoslavians. They were all aliens, all mixed. They were the only people who could do that work. Believe me, you should see what a mess. Boy oh boy, it was something—cold! Because they had those ammonia pipes. I said how the hell do they work here? Dirty, filthy, blood all over, they used to wear the boots. It was a mess. I got to know the guard; I was a kid. He was an Irishman; he had big handlebars. And he used to speak with the brogue, "Hey young Nappi, you gonna go see pops?" I'd say yep. "Okay, don't stay too long, watch out, don't get hurt." With that Irish brogue, he was a pip. He got to know me, I used to go down. I wouldn't stay too long, you know, because they were afraid I'd get hurt. So he used to meet me and I used to give him the bag with the food, whatever was, and then I used to leave there. But I watched what they used to do. How they worked! Believe me! These kids would never do it today. Never. The way those people worked to bring up a family. And all the Italians from Collis Street [Wooster Square], around there, there was a few of them that used to work down there. One guy used to work at slaughtering the pigs. There was one big black man—was a nice man—George—my father used to take him to our house to eat, would you believe that? Every Friday. His job was to split the hogs; he had a big cleaver. After they clean them, he used to split them in two. He used to like the Italian food and every Friday my father would bring him home and my mother used to make pasta fasule [macaroni and beans] and stuff like that and fish because on a Friday that's what we used to have. He was a nice man. But they worked, believe me. They'll never do it today.

❝Good Morning Mister Sargent**❞**

Joseph "Pip" Scarpellino was hired as "hurry clerk" delivering special orders at Sargent factory. He spoke in the living room of his Warren Street home on August 7, 1999.

I started working in 1925 at fifteen years old. My first year I worked in Sargent's. Everybody worked in Sargent's. I was a mail boy. I used to bring the intercom, bring it all. I'll never forget I had the president on [my route], Henry B. Sargent. He used to go to work on a bicycle, all the way down Water Street. I don't know why the hell he wore one—he had it off most of the time, he'd tip his hat to all the girls going to work. One day I walked in [his office] he looked like he was busy, so

JOSEPH "PIP" SCARPELLINO

1919

Scarpellino family album

I put the mail in the in, took out the outgoing and I'm walking out [laughing] and he said, "Son, don't you say 'good morning?'" I said, Well, Mister Sargent, you look kind a busy, I didn't want to bother you. He said, "Nobody is so busy or so important that he can't say good morning. And don't come in here again without saying good morning." And every morning I'd go in there, Good morning Mister Sargent. Nine dollars and one cent a week. I don't know where they got the one cent. They used to dip that damn stuff in that acid and boy those fumes used to come, oh! Of course they didn't mind because they were used to it. How the hell any of them lived more than forty I don't know with all those fumes coming in that air.

❝The Italian Swore at Them❞

Pat Barone spoke in the living room of his West Haven home on May 5, 1999.

My father went to live in a boarding house [after he arrived in 1899] and they brought him to work up in the shoreline. They were laying railroad track at that time. And they made him work hard. They were working sixteen hours a day in those days. And he used to tell me, he used to say, "My chest is got a big hole in it from the sledgehammer." They had him driving the spikes into the track, hold the track on the rails. And he says he used to work and work hard. And they had a man, an Italian foreman, and I can remember like it was yesterday my father kept telling me this all the time. His name was Landino. And he used to come by and he used to swear at him, "Hurry up you son of a bitches, hurry up, we got a lay this track, got a get going." And my father says, "We used to work extra hard, we thought the guy was telling us that we were doing a good job." Then we started to find out what was going on, till we started to know and started to ask questions.

❝They Had the Worst Jobs❞

Rose Marie and Lou Guarino spoke at their kitchen table in their Orange home on August 24, 2000.

The Italians were discriminated against out of their neighborhoods, the way they dressed, the way they ate, their various customs. Dirty word, ghetto. But it was just a place where like people lived. Straight out of that [the neighborhood], they were laughed at, made fun of. They raised chickens in their backyard. And people said they just didn't do that kind of thing, you just went to the butcher store and bought the chicken. They grew their own vegetables and had their various customs and things. So that's why Oak Street and Legion Avenue was an area where the Italians massed because they could speak to one another, they had the same kind of problems and they were all poor. They had to anglicize their names in order to get good jobs. You had a vowel at the end of your name, right away you were labeled a wop or one of those other horrible words, names. You didn't go anyplace. A policeman, a fireman, or anything like that in the '30s, you couldn't get a job because they discriminated against us. It's not a new story, discrimination, it's been going on. And when they came from the old country they got the worst jobs, they worked in slaughterhouses, my father worked laying down concrete in the beginning for Blakeslee's. They got all the worst jobs, collecting the garbage; that's when they used to actually collect garbage. All the worst jobs because they were uneducated as far as the United States was concerned. In their own country they would not be considered so. But they worked. They did the jobs to feed their families. However menial it was, they worked and they didn't look for handouts. One thing that came out of this is that out of their poverty they invented all these wonderful dishes that we eat today, pasta fasule and escarole and beans, all those peasant foods were derived from the pantries because that's all they had and they just combined them. Isn't that something? So we benefited that way from it. Now it's a big business today.

"You Could Work around the Clock at Candee Rubber"

Rosemarie Foglia spoke at City Hall on June 28, 1999. Her voice echoed from the high ceiling of the conference room.

Somehow or other they [my parents] heard about the Candee Rubber Shop and they were far more progressive than we are now. The Candee factory was on East and Wallace, Chapel and Greene Streets, it was like a whole square block. They did the boots, they made everything that was rubber. And everyone in the area, because they were all immigrants on lower Wooster Square, and they all worked there both men and women. They had no need to know English so they all survived because they were working obviously at machines or whatever capacity. So it was fine because they could work—most of these people, remember, had come to this country on borrowed money so their goal was to pay back their trip. And they accommodated the immigrant. You could work around the clock at Candee. Or you could go in and sign in at five and if you had to leave at seven, fine, then come back. If you had the capacity and the strength to work twenty-four hours a day you could do it. And my father was 6'2" and a bull of a person. He would go four, five days straight, then come home one day and just sleep. And he often told the story that there was a bar across the street from Candee where for five cents you could get a beer and a sandwich. And this is what he would do. Then after they were married he didn't do the four, five days routine but he would still work two, three days because the whole point was to save money.

"They Only Trusted You to Go to Work"

Rose Savo spoke at the kitchen table of her home in the Annex on July 28, 2000.

I used to work all week. Hey Mamma, "Bellu pitch 'ncòppa a città," Hey Mom, there's a good movie playing in town. I had a friend—her name was Rose, too. I said to my mother, "Rosie non vo' i,'" but Rose doesn't want to go. So my mother said, "Cuando ti marita, vai allo show" [When you get married, then you can go to the show]. And believe it or not, one time I played hookey—I was goin' with my husband. I couldn't go to the show, you couldn't go no place with him. So I played hookey from work. I was going with my husband. So we took a half a day off and I went to the show with my husband. What do ya think? Comin' out of the show, who's comin' out of the show? Mrs. DiFiglio, the landlady, and "a nonna," the grandma,—my mother! She could go to the show. I couldn't go. But my poor husband he got a calling down. "Oh," she says, "Tu, chésta vo' fa? Ti piglia a figliàma e ti porta addo vai tu?" Oh, so this is what you want to do? Take my daughter wherever you want? Then she said to me, "A casa ci vidimmo," We'll see about this when you get home. When I went home she grabbed me by the hair. Those were the days. They only trusted you to go to work, that was terrible. And you know, I always earned my fourteen, fifteen dollars a week, even more. You'd think she'd give me a quarter. Every day, Ma, dammi cinque soldi, Ma, give me five cents. She used to give me the nickel. Not even to be bothered every day to give me that nickel, give me fifty cents, give me a quarter, so I wouldn't bother her every day. I used to buy a Milky Way for five cents. It didn't bother her every day. Ma, damme cinque soldi, Ma, give me five cents. She never refused.

"We Couldn't Cut Our Hair"

Everybody then was cutting their hair. I had big braids. And me and my sister we wanted to cut our hair too. My mother said, "Aye, patita accussì ha ditto patita, chilla ti taglia a capa," Your father said if you cut your hair, he'll cut your heads off instead. So finally my mother went to Italy. In the meantime my sister and I we cut our hair. So, my sister and I were sittin' around the table with my father. My sister—she used to blame my father, "Aye chilla acussì ditto patita, chilla ti taglia a capa if we cut our hair," Aye, that's what your dad said—if we cut our hair, he'll cut our heads off. So we're sittin' around the table waitin' for my father to say something—he didn't even notice it. He didn't notice it! When she came back [from Italy], "Aha" she said, "E patita? . . . And your father? "Nah, papa nun ha ditto niénte," Nah, dad didn't say anything.

"Going to Work at Fourteen"

Guiannine DeMaio spoke at her granddaughter Laurel's home in North Branford on July 1, 1999.

And now I'm fourteen, I went to get the job. The guy says, "All right, go to work, take this paper to the principal." To the principal? Oh my God, who the hell's gonna go see her? So anyway I went there half past three and the kids were out. We used to go to school till half past three then. I said to her, Miss Mausteder, I want you to sign this paper. "What is this? Why weren't you in school today?" I went and get a job. She says, "What do you mean, you got a job? Why don't you stay till June? You're gonna graduate from grammar school in June." I can't stay in school, I gotta job, I gotta go to work. I wanted to go on my own because I'd already worked on the farm when I was ten years old—I was crazy about workin'. So anyway I said to her, No, I have to go to work, I got the job already. She says to me, "You're not gonna go to work, you're gonna graduate in June." I says, I'm not gonna graduate in June because my mother's poor—we got seven kids and I have to work. They need the money to eat. So she heard like that, she says, "All right, give me the paper."

My mother didn't know a thing. My mother didn't care what I did. But I told her I was gonna go to work. So she signed the paper. Next day I went to work. I used to walk from Brown Place [Forbes Avenue]. The snow was this high. Nobody shoveled snow in them days. Them days a trolley car had a plow in front and that's how the snow moved. The snow that was in piles—there was no cars anyway, there was no cars them days and you couldn't go through, the snow was piled high. The only place was plowed was where the trolley tracks were. And if you had a car or a horse and wagon or wherever you had a walk, you used to walk on the trolley track. Nobody plowed. There used to be a "jigger," I remember even that, it was a small trolley car, it wasn't the big, long ones. He used to start from Granniss Corner drugstore and go all the way down to the train tracks on Forbes Avenue. There was no highway in them days, there was only Forbes Avenue and the train tracks. We used to jump on it [bridge]. The guy used to ring the bell or a horn to let the ships in and the bridge used to go around like that. And us, like fools, we used to jump on it and go around with it, take a ride with it. And once in a while it got stuck. And after that I didn't do that no more. I was afraid of gettin' stuck.

After my mother died, you know, I went to work again. And that Mrs. Hunt, she was the forelady and if there was somebody didn't come in that day—those shoes had a be out. Instead of askin' her or you or somebody, she'd say, "Jen, you wan a take 'em, I'll help you." So I says, Yeah. So I used to take 'em to make more money. Now when I used to give my mother the pay, them days I used to give my mother the pay—we all did anyway—she used to give fifty cents allowance. I was makin' more than my father. In them days, you know—no checks—you used to get the money in an envelope, I used to hand her the envelope. She used to say, "Don't tell your father how much you're makin'." My father used to give her his check, too, just to keep money to get drunk on a Saturday night. So I never told my father, so now after she died, now I got the money. I don't wan a keep the money and all this and that, so my mother's sister—she used to like me a lot, she was like a mother to me, she says to me, "Jenny, when you give your father the money, don't give it to him all, keep three or four dollars a week, 'cuz pretty soon you're gonna buy a "bi-ancheria," linens for your wedding, you're father ain't gonna buy nothin' for you."

"GOING TO WORK"

Rose Durso spoke at the living room table of Joseph and Lena's home in the Annex on February 1, 1998.

Who knew how to take a trolley? Walk every morning, mamma mi! Summer and winter. Walk all the way over the Thomlinson Bridge. And back. Back and forth, back and forth, I'd say to my mother, "Ma, give me the forty cents. My mother would say, "Mi servìno, àggia accattà 'a roba," I need it to buy things for the house. That was it. In newspaper. What bag, what bag? You think they got little plastic bags now, each sandwich is in there, the fruits, the peanut butter sandwich? Addo'? Where? Arrugliato—any ol' way. Pathetic is the word. Well, if you had chickens and eggs you were pretty well off, like we did, you know. But some children had nothing at all. Nothing at all. No farm to plant, produce anything—they were really bad off.

"GOING TO WORK AT CANDEE RUBBER"

Giuannine DeMaio spoke at the home of her granddaughter Laurel in North Branford on July 7, 1999.

We lived in a house on Brown Place. Three bedrooms, three rooms and two rooms—ten dollars a month. No furnace, no water, only a little sink like this, no bathroom, the bathroom is outside, about six bathrooms, outhouses they were. And over there they had a little seat so a little kid could go, a little bigger seat, the bigger one in each compartment. We used to go walk to work, all by myself. In the morning I used to get up. By six o'clock, you know how I used to dress up? Dress up, my winter coat, put a hat, I don't remember about the gloves, and I'd walk to work without even washing my face or comb my hair, nuttin'. I used to put o capel-licchio, a hat, and I used to walk all the way to the shop. As soon as I got to the shop, ahhh, the heat! You'd open that door and the heat. I used to go right to the bathroom, I used to wash my face, comb my hair, I used to make myself present-able and go make my shoes.

When I first started [in 1917], the rubber shop had artics. The mold was made out of oak, oak wood. Now let's say this is the rubber you put over your shoes, it came [mold] this high like this. All this part, the form, was out of wood, it was oak. It was really hard wood. And heavy. Now you take these books—you know these books when you pick out wallpaper? You turn the leaf and they show you the print of the wallpaper, then you turn the leaf and there's another design—that's the way those books were made [inserts]. On each page they'd be, the top part, rubber. It was open, like this. Underneath, on the inside, was gooey, sticky stuff—you could hardly pull it up. It was all gooey like. It was all stuck on the page, you used to pull it up and then the frame—you used to put in on like that, you had a put the insides in first, then the outsides, then a little strip of rubber all the way around like that. We used to do all that kind a work. We didn't finish the shoe because they used to bake them, to cook em' or something.

We used to make about thirty pairs a day. But we never finished the whole rubber. We only did our part, what we hadda do. Then they had a piece a metal, iron. They had a thing over here, iron, another stand like that, another iron. And on that iron they had two prongs like this. On the shoe, on the frame, they had a prong. Now when you got through with the shoe, you used to stick it in the prong. That's how the shoe would stay up. Now you had a bunch of shoes like this, you know, maybe this wide. And two rows, one and two. Everybody had their own section, that was your section. And no matter what you do, like first you had a put the little strip and then you put up there and then you did another little thing, take it down and put the rubber on, you know, all stuff like that. But those things were heavy.

"We Wanted to Go the Movies"

There was a guy, we'd call him Tony. Strong, he used to grab with one hand and then he'd walk around, up in the air, because he was afraid of hittin' somebody in the head, you know, walking. He'd go like this and walk all the ways and bring them to where they used to cook em' or something, bake or whatever they used to do with them. But I didn't make the boots. When I went there they made me make rubbers—I was makin' ladies rubbers with no heels, I made with the extra high heel, they used to give you different kinds you know. And the artics—I never made artics, but the artics were big. I used to go in six o'clock but I used to clean up before. It was seven to . . . I'm pretty sure it was thirty pairs a day. When you finished em' you could a went home. You had a make the quota you got. If you got twenty pairs a day, you had a finish the twenty pairs. My mother and father wouldn't let me go to movies but yet I could go to work at six o'clock in the morning, all by myself, you know what I mean, the Italian people, the way they used to be? So three or four girls would get together, we'd say, "Shall we go the movies tomorrow, tomorrow afternoon?" So now we'd do part of the shoe, like we'd finish our thirty pairs, then we'd do a few more pairs for the day after. The day after we'd be through at one o'clock in the afternoon. And we'd go to the show, to the Hyperion, Poli's, the Bijou. The movies didn't talk though. Rudolf Valentino, he was a favorite.

12

New Haven's Garment Workers: Life in the Sweatshops

At the turn of the century, New York City was the epicenter of the garment industry. When organized labor demanded better working conditions for its workers, production costs rose and factory owners began looking for a more favorable business climate, with a cheaper labor force. They found those conditions in the 1920s in the heart of the Italian community in New Haven, which became a magnet for New York's "runaway shops." New Haven's abandoned carriage and corset factories could be rented at reasonable costs, and finished products could conveniently be shipped by the nearby New Haven Railroad. Italian immigrant women, eager to provide for their young families, became the mainstays of New Haven's burgeoning garment industry; they provided the owners a ready-trained workforce because of the sewing skills they had acquired in Italy and they accepted lower wages than were demanded in New York. City government welcomed the new businesses, turning a blind eye to the deplorable work conditions that prevailed in makeshift shirt and dress factories, calling them a "necessary evil to stave off unemployment and supplement of the work of charitable organizations."[18]

Pre-union working women in the 1920s found themselves at the mercy of owners who cared little about their personal welfare or about the oppressive and hazardous conditions in the factories. New Haven sweatshops were usually set up on dilapidated upper floors of old factory buildings, unheated in winter and poorly ventilated in summer. Women were expected to be at their machines at eight a.m., when the power switch was thrown, jolting thread through rows of sewing machines and causing a surge of production work to begin. Lighting was poor; the constant roar of running machines deafening. Razor-sharp sewing machine needles, pulsating at lightning speed, pierced busy fingers. When that happened, the needle was yanked out by an untrained machine repairman, and the injured girl resumed work at her station. A single unsanitary bathroom the size of a cubbyhole served scores of young women. Factory floors were soaked with flammable industrial oil. Young women inhaled lint particles that punctuated the thick, stale air and gathered in piles in corners of the floors. Mountains of shirts were piled high along the sides of workstations dwarfing fourteen-year-old children working at their machines. On some mornings, young workers reached into their bins to find rats among the unfinished shirts. Talking to co-workers was forbidden. Women conversed by singing to one another, sometimes in Italian. Adding to the gloom were locked exit doors to discourage an early exit or stepping out for a quick cigarette. Sprinkler systems and fire drills that could have saved lives were nonexistent. Ten men died in the New Haven Quilt and Pad Co. fire on 82–88 Franklin Street in February, 1941, and in 1957, fifteen garment workers lost their lives in the worst fire in the city's history, the Franklin Street Fire.

The remarkable work history of the women of New Haven's shirt and dress factories is fading from memory. Most of the forbidding factory buildings that once employed hundreds of sewers, cutters, pressers, spreaders, and packers are gone, many torn down for highways in the 1950s. Few Italian immigrants from the first generation are alive to pass on their stories; daughters who worked alongside them during the thirties, forties and fifties, are passing on. Many third generation Italian Americans have working roots in New Haven's sweatshops, but the legacy of sacrifice and struggle of their mothers and grandmothers is nearly forgotten and lost to history. The first and second generation of women who endured horrible working conditions and placed the welfare of their families ahead of personal aspirations, provided the financial support to send their children to college. As a result, many third and fourth generation Italian Americans owe much of their professional careers and financial stability to the sacrifices of the women of New Haven's shirt and dress factories.

"THE SEWING TRADITION IN ITALY"

Annette Ruocco spoke at the kitchen table of her home in the Annex on November 7, 1998.

My mother—her father and her brothers were all fishermen. They made their living fishing in Atrani. My grandmother used to repair the fishermen's nets because big fish got in them and ripped them and so she would make hairnets the same way you do a net. People with long hair, you would have a net to match your hair. Imagine working with the hair, knotting it, "faccimo a rettina," they called it, making a little net. My mother, all the years that she was in America, she didn't learn one word of English; we always spoke Italian. My mother made the nets too. That tradition of sewing came from Italy because there you send your girls to be taught and they do all that embroidery work and they know how to use a needle and thread. And then working with hairnets—that's a fine art. But that came from Italy. My grandmother did that and the girls went in for embroidery. You know how the Italian embroidery is, all that cutwork they do, all that crochet they do—that came from Italy. My mother taught me to do all that. If neighbors—they didn't have anybody special—if there was somebody

NEW HAVEN SWEATSHOP, CIRCA 1940

Carrano family album

that knew that art of doing that they would teach you in the town [in Italy]. But
I was brought up with the little that my mother knew she passed on to me. But
I used patterns—I did this on my own. My mother didn't teach me how to use a
pattern. She sewed a dress, she knitted but she wouldn't knit the way I would
follow a book, so many stitches this and that. I picked that up on my own. I
never got any training from anybody, got a book, read a pattern and follow it. I
had a knack for it.

"She Made Patterns out of Newspapers"

Antonette Coppola spoke in a meeting room at her nursing home in Branford on May 5, 2000.

My mother was a dressmaker in Italy. She used to sew things for Poli's, because when I was small my father used to bring things after my mother sewed them. My mother, you know what she used to do? Know the newspaper? She used to cut it and fold it, measure you up, make one hole, two holes, she knew what was the waist, what was the back. She made her own pattern out of newspapers. She used to measure you with the newspaper and then cut the material and make a dress for you. She used to make her own pattern. She would put a piece on your arm and then cut it and that be the arm, then the front and the back. I've got a lot of clothes; I didn't buy it. I made it. There used to be a Jewish store on Chapel Street and his brother liked me, he used to save the pieces of material for thirty-five cents, thirty cents. I used to make a dress out of it. He used to call me up and say, "I got material, come." It was next to Grant's and I used to go there, give me the piece of material, was enough for a dress, for a coat, something. She [my mother] used to make everything just by looking at something, she could look at it and do it herself, that's how smart this woman was. I still got my blankets; she used to crochet the blankets.

"All My Relatives Were There"

Mary Ginnetti spoke at the kitchen table in her Annex home on August 21, 1999 with her husband John, brothers-in-law, Al and Orlando Ginnetti, and daughter Antonia.

The day after I was fourteen I had to got Mister Mark to get work papers. It was state law you had to go to school until you were fourteen. My mother was working there already. That's how we got a job. My mother, my aunt, her daughters and I went to work and that was it. Eight to five-thirty; you had an hour for lunch, though. You worked whenever they wanted you to, you know. On the first floor was the ironing and the cutting boards; on the second floor they had the sewing machines. And when I walked in, it didn't bother me because I had all my relatives there. My aunt was there, my cousins were there, my mother was there, keeping an eye on me. As soon as you walked in they put you near the board with the iron and they show you how to iron and somebody watches you to make sure you know what you're doing. And that's it, you're on your own. And I was pressing shirts the day after I was fourteen. And the shirts were inspected; every shirt was inspected to make sure it was done right. I walked to work at the Ideal Shirt Shop all the way to Jefferson Street and back to Irvington Street. No union. Forty-five hours a week [sighs]. It was all right. I remember my highest pay was fifteen dollars for forty-eight hours. Of course it was piecework! The sweat

MARY GINNETTI
In her kitchen in the Annex, 1999

A. Riccio

coming down. It was rough, I'll tell you. Kids couldn't do it today, no! I could picture my daughter pressing shirts! [Laughing] So you worked whenever he told you to work. You had to stay in their good graces or you'd lose your job. I'm ashamed to say that they [owners] were Italians. I really am. Because I worked for Jewish people and they were a lot more tolerant. It's awful to say but it's true. One of them [bosses] just worked you; that's all. The other one was a little more compassionate. I remember working Thanksgiving Day, half a day. You know when we got a day off? When the union came in and it was the fifteenth of August. That was a religious day for us, Santa Maria d'Assunta, Our Lady of the Assumption, and we were able to get a half a day off. Never had a day off. John Lauria, he was a union [representative]. He just come in and kept talking and talking. And there was a shirt factory in Branford so the two factories got together and he kept talking until they signed for it. But I was the only one in the family that went to work that young. Then as the children got older I would press my parents to have them go to school. But I couldn't go; I was the oldest one so I had to support the family.

"PLEASE HELP ME"

Josie DeBenedet spoke in the kitchen of her North Haven home on June 6, 1999. She recalled caring for her parents who "both died in my arms."

I only went to the eighth grade. I used to love to work. My mom used to take work home. She taught me how to sew since I was about five years old. In Italy, everybody knows how to sew. Kids, they learn they go to what they call the "ausilio," like a kindergarten or preschool and they learn how to do everything—embroidery—they do beautiful work over there. She worked at home. Mister Lerner used to bring the work at night when he closed the shop at seven o'clock. He'd bring two or three dozens of blouses with all the beads and things. Then in the morning they'd pick them up so they would have it ready for the pressers in the dress shop. And my mother would be up all night and she'd wake me up about four in the morning, "Please help me, then you can go back and lay down." And I'd get up even to thread the needles, I used to thread the colors that she had to do and put them in the oilcloth, it was plastic and under it was flannel and we used to have that to cover the table. And I would thread all the needles for her and stick it there and there were holes all around the table. So she wouldn't waste time to thread the needle; she'd finish one, put the needle there and get the color she wanted and do it. So I would do that for her. The kids would be playing outside and I'd be working with her. That's how I got to sew and sew; I didn't care. Now I'm glad because my kids—not even my granddaughters when they were small—they never bought clothes, coats, dresses—I always made them for them. So my mom first taught me how to put on the snaps, then maybe make a hem. And I got to love to sew and I always sewed and I didn't want to go to school anymore. After the eighth grade at that time not many people were going to high school anyway. I asked my mother's boss if he'd give me a job and he said, "Oh yeah." I was fourteen. I worked on Wallace and Wooster Street at Lerner's Dress Factory. It was a sweatshop. There was no union and you worked, at one time I was making seventeen cents an hour. That was 1927, 1928. Until we got the union—we got the union in 1933—then it was different. But if not I used to work Sundays, I used to work at night. How many hours! We'd go in at seven thirty in the morning and work until six, seven because I was in charge of the pressers and the finishers. Because I knew the trade from my mother and I worked there. The factory was just an old building, it had one toilet outside and that's all. We had no sink to wash our hands or anything. The conditions at that time weren't too good. They were dirty in other words. And you work and work. And that's it. The bosses didn't like it even if you looked around because you weren't on piecework; you were on day work and you had to produce because if not . . . that's why they called them the sweatshops. Then the union got in, the bosses couldn't control us as much because then we had a chairlady and she would report everything, see? We paid union dues, maybe a dollar, a dollar and a half a week, something like that. Then we got a little better and we started to get a raise. I got a job for a young kid about twelve after school to come and sweep the factory. He had to work two hours for a nickel. But the kid was so happy because he figured he worked ten, twelve hours and make himself fifty, sixty cents and his mother was so tickled, yeah.

66THEY NEEDED MANPOWER99

Salvatore "Gary" Garibaldi spoke at the Santa Maria Maddalena Club on Wooster Street on May 18, 2000.

Jobs were easy to get in those days [early 1900s] because there was a revolution in industry. Every company in this area, in the city and in the country needed manpower—you could have quit this job today, walk down the street and you got a job someplace else. That's the same thing with our sisters. In this area there were so many shirt factories and dress factories in the late '20s and early '30s and '40s. If they quit, say, Ideal Shirt on Chapel and Hamilton, by the time they got down to Wooster and Hamilton, they would go to the Par-Ex and get a job. He [the owner] didn't care where you came from. Matter of fact, he was happy because now he didn't have to teach you the job, you were already experienced. You say to him, "I'm a cuff turner." Or, "I do collars." Well, naturally he had a woman—young girl—already experienced. And they worked. Unfortunately, they didn't have a steady job because they [the owners] were subcontractors with people from New York. And maybe this poor girl would work maybe three days a week; they were at the fancy whims of the owners. Like we saw that the shirts he had to make—when he saw that he came to the end of it—until he got to the next contract in maybe three or four days, so he would say to the girls, "I'll call you." And she would be out of work maybe two, three days. But no pay. There was no unemployment or anything of that nature in those days. So they were at the fancy whims of the owner. Not only in that industry—Sargent's, all them around here. And the conditions that they worked under! I visited those plants because I went to school and I was studying it as an historian. I can just picture Par-Ex Shirt company between Wallace and East. First and second floor. There would be about sixty girls working—the finishers would be on the first floor. The cutters were on the second floor. As they went down, they would bring the work down and there was a shipping platform on Wallace Street and they ship out the completed shirt packages.

66THEY PUT A LOCK ON THE DOOR99

Well now these girls would work and there was only maybe only one sanitary station—I have to use this term, the toilet—there was only one toilet on that floor.

Just think of it—thirty-five, forty girls using one toilet. That was not built as a toilet; it was a section of that floor where they put like a cubicle and made a throne room as a toilet. It was used by both men and women but not many men worked—the only men that might be working on that floor were the cutters. And when they went in there no one could go in that room because the door, as you opened, it would hit your legs. Well now just think of the conditions of that bathroom—we called it a bathroom—at the end of the day. How many girls used that? So you see how dirty it was; there was no wash basin to wash their hands. Then when they went back to their work bench in long rows, sewing machine here, sewing machine there. There would be about fifteen sewing machine girls on this end and I'm in the middle—we had a fifteen watt bulb over the machine and that's all. When you walked in all you heard was "rrrrrrrr." And they were working. Piecework. Unbelievable sanitary conditions—slave work! In some factories here in the city—dress shops and shirt shops—the boss would put the lock on the door so the girls wouldn't get out. And there was a tragedy in New York City—the greatest fire in New York City at that time in the early days—as a shirt factory where over one hundred odd girls died in the fire because the doors were locked. The reason why they were locked was because the boss, if he said something you get mad and you walked out. So to prevent you from walking out put a lock on the door.

"THEY HAD TO GO TO WORK"

And these conditions they worked under were unbelievable. If he [the boss] saw that you went to the bathroom maybe a little extra, he would tell you, "Why are you going to the bathroom so many times?" He didn't realize that the woman maybe had her normal period of the month. Well just think fifty girls on the floor. I'm sure without no question, some of them had their period that day. He knew it but he didn't care. In other words he saw them going to the bathroom three or four times and said, "What's wrong with her that she's got to go to the bathroom all the time." Well, naturally she was a young girl, she was embarrassed to tell him and some girl would say to him, "She has her period." They [the owners] had no respect for their fellow workers. Number one, they thought they were paying them too much and number two, this is it whether you like or not. If she said something, that was the answer she would get, "You don't like it, get out!" Well now that girl needed that job. She couldn't say to him. "Good day." Because when she went home and told her mother she quit hell would break loose with her. As a matter fact some of the girls would go home—not only in the shirt factory but in Sargent's, the other companies—the boss would manhandle her, get a cheap feel and all that. And she didn't like it. But to keep her job . . . so now she come home and told at the dinner table, she'd say how the boss touched her. The father would say, "Fa vede che non successo," pretend it didn't happen. Because he felt that if she took the attitude, "Leave your hands to yourself, I quit," she would have lost her job. So in other words, he was saying to her, "Well overlook it . . . what can I . . ." Those were the kind of conditions these girls were living under, were working under. She was the first generation of the Italian immigrants that came from Italy. So the necessity at home, because of the large families that they had, created a problem because the father was the only wage earner. Say he worked at Sargent, as many did, not making any big money to talk about but to survive, trying to keep up a lifestyle with eight to ten children plus the husband and wife. So it was a necessity when these girls reached the age of fourteen in those days you got your working papers. And naturally there were no personnel departments in those factories—no factory had them—so whenever they needed manpower they would ask the boys or girls in that company. They would say, "We need about five or six young girls who want to come to work." Well everybody's hand would go up because they all had sisters and brothers that were going to school. So right away they would say, "Ho, my sister—she'll be fourteen years old next month." They would say, "Well bring her in." So she'd get her working papers downtown, come in. She left school on a Friday. She was fourteen on a Saturday. And on a Monday she went to work. And at that time the new employee—just think of it, how they treated these working people—they would put her on a sewing machine and say to her, "All right, do this." Never had the knowledge or experience of doing that particular job. But as she went along she learned to sew. So what happened? So she would be given, maybe, say, twenty cents an hour for the first week. And a lot of them did not work a full forty-hour work week. They would make her make maybe five, six hours a day, then send her home. Well he'll [the boss] pay her at the end of the week, eight, nine dollars that she earned. But the following week, now she became a wage earner on the piecework system—whatever she made that's what she received. Well here's a girl, less than a week—what training did she have to elevate herself where she could make a decent wage earning per hour? So then she learned the trade— maybe two or three months from now she knew what she should have known the first or second week when she started her employment there. That's how they existed; they never worked forty hours. Because as soon as that contractor, as soon as that owner of that dress shop or shirt company subcontracted to produce dresses or shirts for New York, he had to go back to New York asking for a new contract, for more work. So therefore when it came where sometimes some girls were laid off. Start in two weeks. He knows he's got the work pretty well done. Well now because you're the cutter he doesn't need you. So he sends you home. Because you're the stitcher of the shirts, he didn't . . . by the time he got through the course of two weeks he would have less girls working—the only ones who were working were those on the three week product. Now they were told, "We'll call you back." Well, naturally, in the meantime, he would try to get work from New York. And when he did, he'd come back and so now he'd start calling them back by piecemeal. Now he doesn't need the packer, the shipper because there's nothing to package, so he would start calling the cutter, the stitchers and all that. And that's how they worked. So they never had a job where they could say, "I could depend on a certain amount of money I am going to earn." They never knew how long the contract of how many dresses or shirts to make. And that's why some of those factories became successful and some didn't. It depended on the owners, how aggressive they were to try to get business in New York to keep up their company here working on a steady basis. And that prevailed in all shirt and dress shops, not only in this area, but throughout New Haven and throughout the East. So don't think for a moment that the early period of our young sisters and loved ones was easy. Even our mothers who some of them had to go work because of the necessity at home, the father died young, and in those days there was no social agencies for financial help—and they had to go to work.

"Working with My Daughter"

Antonette Coppola spoke in a meeting room at her nursing home in Branford, with her daughter Maryanne Santacroce on May 5, 2000.

My name was Rose in the shop. In 1948, my daughter [Maryanne] came to work with me in Ciardi's dress shop. She was on the floor; I was a dressmaker. The whole dress I used to make. It would come already cut. And then I had a put it all together

MARYANNE SANTACROCE AND
MOTHER ANTONETTE COPPOLA
1999
A. Riccio

and then it was all complete. I had a sew it on the machine, put the sleeves in, put the collar in, put it together. When the dress was all made it was supposed to be shipped to be sold. Fifty cents, seventy-five cents, all depends what kind of dress it was. The most I made then was twenty-five, thirty dollars. They were very good to me. They even used to give me dresses to sell outside and I put the money in the bank. My boss, Joe, God bless his soul, he used to take so much out of my pay every week and put it in the bank. I worked for him for forty years. When my kids got married I had money in the bank. I worked all my life. I even made blouses at home, during the night. I grew up all my kids, my brothers and sisters too. In other words, I was a mother to my brothers and sisters. And now nobody cares.

"THE RUNAWAY SWEATSHOPS"

Salvatore "Gary" Garibaldi spoke on May 18, 2000 at the Santa Maria Maddalena Society on Wooster Street.

Naturally these were sweatshops; these are subcontractors. People came from New York, moved into our area into these big, vacant loft buildings that became obsolete at the turn of the century and they were using those buildings for their shirt or dress factory outlets where they were making the shirts and the dresses. You could go around the entire neighborhood and the same conditions existed because they were all dress shops and shirt shops that were moved into obsolete loft buildings, old factories that had gone out of business at the turn of the century. The real estate people or the owner of those properties encouraged you to move into their buildings because they were empty and they had no choice. They figured, "Hey, Mister Gadmatcher or Mister Shapiro wants some room." You're going to get this big factory loft and say to those two gentlemen, "Take as much space as you want." And they gave them a reasonable rental. But remember, there were big, high ceilings, floors already soaked with oil and chemicals used when they were operating that building, windows you couldn't open because they were so rotted into their frames—never cleaned them. They built their own shelves, their own cabinets in the same floor area. So when it came time for lunch they couldn't leave their workbench because it was like an assembly line. When it came twelve o'clock they had a one-hour lunch. Like the Sansone family. All six worked on different jobs making the shirt—they could have gone into the business themselves. And they would have known what they were doing. Yes they [owners] had knowledge but you never saw them sitting there working six, seven hours a day. Yes they knew how to operate certain jobs—I'm not saying they didn't have knowledge, they did—if a machine went out of whack or the girl had problems, they would sit down and say to her, "Well I show you how it's done." Then he'd show it to her and after ten, fifteen minutes, then he would say, "All right, Mary, this is it." And he would leave, go back downstairs in his office. Well, their home was two blocks away so the six sisters, everyday you would see them promenading down Wallace Street into Collis Street to go into the house on the corner where they lived. And say about ten minutes to one you'd see them going back to work. It was comical; it was an everyday thing that you saw going on. In other words, you knew what time it was by seeing those people walking around. It was nice for those who lived within walking distance. They would go home. The lofts were pretty much gone already; they didn't have sanitary conditions, they didn't have the ventilation system or lighting system that was very, very needed in that kind of a trade—a garment factory. The sole reason—ventilation is very important in a dress shop or a shirt shop because of the lint from the fabrics that they are working with—cutting it, sewing, stitching and whatnot—and all these things of that nature flying in the air all around them. There was no vacuum or machinery to take in all that dust and lint that flew around. The entire floor was not ventilated—during the summertime it was hell to work in those lofts. Hot!—steaming hot! So every now and then they would have an electric fan in those days to try to cool off the workers. Unbelievable. And when you entered that floor all you heard—you wondered what the decibel level the roar of the machinery, the sewing machines, was affecting their hearing. Now they had one man and his name was Dominic; very friendly, had a wonderful personality, one of those fellas who loved to talk, always had a little joke. He worked there for so many years and he was the machinist; he took care of all the sewing machines. He would say to some of the girls, "Well the reason why you broke the needle is because you did this— you put too much part of the shirt in there." Just think of it [voice rising]! Of the first aid that these girls needed in case anything happened to them was not there! They would be sewing and all of sudden the needle would go through their finger. The machine would stop [thumping table]. "Call Dom! Call Dom!" They would all get excited because that poor girl can't move her finger because if she does, she'll break that needle. And she's in pain, she's screaming. So right away all the other girls would be yelling, "Get Dom!" Now Dom, maybe was downstairs. He'd come running up and they would tell him, "Run down there, it's the girl down there, Mary." He knew all the girls, where they worked. He'd run down there and he released the machine and took the needle out of her finger. Then he would look at it. And he decided whether you needed any medical attention or not. So he would take out his little kit—a bottle of mercurochrome—and he would dampen the area, and put a band aid on it, "All right, Mary, get back to work." Now, did he ever think that girl could have had a broken blood vessel in her finger, or part of the needle was still left in there? No, she went right back to work. Those were the first aid services they had for any girl who got hurt. During the heat of the summertime they would try to open the windows—a lot of those windows wouldn't open. So they would put a fan or two here—with the lint flying. Sometimes because of the tremendous heat some girls would get lightheaded and faint. And again, Dominic or the foreman would run up and give first aid. Or some girls who were able to . . . but where was the equipment? So Dominic, who carries a little kit, he had the smelling salts. So you fainted. He put the smelling salts under your nose. So you see, these men and women were working under these conditions. They were more or less grouped together in small section because he [the boss] didn't have a big spacious factory loft space to work as a dress shop or a shirt factory. Like for example, Par-Ex on Wooster Street, first and second floor, he rented them and he had we'll say forty and the second floor fifty workers. On the first floor, it was pretty good at Par-Ex because you had the office staff, bookkeepers and then the cutters who cut the fabrics as they came in big rolls. And that's where fellas like Sal Barbaro would cut the fabric to be sent upstairs to be turned into shirts. So the first floor was pretty well cleaned. But the second floor was unbelievable the conditions those girls worked under. Crowded with a table stretched thirty, forty yards in line. Hanging lights; bare lights, just with a little bulb over it, each and every sewing machine. So maybe you had twenty women working, ten on this side and ten on that side working on those sewing machines as stitchers, cuff turners, collar makers, and button holers. And this went right down the line like an assembly line. That was the production department we'll say whether they called it that or not. But they were working under such unbelievable conditions that if O.S.H.A. was an agency in those days, each and every factory that I speak of—not only shirt companies but the average factory in a city or town—would have been closed because of the sanitary conditions, because the lighting conditions wasn't ample for them to work. That's why the name—sweatshops. These are all young girls; a very sparse amount of men, say ten men. And the reason why the ten men were hired was because they were they cutters, the packers and the shippers, where what was needed was more manpower. Naturally men were not conducive to sewing dresses or sewing shirts. I saw men do it because they were the contractors or the owners of the company. And they would pitch in when they had a fast order to go out. But they never hired any man to do that kind of work.

"FROM THE FRONT DOOR TO WORK"

Nick Aiello spoke at the union office on Chapel Street on January 27, 1999 where he still worked.

I lived on Wallace Street in the Wooster Square area were all shirt factories and dress factories. All the Italians, they all worked in shirt shops. You go in a house on Wooster Street and you'll find fifty shirt makers in those apartments. Four story buildings. And rows of machines. And the only industry in those days was the needle trades. Some of the men went to work in shirt shops—in the packing department, some in the pressing department, some stitched. I was number ten in my family. Most of the family above me had to quit [school] to go to work. My brothers went to work in a coal company for a dollar a day, milkman for a dollar a day in those days. There was no refrigeration. There were no hamburgers. Your mother made meatballs, she made bread balls because now they call it hamburger helper—the hard bread was what we used to use. My mother used to get a pound of hamburgers, she'd make a hundred meatballs because you never threw anything away. You saved the hard bread, you cut it and you stuffed and fried the meatballs. You shredded the skin, you made breadcrumbs—you didn't throw anything away. We had fourteen kids. And so everybody had to go to work. Everybody had to

WOOSTER SQUARE GARMENT DISTRICT, 1954
City of New Haven

pull in their share. I had seven sisters and all seven of them either worked in a
shirt factory and one worked in a dress factory. They worked in the shirt factories
for years. One place of employment for forty years. They married people in that
area. As they married, their daughters went to work in a shirt plant—the second
generation went to work in a shirt plant. But they made it. Poor and all they sent
their kids to college, worked hard, paid their dues. The third generation didn't do
it. In the 1950s, we started the downfall when the shops went south, then they
went overseas and now there isn't a shirt factory left in Connecticut. But in that

area there must have been five thousand employees—women working in the shirt or dress shops. Funny thing, the shops were on one side of the street, the houses were on the other side of the street so all they had to do was walk out the front door and go to work. And if they didn't work downstairs they went to work upstairs. Three and four dollars a week, forty, fifty hours a week. Sweatshop conditions. Some had to pack lunch and go to work. They walked to work; they had to take lunch to work. And sometimes they would go to work and the boss would say, "No work." And they would have to come all the way back home again. They did that when the so-called NRA and they had what they would call the minimum wage today. Fourteen dollars a week by labor standards. This was in the late '30s and early '40s. They got paid by cash, three or four dollars a week, would take closed envelopes home. You didn't open your envelope. And everybody brought the pay to the mother. And she would open it and whatever the change was left you got for an allowance or that went to help the family. Then in the 1930s there came the Amalgamated and they started organizing drives in the area. Number one, you want to talk about sexual harassment? It was the worst in those days with the foreman and the supervisors and even some of the owners. Young teenaged girls who had to go to work and took a lot of abuse. No talking. One bathroom maybe for two hundred women. Knock on the door when you went to the bathroom to make sure you didn't waste time in the bathroom. Little lights on the [workstation]—you go blind. The chairs—I had women who used to put cones underneath the chairs to make them stay with the wires—and they sat on that same seat for twenty years. Crowded together. Rows of machines. The spinning wheels with the shafts. And when the thread broke, you don't stop the machines. The boss wasn't going to stop twenty machines to fix a belt—so you had to fix them while the machine ran. As a bundle boy, the machinist taught me how to do it, the way to take off the strap, you punch the holes, you put the clip in, then you take the screws out and you flip it around. So the machines don't stop. It was dangerous. Sometimes if you didn't catch it right that screwdriver flies! But they needed the money and the parents would say, "Don't make no waves, don't tell your father otherwise he'll go in the plant and you will lose your job." One bathroom. The foremen or the foreladies on top of them, make sure they couldn't talk, they had to continue to work and everything was piecework—it was not timework. They couldn't talk; so they used to sing, [singing] "What did you do last night? Oh I went to the movies." You know, singing and that's the only way they used to be able to converse. They used to have to work until the employers started the wages; either change the piece rate. And these girls used to stitch. When New York got completely organized, the "runaway shops" came to New Haven. We called them runaway shops because of the unions in New York. They ran to New Haven where there were no union shops. And they would open up a storefront. They'd put twenty, thirty machines on the fourth floor and most of the stitching plants were on the fourth floor with no elevator so the girls would have to bring their lunch and would stay upstairs and never would come downstairs because they had to go four flights of stairs downstairs and four flights of stairs upstairs. So conditions were horrible.

❝We Started Our Own Shop❞

Alphonse Di Benedetto spoke at the dinner table of Kim and Michael Rogers' home in New Haven on April 14, 2000.

My mother didn't want her brother working in the shirt factory; she worked in Lesnow. So they must have discussed it and my father went ahead and rented a loft on Grand Avenue and bought twenty-five sewing machines and started a shirt factory and let my uncle run it. No problems, there were no unions, no income tax and so forth. They made shirts for other companies. Then the shirt factory started to grow and develop. They needed more space so they rented a place on Chestnut Street and the original name of the shirt factory was the Ideal Shirt Company. He had so many employees he had to have two floors. By that time my uncle Philip had learned how to speak English he and my father used to go back and forth to New York once or twice a week to get their customers to make the shirts. The rent was so much that my father said, "Why should I be paying rent when I can own my own building?" So he found this building on Hamilton and Chapel Street, used to be a spaghetti factory there. And he bought the building and converted it to a shirt factory, both floors, with no problem. My mother was gung-ho for it, naturally, because he was getting wealthy and developing in the community. In the early '40s it became the Planet shirt factory and we opened up a retail store in the front.

❝You Looking for Somebody?❞

Antonette Salemme spoke at the kitchen table of her home in North Haven on August 15, 1998.

My mother's boss was Jewish. His name was Schwartz. She used to tell the stories how they'd be working. She said, "If we ever looked up, he'd go, 'You looking for somebody?'" He used to say, "You looking for somebody?" They couldn't even pick up their heads. Now you're talking when my mother was working in the 1920s. I was shocked—what do you mean? They couldn't do that. They couldn't do that, they couldn't pick up their head, you had to keep working. Oh, those Jewish people, they're very, very shrewd and they are good business people—for themselves. I mean I met good Jewish people but they knew how to make a buck. My mother's name was Vincenza and when she went to work for this guy, she told him. She couldn't speak English. He didn't know how to say her name. The Jewish guy said, "What's your name?" She said in Italian, "Vincenza." He said, "Oh, all right, Jenny, I'll call you Jenny." "Jenny, you looking for somebody?" Because they picked up their heads. She used to make us laugh, she used to say, "We couldn't pick up our heads" or "You looking for somebody?" I said, Ma, you know . . . Of course I thought that was terrible. So he called her Jenny. My mother died with that name. We all called her Jenny. Her grandchildren are named Jenny because we thought that was her name. But her name was Vincenza.

"They Called Me Rose"

Antonette Coppola spoke in a meeting room at her nursing home in Branford on May 5, 2000.

My first job was in a shirt shop on Collis Street. My father's sister took me there, she worked there. Then when the cop came, they made me go run away by the back because I was under age and I had no [working] certificate. When she [my mother] applied for work, she put her sister's, Rose's, name on it—her sister was older than her—but she didn't live here—that's why she always used to say to me, "Your aunt Rose's name is on my working papers." She was three years older so she put her sister Rose's name on the paper so she could go to work. Because she couldn't work at the time. She was sixteen when she came from Italy.

"Hurry Up You Sleeping Jesus"

Mary Altieri spoke at the kitchen table in her Fair Haven home on January 13, 1999.

I went to work in 1927. I was fourteen years old. I went to Mister Marks and I got my papers not even in ten minutes. I passed my test and I went to work. Mister Marks used to give out exams, papers for you if you want to quit the school. If you didn't go to school he'd get after you. But at fourteen years old you could get out of school. I got out of school. They didn't stop me. My birthday was December seventeenth. The day after I went to work. Five dollars and a quarter a week, seven thirty till five, half a day on Saturday and that was it. But then you know these old ladies, they were older than me, they used to throw papers at me, try to initiate me, all that stuff. Take your clothes off—initiate you—see if you were a girl or if you were a boy. They were terrible, I tell you. I had my mother come up there, my mother called them all kind of names, the ladies there. They were all kinds of people years ago. You know because I was fourteen years old, I don't think I weighed seventy-five pounds—I was skinny—but I had to go to work because we needed the money. I couldn't go to school no more or anything. Twelve people, seven brothers and five sisters. I wanted to go to Commercial school nights. I went not even a week, my mother and father said, "Stay home and take care of the kids." So I couldn't have no schooling—I didn't go to school. And then I worked all the time. I did housework and then I went to work after I left Lesnow because he was very mean. Because I wouldn't work fast he used to throw me in the clothes bin, where the shirts were. We used to have bins to clean the shirts and put them in boxes. You wouldn't know but I know, they used to have bins with all shirts—fourteen, fifteen, sixteen—you take a bundle, you had to clean it all, then roll it up and the pressers would take it. I never could make enough for the day. He would say to me, "You're not working fast." I was fourteen years old, how you gonna work fast? I was cleaning off the shirts. They come twelve in a bundle. So now you got a clean all the buttonholes with the thread that they sew on, all the buttons got a be clean, the thread, see the thread hanging there? You got a clip it. Then you fix your collar on and you button your collar. Then you button your cuff and then when you get twelve in a bundle you pack it up, roll it up and give it the presser. That was the cleaning job I had. That's the only job I had in the shirt shop in Lesnow on Collis and Franklin Street [Wooster Square]. He used go by there, he used to throw me right in the bin. He pushed me and said, "Oh you sleeping Jesus, hurry up!" He was no good. The Jewish people. You think they're Italian? They're out for blood them people! But then I quit. I didn't care how much I wanted to stay in the job, I quit. You couldn't do nothing. We had to work. And if you talked to somebody he would fire you and say "Go home." If you stayed in the bathroom five, ten minutes, "Get out, work." It was no place to work. Like now you work in the shop they have a little respect for you. Or if they say something wrong you get a cop and you get them arrested. We couldn't do that. I didn't have a bigger brother that could knock the baloney out of him, you understand what I mean? My brother was seventeen but he wasn't the type to go and fight, you know what I mean? The condition was there. There was no union there; we never had a union in there. They got away with a lot of baloney, the bosses years ago. If they fired you for no reason at all you couldn't get a job back. Unless my mother went there and pleaded with somebody and then everybody would say to Harry Lesnow, "What's wrong with you? Why you got a make this girl go home?" Then he would take me back. But then it was like a cat and mouse, today you go home, tomorrow you come back. That's the way they treated the people. They could have buried us and they wouldn't say nothing to us, you know what I mean? A lot of my friends are dead and they got treated terrible. One day one of the fellas took an iron and threw at him [Lesnow] and missed him because when he yelled at his sister for some reason—he picked up the iron and he threw it at him.

66 My Fourteenth Birthday Present 99

Lena Riccio spoke at the kitchen table of her home in the Annex on April 20, 1997.

When I first went, my father got me out of school. On my birthday, my father came and got me out of school on my fourteenth birthday, the day of my birthday. That was a beautiful birthday present. On my fourteenth birthday he came to school to get me out of school. So this teacher, Miss Austin, she didn't want me to leave, she started to cry—she didn't want my father to take me out of school on my fourteenth birthday. And I was in seventh grade. She begged my father to let me finish the seventh grade in June. "No," he says, "No, she's got a go to work, we have a lot of kids, we need money and all that." Poor thing, she was crying, tears. She cried and she was saying, "Well, let her stay until June, let her finish the seventh grade." He said, "No, she's got a come." Now I wanted to be a nurse or a dressmaker—that's

LENA MORRONE RICCIO
Fifteen years old, 1929

Riccio family album

what was always in my mind. But he said, "No, she's got a . . . we need the money."
So the poor teacher, she was an elderly teacher and she was crying. She didn't want
me to go. But I couldn't argue back with my father that I didn't want to go. So I had
to go. So we go outside and we take the trolley, he takes me to Mister Mark's office
where you get your working papers to go to work. So we got my working papers and
the following day he took me up to the corner and we had to meet this lady. My
father knew this lady that worked in Lesnows Shirt shop; she already had a job for
me in Lesnows. Her name was Philomena and she takes me on the trolley and she
takes me to Lesnows shirt factory on Franklin and Water Street. I was fourteen
years old, what the hell did we know fourteen years old? Well, you never seen a
scared kid in all your life like me. They put me at this big machine—I never saw any

Sewing Dept. L. Wing.
Ideal Shirt Mfg. C

IDEAL SHIRT FACTORY, LATE 1920S.
Chestnut Street, Wooster Square, 1929

DiBenedetto family album

kind of a sewing machine before. I really was scared because there a pile a work here, pile of work there, and I was in the middle learning how to work on the machine because they had to teach me how to work on the machine. Mine was a single needle machine but I was in the middle of this pile of work and what do you think made me make? Pockets. Ten, fifteen cents an hour in 1928. Forty hours a week, sometimes we had to work a half a day on a Saturdays, forty-four hours. Never got an allowance, just money for the trolley so I used to walk to work to save that quarter. That's a long walk. At night it used be dark and cold. Sometimes I had to walk alone. With the big mountain of work here and I was just in the middle. Fourteen years old, I'll never forget that day, I'll never forget it.

"THEY WERE ALL DRESSED IN WHITE"

Antonette Sicignano spoke at the kitchen table of her Wooster Street apartment on August 30, 1999.

When I was fourteen years old my sister Julia was getting married. I said to my mother, Gee, I like to, I want to finish school so I can graduate. I went into the eighth grade at the Greene Street school they used to call that. And they had a room with all girls, you know. And I said [excited voice], Gee, next year I'm gonna graduate. In fact when I was in the seventh grade they made us in the hall watch them graduating. And all the girls were all dressed in white, so pretty on the stage. And they had flowers. They used to perform something after graduation. We had nice regular seats, we didn't have benches; we had nice big seats to see that. Like now you can go [to school] nights, but then they didn't that, no. At nighttime you had to take of the care of the kids. My mother would put the washing machine in the way, wash them and the next morning get up early and you got a chance to hang them. Or [laughing] put them all around the house. We used to go to bed nights and of course you had the coal stove and wood, that's how we used to dry them. My mother had twelve kids, they didn't send no clothes out to be washed and ironed. My sister got married in September. I was fourteen in June 1925. I had to go to work a couple of weeks after. I was in the eighth grade. I was dying to graduate. I couldn't go back to school. If one [in the family] was getting married somebody else had to get out of school to work. My sister Julia got married when she was seventeen and a half, she got married—my birthday was in June—I had to go to work in September. My mother needed another pay. We couldn't take a dollar off our pay. My mother had to have our whole pay. A pair of stockings were only twenty-five cents then. We couldn't even get the quarter; we had to wear the ripped stockings until we got another pair. We didn't know any better then. That's how the world was then, everybody had to go to work. Every family, they all had a lot of children. As soon as they get to be fourteen years old, they had to go work. I had to beg [laughing] to get a pair of stockings. You know when my mother used to see it was a little low, she'd says to me, "What do you make, two envelopes [split up my weekly paychecks]?" I said, they [the bosses] don't make two envelopes, they only make one. She says to me, "Well, there's a lot of people I know who don't want to tell their mother and father what they do, so they make a separate one." I said, Oh, no, what do you see there, a quarter an hour. That's all. A quarter an hour. And you worked seven thirty to five thirty. You had to make a lot, you had a make a lot of work you had to do for a quarter. Maybe they were twenty-five cents a dozen, you had to make a dozen of the part of the shirt you worked on. There were all different parts. They had the two different fronts. One was a button, and one was the button-hole. The sleeves, they had two pieces to make a sleeve, then they had the collars. They used to cut the collars and they used to have to put a lining in between the two pieces, one on top, and on the bottom and sew. The same way with the cuffs. And boy you had to make sure that you got the three pieces together and you turn and make it. We used to sweat like hell to make a dollar. I think the first week [1925] I made about five dollars, that's it. That was sweat. That was a sweatshop. That's why the union came in 1933 because we weren't getting enough. We started paying the union a quarter a month. That's how they started. I went to work at a shirt shop on Wallace and Wooster Streets. We used to call him "Louie-Sal." He showed me how to put the buttons on the shirts. He used to teach us. He taught me about three, four jobs, he taught me. How to put the sleeves on the shirts and in here there's a line they call it the "gores." Do that first, we used to put two pieces together and used to make the sleeves. Then when he taught me that, he said, "Now you got a sleeve." I said, "I dunno, that's a double needle." When I didn't do my hands right, he used to slap them, "This is how you got a do." Oh yeah, I had a learn he used to say. He wanted me how to learn to do the whole shirt, if anything was wrong. I didn't have enough on one job, he would put you on another job, put labels. The first four, five years I did everything then I stuck to only putting the sleeves on.

"I Wanted to Be a Commercial Artist"

Rose Durso spoke at the dining room table of Joe and Lena Riccio's home in the Annex on February 1, 1998.

They were nightmares [the shops], nightmares that work. I wanted to go home at night and forget all about it. You couldn't because you had a go back the next day. And then Miss McGrath—that was my last year in school that I was on the verge of graduating—and Miss Austin got together because I used to draw like an artist, you know, and they said, "Rose, why don't you go into commercial art?" So I said, "Well, how could I? My father needs every penny that I bring home." [They said], "Well, we'll go and speak with him." So they did. They went and my father said, "Sit down a-teach, sit down, sit down." They sat down. [Father] "Wan a coffee?" You know how the old folks are? My mother made . . . "No, no, Mrs. D'Amato, no we don't want any, and we came to talk concerning Rose. We want her to have an education and we'd like to have her go to designing school." They wanted me to make commercial art. My father said, "No! Got a go to work!" They explained to her that I was the best drawer in the grade. My father wouldn't hear of it. They went away crying almost. Teachers were interested, you know. So then when I went in [to school], they said, "Rose, we tried." I said, "I know you did." They said, "Well, here you are, with that, you're intelligent with that category and you could get far." I said, "Well, what my father says, you know, you got a do."

ROSE DURSO
Portrait

Durso family album

❝I Was Fresh❞

Luisa DeLauro spoke at the kitchen table of her Olive Street home in Wooster Square on August 9, 1998.

I wound up in the shirt shop. Oh was I unhappy about the shirt shop, oh. Those machines! You know what they're like, uh. The machines all in row—like three hundred machines, rows and rows of machines. Power machines. I was sixteen and I hated it, I hated it. I was very unhappy. I had to sew on the power machines. They weren't difficult things [to learn]. I made men's collars, used to stitch them for two and a half cents a dozen. That's how cheap they were, for seven, eight dollars a week. Oh it was terrible. Harry Lesnow would come around, he'd say, "Get the hell"—if we went for a drink of water—he was a cruel, very ugly—no class you know? He could've come and said, "Come on girls, get back to your machines." No, he'd scream at them [shouting] "Get the hell over to your machines." And so one day I told him where to go. And I walked out. Because he was always around like a Gestapo, he was a terrible person. And the girls, they cursed him, "You got a die this way, you got a get killed." Let me tell you, he did, he had a terrible death. They used to sing in Italian but they used their own words in [laughing], "You got a drop dead," in Italian they would sing, "Puózze a na' ccide," I could kill you. He was cruel; he was bad. And it used to be so hot in the summer with all those power machines running; it used to be so hot and we would be sweating. No air conditioning, no fans, just open windows—big deal, that's it, no air conditioning, no, none, none. All the time that I worked in the factory never had air conditioning. Never had fans, nothing. Oh, God, it used to be so hot. Yeah, because all those power machines running. It was piecework, you got what you made, what you produced. And I used to work on men's collars. I just walked out, I told him to go to hell because I wouldn't take anything from him. See I had my two sisters Rae and Mary working there but they would never talk back. Me, I was fresh.

"It Was Always Our Loss"

Louise Orefice spoke in the living room of her Annex home with her brother Anthony on October 31, 1998.

It was always our loss. You know, if we wasted time, the machine broke or we had to go get the work or we had to wait for work, it was our loss. It was never their [the owners] loss. Because we were on piecework. We had to write the work on a card. We had to write the bundles that we made on a card and then at the end, Friday, the boss or the foreman used to come and pick the cards and that's how the bookkeeper used to make out your pay for the next week. Yeah, that's how we got paid. I remember the first day I walked in. It was a new experience for me, I just figured, "Well, I gotta work here, might as well." And I had a control that machine. You know the electric sewing machines, they go fast; you had to watch out for your fingers. I went to Lesnow Brothers about May 20, 1926. I worked three days. My first three days they put me on practicing, teaching me how to operate the machine and then the next day they put on piecework and for those three days I got a dollar, one buck. And then the next week he put me on a steady job. I was turning cuffs, they weren't paying very much, ten to fifteen cents a dozen. I had to turn twenty-four cuffs to make fifteen cents. There was an operator before me that used to give me the work. She used to set the cuffs, then the cuffs used to come to me and I had to turn them over and make the stitch on the cuff. I had to make twenty-four cuffs for a dozen because there's two in every shirt. Then I had to turn them, pull them out, get them all set and nice, put them in the box with the rope and tie them up. And that was all my time. I made even less because it was a nonunion shop. Those were the days. Like nowadays, I see all the pampering these kids get from their parents. We had to struggle, we had to struggle. Couldn't get an education. My mother always thought that was a waste of time. She thought that all the girls would get married. I never got married [laughing]. Eh, what are you gonna do, life goes on. We make the best of it.

Then I worked for Schwartz—there's another sweatshop! I was paid ten dollars a week. And the ten dollars was bad enough, you'd go in the shop there, in the back of the shop the boss used to stand up all day. And if you needed a spool of thread or work, you'd raise up your hand [laughing] and he'd take it to you. You couldn't walk around. You couldn't go to the toilet a little extra or a get a drink of water from the stinking rusty sink. Or else he would come and call you down, "What did you get up for?" and this and that. So after a while I got tired and I said, "The heck with you, you can keep your lousy shop." No heat. It was very cool there, very cool. No fans in the summer. Then I went to Par-Ex Shirt. There's another dive. That place was dirty, it was dusty. In the summer they had no fans and they had one man on the floor, he had to be the foreman, he had to be the machinist, he had to give out the work, he had to take the work away from you, he had to do everything. One day I got so mad at him. The machine was skipping. And I was calling him, "Come over and fix my machine because I can't work, can't pass work like this." He started to give me a few words. I said, "You know what? Stick the work, you can stick it." I took my things and I walked out. The best to work, the best shirt factory, I went to work in Brewster's. That was the best, I was sorry I went so late in my life. It was a very good shop to work in. They treated the girls like queens, everything was the worker, no matter what you wanted. The foreman, he was so good. If you had a complaint, you'd go up to the foreman and he'd try to fix it for you, if the machine was too slow for you, he'd get the machinist and make it fast. He was very good. I enjoyed working there.

"I Even Had to Work during My Lunch Hour"

Antonette Salemme spoke at her kitchen table with her husband Sal in their North Haven home on August 15, 1998.

My mother couldn't go to work for some reason. She used go send my brother to the dress shop on Wooster Street. The name of that one was Dave's. He would bring home bundles of dresses to sew at home. My mother had a power machine in her house like I did when I was sixteen. That's where I learned to sew. We would come home for lunch. My mother, she had my brother small then Joe, so I guess she couldn't go to work in the shop so she used to have the work brought to her. When we got home for lunch, we would eat our sandwiches or whatever we got, and she'd have the power machine in the kitchen and all the dresses had belts. That's where I learned how to sew now that I'm thinking about it. I had to sew my whole lunch hour, belts. While my mother ate, I sewed the belts. They were easy. Then we had an iron thing, like a little rod and I had to turn them, you push the top where you sewed it here down to here, you push it in, then you pull it over and it came out and it was a belt. And my mother would top stitch that after.

"A Quarter an Hour"

Antonette Salemme spoke at the kitchen table of her home in North Haven on August 15, 1998.

The lady that owned the dress shop said to my mother. "You know if you want to let your daughter work . . ." It was an easy job, all the dresses were already made, all on hangers. They all had to have tags, so she hired me to go there on a Sunday morning. That's against the law because I wasn't sixteen and I would put the tags on. She used to give me a quarter an hour. But sometimes I'd work longer than other times to finish all the dresses. My mother would say, "Well, she worked long." [The owner] would say, "Well yeah, but she was doing us a favor," so she would never give me my full pay. Me? She used to give it [my pay] to my mother. So I did that.

"Singing Songs at Work"

My father used to say he didn't want me to go to school because, in my father's eyes, only bad girls went to school. He used to call them . . . he'd say they were bad. You learned bad things. And I used to say my father didn't want me to go to school, he was afraid I was going to learn dirty jokes and dirty stories but he put me in a dirty factory—he let me go—where they were all old Italian women. Now if you want to hear dirty Italian jokes, you would hear them then. This one woman, she was a lovely woman and I loved her but she was a nut. And she used to tell us things. And she used to laugh. And then she would sing at her machine, like, "Here comes the guy with the banana," and things like that. And you're supposed to answer. Yeah, we used to do that. I never did it but they did it.

"The Bars on the Window Scared Me"

Brand's, it was a children's dress shop. I worked on a power machine. It was in a building where they used to have wholesale—on Minor Street—they used to sell cheese, tomatoes, and olive oil. When we would go in that building—it was old— stink! And we had a go up to the third floor. We'd go in by eight o'clock in the morning. No air conditioning, they had bars on the windows, all bars, iron bars. I guess they didn't want anybody to steal cuz' the building was like for wholesale but these Jewish people owned the dress shop up on top. No air conditioning, no air, no fans, nothing. When we walked in, between the cheese smell, the provolone down-stairs, we'd go in at eight o'clock, we used to have to light the light. We all had a light over the machine because it was dark, it was not ventilated by any shot. And

PAR-EX SHIRT FACTORY
Chapel Street, Wooster Square, 1950s
City of New Haven

on that side they had all the pressers, on this side they had all the girls that packed dresses and then on this side they had other girls that would take—after the cutters cut out the pieces—they would take the back, the front, the side and make bundles. And then bring these bundles to us. We had a big, big bin and they would tie six dresses together and put them in there. And we had to put those dresses together. With that light on at eight o'clock in the morning in the middle of August. And you were allowed to go to the bathroom maybe once or twice but if you overdid, like some of the girls used to smoke even then—and the boss, he'd be right out there, knockin' on the door, "You know you been in there a long time." I didn't because I didn't smoke then. Then he put me on a merrow machine after I did the straight work he put me on a merrow machine. I used to make the hems on kids' dresses. It had a curved needle that used to pick up just this part and make all these stitches where you can't see it. But now in the summer we used to work on winter clothes and you work in August with this light, the heat, the bars, and no air, let me tell you, it wasn't easy. You couldn't see a damned thing. They had lights—aluminum on top and just a little light on the bottom. It was just a light bulb, it would shine right where the sewing machine was. That was it. I was only sixteen, mind ya. The bars used to scare the hell out of me. By the time we come, you know all the lint and everything, we used have all that black lint. It was awful, awful. But you know I had a work. My mother, you know, things were tough. My brother couldn't work because he had a bad leg; my father was in a wheelchair with a broken leg in eight places and only my mother worked.

"WE PUT COLD WATER ON OUR ARMS"

Lena Riccio spoke at the kitchen table with her husband Joseph at their Annex home on April 4, 1997.

They [in the dress shops] made more money than we did and they thought because they worked making dresses they thought they were better off—smarter—than we were. But our shops were just as bad as their shops. With the windows blocked up and everything. It was like a jailhouse, that's what it was. No fans. Are you kidding air conditioning? Air conditioning, we could put cold water on our arms—that was our air conditioning! They had little fountains. We used to put wet rags on our necks—that was our air conditioning. They had a fan here, maybe another fan down the end of the shop. And the girls that were near the fan would complain that they would get a draft on their neck and they had to shut the fan. Yeah, and you had piles of shirts on this side, pile of shirts on this side and you're in the middle of the machine—what air did we get? We didn't get no air. It was hot. I don't know why they thought they were better than us, I don't know why. Maybe it was cleaner; they made more money. I worked in a dress shop on State Street. I worked a half a day. I came home and I didn't go back. I didn't like it. I didn't like the way they worked. I liked shirt shops.

"IT WAS CONSTANT PIECEWORK"

Antonette Salemme spoke at the kitchen table of her North Haven home on August 15, 1998.

If they ever had a fire in there. And we were hundreds of girls in there. And very close. We didn't have it like that when I went to work later in the bank [1960s] with the difference with the rules and regulations and vacations—it was so different. They'd walk in and say, "Well how many weeks will I get here, do we get a coffee break?" I never heard of that crap. And I resented all that because I'd say, What? They come in lookin' for a job, they're looking for when they can take a week off. And they never worked, they were always lobbin' around. They really do. I could never be a boss. So, our sewing machines, there was a girl right next to the other and we had a bin and the dresses we'd sell would go in there. Then we'd take them out and break them and put them in this bin. It was constant piecework, you know what I mean? And dark, it was dingy. And now these sewing machines were long, long, right? And when they put the power on, you know, they didn't put it on one at a time. At the end of the line they had these boxes with a lever, the lever would be down. At eight o'clock, you look at the clock and they'd zoom it up there and they'd all start up—zzzoom! And all the thread would start goin' through the machines. We had a be at our machines and ready to go when he put that lever up there. You know, like a circuit breaker? You know how they do? That's the way it was. And they had a forelady that would come and see that we always had our bin full. But not that she was on our side by any shot. We had a nice one, she was a nice girl. But I mean basically, they were for the boss. And then you know, they'd be pressing in the corner and all the steam comin' out in this heat. Who ever heard of air conditioning? I don't know how the hell I used to breathe. But if we ever had a fire there was no out door. It was just you come up the stairs and you were in, that was it, you were in. There was no fire escape that I remember. And we had bars on the windows. Bars! Matter of fact I went home one day I said I didn't want to work there no more because they got bars, it's dark, they got light, the light at eight in the morning. But you know I could say anything I wanted, they needed the money. So I had a go to work. We were poor. But we never went without.

66 WORKING AS A DRESSMAKER 99

Rose Savo spoke at the kitchen table of her Annex home on July 28, 2000.

The first dress factory—I worked for Lipman Brothers. I worked for Buonocore, they were Italian people. I always worked on dresses. I used to make the complete garment. My first pay in 1921 at [Isners]—six days a week, from seven to six at night—six dollars a week. They used to teach you. They always had a forelady to teach you and then you took over. If you made a mistake they would correct you. I had a Jewish boss. He was mean. If you made a mistake he would insult you, oh yeah. They used to insult you. One of the girls got so mad at him one day she picked up the box with the work [dresses] in it and she was gonna hit him over the head with it. It was Lizzie Menzel—she was a Siciliano, a Sicilian! She had a temper. She said, "Aye, you're always pickin' on me." She picked up that box, she was gonna put it over his head. He was so insulting, a good-looking man but he had a disposition like a goat. Oh yeah. I'm doing the best I can, I said to him one day, he's correcting me. [He answered], "The best you can is not good enough for me." Oh he had a disposition. We had no choice. They [our parents] couldn't wait till we were fourteen years old—"Go to work!" No matter how wrong it was, they meant right. Right? [Laughing] That's the attitude I have. Yeah.

"THAT WAS THE ONLY SOURCE OF LIVELIHOOD"

Rose Durso spoke at the dining room table with Joe and Lena Riccio at their home in the Annex on February 1, 1998.

That was the only source of livelihood that there was. All garment factories. There was Lesnow, one of the first ones, Ideal was next, Planet on Chapel Street was an old one too. Then came Creighton, then came Jack Small with the shirts and the pajamas. And the industry grew, which was for the good of the people, the women. But then they all moved to the South. When the unions set in they all moved out, they didn't want to pay the money. When the unions came, when they were weak in the beginning the bosses tolerated it. But as they got strong and stuck up for the girls, for the workers to a certain degree and wanted to give them a little raise, then the later years—this was the new era—in the '80s. I always worked on shirts. Shirts all the time. They gave you bundles. So many dozens in a bundle and we got so much a dozen, three cents a dozen, five cents a dozen, that's all. I had to do all the way down to the tail. Some put cuffs, turned them. I did labels for a short while. Me, I got ten cents for twenty-four, and size sixteen and a half. O Madonna! The ones that put the collar, they did twelve, single. Labels, twelve. You're doing piecework, if you didn't produce you didn't get paid. Each dozen, you made a dime. The more dozens, the more you made. Day work was lousy, you got the same no matter how much you made; you got the same. And Saturday. I got four dollars and forty cents, that's all I got [a week]. That was in the early '20s, you know how many years ago that is? And you had a struggle. Single needle [machine] is one stitch. A double needle, it's two stitches. The single stitch is easier. But the double stitch—when one broke—or a needle or something, you were in trouble. Like Lee [Lena Riccio] had the pocket with the single. The shirts had the double needle all the time on the seams, all the way down to the tail. Bad machines. They broke, you know, they were old, then they weren't taken care of properly, maybe they'd have one mechanic in a big factory like that you'd be looking for the mechanic, he'd be on the other side. Lose all that time. But they didn't deduct anything [from the $4.40 a week]. I got a say the truth. But they wanted a hustle for themselves to make more. But if the mechanic was busy on one machine he couldn't come to another one. So there were the losers, you know, then they hustled you up.

"IT WAS STRICTLY BUSINESS"

We didn't get any breaks. You could hardly get a lunch break. We were day work you couldn't talk too much. Lesnows was the worst. There was one there—I don't want to mention names—he would with hands, would come when you didn't think. Surprise—I used to call him, "the surprise." He'd stand behind you and just look. He'd make fun of the girls, he used to swear a lot, bad profane words, he was just a bitter man. Think nothing of it. Like I said about the grapes, he said, "Throw it away." I said, "Before I throw this away I'll quit my job, Harry." I didn't even . . . I'll quit my job. He turned around and he went away. He was the son of the owner. Mister Diamond wasn't bad, he was a nice guy, you know. But him—oh Madonna! His Uncle Sam was nice too. He had compassion for the girls working there. All Jewish guys. They were good people but they were business, just strictly business and nothing else, never a smile, never a pleasant word, nothing. It was strictly business. They never hurt anybody or touched anybody but it was strictly business, see. So that's it. But we had a work hard. The machines were always breaking down because they were old machines, rusty and everything. Poor lighting over the machines, terrible.

"I Didn't Even Get the Forty Cents"

The harassment. The abuse. For four dollars and forty cents for forty-four hours. Even as late as 1935, 1936. My first job, I was fifteen years old, I had to go to Mr. Mark, get my permission, and my father had to sign to get the job. You had a go through this man, Mr. Mark and he was a stinker, okay, in those days. Well, we went there, he signed, he gave us the okay, and I lied. I lied. I told Mr. Diamond I knew how to run a double needle machine. I never saw one until I went in the room and saw this big huge thing in front of me, I got scared, you know. It was 1929. So I got in there and there was a big, tall, nice man with gray hair said to me, "What can I do for you?" I said, "I'm looking for work." He made signs with his fingers and said, "Come with me." And walk through the corridor. He took me and I see this big machine in front of me—my god, and I got scared, I got nervous. Finally, I looked on the side and there was Anna, Anna DeFrancesco. Well I looked around and I said, "Ooh Anne, I'm so happy you're here. How do you run this machine?" She said "Ro, I'll show you." And she did. This was Lesnows on Franklin and Water Street. It was a big concrete building, ugly and cold inside with a bad atmosphere. Gloomy, gloomy, the lighting was bad, the floors were full of oil, you name it, the machines were old, machines that you had to struggle to work on it. [The man] said, "All right, come with me," with the Jewish accent that he had. I sat there and by one or two o'clock in the afternoon I had kind a sorted everything out. So he gave me scraps to work on, and then the next day he gave me the regular. Ten cents an hour. [You produced] all you could in an hour. My job was, starting from here [top of the shirtsleeve] closing all of this of the shirt, on both sides. The sleeves were all opened when it comes and you had to—without the cuff included—you started and you had a match it under the arms and go all the way down to the gusset. And match the gusset. And I got on to it. And I worked a week. At the end of the week, I went and look in the pay—four dollars and forty cents, even a half a day on Saturday. I stuck it out anyway. When I brought my mother the first pay, my mother, she was radiant that I brought her four forty. And with that she did the week's shopping. I didn't even get the forty cents out of the pay. We walked. We never got the trolley car, back and forth. I said, gee, I was hoping she'd give me the forty cents, but they were so poor and pay the taxes on the property, the forty cents was forty dollars to her at the time. So therefore we continued doing that year in and year out. You could talk. But not while you were working. They watched because you got a produce. And they watched every little move. One of them came and he got behind you and he looked to see if you were working and if you're talking you had a stop—real quick—and put your head down and work. Like slaves, just keep going, keep going. Those machines, if one thread breaks, you're in trouble for an hour. All those four spools of thread going all the time. But all in all, the factory gave four dollars and forty cents—for a long time. Then the unions settled in and little by little they improved and maybe you got like a nickel more or ten cents or fifteen cents and so forth and so on. Then there was the nephew—the devil himself on this earth! The devil himself. He didn't miss a trick. And really, he enslaved the girls, he really did. Mean. He was mean, very, very mean. You couldn't make a move. One time, one Saturday I brought a bunch of grapes, I didn't have lunch. He put me on trimming all the threads off the shirts to make them nice and neat before they went to the pressing department. So I was eating my grapes and he said, "Whadaya doin?" I said, "This is my lunch." The boss said [mean tone] "I want ya to stop and keep going, stop eating or throw it away!" I said, "Before I throw this away, I need the job, but I'll leave, I don't care how desperate I am." You know, he walked away, he didn't say anything else to me and I kept eating the grapes. I defied him, right? I worked every minute. For four forty a week. I wish I get [kept] the envelope—all the envelope had was your name, your number of the machine, and how much you made, that's all. Nothing fancy, four forty, that's all I got for years.

66 WORKING AT CIARDI'S 99

Maryanne Santacroce spoke in the kitchen of Angelina Criscuolo's East Haven home on December 21, 1999 with her husband Anthony and friend, Tony Vitolo.

The Ciardi dress shop was on Wallace Street. It was really a sweatshop. Because there was only one entrance to come in and only one way to come out. They only had one front door to get in. And they had a freight elevator you never could use, the only entrance to the place there was, the only entrance. To go out, the same entrance but you couldn't use the freight elevator at all—that was the only way. And the old ladies, they used to be there that the material was under their sewing machines when the power went on. Half hour for lunch. You ate right at the machine because the people didn't want to get off the machine because when the power went on again they had to do because they were on piecework. They wouldn't even go to the toilet, the old ladies because they knew they had to make enough dresses to make enough money for the week. So they would just sit there and not even have lunch sometimes, just sit there.

These were all the people who came from Italy. They were piecework, every item you made that's how much you made. As you go in, you walk up these big flight of steps. Then walk up a little further and there was a fire escape—it was all boxed in but you could see there was a fire escape there. And then you walked right into the factory to get into Ciardi's dress shop. And I was petrified because you could see down. It was the top floor. There was the Sunbeam shop downstairs and the rubber shop was downstairs because during the summer you'd smell all that rubber and when you walked you saw all the sewing machines. You couldn't open the windows with the smell in the summertime with the rubber company downstairs. It was so cold in the winter. And with the old people it was too cold to open the window, so you didn't open the window. It was really a factory, you know. It was interesting, the factory, because the way you saw all the sewing machines, power going. In the back was the pressers, the finishers, the buttoner machines to put the buttons on, because they made the whole dress but they had other people to put the button holes in, the buttons on, they put whatever used to go on the dresses, the belts. Then they had a place where they sorted in bundles, all the dress sizes in bundles and they would give the bundles to the ladies and they would have to make the whole dress. All the pieces for the dresses were in bundles—size twelve, fourteen, sixteen, eighteen. And then after they made them you put them on a model to see if the darts were right. If it wasn't they went back to the operator to fix them. And then if they had anything to be pressed—you know like the collar would be pressed, before they put them onto the dress, you have to bring it to the presser and they would press it and then you'd bring it back to the lady. And then they had to clean all the threads, they had the machine to clean all the threads like an electric razor, you would clean off all the dresses. Then you'd put the tags on them, the size on them before they would ship them to New York. Then they used to ship them out. Then for these same dresses that they got a dollar fifty were selling for ten, fifteen dollars, even more.

"I Worked Three Jobs"

Antonette Coppola spoke in a meeting room of her Branford nursing home on May 7, 2000.

In my time I used to go home and put them [children], let them eat, dress them, make them everything, then I used to go to another dress shop till one o'clock at night. I'd walk home after, back and forth. And then in the morning, I had a get up at five o'clock to get them dressed and bring them to the nursery and then I'd go to work. That's the life I lived. My husband was sick for eleven years. But I had three [jobs] because I used to work at home, the shop in Fair Haven used to make blouses, so I went there and they used bring me the blouses because it was cheaper for the government [taxes], like if they had to pay the government fifty cents, they would pay me only a quarter, and used to make blouses till three o'clock in the morning. And then I used to go to sleep for a couple a hours and then I'd go back to work.

❝Go Back Mary❞

Mary Marino spoke in the living room of her Warren Street home on August 24, 1999.

Once I was out of work because I wasn't feeling good. Now my boss didn't know who to give my job to. So they gave it another girl, Mary, "Pretty Mary." So after, when I went back, my boss said to me, "Mary, this here is not right." The thread broke and she never ripped it out and did it over again—she left it like that. Now they had to repair that—when you repair that it don't look right. I looked at it. I said, "That's not my work, you know it." I said, "This is Mary's work." The boss said [soft voice] "Oh, I'm sorry." I never passed a shirt. If the thread broke I took the shirt; I ripped it, made it over again so it wouldn't look repaired. There was a lady, Maddalena that used to fix all the repairs of the shop. She said, "Since you came to work here I got no work." One day I said, I'm mad. He don't give me the job I want. I used to love to put the top center on the white dress shirts. That strip was like a yard long and that wide. And you had a two-needle machine. You put a piece through the steel folder, it folds it in on the top and the bottom and then you take the shirt and you put under another folder. We worked hard. Then you attached it by two needles on the top. So I heard that a job opened up on Prince Street. I wanted to leave. So I went in this new place and who comes out? Lesnow! He said to me, "What are you doing here?" I said, "I want top centers, you don't want to give it to me? And I don't want to work." He said, "Go back." Because he had that shop [laughing] and the other shop. He owned both shops. "Go back Mary." He made me go back. He had just opened up. There's no more factories around. They all went down to the Caribbean.

13

Workers Organize: The Labor Movement in New Haven

When a group of courageous young Italian American men and women decided to leave their machines and cutting tables in protest of the terrible sweatshop conditions, owner demands for more productivity without pay increases, and miserable wages at Lesnow Brothers in the Depression winter of 1933, it marked an important chapter in New Haven's tumultuous working history. As early as 1884, women shoemakers protested the lack of fire escapes, poor ventilation, and owner demands for increased piecework production without fair payment and organized a strike against the L. Candee Rubber Boot Company. In 1886, women corset factory workers followed the shoemakers and went on strike for better work conditions. That year, after twenty-one work stoppages had occurred in the city, an article in the *New York Times* appeared, "This town (New Haven) has picked up the reputation lately of having more strikes than an other city of its size in the country. Very likely it deserves it; at any rate the labor problem is in everyone's mouth."[19] During labor unrest in the 1880s, women formed representative committees with elected leaders, forerunners of the union-elected chairlady of the 1930s who monitored abuses in the workplace and reported violations in the union contract by owners.

In the 1920s, New Haven's needle trades employed thousands of Italian men and women with some African Americans, Jews, and Poles. Despite working in dangerous, inhumane conditions, enduring daily verbal and sexual abuse from bosses, and toiling long hours for poor wages, owners, and even union organizers, believed immigrant women could not be mobilized because of their strong commitment to the economic well-being of their families, respect for parental authority, and inability to comprehend the dynamics of union management disputes. But with the Depression in full swing in 1933, New Haven's workers in the needle trades had reached a breaking point: spreaders in cutting rooms earned $4.50 for a fifty-four hour week, cuff turners $4.00 for a sixty hour week.[20] To make matters worse, Sargent Manufacturing Company, a major employer in the city, was reeling in a recession that forced many men out of work. L. Candee Rubber, another economic mainstay for hundreds of employees, had already closed its doors in March, 1929.

The movement to unionize New Haven's workforce had already been set in motion in 1932, when Sidney Hilman, an experienced organizer from New York City and General President of the Amalgamated Clothing Workers of America, began a campaign to unionize runaway shops that fled to New Haven. His wife Bessie, who had family ties in the New Haven area, knew first-hand of the terrible plight of Jewish and Italian working women and she strongly supported her husband's efforts. Before organizing strikes at any of the factories, the Amalgamated negotiated with the Shirt Contracting Association as the numbers of union members increased. The first union contract was signed between the Brewster Shirt Co. and its 125 employees in the spring of 1933 with no job action. The owners of the D & I Company, Ideal Company, and Par-Ex Shirt Company soon followed, agreeing to union contracts for its workers. Owners wisely settled disputes and accepted union contracts when they saw the disruption in production caused by the standoff at Lesnows, where owners had demanded hourly raises in piecework production without increases in pay rate and refused to negotiate new contracts for its workers.

The 1933 strike at Lesnow Brothers, the largest employer of garment workers in the state with five hundred workers in the heart of New Haven's garment district, ranks as one of the most dramatic confrontations in the city's labor history. Protesters who braved freezing temperatures walking picket lines and organizing the local community against Lesnow Brothers during the winter and spring of 1933, received little attention from the *New Haven Register*, a staunch antiunion newspaper. The police used force to break up union rallies and the city refused to let protesters use the auditoriums of the local Columbus and Dante schools for meetings. Strikers deprived of meeting places met at Waterside Park where park officials refused to issue them permits to assemble. Undaunted by outside efforts to discourage the protest, Jennie Formichella, an organizer from Bridgeport, and Jill Iannone handed out fliers outside shops and met with Italian-speaking families. Two Italian-speaking union officials, John Lauria and Aldo Cursi, met with immigrant parents of the rank and file, convincing them of the union's benefits. Many immigrant parents who had been against striking for fear of losing critical sources of family income and the threat of physical harm to their daughters, now encouraged them to walk in picket lines. With the ominous threat of losing desperately-needed jobs, the women inside Lesnow Brothers factory finally decided to strike against long-standing abuses by their bosses. Jennie Aiello Alfano, a tough-minded young woman who worked on the second floor cutting room, dodged fellow workers loyal to the owners by sliding down the clothing chute with bales of unfinished shirts to the first floor stitching room where she rallied her friends to strike. In the face of the Lesnow ultimatum, the Italian community's reluctance to strike had changed to overwhelming support of their children's efforts to win union contracts.

On April 18, 1933, Amalgamated called for a national strike of all nonunionized shops. On May 1, 1933, a picket line composed of other striking shirt shop workers and members of the Yale Divinity School gathered outside Lesnow Brothers. Hired thugs stood ready to intimidate the strikers. On May 1, the male cutters joined the striking women and walked out. Two days later the factory closed its doors. On May 3, 1933, Lesnow representatives met with union officials and Sidney Hilman and agreed to a union contract with provisions for a ten percent pay increase, health insurance, and pension benefits.

In August, 1933 the International Ladies Garment Workers Union called for a similar campaign for the dress shops. Women marched from shop to shop urging workers to strike, the number of women growing with each successive closing. Fist fights broke out between women loyal to the owners for their favored positions in the workplace who "would not walk" and strikers who taunted them from picket lines, calling them "scabs," "traitors," and "Judases." The police intervened to break up these skirmishes between women on both sides. By the mid-1930s two local unions, the Amalgamated 125 of the Shirtmakers Union and ILGWU Local 151, which comprised the dress factory workers, were established in the city.

Local unions became social and cultural institutions for many second generation Italian women who missed the chance to attend high school, providing them with educational programs. The union organized company picnics, cultural events, sports teams, child care for children in the factories, and legal assistance. In the mid-1930s, the union sponsored one of Italy's leading Italian socialists, Giuseppe Emanuele Modigliani, to speak against Fascism and Mussolini at a huge rally at Fraternal Hall on Elm Street in New Haven. Many of the courageous women who walked picket lines and risked personal injury during job actions were elected chairladies of their shops where they monitored potential workplace abuses, fielded complaints from coworkers, conferred with union business agents, and made sure earnings were equal to the number of finished pieces. After the strike at Lesnow Brothers, many members of the Aiello family became officers of the executive board of the Shirtmakers Union.

The victory at Lesnow Brothers ushered in a new era for unions in other sectors of the city: workers at Sargent and Winchester's unionized as well as the city's service and maintenance employees at Southern New England Telephone and Yale University. On the national stage, Sidney Hilman's demand for "a seven-hour day, a five-day work week and a living wage," for workers, which many owners, a governor, congressmen, and senators fiercely resisted, finally won approval in 1934 when President Roosevelt enacted a thirty-six hour week and ten percent pay increase. By 1938, second generation Italian women began attending high school instead of working in the needle trades; Lesnow Brothers left for East Hampton, Massachusetts, a town with a larger labor pool, followed by Brewster Shirt Company to Ocala, Florida. In 1959, there were eighty-two apparel manufacturers in New Haven and thirty-seven of these firms manufactured shirts or dresses. In 1989, New Haven's last shirt shop closed, followed by the last dress shop, which closed in 1991. The needle trades had fallen victim to foreign competition in the Pacific Rim and Asia where workers were paid a fifth of salaries that had been won by the union.[21]

"We Were Afraid"

Lena Riccio spoke at the kitchen table of her Annex home on April 20, 1997. Like many of her young co-workers, she often walked four miles from the Annex to the shirt factory and back.

When they wanted us to join the union. We were young. We were scared. We didn't know what this union was and the boss [Ed Lesnow] used to get us scared, "You're not going to have a job if you join the union." So the girls used to hesitate. Some would go; some wouldn't go. They were really afraid. We didn't know what a union was; the boss used to tell us, "You aren't going to have a job if you go join." And then the union guys used to say, "If you don't join you're going to lose the job, you can't get a raise." So we were afraid—now we didn't know who to listen to. And we used to go to the union meetings but we were more afraid to go to the meetings sometimes—we didn't know what it was all about. We were afraid to go to this union hall and we knew the girl that was with the union, Julia Formichelli. So we knew her and we weren't too afraid because we knew who she was. But she used to talk to us nice. And this lady had a little store and we were afraid to go to the meetings so the lady used to call us three, four girls in the store, make believe we went to the meeting and we would be in the store. So they used to tell us "You'll get a raise, you'll make more money and the boss can't fire you because you'll be in the union." So we had to join. But we were afraid because these guys that were in this union, they were like threatening us, forcing us to join, "If you don't join you won't have a job." You listened to the boss, the boss would say, "If you join the union you're not going to have a job." You didn't know who to listen to. So that's how we started the union. The majority joined—the girls, one by one, one by one, they all joined, so we all joined. John Lauria would meet with us at the hall. He used to be real wild; he used to get real mad. So they girls were afraid—we were young compared to him. We were afraid if we had to answer him. I know I wouldn't tell him anything because I was afraid. We were fifteen-year-old kids in the early 1930s. The [union] used to take advantage of the girls because they knew we were afraid [of losing] our job and they would scare us about our job. We needed a job so we used to go along with them. I was the oldest in the family and I had to go to work, even though we earned a few dollars a week but that few dollars came in handy at home. And we used to hand in the whole envelope [pay] at home. Used to get a quarter a week for trolley fare. Sometimes we would be afraid, if you didn't go to the meeting they would threaten you, that you had to come to the meeting. So we used to go to the meeting. But we knew this girl Julia here and when she was there I wasn't afraid to listen to him talk because she knew us girls. But he wasn't very pleasant. They told us how much we had to pay dues. Every couple of months they would raise the dues. I don't think it came to a dollar when they started and before you know it we had to pay a few dollars that they took off our pay. They used to tell us the union is good because if you got a gripe with your boss you come and tell us and we go to the boss and fight for you, fight for your job or whatever complaint we had that our boss did. I was afraid; I never talked.

"THE STRUGGLE TO FORM UNIONS"

Salvatore "Gary" Garibaldi spoke at the Santa Maria Maddalena Society on
Wooster Street on May 18, 2000.

The term was boss. The boss owned the company and some bosses locked the
doors so that the girls didn't leave unnoticed. So now what happens? These girls
are now working and word is getting around that someone is talking to them on
the outside about forming a union so they can upgrade their working conditions.
Well, naturally, you found that, say out of one hundred girls, maybe you might find
about eight to ten girls to be a little more loquacious or outspoken and brazen
[voice rising] enough to bring it to the attention of not to the boss—but they did it
indirectly to the boss—they would talk to other fellow workers. "Hey, I know
there's a couple of guys that want to unionize us. We're going to have a meeting.
Can you come to the meeting? Secretive—don't tell no one." So they would meet
in Waterside Park. Outside, on a Saturday morning—you couldn't do it during
working days. So what happened? You always had someone—I hate to use the
term stool pigeon. Monday morning they would go back and tell the boss who was
generating this movement. This is 1932. Now you have men and women meeting
on a Saturday morning, very quiet, not announced, very careful who they are talking to because now they don't want to lose or jeopardize the poor girl's job. So
when the boss found out who were these so-called people interested in forming a
union he would call them and say, "What's this?" Because he knew maybe one or
two were really outspoken and they would say, "Yes, we're trying to unionize."
Well, he'd keep quiet. When it came maybe a day or two later, he would say to the
girl, "Um, I don't need your work time today." And he sent her home, retaliating
because she was doing something he doesn't want to accept. So before you know it,
the girls are picking that up, that when you talk, there's [singing] somebody talking
to the boss. Now between themselves they're trying to find out who it is. Well then
you had some lovely women there, for example, Jennie Aiello and Lucy, her sister.
They were very outspoken in the formation of unionizing. And she would talk to
the boss—not disrespectfully—but in those days it was considered disrespectful to
talk to your boss, like say, "Hey look, who do you think you are?" That was like,
whoo! Murder for a worker to talk like that to the boss, question him or his integ-
rity or his honesty. Or "You're lying; you're against us." Well that was talk . . . you
never dare talk to a boss because that was more or less a movement where you got
fired right on the spot for talking like that to him. So that's why a lot of those
workers feared in speaking outward because they would lose the job, which because
of the necessity of the home meant they had to maintain their peace. For example,
a young girl goes home and says to her father that the boss has roaming hands and
she doesn't like it. So the father would say to her, "Well, overlook that as long as he
doesn't touch you." He's talking like—he's a father—but he's talking because he
knows that if he tells her to quit or goes there and beat him up she would lose the
job. But what kind of conditions was that woman working under? And why should

she have to accept that kind of condition? See, but that was more or less an accepted thing. So you had people who had to live under those conditions—not because they wanted to—but because the necessity at home. So now, as the movement is getting bigger and bigger and the stool pigeons are going back and talking to the boss, it's not twenty, now it's forty. Well [defiant voice] now they find out we're at a meeting at Waterside Park. Naturally, they were business people in the city of New Haven and a lot of them had friends that found out what they could do to stop this movement. And they would call upon the City of New Haven officials, the mayor. See, the town and cities in those days were not unionized—unionization came because of President Roosevelt advocating it. But prior to that—whew!—you mentioned unionization anywhere you worked, you got fired immediately. And now to get a job someplace else, you were blackballed because you were a troublemaker. Like if I were a troublemaker at A. C. Gilbert and I wanted to go to New Haven Clock Company, they would call up each other and say, "Hey, no, don't hire him, that's why we got rid of him." So if I went to New Haven Clock Company looking for a job: not wanted. They wouldn't hire you. So you see what happened? Your lifestyle, making a living, was at the hands of those people. As far as I'm concerned they were corrupted, dishonest, and slave employers. If you told them that, [chuckling] right then and there, you got fired. Well now getting back to Waterside Park. Well the Chambers of Commerce in New Haven were members of it, they said to the leaders "What will we do to stop this movement? You know what happens, we unionize our factory, there's the open door for other factories in the community." So the powers to be in the Chamber of Commerce would do everything to stop that movement. In the work area condition [issues], it was the Chamber of Commerce—how to control the people. We didn't realize it that not only those working in shirt factories or dress shops—they were also controlled to a certain degree. The mayor at the time was John W. Murphy, a Democrat, who served a number of years. Now, what did he do? He didn't do it openly because he's still looking for votes. But he would send down maybe four or five police officers to see what was going on down Waterside Park on Saturday morning at ten o'clock. Well, the first thing they would do, they would hear what they were talking about and stop the procedure, "Ho, you have no permit to assemble in the park! Stop what you're doing—out!" And they would break up the sessions. Now these men and women were trying to unionize. They did not know that they had the right to assemble on city property in a just order but because they didn't have that knowledge and there were men and women who grew up to respect authority, they respected those police officers. And they were disbanded. They tried to hold a meeting someplace else, secretly, but they couldn't get the large number because wherever they went it was too small. As a matter of fact, some factories in this city, when they started unionizing, they hired Pinkerton Guards because they were known as union busters in the East. So they bring them down to break up these assemblies of men and women trying to unionize. It would get physical, like you would be talking to one of those guys and they would rough them up—they didn't talk impolite because they had clubs and they'd break it up [menacing voice], "All right, move, move, move," and maybe hit you with a club. Well naturally, you're a young fella, you feel, who is this guy hitting me? And you turn around and let him have it maybe. It did happen many a times. And what happened to you? You were subject to arrest. See, in other words, it was all manufactured what they had to do to you and I [for] trying to unionize. You have to remember our parents taught us upon their knees, you and I have to abide and respect every person you come into contact with, particularly your school teacher, your police officer, your clergy people, and your elderly people—that was the training upon the knees of your mother. They were religious, peace-loving people. So, therefore, you were trained—ingrained—you were educated to respect, regardless of what nationality you were. So along comes these ruthless characters.

❝My Glory Day❞

Nick Aiello spoke at the union office on Chapel Street on January 27, 1999.

I got interested because I remember the two organizers were Italian. Before them came August Belanca and Mamie Santore. They came from New York. They brought in these two clothing workers, one named Aldo Cursi, the other one named John Lauria. Cursi was the manager; John Lauria was the business agent. We had our own local, local 125. And the first time I remember, I think I was about nine years old, in 1933. He came to my house to talk to my father and mother to convince my sisters that they should belong to the union. They were able to convince them that this was the way to go. You see, my mother was born in Sorrento, Italy, my father was born here. They convinced my father but she was unconvinced. What my sisters did, they used to find excuses to go on the picket line or to go to meetings. So I got interested one morning when I heard this fella telling my sisters, "This is a union, we're going to get you raises, you'll have security, you'll have seniority, we'll get rid of this harassment, get rid of the sweatshop conditions." Anyway, he made the story convincing that my sisters went to the meeting and they used to meet at the Fraternal Hall on Orange Street. So as he's organizing then they got together and the shop where my sister [Jenny Aiello Alfano] worked decided that enough was enough. They had a walk out at Lesnow. Lesnow was the first shop they hit. And he was the worst. Then there was Brewsters, Fairfield Manufacture, D & I, there was Planet, there was Creighton—there were twenty-two shirt shops in the Connecticut area, used to employ 2,500 people statewide. And they were able to close down all shirt shops in the city. And I listened and watched and my sisters used me as an excuse to go on the picket line to do their time. Until my aunt one day came and saw me sitting on the doorstep and wanted to know what I was doing and she went and tells my father. And of course he raised some hell but that didn't stop my sisters from doing union work. And then they got a contract and then the so-called conditions improved and that made me interested in that. Lesnow moved out and went to East Hampton. So my sisters used to take me to the union meetings when I was fifteen years old. You went to a party; you went to conferences. I would have never seen the World's Fair in 1939 if it wasn't

NICK AIELLO

Protesting foreign imports, 1970

Greater New Haven Labor History Association

for the union that had social activities. In those days the unions not only took care of hourly wages and working conditions, they also had social activities. After the meetings they had bowling clubs; they had sewing clubs; they took us on picnics. I went to the World's Fair from New Haven by train to the Richard Peck in Bridge-port to the World's Fair. They used to have family picnics at Lake Compounce; they had togetherness. We used to have a bowling club, which I used to take care of when I worked in the shirt factories. We used to pay a quarter a week and then I used to make the schedule out. Then at the end of the year we take the money and

UNION-SPONSORED SUMMER PICNIC

Sunbeam Dress Company at Boystown, Milford, Connecticut, 1942

Greater New Haven Labor History Association

go to New York for a weekend. And the manager and the business agent and the girls would go and stay at the hotel Piccalilli, they knew the management, we used to watch the stage show, we use to go a night club, we used to a ball game or go to a track. We used to spend a weekend. But in those days you had to go ask your mother and father to be able to go and amazingly they let them go. But they were chaperoned.

   I went to work as a bundle boy in Uchitele's on Brewery Street. They made army jackets. A wealthy thirty-five-year-old manufacturer went into making army jackets so he could stay out of the army. The pants were made some place else but we made the jackets. I used to go to high school and I used to go in the morning—I was a junior—I would walk to the factory on Tower Parkway, punch in, and work till four, five o'clock as bundle boy carrying the bundles, fixing the sewing machines, fixing the straps around them. I learned how to put the work together, where it went and I used to be able to stack the work and by the time I got in I knew which girl was going to need a bundle. Or they'd call you. Or they'd call you and you have to fix their belts. I came back from the Navy in September, 1946. I couldn't go to college because the semesters were already filled under the G.I. Bill so I decided to go to work for a year. And I went to work in Elm City Shirt as a spreader. You lay material for the cutters to cut. They make the pattern; the marker makes the pattern. Then the spreader spreads the material, maybe five, six inches high. Then he put the marker on and the cutter would cut the parts of the shirt. And so from a spreader I went under the G.I. Bill and I learned how to become a cutter. But I was active in the union. I got active because I was on the executive board; I was the chairperson of the plant with a committee. I worked for nine years and in 1958 I got a call if I wanted to be an organizer. And I talked with my family, I talked it over with people and I took it on a temporary basis for six months and I would keep doing it for forty years. An organizer would travel and you live out of a suitcase seven days a week. You would go to New Hampshire, Maine, Vermont, you would go wherever they sent you. You'd be assigned to a factory, check the factory, try to get names and addresses through the city directory and then you get the names and after five o'clock—we waited till six—you would go up and knock on the door and say, "I'm so and so—I understand you work in this factory. I represent the union." Most times you would get the door slammed in your face. But you did find that they were receptive and you go in and explain your program, you explain what you want to do, how you want to do it, the law protects them to join a union. They sign a pledge card, they intend to join the union. Under the labor rules when you get at least fifty percent you could petition for an election but we used to try to get sixty and seventy. Then you try to negotiate for a union. They say, "No," you file a petition and you have an election. And so you follow that up. And if you finish one you go to another shop. I did that from 1954 to 1962. The places that were toughest to get were where the employer was hostile. Where you go into a town, the police follow you. You stay at a motel. Sometimes you couldn't get a room; sometimes they wouldn't give a room. Two days you're in town, you get a call or you get a knock on the door saying, "What's your position?" You'd have to go in the suburbs to get a room because they wouldn't give you a room in the town you were going in. And they were tough. They were not cooperative. The toughest place was in Ware, Massachusetts, a place called Ware Knitters. Guy had a plant in Ware, he had a place across in Canada and he had another one in Massachusetts. Very hostile. The police department had two officers that used to work part time in the factory. And you would get a call from—nothing threatening—but they would make you know you're not wanted. And I did that for nine years. Then the business agent that was here got sick. So I came in 1962 to help him out. Two years later he couldn't talk so they assigned me here with the approval of the board and the membership, which I came out of and I became the business agent. And then I became the manager. And from the manager I became an international representative; we merged, we made the New England Joint Board. And I've been doing it ever since. And let me put it this way: you know a doctor treats you when you're sick, a lawyer treats you when you're in trouble. We in the labor movement made sure you had good health care, a fair shake for their money, we made sure you get good legal advice and I made sure they earned money that they can pay whatever it is. We help you twenty-four hours a day. We socialize. We help you with your children; we helped you with your family. It was an outlet for people who didn't have anything to be united in one cause. The labor movement does more for people than any manufacturer does, than any government does. We do more for the people. Now I'm not saying that we're all the best—everybody has their bad apples—but most of the labor movement and the unions are honest and decent people and were committed to their neighbors and the people. Some got involved in politics—let's face it. We knew under the socialistic rule and the labor movement rule, if you couldn't do it, you do it by the ballot box. And the Amalgamated ILGWU were one of the very few unions that were out there pushing politically. Sidney Hillman—one of the best labor leaders in this country—was with the Roosevelt cabinet during the war years and it was the labor movement that made the thing work and did what we had to do in order to keep a democratic country and people getting fair wages. The equality—getting up there on the ladder. If you look today at most of our elderly, they made it from their bootstraps and sent kids to college through the union and through the wages that we got for them. We got scholarships, we got all kinds of health benefits, unemployment—the labor movement. It wasn't just with the union people—it was for everybody. When we got unemployment, it wasn't just for union people, it was for everybody. When we got workmen's compensation, it wasn't just for union people, it was for everybody. When we got health care, it wasn't just for the union people, we got it for other people. So we got it even for people who didn't belong in the union because—the minimum wage—union scales are not minimum wage anymore. But the minimum wage helps the other people get more money. And the more they get, the more we make in the experienced world. So we were a vital effort, a vital cog in this democracy in getting a better world, a better people. And I'm still doing that. I call it a labor of love. There's no organization that does more for people than organized labor—that's my feeling.

Another gimmick. They had child daycare centers. The schools were in the neighborhood. And the school used to start at 8:30 so the married women used to come in at 8:30 after they dropped the kids off to school. The kids got out at three o'clock. They worked until five. So what the employer did, he took the lunch room, brought in a couple of nurses and the kids, when the kids used to get out of school they used to go upstairs to the factory and sit in this room or go down to Sargent Park [Waterside Park] and play in the park so the mother wouldn't have to go home early. And so the kids were in that environment. I've seen pictures of the children in Brewster's—it was child daycare. And we had one employee told me that, "You know, we took the kids off the street, we gave them milk." But they didn't know that the kid used to go to the factory and help the mother take off the threads. They were home workers. In the tie company, Siegman Tie used to have home workers. And the women couldn't see. They call it a slipstitch, with a needle they used to stitch the inside. They fuse it now but that used to get stitched, they called that slipstitching. And you do hundreds. I went to visit a woman one time and she had all these needles all over the house. All these needles on the arm of the chair. She used to thread them at home, take them into the plant. As one finished she would take another one out so she wouldn't have to waste time to thread it in the plant because she was on a quota and had to make so many ties a day to make the minimum wage. See, even if you got the minimum wage, they had a price on the article. And if you didn't earn whatever the piece rate was—the minimum wage—that meant you were at a deficit. You had make up your pay, to maybe a dollar and quarter or two fifty, whatever the minimum wage was. So you had to make the minimum wage or if you wanted more you had make more than the minimum wage, the more ties you stitched, the more money you made. So what you call that? You had to work speed up. So in order to help herself she used to bring the needles home, stitch them and then bring them into the plant. Girls used to have repairs. They would take the repairs home, repair them so they wouldn't have to waste the time in the plant. All these conditions. You had a quota to meet. You had to produce. If you didn't produce you didn't get anywhere. Poor lighting. Oil-soaked floors. You opened the window [for air]. You had the fan. And the trouble, who didn't want the fan, who wanted the fan, who wanted the window open, who didn't want the window open. There was never air conditioning. That came later. But very few plants had air conditioning. Heat? And especially the pressers, it used to be eighty, ninety degrees in the plant—they used to sweat those pressers. And you want to go home, eh, the boss would say, "You want to go home, go ahead." But nobody else did—if you didn't go home they didn't go home because you felt if you went home the other girl would do the work and she stays in and you're home? And you lose out. They would very seldom shut the plant because the employer would say, "Well if it's too hot for you go home." Cold in the winter. To heat those big plants. You know they were all old factory buildings. All the along Chapel Street you see these tall, big, red buildings. They used to house shirt shops at one time.

My biggest thrill is when I came back to service this area and sat across with the same employers who had my sisters—"Oh I had your sister." I said, "Yeah, you had my sister and I know what you did to my sister." They worked hard! They worked them to the bone! Cut their pay, shortened their pay. One employer used to pay them cash. And when the people used to go home they used to find fifty cents short in their pay. The boss would say, "I don't know, you took the pay home—I didn't open it." And it took a while before somebody stood out there when they got their pay and said, "Let's see my pay." They found out the guy was shorting them a half a buck, a quarter. They said, "Why?" And he'd say, "I was saving it for a Christmas club." Another employer was paying a girl by the pound to trim shirts. You know how many strings you got to have for a pound in the shirts? He paid her four change for forty hours a week; he was paying by the pound he said. Or the employer who the girls didn't count. Instead of twelve dozen, he would put thirteen but mark twelve. They never counted. And he would get a dozen for free. These are the things they did. Favoritism. Favoritism by the one who would cooperate over the ones who wouldn't cooperate physically, sexually. It happened. They had girl-friends, the ones who they catered to.

Sitting across from the same employers. My glory day. And I had employers who used to say, "Why don't you come in at lunch hour?" I'd say, "Look, I got to visit plants. I can't be in everybody's shop at lunch hour. But, however, if you want me to come in at lunch hour, I'll come." I go at lunch hour, nice. Sit at the lunch table. Before you know it the guy says, "Oh, I didn't know I had to get paid four hours if the boss sent me home." They violated the agreement every day. "Oh you mean, well, he made me come in on Saturday to make up the day I stayed home but he didn't pay me overtime." I said, We have overtime on Saturdays regardless of the hours you put in. But they never paid the employee, saying, "Oh I make him make up the time," and tried to pay them straight time. These are things they were doing with a union there! Just think if . . . then the guy said to me, "Don't come lunch hour no more." Because after I got through with the girls, "Hey did you know we didn't get paid time and a half?" I'd say, "Do you know that you didn't have to make up the time he had to pay you on Saturday? Holiday pay—you worked the day before, the day after, stuff like that"—"He didn't pay the holiday, I didn't come to work." I'd say, Why? They'd say, "I was sick." I would tell them, He's got to pay you because that was the union agreement. Girl was to come in, he'd tell her to come in eight or nine o'clock. And make her wait. Then she'd go to work and lose the time. The girls would never complain because they felt they didn't want to make waves, they felt that was the norm to do. Because you know we had a contract, we had an agreement and we explained the agreement to these young la-dies. We had what we called an industry-wide agreement—one agreement covered all the shops, same holidays, same rates of pay, same hours. Piece rates may be dif-ferent on different operations—one employer might pay a little more piece rate than somebody else depending on the work you do—but the normal holidays, all the fringes were the same. Two weeks vacation with pay, holidays whatever it was, it was the same. But a lot of them didn't know, and when you told them that—you had to explain to them—your convenience and the boss's convenience. If you worked—you're on a forty hour week—and you go home and you're laid off or you don't work. That's not your fault. So you get hours. But if you tell the boss you want to work nine to three, that's your convenience so he pays you nine to three, when you get a holiday it's based on nine to three, you get a vacation pay, it's based on nine to three. But if he sent you home you're allowed so many hours. You figure the layoff time added onto the vacation hours, you're entitled to two, three weeks. They knew but they didn't know about convenience versus the boss's convenience. They fig-ured, what the hell, they got laid off. But we made sure that they got time. The va-cation rule would give them so much time for layoff and sickness so you get credit for the time. And that would come up to the 1,800 hours you needed for the two weeks vacation. You had to administer that contract—you had to police that contract. Of course not all the employee's complaints were legitimate. Our indus-try was you negotiated through your contract but you had to negotiate it every day by . . . I mean the rules, they break the rules. If they get away with it fine, nobody complains. And I would never look. They'd have to give me a grievance; they'd have to give me a complaint. Sometimes they would talk to me and they would explain. I'd say, "Are you complaining, is this a conversation or . . .?" They'd say, "Oh, no." I'd say, "Well then if you're going to complain then have a grievance." And my job was to go around and when the employer and the employee—the shop chairperson couldn't agree—I would have to make the decision. And if the decision was not applicable, then we had arbitration. We were the only union that had an arbitration clause. If you got into a dispute and you couldn't resolve it, you go to arbitration automatically. And the arbitrator's decision was automatic. The cost was shared by us and the employer on a fifty-fifty basis. Now there's dismissals. I've been to arbitration cases, labor board cases—you're constantly helping them. So that doesn't make you a nice guy with the employer although you got some employers who cooperated and agreed were decent employers. Some were decent. Some were hardnosed.

"He Was Happy to Pay"

Alphonse Di Benedetto spoke at the dinner table at the home of Kim and Mike Rogers on April 14, 2000.

In order to compete before Roosevelt got elected and the NRA came into being and the unions, he had to pay his employees the same as everybody else. And he was not happy about that. He realized it wasn't enough, it was sweatshop conditions, but he had no choice. This is what people didn't understand. They'd accuse a man like my father of operating a sweatshop. But he had no choice. I could remember his making a dozen shirts for six dollars; that's fifty cents a shirt. How the hell can he pay an employee a living wage with that kind of money? So now Roosevelt gets elected and even though my father was Republican the NRA comes into being and the unions and so forth. And now he got to pay minimum wages, got to pay according to the union standards. So one day I was talking to my father about it, I said, "What do you think about that? Now you got to pay all this money." He said, "Oh, I'm happy because now that I have to pay that kind of money my competitors have to pay that kind of money too." So he was very happy that now he could treat his employees a lot better. But as time went on, the unions stopped him from doing things for the employees like taking them on trips. They didn't want the employees to think he was a nice guy. The unions don't want the employees to feel good about their bosses because they're on the other side. They always have to challenge the bosses. I can remember one day, there was some problem and we had to go to the union office. I was now a young lawyer, just out of law school. I thought this was going to be a big deal, I was really going to impress my father. And the issue came up, we were discussing it, and finally I got angry and I said to my father, "Give me your keys to the shop." I said, "Here." I threw the keys on the table, I said, "Here, that's what you guys want? Then you operate the business, you take over the business." So this old-time union leader, his name was Mister Cursi, a nice guy, he said, "Young man, don't worry, when the time comes for us to take over, we'll take over." One day Mister Cursi's associate came into my father's office at the shirt factory. He said to my father, "Look, some of the girls upstairs have got a beef, they've got a complaint. Now I got to go up there and show them I'm on their side so whatever I say, just ignore it [laughing]." And he goes upstairs blasting my father and so forth and so on. Made the girls feel good. He liked my father.

"So What's Two Cents?"

Clorinda "Schoolgirl Mongillo" Ruocco spoke in the living room of her Fair
Haven home on August 18, 1998.

I wanted to go to college. Forget about it. I wanted to be a physical education teacher, that's what I really wanted to do, but I couldn't because I had to go to work to help out, feed the family. There were nine of us then at the time and I went to work and I was a presser in the Ideal shirt factory from 1936 to 1942. The cleaners used to clean the shirts; cut the strings off the shirts and everything and then we used to get them. We had an iron with a long hose and then we had a spray bottle like a pint jar with starch in it. You held it in your hand and you press. But what we had to do first, when we got the shirts, we had to press the sleeves and press the back of the shirt. Then we lay it flat on the table and pin it. And then we had a ring with different sizes, fourteen shirt, fourteen and a half you put the ring in, fifteen, fifteen and a half, sixteen, and then seventeen. So, if I'm pressing the shirt size fifteen, I put the fifteen ring in it, lay the shirt flat, spray it, press it, turn it around, put a piece of tissue in the back of the shirt with a cardboard, slipped into the collar. And then you fold it, you pin it, pin it all up, and then you put aside and then you get paid for so much a dozen. This was 1930s. I don't think bread was even five cents. It was a hard job, eight hours a day, sometimes on Saturday. And after working hard you had to go home and help in the house a little, right? It was tough, tough. I enjoyed working you know because I love people and I was friendly with everybody and we used to have some good times together. While I was working as a presser—we had two bosses, they were brother-in-laws, Sal DiBenedetto and Philip Planeta. Sal DiBenedetto, he was kind of rough. Well anyway, we had a meeting; they had a union at the time. The union was in there when I went to work and when we used to go to meetings; they elected me chairlady of the union. So, in other words, I was able to talk to the bosses, you know, if you wanted a raise if things weren't going right—straighten them out and everything. We had a hard time with them but call in the head guy to come in and before you know it we used to get our way because at that time they called them the sweatshops. And that's what it was, sweatshops. You really had to work hard for your money. So I was the chairlady all the time I worked there. I remember one incident there when we were pressing these shirts. They were kind of difficult because not only did we press them, we used to fold them, get them ready and then the packers would pack them in the boxes. We used to have to pin them together and everything. So we asked for two cents for each dozen, you get so much a dozen, I don't remember the amount we were getting, but we wanted two cents more a dozen. And we had a tough time. And he [the boss] said, "No way," this and that and everything. I said, "Well, then, you don't want to, forget about it, we'll go out [on strike]." Blah, blah, blah, back, blah, blah, back and forth, back and forth, and then finally he gave in. He gave in because they were making enough money—if they weren't making money they wouldn't give in, right? They're making money. I mean if it wasn't for the people that worked in the shirt factory, he wouldn't be making anything. So, what's two cents? So we got it.

❝The Showdown at Lesnow❞

Mary Marino spoke in the living room of her Wooster Street home with her sisters, Rose and Anna, on August 24, 1999.

I was 14 but I didn't look it; I had braids. My aunt made me a tam [two sisters laughing]. She gave me her daughter's coat to wear. I went out for a job. I knocked and I went in the office. Now we called this guy, the head one, "'o cane" [the dog] we used to call him because he was stern. So when we used to see him, we used to say [excitedly], "'o cane! 'o cane! Mo venne 'o cane!" The dog! The dog! Here comes the dog! When the boss at Lesnow Brothers shirt factory saw me he said to me, "What do you want little girl?" I said, [soft, innocent voice] "I'm not a little girl. I came here to ask you for a job." All braids. He said, "Go back to school, huh?" I said, "No, I'm of age." He said to me, "Do you know anybody in here?" "Yes," I said, "I do." He said, "What's her name?" "Mamie Esposito." She came out and said, "She's old enough to go to work." And I got a job like that. I asked for that job. And I got all my sisters jobs too. It was a big place and I'll tell you something— I preferred working for a Jewish concern better than the Italians, all right? My first pay was seven dollars; I worked all day Saturday too and late at night. My mother said, "See, bella'e mamma, this helps me, mi aiuta a me, i teng' due mortgage!" See, my beautiful, this helps me because I have two mortgages to pay. I didn't know about the mortgages. Mortgages? Then there was a strike. I no sooner get in there . . . one morning I went to work. What the hell is going on here? The whole street was full of people. They were hitting one another—hey, I'm not going in there. They were hitting one another because Lesnow didn't want us to join the union. Then the cops came. I don't remember who the people were but they were fighting with one another. I ran away; I got scared. They were trying to keep the people from going into the shop. So then they called two or three of the workers—Anna Giuliana—in the office. Mr. Lesnow said, "We don't want to join the union but . . ." I guess they threatened him or something, I don't know. And so we joined the union. And then they told us, "All right, join." They had no choice but to join the union. And that's when everybody went back to work. That was 1933.

"When the Unions Came In"

Antonette Coppola spoke in a meeting room in her Branford nursing home with her daughter Maryanne and son-in-law Anthony Santacroce on May 7, 2000.

Then the union got in. And we had a go piecework. And the first pay I made nine dollars. And I brought them [my children] down to Grand Avenue, to The Little Folks store, I bought a white fur coat, shoes, stockings and my boy, I bought him knickers and a coat and a kelly. And the pink suit, I'll never forget it, the leggings, the hat, everything. And I had money left over. They used to get tickets for how many dresses they made. Then they used to have to give it to the boss and from then he used to tell them how much. They used to make a three-piece outfit, the dress, the pants, and a jacket. A dollar and fifty cents. I remember all these things because she [mother] used to have a little book with all her tickets used to come in, that's how they got their money.

"Turn Off the Power"

Annette Ruocco spoke at the kitchen table of her Annex home on November 17, 1998.

I got into the Par-Ex shirt factory. That guy used to make me go all the day, until finally he decided to hire me and he put me on cuff setting, you put the cuffs. There was no air conditioning; it would be very hot in the summertime. As a matter of fact, when we had the hurricane of 1938, we worked until it was time to go home. No one ever warned us, "This is a hurricane, close the power, go home." No, we got out and found that the streets were flooded, some of the trees were down. The shops they didn't turn off the power. You worked—regardless of what the weather was. And when they came to inspect our work, you see them coming down the row from the beginning where all machines were connected in a long table, the length of the room and each one had bins on either side and they had the machines. Either the work was brought to you or you'd go get it and you'd have a whole bundle and it was piecework, so much a dozen. Sometimes there was no work, you'd be walking around and spend all day hardly earning any money. Until one day one girl took over and she said, "Today we're going turn off the power and we're going to have a meeting." And that's when the union came in. That was Carol Paollilo because her brother was an alderman and she got involved with the unions. So she was the one to start the unions. And at a certain time she got up, she went to the power box, turned off all the machines and we went into her backyard to have our meeting. That was the first union meeting we had. And after that they talked and from there they went to a convention hall. She met the union men and so she was in charge of starting this thing, starting the union. She talked in her yard on Collis Street, the few that were able to get there, and that's how she started the factory to get into the union. Some of the girls were older than me; I went in, and I was real young so I followed them. But the older ones who had worked in the shirt factory for a longer period of time than I did, they were for it. They were maybe seventeen, eighteen and they were older and they wanted a union. The bosses didn't want that. Hey, those factories were getting away with murder. Inslers was giving you fifteen cents an hour to turn cuffs and collars and have it ready for whoever set the collar. Then somebody from the Board of Education came to my house to investigate that they were paying so little and hiring—they wanted to know that I was fourteen. I might have been less than fourteen and they would hire you to turn collars. That's why they started the unions because these shirt facto-ries—they were sweatshops. You didn't earn any money at all. And then you had some of the foreladies that pushed hiring these kids. Now it's against the law to work like that. And that's how our union started.

"A Chairlady at Standard Dress Company"

Renee Vanacore spoke on the back porch of her North Haven home on No-vember 20, 1999.

I used to love dress design; I have closet full of clothes. I said, "Gee I'd love to be a dress designer." The guy said, "There's nothing here, you got to go to New York." I said, "Yeah, I know it. I can't go, how am I going to go?" So I told my mother that. My mother said, [sassy voice] "No, all the bums go to New York." That was it. I went home, I told the guy; he was a dentist. When I worked in the dress shop they wanted me to become a chairlady of the Ladies Garment Workers Union. All the women elected me. I went to New York because I was the chairlady and they were fighting because my boss [Izzy] used to make them work overtime and not pay them. The girls said, "Gee we're working an hour, two hours overtime." And I used to say to the boss, "You let them work but you got to pay for them because I'm not going to let you get away with it." He said [cocky voice] "Nah, nah." So we went to New York. My boss took me; he drove us down to New York. Years ago there was no highway so we went through the back [roads]. Well anyway, I got up there and I had to say who was right and who was wrong. He thought by him bringing me that I would stick up for him. Ont-ah! I said, they're right and you're wrong. You know what the [union] boss said down there? He said, "You want to come and work down here Mrs. Grigione?" I said, "Not New York—how am I going to get back and forth?" They wanted me to work there. The big [union] boss came down and he took me to lunch. They all liked me. In fact they used to say to me, "Jesus Renee, why don't you go to New York and work—you'd make a helluva . . . because you're truthful." I said, Well, that's the way I am. I don't care. I used to say to Izzy, "You do me a favor. You work these girls overtime you have to pay them. I don't care; other-wise I'll report you." He said, "All right, I'll pay them." Because he didn't want to pay. My boss liked me. Because I wasn't a two-faced hypocrite. Because he didn't want to pay the girls. Because he had a lot of work all of a sudden and he needed the girls. I said, "How could you let the girls work without paying them? You got to pay them." You see what it is? If you're wrong, you're wrong—I don't care who you are. I said to my boss, because he used to give me a dress every Christmas for a gift. Nobody ever got anything; I was the only one. So I said to my boss, "Don't give me anything, don't expect any favors from me because if you're wrong, you're going to get wrong—I'm going to report you." He said, "Oh, don't do that—I'll be fair."

66 THE UNION IN SARGENT'S 99

John "Johnny Blake" Calamo spoke at the table of his elderly complex apartment on December 29, 1998.

In 1940, when the union came in everything changed for the better. You could make more money. Before the union, some of the supervisors used to cater to some of these workers, and those guys would get to work on Saturday. They used to bring the guy stuff—wine or this or that. I never did. I didn't bring nothing. I was working with a guy and he told the supervisor something about me to him. I was getting all tough jobs—my fingers used to bleed. I went up to the supervisor and I said, "Somebody has been telling you something about me?" He didn't want to admit it. I said, "I get jobs, my fingers bleed. I ate with you, I drank with you, and I've been in your house—you treat me good and I should talk about you?" So he found out after—that was before union got in—he was out, because the people in the department didn't want him. He was catering to the guys that were bringing him things. In 1940, we all signed up for the union because things weren't being done right, you understand? You get all the good jobs: I get all the bad ones. Why? Hey, I got to make a day's pay too, you know. When I was on the floor—the supervisor—and I used to hand the fellas the work to do on polishing. There was about five or six boxes of work—it was a good job. One guy wanted the whole thing. I said, "You take one box, that's all—one, and don't take any more. The other fellas got to get a box too." That was a beautiful job, it was about three, four dollars a hundred, a steal. But I gave them all one. And they were black fellas. Today if I see any one of those black fellas—they called me—because they knew that I treated them all right. One thing I always did when I was supervisor. I used to ask them if they made a day's pay polishing. If they were short, how many? So, okay, put them in, tomorrow . . . I never cared. At least they made a day's pay because I knew that they were bound to have some trouble with some of the parts. But they respected me. When they retired they got four, five times more than I did.

And we had stewards in the department and they used to fight for you. Oh yeah, it was good. When we signed the card for the union, I never let the guy I worked with know about it because he would have went to the supervisor, says, "Hey, he signed for the unions." Didn't tell them nothing—no way. They [management] didn't give them no hard time. After we signed, they went into the factory and said, "Look, the people signed for the union. What do youse wan a do?" Only at negotiating times, but at that time they never fought much either. We used to get ten cents an hour more. What the people didn't understand sometimes was this: if the company made money they would give you the raise but if they didn't make money they couldn't give you the raise. And you get some instigators—whether they made it or not—they wanted a raise and they used to instigate some of the other people. We went out on strike twice. That's why: the instigation. A lot of the people—they were in the union—but if they had to say something or get the steward—they wouldn't. They'd keep quiet. Not me. When I was steward, the other people—I told them. The guy had a grievance. Well I says, "Come on in to the foreman, I talk." He said, "No, no, no, you go." I said, "I go? I haven't got the grievance, you have." So he didn't do nothing, see? I had a foreman—he was good. I went in there for a raise on the price. He used to ask me [laughing] if it should be. But I used to give him a fair price. He never said a word. He said, "Okay," he used to change it on the card. It was good with the union.

"THEY WERE SLAVE SHOPS"

Josie DeBenedet spoke at the kitchen table in her North Haven home on June 6, 1999.

They were slave shops at that time [in the late 1920s]. No union, nothing. Because when I was working in the dress shop, I went to work at fourteen years old. And there was no unions. We used to go in at 7:30 in the morning and work all day until seven, eight o'clock at night. And you couldn't say anything, if the boss didn't like you, he'd tell you to get out and you couldn't do anything. See, after 1933, we started with the union. The dress shops were one of the first [to organize]—the Ladies Garment Workers—I got married in October and when I came home from my honeymoon my mother said we had to go and picket. My mother and I worked in the shop where I was. We had to go to the Fraternity Hall on Elm Street where Harold's is today, right next door was an old brick building. And over there we used to have the meetings organizing the union. And then we had to picket another day on Orange Avenue in West Haven. There was a big shop there—they used to make velvet and thread—we had to picket up and down all day, picket, to make them join the union. At that time we didn't have strikes. Everybody, if they wanted to work, we had to join the union and we did. We had a chairlady; every shop had their own chairlady that would go to New York once a week, once every other week, to report.

"THEY WERE HITTING THEM"

Antonette Sicignano spoke at the kitchen table of her Wooster Street home on August 5, 1999.

We were working and over on Hamilton Street [Wooster Square], there was Saint Andrew's Hall. They said we had to get out, we had to walk on the picket

ANTONETTE SICIGNANO
In her backyard on
Warren Street, 2000

A. Riccio

line. There was Nick Aiello, there was another one, his name was John Lauria and we had to do the picket line. Then when we used to see that it was bad weather or we used to see that they used to start hitting us, we used to go to the hall. They hit the ones that were the head ones, the policemen. They used to hit all the union people they didn't want them to be in . . . Oh yeah, the policemen came. And we used to walk up and down, and if you said a word, boy, they come and get you out of line and they hit you with clubs. Yeah, clubs! They must have called the policeman and the policeman used to come in. I'll never forget a girl-friend used to live on Franklin and Collis Street and across the street was the shop. So I didn't go, I went up to that girl's house on the third floor. And I'd be looking out the window, these cops were just hitting them and laying them down. And me crying. I was crying because they were hitting them. They looked like—doong-doong—when they used to shoot them and they used to fall—that's what it reminded me of. And they were all out the street there and they used to get up. They were hurt. A lot of them were hurt, oh yeah. They used to go more after the men—even women, too. Then they said to us, "On the corner, there's a hall. We're going in there." They used to give us coffee. Nick Aiello's sister Jennie, they tore off her coat. They used to get hit. A lot of them got hit. I remember one girl, I think she was bleeding, they tore all her coat. Oh, yeah, it was in the wintertime and it was cold. John Lauria, I think they cracked his head once. So we used to run into that society club hall on the corner of Hamilton and Collis and there was another one on Franklin Street, Saint Trofemina or Saint Andrew—we used to go to either one. And they used to bring hot coffee in there, sandwiches. They used to make us get warm, then we had to go out again to picket again. We used to have our meetings, we'd stay there and then sometimes they used to change. Some used to go march, used to go up and down the sidewalk and then they used to say; "Now it's your turn, go out." I hated that, oh, I hated it. I used to go more near the buildings so anybody hard they were hitting, not near the street, so I wouldn't get hit. We were in a line maybe four or five of us; I was small anyway. I used to hide. I wouldn't answer them anyway, no. When we would see we were going toward the hall we used to walk a little faster. It was cold; it was in the wintertime. There used to be a lot of fights out that street. When I used to go home, I used to tell them [my parents]. They didn't know what was going on but I used to tell her when I got home at night. They used to say, "What did you do today?" I used to say this here, I walked only a little bit but I was afraid. You didn't even have a nickel to take a bus, you used to run all the way over the bridge and it was cold going over that Chapel Street bridge. You think they'd say to stay home? Aayye, you gotta go to work tomorrow! They'd make sure, they needed the money. They needed it bad. We didn't stay too long on strike [1933], maybe a month I think. And when we went back [to work] that the union was in, then they started giving us different prices. And every now and then, you get a little more. That's how it started going up. After that, then the union came in because when I retired they wanted to know what year I was, so they counted my years from 1933. They didn't give you too much, the union. Before, [prior to the union], we were working and whatever price they gave us, we had to take it and you made sure—they used to give it to you by bundles, finish, and put down the name there and how many of them were in that bundle. They used to give you a card. With the unions, you were treated better. You know when we didn't get our price we used to call the union. They used to come up. And the bosses to get . . . they used say, "Hi girls, how you doing." They used to shake hands with us. They would ask, "Any better?" "Yeah, it's better, much better now." And somebody else would say, "Well, they cut me down, I was getting so much and now . . ." And they would want to know why and they'd go into the office and talk to the bosses. Oh yeah, things used to change there. But toward the end, they wouldn't listen to the union no more. No, that's why they all left. A lot of them died, they got old you know, yeah.

"They Went South"

Louise Orefice spoke in the living room of her Annex home on October 31, 1998.

I remember the first day I walked in. I went to Lesnow Brothers about May 20, 1926. I worked three days. My first three days they put me on practicing, teaching me how to operate the machine and then the next day they put on piecework. And for those three days I got a dollar, one buck. And then the next week he put me on a steady job. I was turning cuffs, they weren't paying very much, ten to fifteen cents a dozen. I had to turn twenty-four cuffs to make fifteen cents. I made even less because it was a nonunion shop. Then the union came in; the union was trying to organize the girls to join the union. And we even had a strike. And we lost more time because the boss didn't want the union in the shop. So finally, he had to join. Then after a while he got disgusted with the union because he didn't like what the union used to tell him to do. They had to pay us more and give us better working conditions. We had to work like anything, we had to pull out our own work, we had to tie up the work, that was all piecework. When the machine used to break that was our loss of time. No gain. So they [Lesnow Brothers] had trouble with the union so after a while they didn't stay too long. They closed the shop and they went down south.

"We Tried to Start a Union"

Antonette Salemme spoke in the kitchen of her North Haven home on August 15, 1998.

We tried to put in a union and we almost all got fired. And then all the girls chickened out. Well, somebody started, "Let's make a union, union, union," and we were all kind a encouraging each other. But when the time came that we weren't supposed to go in, they all chickened out because these girls all needed jobs, it was Depression. So we were scared. If we got fired our parents wouldn't accept that. No, I was afraid to go home and tell my mother I got fired. Not meetings or nothing, you know we would talk amongst ourselves like if we were eating lunch and say, "You know, we oughta have a union." People were startin' to talk unions then. I didn't even know what it was but you know you learn as you go along. But then when the time came, the day we were all supposed to stay outside. Somebody said, "Nobody go to work, everybody meet downstairs." When we got there everybody was upstairs. There was a lot of old ladies in that place that used to—we were only kids—and they used to rile this up and then they'd chicken out and they'd go to work. So we used to follow them, you know, never really fully into anything. That blew over like nothing. I left there and after I was married they never had a union, never had a union in that place. We worked about forty hours a week. Ten dollars [a week]. I used to give my mother nine dollars and fifty cents and I used to get fifty cents for an allowance. And out a that fifty cents I used to save up and buy my own stockings, personal stuff. But you know what? My brother Davey, he didn't work and he had bought his girl a cedar chest and he had a pay fifty cents a week. You could buy things [paying weekly]. And he never had the money, so he'd always, "You got a half a buck?" So I'd give it to him so he could pay on his chest. Oh yeah, I used to give it to him. It was my brother. We were very, very close. And I never got a cedar chest. My mother had a go buy me mine.

"The Chairlady Fought for Us"

Rose Savo spoke in the kitchen of her Annex home on July 28, 2000.

It was the 1930s. There was a lot of trouble in those times, you know the bosses didn't like the idea. How many times we walked out. They didn't go along with what the union was demanding. Yeah, many times we walked out. One time the bosses changed, "Come on, come on, come on back to work, come on back to work." But we couldn't because we had a chairlady and she used to tell us what to do or not to do. Vera Colavolpe—she was the chairlady. She had to make sure that things were run the way they were supposed to and the prices. She used to fight on the prices. If they didn't give us enough on a garment she used to fight for more money, yeah.

The Litman brothers—they were from New York. They used to come down once a week to bring the payroll. But this Sam Garfinkel and Mr. Raffa, they used to run the place, you understand? And they used to have to answer to the Litman brothers. They used to debate in the office there, who knows what used to go on. But they used to get—the chairlady used to get what she wanted. She didn't think the price was right, she would get more money for it. You used to get so much on a garment. Sometimes, you know, you didn't make the whole garment, who made the sleeves, who made the body, who made the skirt, you understand? So each part was a different price. So if the chairlady didn't think it was right, they would fight for more money. She was an operator herself. Most of the time she got her price, oh yeah.

14

Northerners and Southerners

In the 1930s, the Italian government exiled the antifascist Carlo Levi to the remote town of Eboli in the poverty-stricken region of Basilicata in southern Italy. In his book, *Christ Stopped at Eboli,* Levi chronicled daily life in the town, adapting the title from a local proverb that described the surrounding territory steeped in archaic peasant culture and pagan folklore, a primitive territory so separated from history that Christ himself could not redeem it. Images of southern Italy as an uncivilized outpost of Europe had a long tradition. In 1806, the French traveler Creuze de Lesser wrote in *Voyage en Italie et en Sicilie,* "Europe ends at Naples and it ends badly enough. Calabria, Sicily and all the rest is African."[22] Generations of southern Italians in the Mezzogiorno who had lived through centuries of political and economic exploitation by foreign rulers reached the breaking point during the occupation of the ruthless Spanish Bourbons in the 1860s. The military success of the Risorgimento, or the Unification, resulted in the removal of the Bourbons from political power but failed to unify Italy. The newly-installed northern-based Piedmont government did nothing but continue the tradition of southern exploitation by imposing disproportionately high taxes on the poor, and levying high tariffs on its industries while promoting industrialization of the north. As a result, the south lost virtually all its manufacturing; corruption of government officials was rampant and bribery by the most affluent exempted them from paying taxes.

Socialist party members did not point to their miscalculations for failing to unite the country but blamed southerners as "congenitally flawed by anarchic individualism which made them unsuited for political organization."[23] In Reggio Emilia, *La Guistizia* reproduced an overtly racist pun made by Deputy Gabelli in the House, referring to the north-south question as "i nordici e sudici," or the northerners and sweaty southerners.[24]

Reconciliation of the historical economic, political, cultural, and social divide that separated the country between north and south could not have occurred in Italy at the turn of the century. Industrialized cities like New Haven provided Italian immigrants—southerners from Campania, Calabria, Puglie, and Sicily,

Marchegiani and Abruzzese from central Italy, and northerners from the Piedmont, Emilia Romagna, Tuscany, and Veneto regions—a new urban arena to interact with their compatriots for the first time. Of the 2.3 million Italians arriving in the United States, 400,000 were northerners who arrived with twice the amount of money as southerners, many were considered skilled workers in building trades and only twelve percent were illiterate.[25] Northern immigrants had the benefit of a sound educational system with adequate funding and more industries; many learned building trades and had worked in large cities in Europe. Many of the first northern arrivals went to California where they bought land and started farms. Southerners, by contrast, had a fifty percent illiteracy rate, poorly funded schools, were less skilled, and lagged behind in the financial resources needed to buy land. In Italy, northern politicians and academics viewed the south as an economic burden, a barbaric civilization whose people were lazy, corrupt, and culturally backward. The same bigotry against southern Italians followed them to America when Massachusetts Senator Henry Cabot Lodge unleashed his racist statements of southerners as an inferior race, in comparison to superior "Teutonic" northerners.

Italy's "Problema del Mezzogiorno," or the southern problem, was transported to New Haven's Italian communities where cultural differences and old suspicions between north and south persisted. New Haven's immigrants brought Italy's diverse cuisines, religious customs, political views, and even mannerisms that varied from region to region and village to village. Language barriers between New Haven's Italians prolonged divisions. Regional dialects familiar to those from the same towns sounded like different languages to those unacquainted with them. Beyond differences in dialects, southerners were sometimes looked upon as too demonstrative in behavior by conservative, understated northerners. Northerners sometimes disparaged southerners as "conigli," or rabbits, for having large families much the same way a northern political leader in Italy had stated: "People are the only commodity the South can produce in abundance."[26] Southerners knew little of northerners other than that they were responsible for collecting taxes for the northern-based Piedmont government. Skilled northerners owned homes and looked down on southerners for accepting poor housing conditions in cold water flats and they belittled unskilled southerners for not having useful trade skills. Social clubs and societies were strictly segregated by region and membership was prohibited to outsiders. The Societá di Mutuo Soccorso Settetrionale accepted non-Italian husbands married to northern women but prohibited southerners. Intermarriage between northerners and southerners was often discouraged.

Historical tensions between north and south continues in Italy. The old "southern question" still sparks heated debate not only in political circles, but in the streets as well. La Lega Nord, or The Northern League, a northern-based political party, preaches the extremist politics of separatism from Italy with the same hate-filled rhetoric of the past, pointing to the less-industrialized south as a major obstacle to the north's economic progress and southerners as an inferior race of people who stand in the way of greater industrial development.

"North and South in New Haven"

Salvatore "Gary" Garibaldi spoke at the Santa Maria Madalena Society on Wooster Street on April 10, 2000.

I know both parties because I lived in the Hill section for a period of time because I was forced to move because of redevelopment. And naturally I met people at the Marchegiano Club down the street. And I know from talking to these people, they always felt that they were better-educated, trade people and they considered themselves a little better than the people from the Wooster Square area. And it's like that everywhere. And we look down on—yesterday—not today, those that came or lived in the south or those who lived in the hills, we called them hillbillies. Well today that's changed. But in that period of time an easterner was considered above intelligent than the guy from the south. And you had that right here too. So the Marchegianis said, "Eh, Amalfitani, Atranese che sanno?" The Amalfitani and Atranese, what do they know? Well you see—rightfully—they were bragging for bragging rights, and even though you and I may not like to hear it because he was downing our loved ones . . . but . . . let's be honest about it; he was right. Because they knew how to read and write, they did a lot of things different, they didn't have to rely on someone . . .

"The Marchegians Adopted Me"

Josie DeBenedet spoke in the kitchen of her North Haven home on June 10, 1999. She spoke with pride about inheriting two different Italian dialects.

I was adopted after my mother died in the Spanish Flu. My oldest brother Louie, he was twelve, so at that time at twelve you were on your own. In those days at twelve you were an adult. He went to work with a fruit peddler. We used to have fruit peddlers come to our house and the fruit peddler liked him and felt sorry and so he told him, "As long as you don't have no place to go you can sleep in the barn with the horse, it'll be warm there and all." So my brother, that's where he stayed, in the barn. My younger brother Andrew, they put him in a home, the orphanage on County Home up on Orange Avenue. And me, the people that adopted me, she happened to go the grocery store on Columbus Avenue and this salesman overheard my mother say she would love a child. "Oh yeah," she said, "I've tried everything but here I am almost forty years old and I can't have any children." He said, "Would you like one? I have a "compare" that his wife died last week and he can't take care of the kids so if you would like one I'll get you one." So she said, "Yeah." So he said, "What do you want, a boy or a girl?" So she said, "Oh, I'd like a girl." This was on a Friday. On a Saturday my father took me to her. Now they lived on West Water Street, across the street from the railroad station and my dad lived way on Hamilton Street. My dad was from Naples and the people that

WOMEN FROM LE MARCHE

1920s

Innocenzi family album

adopted me were from Fano, in Le Marche on the Adriatic coast. So he said, "Do you want a child?" And my mother said, "Yeah, but I never thought anybody would give away children." So he said, "Well, if you want to take her because I'm a busy man." So she took me out in the veranda outside and showed everybody that she had a daughter and even her husband didn't know it. They adopted me. He wanted a hundred dollars for me. And my adopted father said, "When I want to buy meat I'll go in the store, I won't buy it from a human." So my mother was so scared that he was going to take me back. So she had twenty dollars and she gave it to him. So, [laughing] I was sold for twenty dollars. And when I went in I just looked and my dad wasn't there any more. So my foster mother always said to me, "I went like that sigh of relief." She gave my father permission to come and see me. But, she said, "You could come to see her but she is our daughter, we're going to change her name. You cannot have her back once we get the papers done." It was in the Journal Courier for three days, if any of my relatives—my mother had two sisters and two brothers—if any of my relatives wanted me then this woman couldn't have me. But nobody showed up. Nobody wanted me. And they brought me up; I couldn't get better parents. And everybody loved me—all the old folks, they all loved me because I was adopted. To think that nobody wanted me and that someone took me. These kids can tell you—she [my mother] loved them. They all called her "mamma." And for three days I didn't talk. Well you know what? They were Marchegiano; we were Napoletano, right? We don't talk like the Marchegiano; they didn't talk American so I was stuck. I didn't know what they were saying. Because I never even heard of Marchegiano. I was only four years old. That's the way it was. Then one day, my mother said, I went over to her and I pulled her dress and I said to her, "Mamma, i muore e fame," I'm dying of hunger. She said, "Ooh, don't say that." She said, "No, no, no, don't say that." Because maybe that's the way I was used to [saying it]. We didn't have anything to eat. As a matter of fact, I always have a big stomach and I went through different tests and they said it was from malnutrition when I was a baby. And these operations I had they told me that it was the milk that I drank when I was baby was no good; the cows had tuberculosis and that's how they had to remove the glands on me. I was born Neapolitan, I was raised Marchegiano, and I married a Veneziano—I went right through Italy.

"They Didn't Understand Each Other"

Now everybody is mixed up, but before we didn't care for the southerners, the southerners didn't care, they used to have the war over here. The South and the North, they had the [civil] war. Same thing in Italy, they hate the Neapolitans or the Sicilians down there or the Calabrese. You know what it was? There were a lot of Marchegians in the Hill section, on Carlisle Street, Portsea Street, all up Washington Avenue, Columbus Avenue and everybody got along all right. But then you go down Wooster Street—that section was all Napoletano. First of all, they didn't understand them because at that time they didn't have schooling. Before, when they didn't have schooling, so they talked the dialect. So then they didn't understand them, the southern. They didn't understand anybody. The same thing with the people from the south. They didn't understand what the northerners [were saying]. I remember my girlfriend. She used to make fun of my adopted mother because her people were from the south and when she'd come up my house, my mother used to say, "Vimm acchi, vimm acchi." And even now, she's what eighty-eight years old, when we talk she says, "Remember your mother, when she used to see me, 'Teresa, Teresa, vimm acchi.'" And she used to say a lot of [Marchegiano dialect] words because of hanging around with me.

VENEZIA SOCIETY PICNIC, 1942

DeBenedet family album

"Intermarriage"

Ron Mortali spoke at the Marchegiano Club in the Hill on August 3, 2000.

I went out with my intended wife from grammar school, from 1948 to 1957; nine years, all through high school, all through college. She went to Saint Mary's, I went to Notre Dame; she was a year behind me. Senior year in college I decided to tell my grandmother. My father was the oldest of eight and I was the oldest grandson. It meant a lot to my grandmother and it meant a lot to me because she would actually run things by me, family things, and get my opinion on them, which was kind a neat. Always did that, mostly in Italian. I understood it better then because we were using it all the time. So I told my grandmother, "Nonny, Lucille and I," who she knew for nine years and also made pizzelles at Saint Anthony's Carnival with her paternal grandmother, who was an "Alta Italia," northern Italian, her maternal grandmother was a "Bass Italia," southern Italian. So she knew the family very well and she knew my wife very well. Where did you go when you were kids? You went over visiting relatives, you spent Sunday afternoons at somebody's house eating or watching TV. I said, "Nonny, Lucille and I are gonna get married the week after I graduate from college. The very first thing she said to me was, "What church are you gonna get married in?" I said, Sacred Heart, that's my wife's parish. She said, "What's the matter with Saint Anthony's?" I said, "Nonny, it's her parish, you get married in the girl's parish." She said, "It's no good." I thought she was still talking about the church [incredulous voice]. I said, "Well, nonny what's the big deal?" She said, "It's no good because she's a 'Bass Italia,' you're gonna mix your blood." I said, What are you talking about? She says, "It's not right, you have to marry a Marchegiano girl, you're my oldest grandson." I said, "Oh come on, don't be old-fashioned."

Family roots from all the small paesi's, towns, we're talking three hundred to four hundred in a small little community, every family knew everyone. So the same thing happened when they migrated here, they had in back of their minds, Well, I know this family, I know that family. Wouldn't it be nice to have my daughter or my son meet their daughter or son and wouldn't it be wonderful to have these people that we all knew so well back in the old country, same paese [town], salt of the earth, good people, these are the people we would like part of family and extend the lines. You could understand their reasoning because they said, We know their roots, we know their fathers and their mothers, their aunts and their uncles and they're good people. We don't know who this person is that you're marrying, or what their background is, who knows if they are highwaymen or something like that. They tended to stay with the things they knew. They were comfortable in their own environment because they all came from the same region, they were all familiar with the same culture, the same foods, the same societies, and the church and in particular, the language.

"A Question of Sauce"

In those days with lack of communication like we know it today, there was word of mouth of neighborhoods. My sauce is better than your sauce, it boiled down to that kind of thing. "Oh no, no 'Bass Italias,' southern Italians, they use the oregano, you know. Marchis don't use oregano. Totally different sauce, ours is very light, it's Italian, but the ingredients to making the sauce is done differently. We do the thing with the 'en potaccio,' with the wine. It's a way of preparing chicken, the wine is cooked down so the wine is absorbed in the food and it makes a nice tight sauce. They were very adamant about it.

"It Was a Competitive Prejudice"

Bill Zampa spoke at the Marchegiano Club in the Hill section on August 3, 2000.

They all found themselves competing for jobs, status, and everything else. The ones that migrated here—the Amalfitans, the Napoletans, the Marchegians—there was nothing left in Italy for them. This was the place, there was nothing left. They were the people who worked on the farms, tenant farmers who had no property, they had no life. They came here for a better life. The ones that had resources and prestige, they stayed in Italy. So in essence, everyone was competing for those menial jobs. And of course it was means for going up the ladder. It was prejudice but it was a competitive prejudice because everyone was competing for the same jobs.

"It Was Another Language"

Joe Panicali spoke at the Marchegiano Club in the Hill section on August 3, 2000.

Well first of all you got to understand the Italian language had its dialects too. There are very many dialects. The true Italian is Tuscany. But since schooling has come about prior to my parents' situation, there were dialects relative to the area they were in, so when the Marchis talked they talked with a very fast, choppy language whereas my mother-in-law, when she spoke to me at first I found it very difficult to understand. She spoke Italian but it was all [southern] dialect. She used words that I never heard before. She used to call what we call gnocchi, they call them "strangolapeopola," [strangulaprièvete]. Where is the relationship? Now we to say "bacio," kiss, they would say "vaso." There is no relationship but apparently that's a derivative or a slang of that. So when I started to listen my mother-in-law, it wasn't till after a while I started to pick up things from her, and then I'd have to nudge my wife, "What did she say here?" I would understand it after a while but it was almost another language, it was a dialect like the Marchis too.

"They Called Her 'The French Woman'"

Rosemarie Foglia spoke in a conference room at City Hall on June 28, 1999.

When my mother came to New Haven she often tells the story that off the train and it was a sixty-year honeymoon because that was it. She was married in the afternoon and they came to this three-room apartment on the corner of Greene and Hamilton [Wooster Square]. This was a seven-family house and there was a grocery store downstairs. And their anniversary was January 29th so when I conjure up images of January 29th—a cold, miserable day—I mean it just seems so cold and so unlike what we were all accustomed to, you know the warmth of the family. And then my father went to work the following morning and said, "You know there's a grocery store downstairs." And the only thing mother could think of making in the winter was soup. And she went downstairs and she had seen someone walking out with celery. And that was okay because my father had told her the owners of the store were Italian. And my mother went in there and started asking for vegetables in what we call in the fluent Italian, Roman Italian, and no one had any idea what she was talking about. So then she reverted to the Piemontese [dialect], which is very different. They had no clue. And they called her "La Francese," the French woman, even to the day she died she was "La Francese," because of the Piedmontese.

"It Was Like a Double Foreign Language"

Piedmontese is in northern Italy and very close to the French borderline and the dialect sounds very much like the French. We say "pang," bread, the French say "pan." So many words are like the French and when the southern Italians heard my mother speak, the idea of the northern Italian dialect it did not register at all. They just assumed it was French and could not understand why my father said he had married an Italian because in reality she was a "Francese," French. And this debate I guess went on for years that we were not really Italian, we were French. Now remember you're talking about a couple that had no family here, no relatives, nothing at all. My mother said she sat in the house for days because obviously nobody knew what she was talking about. And she went down to the grocery store every morning and just picked and finally my mother was asking for "sedano," celery, and they showed her everything in the place and, "We don't have it." And finally at one point when she was down there—remember she was embarrassed—this was all strange, this was like a double foreign language, the owner of the grocery opened what they called their ice box in the back, what was their refrigerator area and my mother saw the celery and like kind a jumped for joy and pointed to it. And he explained later, "This is what you're lookin' for but who knew? Why didn't you call it. . . ?" For whatever they called in southern Italian [alaccia]. So that kind of broke the ice for my mother because this was days later. At this point they had developed

NORTHERN AND SOUTHERN
ITALIAN WOMEN
In the Hill, late 1940s
Mortali family album

a rapport so she always said her first friends were the grocer and his wife who happened to live in the same building.

At this point she came to know some of the women in the building because most of the women left very early—like four or five o'clock in the morning—and they worked in the sweatshops around there so all my mother had exposure to was the children because the mothers would run home and prepare a quick lunch and then off to work again and my mother knew no one. And my father came home all hours because he was working. But she managed to cook. And within the course of a few weeks my father had taught her the route downtown and she just learned how to point because the other families of northern Italians were in the Hill area and not in the Marche area, somewhere off Legion Avenue. But from Green and Hamilton to there was like an eternity. And she could not get her bearings but it was the only other cluster of northern Italians that they were exposed to. But what came of this, being that she had no family, that neither of them had family, her best, closest, and dearest friends were her neighbors. They became our extended family. My brother is seventeen years older than I am and my mother's fear was what would ever happen to either of her children if something happened to her or my father. So these women that lived in this tenement house truly became her sisters. And they shared everything until the day we moved—and we moved for what was then the redevelopment days. And the cursing to Dick Lee was unbelievable in those days because it disrupted entire families. There were a number of families that wanted the opportunity to move but there was still an older group that just didn't have the courage to move out of what was our Italian ghetto, our very secure world. But to the day we moved, most of the families, if one made coffee it was for all and if there was something different being made everyone tried it.

"Zambaione and Malocchio"

And my mother cooked the weirdest as far as they were concerned because they were not polenta eaters. But my mother made polenta as a staple and my mother made very different things like "zambaione," custard, which is in now, was something we had every day. You know zambaione is the eggs and the marsala and the sugar and now they serve it for ten dollars over strawberries. We had it as a nutritional drink. And this particular group of southern Italians had never ever seen the zambaione, it was not their thing, marsala was not their thing, but my mother made this as a matter of course and whenever someone was ill they would ask my mother to make the zambaione. But by the same token, if anyone had a headache, we'd ask one of the neighbors to do the "malocchio." So it was an even exchange of talents—the zambaione to get your strength back, the malocchio because you know with the water and the oil. I don't mean to generalize but at least it was in my household and most of my mother's friends, the northern Italians are very conservative people. They're not demonstrative people, they're snobbish for the lack of a whatever, but I think it is more their conservatism that takes over, what we call snobbery. They're a lot more in control, they love just as hard but they're not as outgoing and every time I went to Italy it just reconfirmed that this was what it was all about. And you have to remember that the northern Italians suffered at the hands of the Papal Wars, so the church was really not their buddy, for so many of them. My father really did not believe it what was the church per se, yet we had priests that were in Saint Michael's and there were a few northern Italians. They were at our house every Friday or Saturday night. And that was great. They were his friends. But don't expect me to go to church, this was my father's philosophy. So I think some of the cynicism that they had they were reared with because—maybe their grandparents and great-grandparents had suffered at the hands of the Huns and Papal Wars and whatever, I don't know. But they were not as churchgoing, as we know. I could not go out on Sunday unless I went to church but there was no "moine," a big production shall we say about it, it was just a given. And I was never allowed to go to Wooster Street to these feasts because my mother would say, "Where do you hear of people carrying statues? Or pinning money on statues?" As she got older she got very much into it but I was not allowed on Wooster Street when they had the feasts. It was kind of different for them.

My mother had never seen the evil eye, malocchio. There was just no such thing. As far as she knew, or at least her part of the country and she said when she first saw it [performed] she just couldn't understand it. But interestingly enough my mother was kind of considered the smart one in the group because she could read and write. As a matter of fact she spent a lot of her time—she never worked in factories—she went one day and told my father no way—but she spent a lot of her time writing letters for the people in the neighborhood because most of them had not gone to school. And this is where she would get the fresh eggs and who would bring her a pillowcase and it was a wonderful way of exchanging and using each other's abilities. And we had some different things, there was always some kind of weird dessert or whatever because that was the gift my mother had gotten for writing a letter. And then, because my father had a little more money than the average and my mother was very frugal, she would give out loans. And this was her way of holding up her share.

She cooked and canned everything. I think my favorite story is when I was a freshman at Sacred Heart Academy and went to my first Irish friend's house and came home and I was absolutely devastated. I thought, I can't believe we're this poor because when they opened their cabinets there was Campbell's soup, there was pasta, there was everything. We had cloths filled with lemon oil and cases of oilcans in our cabinet. That was it. And I went home and started to cry and I couldn't believe we were so poor. And my mother really sat me down and oh, let me have it, that yes, those were canned soups. She made fresh soups and mother not working, my mother made ravioli twice a week and pasta for the remainder of the week. She didn't make bread but she did all of the canning, which to this day conjures up mixed emotions because all I can think of is tomato all over the place and paste sitting on the stove from September to November and little tomato seeds because—remember—we didn't have running hot water and all that other good stuff. And just lots of work. She canned fruit and made their alcohol drinks, sport coffee. Someone would steal the alcohol from the hospital—they would share it and make their own strega. And they would buy the unbleached flour sacks and make sheets. And the only time the good sheets went on the bed was when the doctor was coming. And most of the time we lived with seams on our back. And maybe the half-picture of a body because I think there was a flour company that had Mister Atlas [laughing] so it was almost like early porn, you had this body you sleep on all the time! But then as they would keep them in the other part of sink and you smelled the Clorox for a week, then they'd be bleached out and they became sheets and my mother would go, first they became sheets and then, as they wore out, they became mopines. So these half-bodies lived with you an entire lifetime and then they became dust rags. So that's how my mother compensated for not going to work and my father never questioned it all and it worked out just fine. My mother was considered the more educated one but not necessarily the smarter one because she had some schooling, could read and write. So as a result, someone passed on the prayers and the process, not to me, to my mother. And from what I remember the prayers had to be passed on to them at a certain time of the year, it was Christmas Eve. And I have to tell you, I think my mother faked half of it. But it worked. And I can remember as a little girl there was always someone coming in with a bowl of water and the little dish of oil. And I remember having it done—I still get these headaches and I still sometimes think I wish someone would do "'o malocchio." Now they call it allergies or whatever, but I remember the soothing fingers on my forehead, almost hypnotizing that I didn't want it to end because it would be this whispering and all I remember is the s's because saying these prayers—and I don't know if they were jumbled words or prayers or whatever—but the power of faith in healing truly worked because there would be these crosses over your forehead and the oil and then the fingers being poked into a bowl and then they could tell you—it required an extra prayer—if it was a man or a woman or a group, which always fascinated me. I'd look down and I'd just see blobs of oil. Like someone put the "malocchio," [the evil eye] on you because, it was either a group, a man, or a woman. Now how could you tell? Only those that were blessed could tell whether it was a man and "Oh, it's a man, oh it was a woman, oh this was a whole group, put the eyes on you." And my mother interestingly enough sewed, not well, but she sewed and a lot of women in the neighborhood would bring things to her. And I realized as I got older they would get their little housedresses from around or their aprons, the mantecines, but they didn't have pockets in them. And my mother always had to add a pocket. And why did she have to add a pocket, other than for the handkerchief or for the dollar? That whenever these women would step beyond their house, if someone said, "Gee that's a nice dress, or a nice hairdo, they could put their fingers in their pocket and cut off the evil eye [thumb holding down third and fourth fingers, second and fifth finger extended]. Now my mother convinced herself that she believed in this but I never had a horn, le corne [amulet to ward off the evil eye], around my neck and all of our neighbors except our house had the red corne at the door and scissors that were opened—that blocked the evil eye. We were the weird ones. We didn't have this at our door. I guess it was the beginning of wreaths, we did not have one of those, the thing that was near our door was the stretcher for the curtains, which I always hated, because it gave me blisters.

The Pappacodas were one of the heirs to the building. The Avitables, when I was growing up, there was a Crotese, the Santoros, the Purgatores—that entire group is all gone—Protese and Santoros.

15

Going Back to Italy

By the turn of the century, improvements in the reliability of steam ship travel allowed shipping companies to advertise predictable arrival and departure timetables, capitalizing on the desire of millions of peasants stricken by the pull of "American fever" to heed the call of distant American jobs. Italians who had been accustomed to seasonal job seeking in nearby countries expanded their horizons beyond Europe where the convenience and flexibility of a "round trip" ticket guaranteed frequent trips back and forth to the United States. Many Italians viewed the high cost of passage as a long-term investment that would pay itself off when earnings from American jobs could be used to buy farmland.

Italians departing for American shores received the blessing of the Italian government which believed that remittances received from returnees would eventually stimulate the south's failing economy. In 1903, 78,000 of the 214,000 Italians who crossed the Atlantic returned.[27] During the years 1862 to 1901, nearly 2.5 million Italians, mostly "detached males," worked abroad for several months to support their families and returned home for the rest of the year.[28] In the period between 1900 and 1914, 1.5 million Italians returned home.[29] At the same time nine million southerners had left Italy and found work in other countries leaving villages severely reduced in population and others as ghost towns. Loss of farm laborers who left Italy led to hiring new hands at higher wages, triggering higher prices for wine and wheat. For some tenant farmers who stayed behind, the loss of farmhands meant the loss of farms. Some immigrants were ambivalent about where to settle and made numerous round trips before deciding. One coal miner made twelve round trip journeys before deciding that his family of nine children would fare better in Scranton, Pennsylvania.[30] At the same time steamship company agents combed the rural south assuring the most unconvinced peasant of a return trip home should he fail to find work in the new world. In some cases, returnees, eager to purchase land on which they had worked as tenant farmers or day laborers, bought poor land that produced small harvests and marginal profits. As taxes rose, and the availability of loans was nonexistent, the new landowners were forced into bankruptcy and returned to the United States.

Italians returned to native villages for reasons other than economic necessity. Rather than risk marriage to American women, young men in search of brides returned to marry daughters of families they had known from childhood. Married men with jobs in America returned home long enough to know children born in their absence. Some immigrants who recalled the "miseria" they had experienced in youth stayed in America with the idea of retiring with American pensions, returning to small villages where they would live comfortably as "signori," or the well-to-do. Immigrants who had fared well in the new world returned home with enough American money to build handsome two-storey homes with balconies on land where feudal hovels once stood. American dollars were also responsible for the passing of land ownership from the idle rich to farmers: from 1901 to 1911 the number of landowners increased by 280,000.[31] When the market crashed in 1929 causing the Great Depression, back and forth voyages for 'birds of passage," as Italians were called, came to a sudden halt.

"Hangings on the Green"

Lucy Pastore spoke in the living room at the home of Kim and Mike Rogers on February 16, 2000.

My paternal grandfather came here after the World War I. And on the center of the green in New Haven we had a gazebo. They had a hanging; they used to have hangings out on the green. The man committed some kind of a murder that they had this hanging. My grandfather was here at the time and he saw this hanging. The man after three minutes you're supposed to take him down. But they didn't take him down. He went back to Italy and he said, "I'd never go back to the United States again." He never came back.

"Is That How You Talk to Your Aunt?"

Giuannine DeMaio spoke in the family room of her granddaughter Laurel's North Branford home on July 11, 1999.

My mother's brothers and sisters all came to America. But one brother and one sister—the sister married, well, she married the lawyer. The brother lived way up in the mountains with his wife and kids. He never wanted to come to America. Then finally, I dunno how he got talked into comin', so he brought his wife and a little boy, maybe a couple a years old. The minute she landed, she cried, morning, noon, and night, "I want my mother, I want my mother." She couldn't make up her mind to live there [Italy] like my mother and her other sisters—they all made a go of it. Not her—she cried every day. Her husband got a job in the lamp shop on Chestnut and Water. They all went to work in factories, mostly in Sargent's. So he used to go to work and, oh, she cried every day, every day. So finally she got another baby and she was rippin' because she figured she's stuck here. So one day she says to my mother, "Would you like to see your mother?" See, my grandmother was still in Italy. She never came back here because she had her other daughter that married

GIUANNINE DEMAIO
North Branford, 1999

A. Riccio

the lawyer. She said, "Sure, I'd like to see my mother, how am I gonna see her?" "Ask your husband, I wan a go back to Italy, maybe your husband will make you go." Because she didn't wan a live here, but my uncle didn't want to go back. So she said to my father, "Gee I would like to see my mother in Italy, do you think you could let me go to Italy?" He says, "Yeah, you could go, you got a take the three kids." My mother had three kids, the baby was two years old, then she had my sister who was four years old, I must a been six or seven. So we went to Italy. I always remember by the train, we slept overnight on the train and then we went on the boat. It took us seventeen days and eighteen nights to get to Italy. I remember everything. It was a big boat. A bunch of us kids would get together—we'd pull the rope out of—I dunno what it was, where it belonged—but we used to pull it out and jump rope with it. That's all we did. All the kids got together a-boom, a-boom, we used to jump rope all the time. My mother was in bed all the time. She couldn't stand the motion. She'd be layin' down, you know. But my aunt, she was a frigger—she used to say to me, "Vammi a piglià' 'nu bottiglia 'e acqua," Go get me a bottle of water. So I used to say, All right, i' vaco a piglià', All right I'll go and get it. So I used to walk the whole length of the boat before you came to the faucet. I used to fill the water, bring it to her. By late afternoon, she'd say it again. Without saying a long story, she was on my heels all the time. Now why she never sent her son? But I was the sucker that would go all the time. So one day I got so disgusted with her I says to her, "'A zi' piglià 'o figlio tùjo e va a piglia l'acqua," Aunt, get your son to go and get the water. She said to me [voice rising], "Scustumàto! Accussì parla 'a zia tùja?," You have no manners! Is that the way you talk to your aunt? Now my mother is sitting next to her. And she sayin' to my mother, "Accussì impara e figli tuòje, parla con me accussì, a-poo-pung, a poo-pang?," Is that how you teach your children to talk to me? And on and on. So I got tired of listenin' to her, I walked away from her. And I went back to the kids jumpin' rope. So now she's after my mother, "Miéte scuórno, e 'a figla túja è accussì, e i' songa viècchia, e éssa non mi respónna," You should be ashamed of yourself, your kid is like that, and I'm old and she won't answer me. So finally, I guess my mother got tired of listenin' to her, she was waitin' for my mother to give me a beatin'. In them days Italians, they used to hit the kids like hell. There was no abuse them days. So anyway, we were jumpin' rope. Pretty soon one of the kids says, "Your mother's comin' with a shoe in her hand." I says to myself, here's where I'm gonna get a beatin'. 'Cuz my mother couldn't listen to her anymore, cuz she's hollerin' at my mother for not teachin' me better. So I got on the deck, like this. I could remember it like it was today. Pretty soon my mother came with the shoe—poonck!—blood all over. "Oooh Jen, you got blood all over!" Pretty soon the captain came, he grabbed my mother. He wanted to bring her to jail because the kids said my mother hit me with the shoe and I was cryin', "I don't want my mother to go to jail, I don't want her, I don't care what she did, no it was my fault, it was my fault."

"Ma, I'm Back"

Andrea Colavolpe spoke at the Saint Andrew's Society Center on Chapel Street on June 14, 1999.

My first thing I do when I get to Amalfi I got to go the cemetery to visit my mother. Oh yeah. That's my first trip. Soon as I arrive at Amalfi—if it's at night I can't go because the cemetery is closed, but the next day I have to go the cemetery. And you know how many steps you go to get there?—there's some five hundred steps. It's behind the church. That's where my mother and father are buried. If I get there in the afternoon I don't even go home and eat—I got to go to the cemetery and see my mother. I got to salute my mother, "Ma—I came back again, I came to see you." To me, it looks like she wants to come out and say, "I'm glad you came up and see me." Because in Italy, everybody has their pictures on the grave. Not like here, just a stone, nothing. They have a picture on the grave, on the stone of my mother and a picture of my father, the date they were born and the date they died. They don't put Lucia Colavolpe, no. They put Lucia Carrano Colavolpe. Carrano was her maiden name.

"America Is My Home"

John Nappi spoke with great pride about the love of his father for America at the kitchen table of his East Haven home on September 15, 1999.

My father told the American Consul in Naples, Italy. He told them in 1950, "I want to go home." He was very sick. The consul said, "But Italy is your home." He said, "Oh, no, America my home—I got my boy, [thumping on the table] he fight for country." He [the consul] said, "When I heard it, I couldn't get over it," and I told my assistant, "Get him a ride a soon as possible, this man is very sick." So when I picked him up at pier 59 in New York he was in bad shape. He didn't last two months after that, he had prostate cancer. But he wanted to die here. He kissed the ground when he got here. He was glad to get home. We were surprised because up until then, forget it, Italy was everything to him. There was nothing like Italy because he had everything there. But then when he went back he saw, when he was sick, they had to drive him from Sarno, Nola to go to the doctor in Naples. He had to depend on his nephew. He couldn't get no medication. Couldn't get the care he needed. And then when he came back, he was too far gone.

"Pack It Up for Me"

Rose Savo spoke at the kitchen table of her Annex home on July 28, 2000.

One time when I went back to the town I lived and said to my uncle, "'O zi', non steva a casa la?" Uncle, isn't that my house over there? My uncle said, [excited voice] "Ooh, chi ti ha creato!" My goodness! Who made you? I was only a little kid, I was only three, four years old but I remembered—I picked out the house where we lived [in Italy]. There was a stone staircase and at the foot of the staircase there was a fountain. Everybody used to come there to get their water, you know? One day I got a new pair of shoes, and I'm sittin' at the foot of those stairs, in one corner. So I got brainstorm, I said "I'm gonna take my shoes off, I'm gonna see what happens." They stole my shoes! I went home and I got a beatin' [laughing]. My father's town was Nola. That's where I was born, I was born in Nola, in my grandmother's house. They had a lot of property there. My uncle lived on that land. He had it rented. They used to raise tobacco. And every time I went back my uncle would say, "This is all your property." They got a funny system. Whatever property is in the family, when the old folks go, it goes to the first son. If the first son goes, then it goes to his kids. My uncle always said to me, "This is all your stuff." And I said, "Yeah, when I go back to America, pack it up for me—I'll take it back." [laughing]

❝I Was Made in America and I Was Born in Italy❞

Rose Savo spoke at the kitchen table of her Annex home on July 28, 2000.

I was made in America and I was born in Italy. My mother was six months pregnant with me, she went back to Italy—my mother went back and forth I don't know how many times. My brother was made in Italy and he was born in Brooklyn. I was made in Brooklyn and I was born in Italy, yeah. And I have a younger sister, she was two years younger and we have the same birthday, two years apart. Her and I were born in Italy. But I was made here in America. In Brooklyn.

16

The Depression in New Haven

During the Depression in New Haven, the majority of Italians in the workforce found themselves at manual labor and semiskilled jobs. Most were far from affluent. Few had yet entered the professional ranks, although some had made gains apprenticing from unskilled to semiskilled jobs as barbers, carpenters, masons, and shoemakers. In 1933, half were employed in factories and few were afforded the opportunity to attend high school, which excluded them from clerical positions.[32] In the Italian community, splintered allegiances to different self-help and religious organizations according to region and village kept Italians from the political unity needed to support a mayoral candidate and win patronage jobs. New Haven's municipal departments, especially the police and fire departments, were in the domain of the Irish and few Italian surnames could be found on city employment rosters. Prejudice and discrimination in the workplace kept many Italians from finding work during the Depression. In desperate attempts to find enough work to provide for their families, Italians disguised their ethnicity, cutting vowels or completely changing their last names to sound more "American."

The Depression claimed about 16,000 jobs in New Haven, forcing many immigrant families to accept terrible work conditions.[33] Sargent Manufacturing Company and Winchester Repeating Arms were in recessions and many men were out of work; L. Candee Rubber closed its doors in 1929, forcing eight hundred workers to lose jobs. At the same time in 1933, hundreds of underpaid women who worked for the Lesnow Brothers, the city's largest manufacturer in the needle trade, were told to produce more shirts per hour with no increase in pay. In an economic climate of heightened fear and desperation, young Italian-American men and women decided to join the union movement, protesting dire conditions by walking picket lines and staging a successful strike for better wages and benefits. Many of the eighty Italian self-help societies were flooded with requests for financial help, and funds were quickly depleted.[34] In 1932, the city declared itself fiscally bankrupt and could not provide relief for the unemployed. In 1934, over seventy-five percent of households in Wooster Square had contact with relief agencies and a third were surviving on relief funds.[35]

When the city's largest depositor declared bankruptcy in June, 1932, it set off a wave of foreclosures on properties throughout the neighborhoods of New Haven. From 1929 to 1933, nine banks failed and property was repossessed, causing a number of working-class Italians to lose cherished homes bought with hard-earned money. Italian-born fathers, who had purchased parcels of land with dreams of building homes for their American-born children, lost them during the Depression in some parts of the city. The Depression forced many neighborhood banks founded by Italian-American businessmen to close or merge. Italians in rural sections of the Annex and Forbes Avenue neighborhoods fared better than those in the inner city, surviving on crops grown in their vegetable gardens and local truck farms. Using the familiar Italian hand gesture of twisting the wrist with the index finger extended and thumb pointing upward, Italians expressed the anxiety brought on by the Depression with the phrase, "Ci sta a leggiera," or "These are tough times." For those who could not find enough work to support their families, the alternative of "going to the city" or relying on a handout from the city, was considered "scuórno" within the Italian community, a shameful thing to do.

"THEY SENT THE CHILDREN"

Frank DePonte spoke at the dining room table of Joe and Lena Riccio's Annex home on November 21, 1999. Frank recounted his father working a sixty-hour week in Sargent for twelve dollars to feed his family.

There was poverty in the 1930s; there's no question. We had a little grocery store right by Sargent's and I'll never forget. They wouldn't go get what they called charity in those days because it was embarrassing to the family and implied that the father was not adequate to take care of his family. So they had literally to be starving before they would go and they could go to the city, what they called city hall and get what was called a city ticket. The reason I know is because they used to cash them in our store like food stamps and you would buy so much food, maybe fifteen, twenty dollars, which in those days was sufficient, it was a lot. But you know I never saw an adult cash one of those tickets in that store. They would always send a child because they were embarrassed. They'd say, "You can't feed your family, what the hell kind of man are you?" It was that kind of thing. But there was no work. I mean they would do anything. People had jobs but they were just scraping by.

"IF YOU DIDN'T WORK YOU DIDN'T EAT"

Alfred Nargi spoke at the kitchen table of his nephew Louis Nargi's home in New Haven on July 15, 1999.

Nobody had time to lay around in the old days. You were either selling newspapers at six years old or shining shoes at six years old or working on the farm [in North Haven] picking strawberries, tomatoes, or string beans, all right? We picked

ALFRED NARGI

1999

A. Riccio

strawberries for two and a half cents a quart. And if you made three dollars a day you were doing exceptionally well. We were just kids, twelve, thirteen years old. Today they would say that's abuse of child labor. But if you didn't work when you were a kid, you didn't eat. We didn't have nothing much to eat. Today they got vitamins, special foods for the kids. We had beans and macaroni, beans and potatoes. I never saw beans made so many different ways when we were kids. And that's the way it was. Who ever heard of cereal in the morning? Who ever heard of corn flakes and all-bran? Forget about it. Never. But the old days were the best. Today they got everything but they don't know what they missed. There was a Depression and people still got along. They didn't go out killing each other because they couldn't eat. But they got along. They always managed to have food on the table. We never went without food on the table, never. I would always say to my brother and a lot of friends. If I had one wish in my life, I would not wish for money. I would wish they could turn back the hands of time for one year for the generation of today to 1932, Depression time. You know what would happen to a lot of these people? They'd blow their brains out, they wouldn't be able to survive, they couldn't take it. But our parents did. With twelve kids, who had fourteen kids. The Mariano family, the Sansaverino family, they all made it fine.

LOU AND DIANE LANDINO
In their backyard, Annex, 1999

A. Riccio

"Come Back Next Week"

Lou Landino spoke on the back porch of his Annex home on August 21, 1999.

Going into the Depression, 1928, '29. I lived through it. I used to go out, go down to firehouse on East Pearl Street, come home with two bags of oranges and whatever it was that they would give you. Sometimes if they had butter, you got butter. If they didn't you got oranges, you got potatoes you might have gotten onions, maybe you got a couple dozen eggs. Government surplus, that's what it was called. Then I'd walk from East Pearl Street all the way to Blatchley Avenue, we'd go to Emmanualson's Bakery, fifteen, twenty cents, and they would fill up two bags with the day old donuts, bread, whatever. Hopefully you guys will never see this [Depression] but then again maybe you should see it so you'd appreciate it. I ate a lot a bread with a lot a mold on it. It's true. My cousin's wife-to-be, her uncle had connections down at City Hall and he would go down to Emmanualson's Bakery or Tip Top or Ward Bond Bakery and they would just throw—he had an open rack body truck—they would just throw loaves of bread onto his truck. And he had a list. At this address drop off so many loaves of bread. And that's what I used to do. The guy would give me five or six loaves of bread, take em' up to the third floor, you run up the stairs, knock on the door, five loaves of bread, come back downstairs. This is what people had. We toasted bread. We made bread pudding. We did everything [laughing] we could with bread. Make croutons. Toast every morning. You'd go like this, scrape off the mold and eat the bread. No butter. Just plain toast. You guys wouldn't be able to handle it, I don't think. I used to go to City Hall. I needed a pair of shoes so I'd go down, the teacher would say to me, "You need shoes," and she would give me a slip and I'd go down to City Hall, down the basement on Orange Street. Mr. Gartland. Yeah. And I'd show him the slip. And he'd say, "Let me see your feet." And I'd pick up my foot. "The holes aren't big enough," he'd say, "You can go another a week, come back in a week and we'll give you another pair of shoes." And walking, wear out more socks.

17

Witches, Healers, and Herbs

Some scholars believe that belief in the evil eye dates as far back as prehistoric times and that it precedes man's belief in God. The first traces of the evil eye appear in images on Mesopotamian clay tablets at the dawn of writing around 5000 B.C. Belief in the evil eye was not confined to Italy but understood in Greece, Spain, Turkey, Scotland, Ireland, Finland, Germany, and Poland and in countries of the Muslim world. The prophet Mohammed believed firmly in its powers. To understand the concept of the evil eye is to imagine an age before the forces of technology and industry overwhelmed nature, a world where man considered himself an integral part of creation, and where the necessity of sharing and reciprocity was the only means to assure human survival. Some theorize the evil eye evolved as a consequence of an individual who failed to follow the norms of cooperative behavior.

Mediterraneans avoided boasting of success or gain for fear of arousing envy in neighbors. This code of behavior was coined in the old Latin aphorism used frequently by the Romans, "Laudet qui invidet," or "He who praises, envies" that cautioned against accepting praise in any form because good fortune might arouse envy in someone with the power to cast the spell of the evil eye. In the Italian south, those who possessed the power of the evil eye were thought to bring calamity or even death. For Italians who believed in the phenomenon, a seemingly harmless remark made by an evil eye caster admiring the beauty of a child could mean the opposite. Suspicion and fear were part of daily life in southern Italian society and protective "corne," or amulets, "mano cornuta," or hand gestures, and "fattuchiera," or sorcery were all used to defend home and family against evil spells.

Many southern Italians transported the belief in the evil eye, or "'o maloucchio" to New Haven where a spell cast over an innocent victim by a simple glance foreshadowed certain bad fortune or sickness. Every neighborhood had a network of women healers who recognized the power of an "ianara," or witch, who could cast evil spells by the act of "iettatura," a simple look. An ianara had the power of being an "iettatore," or one who cast evil spells. An ianara casting an evil spell was said to be in a state of mind of "una che tiene a 'mmìria in cuollo," or someone in a jealous state of mind. The "mammare," or midwives, were usually elderly women who also assumed the role of "guaratrice," or the healer. They were called upon to exorcise "a fattùra," or a spell placed on the victim which caused sickness. To break the spell, the woman performed the ancient rite of "'o maluocchio," or "doing the eyes" as it was called in New Haven, invoking special healing powers through secret prayers and rites passed down from mother to daughter, usually on Christmas Eve. Often the ceremony began with three dishes filled with water, a teaspoon, and olive oil. The woman made the sign of the cross on her forehead and blessed each dish with a sign of the cross. After dipping a finger into the teaspoon of oil, the sign of the cross was made three times on the sick person's forehead. A secret prayer was said three times and dipping the finger in oil, either three drops were made in one dish or one drop in three dishes. Odd numbers were always used. If the oil droplets spread too quickly in the water, a person retained "the eyes" and remained under the evil spell. Some healers placed a lighted match to the droplets of oil in the dishes, symbolically burning the "bad eyes" or making criss-cross incisions with a knife on the oil droplets to dispel the evil eye in the sick person. Other women healers claimed to have the power to interpret whether a man or woman had cast the spell of "the eyes" by the shapes the droplets of oil formed in the dish.

"I Ran Out of the House"

Fred and Rose Nuzzo spoke at the dining room table of their Fair Haven home on July 22, 1999. They opened Grand Apizza on Grand Avenue in Fair Haven on March 3, 1955.

Here I am [Rose] from a big city, from Philadelphia. I never was faced with anything like that. The only thing my family used to do when the children were born, you wouldn't say, "How beautiful" without saying, "God bless them." We wore black—that was our superstition—they put black velvet ribbons with the medal on our undershirts. That was the most I knew of witchcraft. And one night I was living next door with my aunt before we got married, up here on Clinton Avenue. And he called me over one night and my mother-in-law to be was very sick and I guess she had a headache or something. So his Uncle George came over and his Aunt Elizabeth. And they said, "We're going to do maluocchio." And I said to him, "What's maluocchio?" You have to remember I'm a city kid that's been out and everything, What's maluocchio? Well, he got the dish with the candles and the oil and his started criss-crossing in the water. I ran out of the house. I said, "What the hell are they doing? What have you got a bunch of witches here?" I didn't know what was going on. Well, they explained it: people get migraine headaches, it's a way of pushing out the devil. They figured you're obsessed or the devil's trying to do something, whatever. It has to do with the devil I know. And you get these migraine headaches or you get a pain here or your eyes hurt or something so they do the "maluocchio" and they throw the oil and they make the sign of the cross and then they put the matches in. You know the stick matches, the old wooden matches? You light the wooden matches and you stick them in the water at the end. You burn the witch, the devil, whatever. Years ago when they got done with the maluocchio, they used to throw the dishes out the second story window.

"Getting the Eyes"

Lena Riccio spoke at the kitchen table of her Annex home on July 23, 2000.

Like if you saw a pretty kid and say, "Oh, cuand' è bella," Oh what a beautiful child, and you don't say "God bless you," then they say it's evil eyes. Or if somebody is jealous of you. We don't know anybody that is jealous of you—you never know. It's just certain people that you have to watch out for. My mother used to have a friend, I don't know if she was a cousin or what—came from Providence, Rhode Island. And every time she used to come to the house, my sister Jeanie would get deathly sick. She would get deathly, deathly sick. And my mother would do the eyes. Before you know it, she would be all right. Every time she came, it would be the same thing. So finally she came another time, my mother got so mad at her; she kicked her out of the house. She was evil that lady. My mother would have three soup dishes of water. And a teaspoon of olive oil. I don't know the prayer [she would say]. She would dip the thumb in the olive and then she would make the sign of the cross and recite this prayer and then the residue oil, she would flick it down into the soup dish, in the water. Now if somebody had given you the evil eyes or the curse to give you this headache, the oil would settle at the top, make a big circle and spread—you wouldn't see it. If they were not an evil spirit, the oil would go right down to the bottom of the dish and would stay there. And you would do this over the three dishes and your headache would go away if it were caused by "i maluocchio," the evil eyes. If it wasn't caused by the evil eyes well then she couldn't help you. You suffer.

"Science and Malocchio"

Edward Morrone spoke at the backyard family picnic of Joe and Lena Riccio's Annex home on June 13, 1999.

I read there's a scientific basis for the 'o maluocchio, to make your headache go way. If it's a stress induced headache there's slight perspiration on your forehead. And the perspiration mixed with the oil going into the water, you're now putting in a mixture of olive oil and water and it spreads on the top. If there's no perspiration on the forehead it's just pure olive oil going right down to the bottom. So there is some scientific basis for it. So if it was stress induced it was purely in the head. And if you believed that these wide circles were going to make your headache go away and it was not a physical thing, they indeed go away. There's some scientific basis to it: if it was psychological, it would go away; if it was a physical thing it wasn't going to go away and there was probability that there would be no perspiration on the forehead. I'm not sure I believe it either. That's what I read.

1

2

LENA RICCIO PERFORMING "IL MALOCCHIO" FOR HER GRANDSON, JOHN GORMAN, 1999
From top left: 1. Blessing herself; 2. Blessing the water; 3. Saying the prayer and making
the sign of the cross on forehead; 4. Dropping oil into dishes

A. Riccio

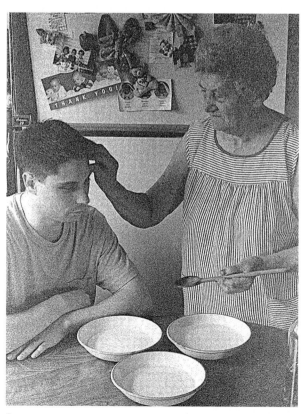

3

4

❝Giuanne-Giuanne❞

Al and Betty Jones spoke at the kitchen table of Jennie and Dominic Randi's
East Haven home on July 22, 1999.

My grandfather [Giuanne-Guianne] was studying to become a priest but we don't
know what happened as to why he didn't continue. And he came to America and
he was a longshoreman in New York. He and my grandmother opened a grocery
store on Wooster Street. From Wooster Street they ended up on Main Street in
the Annex. My mother went to school—she couldn't speak any English because
all my grandparents spoke was Italian. He started being a healer on Wooster
Street and then he went to Filmore Street [Fair Haven]. He started because he
had a book and he to say "le preghiere," the prayers, and when he said a prayer,
like if you had a headache, he used to say these prayers and right away the headache used to go away. And word started getting around, and before you know it
they came from all over. He was, they called him "'o fattùra," he was a healer. They
used to call him "Giuanne-Giuanne," John-John. They people used to say, "chillo
fa la preghiera fattùra," He says the prayers of a healer. But people would come to
the house and in the back—I was ashamed because we were Italian, they were
American, and they would come. We never talked about it in school; we never
talked to anybody about it because my sister and I were embarrassed. I mean
maybe we knew but we don't know what they knew—what did they think, that
my grandfather maybe was crazy. But he was so kindhearted. You never heard him
yell at anybody, never raised his voice. You never heard him say a mean thing; he
was so kind. He was so goodhearted; he helped everybody. He was a very, very
calm man. In the back of my mother's house was like a great big entry hall. And
they would go in the back and we'd see these people sitting there. He never made
any appointments, they would come and sit there all day if they had to. There was
a waiting room and they would just sit there and wait their turn like you would go
to a doctor's office. He would take them in there one at a time, they'd go in, and
find what was wrong with them. In fact, sometimes they'd come and we'd be eating and we'd have to say, "Gee, I'm sorry, he's eating. If you want to wait you can
wait, but he just sat down to eat his dinner." And they would sit there at night
some of them and they would wait. A lot of people really believed in him, they
would come for years and years. A while back somebody called me looking for
him. He died in 1953. And then behind my mother's apartment there was an
empty room and that was like my grandfather's little office that was off the little
hallway. So people would sit there and wait to go see my grandfather and then
we'd have guys dating us and they'd say, "Why are all these people sitting in the
back room?" Sometimes you couldn't park in front of my mother's house because
so many came to see my grandfather. And they came from all over. They came
from upstate New York, they came from Hartford, from all over. And they would
bring my grandfather eggs and baskets of fruit and chickens. He didn't use anything, he just used his hands—he never gave out medicine or anything. He didn't

"GIUANNE-GIUANNE"
GIOVANNI RICCIO
1940s
Randi family album

want to take money—I mean some people forced it on him—but he really didn't want to take it so they would bring him chickens and eggs and all that kind of stuff. He used to make his own medicine, an herb medicine. He used to get different kinds of wild herbs; he used to grow his own herbs. I used to go and pick them, some of them used to grow in the yard. He had different plants. He used to make a tonic for blemishes and sores, some were for stomach problems. People used to come there with sores on their legs, like canker sores. He used to say prayers for them. And people kept coming back. I never saw so many people come from all over, even from California they used to come down.

They used to compare him to a medicine man, Chief Two Moon, an American Indian from Waterbury who used to make medicine like him. He had a recipe of what he made. He had a patent for it. But the doctors didn't like it. People would go back to the doctors and say, "Gee, you couldn't cure me, but Giuanne-Giuanne did." And they would get mad; the doctors didn't like that at all because they figured, "Who the heck is this guy?" He's not a doctor or anything; he doesn't have a license, so why would they go? But people used to flock to him and he never charged or asked for money. After he got through saying the prayer and everything, and they were ready to leave, if he turned his back or got up to get something, if they left a five dollar bill or whatever denomination on the table, that was it. He didn't ask for money. He would pray for them. I remember he had the most beautiful handwriting. He would never say what he did. If you had a headache, he'd say the "maluocchio," used to say a prayer and it would go away. Somebody put the curse on you or something like that, he would put his hand on your head, he'd talk, like a prayer, and then at the end he'd make the cross. He used to make three crosses. One time his son-in-law, Dominic [Randi], had a headache and he took him and he did something. He put his hand on his head and said something in Italian, praying, did the oil in the water, "the maluoc-chio"—if the oil separated in the water, that meant you had the "maluocchio," then if went together in the water, it had gone away. He came out with no head-ache. He felt like a million dollars and that was it. Nobody ever went in the room but the person; they just went in by themselves. People on crutches and after a few times with him they were walking away with no crutches. There was a woman from the New Britain area and she was deaf. And my father said a certain prayer for her and she claimed she became deaf because she had a child out of wedlock. Now sixty years ago, that was a no-no. And she kept coming and coming. Turn around, next thing you know, she could hear. Those stand out vividly in my mind. He never talked about it; you just took it for granted. If he didn't cure them, they wouldn't have been there. Am I right or wrong? So they came from all over. Word spread like a grapevine.

"'O Maluocchio"

John and Mary Nappi spoke at the kitchen table of their East Haven home on July 8, 1999.

My mother used to do it; she believed in it. All the old people believed in it. And you'd be surprised if it didn't work. They used to do it with the oil in the water. They used to get the water and olive oil. They used to make a cross here, a cross there and dip their finger and let a drop fall in the oil. I don't know what it was—if it spread or got smaller that means somebody had their eyes on you, a lot of people were talking about you or they said something. Believe me, when you got that, you felt nauseated and all that. That's what it is. But after she did it—I don't know for what—it was gone, I swear to God. She'd go, "You did have the eyes! Somebody's talking about you."

"She Was Like a Chiropractor"

The old woman, Cuncietta Amatruda, she was a big woman. If you had a sprain or anything—if it was broken she wouldn't bother—but if you had a stiff neck or you had something, she rubbed it. Everybody used to go there; she would take care of you. She used to go, "Oh you got a bump here, I think there's a blood clot like." You go there, she rubbed you down two or three times, forget it, it was like a chiropractor, like a doctor. They used to send you there on Wooster and Franklin Street. Everybody used to go up her house. You know what she used to do if you had boils or something like that with pus? She'd say, "Go down the [waterside] park, go get these leaves," they used to call them the "cinque punti," leaves with five points, "pick those." You used to take them, put them in salt, in olive oil and then put them on the thing and in two, three days all that pus used to come out.

"Taking Care of a Cough or Cold"

Sabatino "Sam" Troiano spoke at the dining table of his North Branford home on May 27, 2000 with his wife and son Gino.

There was a round plant they called "a maura." It'd run, it had vines and my mother'd take that in the summer, dry it, hang it up and dry it, and if you had a cough or a cold, she'd take that and make a tea out of it. And we used to drink that. Down on Eastern Street it used to grow all over the place, it looked like geranium leaf, you know, like that, but it was a vine. And that used to work all the time. You'd drink it nice and hot. Sometimes they'd put a little whiskey in it, a little wine. Doctors? Like with a cold—hot mustard plasters, oh I used to hate that. Burn. In the front, the back with the hot wool cloths, put em' in the oven, get em' good and hot, put em' on my chest.

"Maria Piezz' e Pasta"

Rose Sansone spoke at the kitchen table of her Fair Haven home on June 2, 1999.

If we had sore throat, my mother would take and she'd let us close our wrist and with oil she would rub it. And do you know that you feel that lump in your arm, and when that lump went down, your throat was all right. She used to do it for three days. There would be a lump in your wrist. And when she rubbed with that oil, how that used to hurt until that rubbed out and rubbed out. Then we had another old lady on Wooster Street, they used to call her "Maria Piezz' e Pasta." She used to live next door to the Farnam House when it was on Wooster Street. It used to be a big, big brick building—I can still picture it. You go there for three days to "ingamma," heal your stomach. On the third day she would take a big steak and put it on your stomach and you had to keep it there for the night. The next day you go there, she would take the steak off and then your stomach was all right.

"Call 'A Mammara'"

Nick Vitagliano spoke at the kitchen table of his Branford home on June 2, 2000.

My mother never did it [the maluocchio]. But she always had friends that were always willing to do it. And she knew how to call upon them and they would come. She would walk down the street because they lived in the neighborhood. She'd say, "Do me a favor, my son, fa mal' 'e capo accussì," he doesn't feel well, he has headache. "Aspetta, dopo mangiato a mattina," wait until after I eat breakfast, and then

ANGELINA PONGETTI, HEALER

1940s

Calzetta family album

she, "a mammara," the woman who would do the eyes. There was one a woman who did it for everybody. But as soon as she'd come in the house she would bless everybody as she was going, clean her way into the house so she'd be nice and clean to tend to the sick. We used to be in bed, sometimes we were so sick. She'd make the sign of the cross, say a prayer or two and go like this and like that, take a little water and put it on your forehead. You as a kid you'd say, "My God, what the hell is she gonna do now?" And you're staring and looking. You'd roll your eyes. And she used to say [excited voice], "Ooh, vidi, vidi, l'uocchio, come fa!" Look, look at the eyes, how they are! You got scared. For some reason they knew when it worked. Sometimes it wasn't working. She'd have to do it again and again.

"My Grandfather Healed the Little Girl"

Antonette Coppola spoke in the conference room of her Branford nursing home on May 7, 2000.

They [Amalfitani] used to say that he [grandfather] knew how to do something to harm but he never did anything to harm, he helped people. And he used to get arrested. They used to put him in jail a couple a days. My mother used to get mad at me when I used to run away and go with him. But he used to give me two cents to buy lemon ice. And my grandfather liked me because I had my grandmother's name. When I went with him this is what happened. I said, "I wanna come with you." He said to me, "Would you stay in one room with the other people?" I say, "Yeah." He had a crib made out of straw on the floor, there was a girl—she was beautiful. She was so sick they had her in that thing. So they called my grandfather. He said, "You got a stay in the room, you can't come in there." So the mother and the sister used to look through the hole. So I used to look too. I don't know what he used to say, he used to say some words. That crib jumped up. At the end, he came out, he said to the mother and father, "Go downstairs, there is the a pecora, goat, with ribbons on the head. Take all the ribbons and throw them in the river." Now I was a young girl, I said to the girl's mother, "Chill' è shèmo, come 'o sapè a isso?" He's a fool, how does he know? So they unknotted all the ribbons [on the goat], threw it in the river. At the end, he came outside, he said to the mother, "Prepare a big table like a wedding." And she made homemade macaroni and everything. The girl came out with him, out a the crib. He never did anything to harm anybody. He tried to help them. They used to arrest him because he wasn't a doctor. And my mother used to say to me, "You gonna go to jail with him" [laughing]. But on account I had my grandmother's name he liked me, he used to give me two cents. I used to run away from my mother and used to go with him. She didn't like the idea of me goin' with him. She tied me near the bed, she said, "You're not gonna get out a there till you promise never to go to grandfather's. So she untied me and I went back to my grandfather's house. Because he used to give me two cents [laughing]. You know what he looked like? He looked like a king. Everybody said he belonged to the family. The mother that grew them up wasn't really the mother; she could nurse him. He was born to a servant of rich people in Salerno.

"SHE WAS RELIGIOUS"

Rose Savo spoke at the kitchen table of her home in the Annex on July 28, 2000.

I don't know if you ever heard, years ago, when anybody had a headache, they would make "l'uocchio," the eyes, the maluocchio, the bad eyes, they used to call it. She [my mother] used to do that, she had a lot of customers—not that she charged, they used to come for her. And you know something? It used to work. She used to say prayers, she used to make signs of the cross on your forehead and she said different things. The headache used to go away, unless you just imagined it, but it used to go away. She had a lot of customers. My mother [Assunta Nappi] was on Wooster Street for fifty-five years. She used to take a dish with water and she had oil. She'd say some prayers and then she'd drip the oil in the water. If the oil spread, you had "the eyes," [il maluocchio], if they didn't spread—if it just stayed the way you dropped it—you didn't have nothing. Sometimes the oil used to spread, you know and [my mother would say] "Oh! teneva l'uocchio!" You had the eyes! Then, it didn't spread, it would stay just the way she dropped it, [my mother would say] "Non tiene niénte," You don't have anything. She was very religious.

Veneration for patron saints who possessed supernatural powers to protect the faithful and to grant special favors was deeply-rooted in the southern Italian soul, an ancient belief that predated the birth of Christianity. The images of the saints, whose forbears had been Greek and Roman gods, were carved into stone and wooden statuary and carried on the shoulders of townspeople through the winding narrow streets of hilltop towns, fishing villages on the Mediterranean, and through major cities across the south. As protectors of towns they were petitioned to ward off plagues, stem lava tides from nearby volcanoes, and guard against earthquakes. Saint Rocco was the healer of sickness, Saint Francis the protector of animals, Saint Lucy the guardian of eyesight, and Saint Anthony the finder of lost items. Patron saints also protected those at work: Saint Joseph watched over carpenters and Saint Damiano protected barbers. During thunderstorms in New Haven, Italians invoked the prayer of Santa Barbara, the patron saint of thunder and lightning, for protection:

Prayer of Santa Barbara

Santa Barbara!
Sei padrone di tuóno e lampe,
Tuóno e lampe.
Fatta indietro,
Questa è la casa di San Michele,
San Michele e La Madonna,
Questa è la casa di San Antonio
Sant Antonio,
Tredici grazie!

Santa Barbara
You are the master of thunder and lightning
Thunder and lightning,
Go back,

> This is the house of Saint Michael,
> Saint Michael and the Madonna,
> This is the house of Saint Anthony,
> Saint Anthony,
> The Thirteen graces!

For the people of the Mezzogiorno, the feasts signified the high point of the year, a time of celebration for many who lived a threadbare existence with few enjoyments. Festivals began with a mass where afflicted devotees prayed for the healing power of the saints to heal them, sometimes leaving braces and crutches on church altars as reminders. A procession marching to the music of a band made its way through decorated town streets where people chanted hymns and pinned money on the saint as it passed by. Some gave small donations to help cover expenses of the celebration. In the town center, booths were set up by vendors selling specially prepared dishes.

From cobblestone streets of Italian villages to the main streets of New Haven's Italian neighborhoods, feasts were replicated with the same reverence and dedication as in the old country. Women prayed and wailed in sympathy for Mary who lost her son on the cross during the procession of the Madonna d'Assunta that began at Saint Vincent DePaul's church in East Haven and proceeded up the hill to Main Street in the Annex. Families continued the Italian tradition of bathing in local waters, thought to have spiritual cleansing and healing powers on August 15th, the day of the feast. In Fair Haven, the Madonna di Monte Carmelo procession passed through major thoroughfares strung with festive lights. In the Wooster Square neighborhood the Saint Andrew's Feast procession proceeded to the waterfront where the statue of Saint Andrew was taken aboard a fishing boat for the Blessing of the Fleet ceremony. In 1921, members of Santa Maria Maddelena Society raised and spent the considerable sum of three thousand dollars for their feast and were known to offer money, jewels, and even a bride's wedding dress as thanks offerings.[36] In the early days of immigration, local citizenry unfamiliar with Italian customs viewed feasts as un-American. Irish parish priests looked upon Italians as suspect for their belief in saints as pagan worshippers whose polytheism ran counter to mainstream Catholic beliefs.

"La Madonna d'Assunta"

Nick Sorvillo and Lena Riccio spoke at the kitchen table of Lena's home in the Annex on January 27, 1999.

La Madonna d'Assunta is August 15th, a holy day of obligation and you to go in the water. You had to put just your feet in the water, it was supposed to be blessed or something. If you had a sickness or something it would cure you. They had these beliefs. It was a big, big feast and my mother used to carry the saint. They used to have a feast in Saint Vincent's church in East Haven. Then the ladies of the society had to carry the saint. They had it on a board like they carried Saint Andrew when they carried him down to the docks and take him for a ride on the boat to the breakwaters. Madonna d'Assunta and the ladies used to carry the saint. It was outside. People used to pin money on it when they had the feast. When they had to bring into the church the ladies used to carry the saint in church. It was like two thick sticks but four people had to carry it and the saint was on a board on these two sticks. And four ladies used to have to carry it on their shoulders. My mother, Antonia Morrone, she was one of them that had to carry the saint in the church. Most of the ladies would cry when they brought the saint in church. My wife Louise was born on that day. August 15th was a holy day of obligation. And she said to her mother, "Gee, what a wonderful thing, everybody goes to church for my birthday."

"The Tranese and the Amalfitani"

Pasquale and Theresa Argento spoke at the kitchen table of their Annex home on May 23, 1999. Theresa's grandfather was a sailor from Amalfi.

Where do you find people on a very beautiful day and the sun is out walking the streets with an umbrella? They [people from Atrani] were waiting [hoping] for the rain. I remember my mother used to have a next door neighbor and it was the feast of Saint Andrew. She'd come out with the umbrella [laughing]. My mother would get so mad. She said, "Tu fai appost'?" So, you're hoping for it to rain on purpose? Take away the umbrella, the sun is shining that they wanted it to rain on the feast.

"Take Offa You Hat!"

Joseph "Babe" Dogolo spoke at the kitchen table of his East Haven home on September 15, 1999.

The band was coming down Wooster Street, near Brewery Street, the people were all over there. And in front of us was this big Irishman or something like that. And the band came and they stopped. The band first played the Italian march—pa-da-ping-ba-da. And then they played "The Star Spangled Banner." And this Irish guy had his hat on; he didn't take it off. My father took it and hits him a shot and he knocked his hat off. My father got pinched. My father said to him, "You America citizen? And you don't take offa you hat in front of the Star Spangled Banner?" In those days it was a big thing and my father got arrested because he whacked him. But my father said, "You're from over here, I know better than, you got a take off a your hat because they play the "Star Spangled Banner." There was almost a riot; they wanted to jump on him, the Irishman.

"Santa Maria Maddalena"

The feast of the Maddalena was something out of this world. Wooster Street was lit from Olive Street to East Street, all the lights. They used to come from New York to put the lights. They used to wait all year long. That was the Tranese [from the village of Atrani]. Then the Amalfitani wanted to do better and they had to do better, back and forth. It was a rivalry. They were always arguing among

"THE FLAGPOLE WALK" AT THE WATERFRONT
Santa Maria Maddalena Feast

Argento family album

THE FEAST OF SANTA MARIA MADDALENA
Saint Michael's Church, Wooster Square, 1923

Argento family album

themselves, always arguing, not violently, but "You're this and you're that, we're better than you." They used to have fireworks down the waterside park—my god! Out of this world. There were stands, all food. That's why they stopped it; it turned out to be like a carnival at the end, throwing balls and everything. But in those days there was none of that. The streets were clear and the people enjoyed themselves because the music played, Italian music, and they danced and they did everything. And they couldn't wait for the feast to come. But today, towards the end, they started selling beer. In those days there was no beer there—you didn't sell no beer way back then, just cold drinks. Then they started getting drunk and that was the end, no more. That was the end of the feast. But the saint! They worshipped that saint. My God! She was full of rings and jewelry. As the people died they left their jewelry to Santa Maria Maddalena. And after the feast they would go down to the society [hall] and they would take off all her jewelry and put it in the vault and lock it up in the bank. Every year they did this. People didn't know that—people thought that maybe the jewelry was around the place. No, nah, nah—in the vault and still today it's in the vault. The things that people left them—jewelry, diamonds, earrings, you want to see the gold. Then when they used to come through the streets with the saint with the music playing and all that, they used to hang out twenty dollar bills, ten dollar bills, five dollar bills—hand them down like that. My father used to be in the front—stop, the old lady came. Some who couldn't walk believed that they could get better and who gave five dollars, ten dollars. They used to take with the pin and all the money was all like a big flag. At the end of the day take all the money off into the society. There was no robbing or anything like these thieves today—everything was in order to them. When somebody died in your family who got a hundred, who got fifty for funeral expenses and everything else. It was a great, wonderful thing.

"It Was a Holiday"

Tony Vitolo spoke at the kitchen table of the home of Angelina Criscuolo in East Haven on December 21, 1999.

Santa Maria Maddalena Day in those days was a holiday. People didn't work; the Atranese didn't go to work. It was a big holiday. And the official thing for Santa Maria Maddalena was "'o sarchiapóne," long squash. Stuffed. You'd bake it and cut it. My mother used to make it. You take it and you cut out all the seeds out and you stuff it, chopped meat, garlic, all that. And then they'd bake it. And that was the official dish.

"The Feast of Saint Andrew"

Lou Landino spoke on the back porch of his home in the Annex on August 6, 1999.

The three days to the feast, leading up to Sunday night, they would have a couple of old Italian boys would be down Waterside Park, and they would shoot this—boom!—every so often, which was the signaling of the beginning of the feast. And you'd hear this, like a cannon, boom! Then maybe after they'd a couple of wines, set another one off. When they had the Italian feasts on Wooster Street when we were kids, the Italian band—maybe a dozen guys playing instruments and drums would come down from Saint Michael's church, down Chapel Street, down Hamilton Street and then down Wooster Street because they had all the

SAINT ANDREW WOMEN'S SOCIETY
Marching down Wooster Street at the
Feast of Saint Andrew, 1920s

Argento family album

lights over and naturally we as kids would run behind the band like you see in some
of movies and just raise holy hell in general, that's all. I mean no harm, just jumpin'
around to the music and clapping—it was one big show. Then it was like a three
day affair, and Sunday night down Waterside Park, back toward the water, where
the Rusty Scupper is now, that's where they used to set off the fireworks on a Sunday night. At the end they used to have this huge framework and the American
flag would come out, stars and stripes and there'd be color and the little Italian

band was over there playing. The flag was all fireworks, beautiful, red, white, and blue with the blue field with the white stars, the red and white stripes. It was just tremendous color. And the music would be playing and that was the climax of the fireworks—it was beautiful. You really had to be there. It just can't be described in words.

"Blessing the Fleet"

Andrea Colavolpe spoke at the Saint Andrew Society in the Wooster Square on June 14, 1999.

Years ago, the four Gargano brothers were the first people that got involved with the blessing of the fleet. They used to take the boat, take Saint Andrew and bring him down Waterside Park where they had their boat. They were the original ones—they had to carry Saint Andrew. If the four brothers didn't carry Saint Andrews, the old lady would have told them, "You can't eat here today—you got to carry Saint Andrew before you come home and eat." I think there's only one left. And the four brothers, believe me when I tell you, they were very devoted to Saint Andrew. They were the commanding chiefs—they were the first one to carry Saint Andrew—nobody could have gotten underneath Saint Andrew but the four Gargano brothers first. Then they had a different gang that got underneath. It was a tradition from the old lady, the mother. She told them, "You got to carry Saint Andrew otherwise don't come home." That's the truth. And they used to go down on Franklin Street where the Gargano mother used to live, go right underneath the house, oh yeah. The mother had to see it; she was very devoted, the old lady, very devoted to Saint Andrew.

Italian Societies

After the Unification in 1870, economic policies enacted by the new Italian government further deepened cultural and economic differences between north and south. Especially hard hit were small farmers in the south whose meager profits were wiped out by increased taxes on farmland. In the Unification's aftermath, Italy had the highest taxes of any European country except Spain; 54 percent of income went to taxes. Describing inequities between the poverty-stricken areas of the south and the rapidly developing industrial north a professor remarked, "[In Italy] the less a man has, the more he pays."[37] The new northern-based government in Piedmont organized Italy's 40,000 charitable foundations but the majority of funds were funneled to northern regions for road-building projects, industrial development, and school systems improvements.[38] Poor families facing increased tax burdens turned to local societies named in honor of the town's patron saint for help. With meager contributions from members trapped in a steadily worsening economic climate, societies could offer little financial assistance for burials, sickness relief, or unemployment benefits.

Many of New Haven's Italians harbored memories of bad experiences and a lingering suspicion of government officials whose only function was to collect taxes. Few applied to the city for relief; in 1887, only 4 out of 350 adult recipients were Italian.[39] Fiercely independent and loyal to village and region before nation, Italians transported their own grassroots self-help institutions to the street corners and storefronts of their neighborhoods. Society members who derived steady income from full-time jobs and small businesses filled the coffers of local "fratellanze," or brotherhoods, "circoli," or clubs, and "società di mutuo soccorso" or mutual aid societies, which flourished into political, religious, social, and cultural centers all over the city. By 1930, over eighty societies had been established in New Haven with a membership of 10,000.[40]

In 1884, the first society, "La Fratellanza," or "The Brotherhood" was opened by Paul Russo to anyone of southern ancestry and "La Marineria" was started to aid visiting Genoese sailors who settled in the city. In 1897, Angelo Mazzarello founded the Circolo di San Carlino in the Fair Haven neighborhood where benefit performances in the building's five-hundred-seat theatre raised funds for the reconstruction of Saint Michael's church. Ties with Italy were kept and funds were raised by the societies for victims of the 1905 earthquake in Calabria and for the 1906 earthquake at Vesuvius. The Circolo del Sannio, comprised of the people of Cerreto Sannita, was founded in 1897 in the Oak Street neighborhood and offered members courses in Italian history, language, and drawing. The Regional Marchegiano Society was founded in 1909 in the Hill section by thirty-six men who joined together to help one another in times of need with death and unemployment benefits. Italian women became active in the affairs of the societies. In 1924, 132 women formed the Societa Femminile Marchegiana with its own bylaws and by 1936 were in equal partnership with men. The Venetia Club, which began in the Hill neighborhood, had a women's society. The Saint Andrew Women's Society marched in white uniforms in the Saint Andrew feast parade. The Societa di Mutuo Soccorso Settentrionale Italiana was opened to all of northern ancestry and provided burial funds and a sickness stipend for the unemployed based on weekly contributions.

In 1906, the Ullman brothers, owners of a corset factory, recognized the voting potential of societies and brought the members of the Santa Maria Maddalena Society into Republican ranks. In 1906, Antonio Vannacori from the Wooster Square neighborhood was elected the first Italian Alderman as a Republican, a political affiliation of the area that continued through the Mayor Richard C. Lee years of the '50s and '60s when the city was overwhelmingly Democratic.

In the large meeting rooms of society buildings like the Marchegiano Club in New Haven's Hill section, where men played cards, prepared old world meals in large kitchens and organized pig roasts on outdoor spits, Italians found refuge in an alien world around them, keeping the memory, traditions, and language of Italy alive and supporting yearly festivals with financial contributions. The societies played an important role in maintaining close ties with Italy, especially when a returning "paesano," often someone who had tended the same soil and strolled the same village streets, came back with the latest news from home. Newly-arrived immigrants learned helpful ways to make the sudden transition from an agricultural small-town lifestyle to an urban, fast-paced way of life from more experienced compatriots who spoke the same language and understood their needs. By the 1940s, the function of societies changed from mutual aid to social and recreational activities where the second generation attended dinners and dances. By the 1950s, the pull of assimilation was greater for second- and third-generation children than the need to retain their Italian identities and society membership waned. New Haven's once-thriving societies and clubs are now populated by elderly men who return from the suburbs to be with old neighborhood friends.

"THE MARCHEGIANO CLUB"

Larry Baldelli spoke at the Marchegiano Club in the Hill section on October 11, 2000.

They would come down to play cards all dressed up in jackets and they all had the vests, they all had the long sleeve shirts and they had the little chains that went from one pocket to the other. And they all played and that's all they did and if you didn't get here early you didn't play cards. This place was jammed from pillar to post. In the late '50s, early '60s it all changed when they came through with the highway and put the connector in and they tore things down for Lee High School, it was all over. And of course people moved out of the city to the suburbs. I never felt threatened in this area for whatever and I don't feel as though it's an area to look down at, but not everybody feels the same.

They used to find an abandoned road somewhere; didn't have to be blacktop. A road where cars did not pass through regularly because that meant they would have to stop. The straighter the better but if it had curves that was part of the game—you had to take that into consideration. So the first person would shoot and his ball, if it stayed on the crown and kept going, he didn't have to have a lot of power but he had to make sure it stayed on the crown wherever that stopped . . . so now eventually it's going to fall off the crown as it slows down so wherever that stops his next team player starts from there. Whoever went the furthest with their four players won that point and they would just keep going and come back. So sometimes you could have a real powerful arm that couldn't control the ball and it just went flying off the side and it was all over. There was a lot of skill in that because you had to throw it just so hard to keep it on the crown of that road. We had some bocce players who were phenomenal; you would not believe what they could do with a bocce ball. The could hit that pill [little ball] from ninety feet in the air, just make it come right down and not touch anything around it. Not touch any other ball around it and your ball would stay there. Actually they didn't always hit for the pill but hit the opponent's ball. We had soccer teams, baseball teams here. We were a pretty progressive society when they first started. For the members who were indigent they actually bought grave plots for them. Anybody who couldn't afford to be buried at Saint Lawrence cemetery, they actually gave them a plot if they didn't have any family, they actually buried them. That's the way it was founded because in those days, let's face it, there was discrimination against Italians. There was discrimination against any ethnic group who came in. There was a need to stick together and band together and that is what this society was formed for. It was formed as a mutual aid society to help people who came over. We still have the death benefit—when somebody dies we still pay the mortuary.

"THE ACERNESE CLUB"

Orlando Ginnetti spoke at the kitchen table of his brother John's home in the Annex on August 28, 1999.

I wasn't a fan of Roosevelt. I was young then, but I read a lot and I didn't think he had what it took. He was a good politician. Of course, I was probably influenced by my father and the club he belonged to in Fair Haven, the Acernese Republican Club on Grand Avenue. These were all people that came from Acerno. The club was where all the Acernese gathered; they used to play bocce in the backyard, play cards. Very helpful, it was a house and they owned it. I used to go in there a lot, chase my father, but mostly because I knew the paisans, friends, were going to buy me a soda. They would, they would, yeah. They had a cooperative where the members could go in and borrow money and then pay it back. If they borrowed a 100 dollars, they paid back maybe 102, 103 dollars—it was reasonable. My father used to borrow every year to make his wine. He'd make about six fifty-gallon barrels of wine. And by the time the next season came he didn't have any more. Because he had a lot of friends. And anybody who walked in the house didn't walk out without a gallon of wine.

"THEY PAID FOR EVERYTHING"

Joe and Pat Amarone spoke at the Santa Maria Maddalena club on Wooster Street on October 9, 1999.

The Santa Maria Maddalena di Mutuo Soccorso Society was founded as a mutual aid society to help the immigrants. They started that club for that simple reason: to help the immigrants from the town of Atrani. I'm not saying that they wouldn't help other Italians but their main focus and their main idea was to help the Italian immigrants get settled, find them a job, give them financial help if they needed it. My father was born in Atrani in 1888. And he came to this country in 1903 when he was fourteen. He came with his dad, it was just him and his father. And they were here about a month and a half and his father was killed in a construction accident down where Sperry and Barnes was, where the freight cars were. He slipped on the rails where the cars were coming in with coal bins and they used to pick up the scraps of the coal and store it for sale. So my father was left here by himself. So naturally he came down to the Society of Mary Maddalena, which at the time I don't know how big it was—maybe fifteen or twenty older Italian people started this club in 1899. He came down here to this very spot and he asked for help. He had no money, no family. So the club president at the time—they made arrangements for him to live someplace here on Wooster Street. In the meantime, they sent for his mother, his brother, and two sisters at the club's expense. They had his grandfather buried, paid for his funeral and all expenses, paid for the family to come here. It took about six months before they got here between paperwork and telling the situation to the immigration people. They finally got here, set up home.

"THE ANNEX Y.M.A."

Charlie Mascola spoke in the living room of his home with his son Chuck and old friend Joe Riccio in the Annex on January 5, 1999.

I can remember they [young men in the neighborhood] had nowhere to go. So I said to my father, Well, we got the barn back there, let's do something. My father said, "Well, what can we do?" I talked to my father. If it wasn't for my father we would have no club. The Vanacore boys wanted Annex Boy's Club and I said, "Annex Boy's

SAN CARLINO SOCIETY THEATRE
853 Grand Avenue, Fair Haven
Founded in 1897
"La Colonia Italiana"

Club is small, we're looking for something further ahead." Tony "Kelly" Ferraiuolo came up with the name Young Men's Association. The week after the Hurricane of 1938, the 25th of September, we had a meeting upstairs [in the barn]. The club used to be called The Italian Club. We used to go get pizza down the club, and there would be eight or nine of us girls and guys sitting on each other's lap; all brothers and sisters. I think there were about eight or nine marriages out of it. We had minstrel shows [at Fort Hale School]. They had baseball teams here; we never had basketball because we never had a gym. We played basketball; we always got beat. In amateur football, we were one of the best in the state. The Italians in them days, they were short and fat, they were two hundred pounds but they were tough, they were dumb, they'd fight at the drop of a hat. We had teams over here, The Woodwards for the guys who lived on Woodward Avenue, The Forbes, The Townsends, The Oakleys, everybody had a little team. On a Sunday there would be four games, the first would be the Annex Ants, the little guys would play, they started at nine o'clock, then it would be the Annex Midgets, then the Boys Club and then the big team at one o'clock, the Big Annex would play. Every Sunday there were four games. They would draw maybe eight or nine hundred people.

"Come With Me, I'll Take You to the Job"

Bill Zampa and Ron Mortali spoke at the Marchegiano club in the Hill section on August 3, 2000.

If you came to the [Marchegiano] Club, the society, Joe or John would say, "You just got off the boat? You come with me—I'll take you to the job." There were boarding houses all were all along Christopher and Water Street—they were all run by Marchegiano ladies or Marchegiano families. Ever hear of the Underground Railroad for slaves? Well, this was the immigrant railroad for the Marchegians. Marchegiano guys, they came right out of Ellis Island, Grand Central Station, right here to Union Station, and this is why this section was so heavily populated with Marchies, they didn't have to go that far from the railroad station. So the whole Hill section is all Marchegianos, and they stuck together and this is where the club is, not far from the railroad station. They had to walk two blocks from the railroad station to the club. No big deal, no taxi cabs, no buses. They sponsored all the immigrants that came over, they would see to it that they would place them in some workplace where they could keep an eye on them and make sure that they produced and kept them right on line. They didn't take risks. They made sure they were upstanding, paid attention to what they were doing and do what they were told to do. They'd go with them to the jobs and made sure they produced and perpetuated themselves in the workplace as good workers and if I told you that I'm bringing someone on a job, they could count on it that they could produce for them. In the early days they worked in the labor trade primarily as laborers, at Blakeslee's, all the construction that took place at Yale, the Bijou theatre, the Poli theatre, they built all that, all the stonework.

"THEY USED TO COOK AT NIGHT"

Tony Sacco and Salvatore "Gary" Garibaldi spoke at a table in Tony and Lucille's restaurant on Wooster Street on May 19, 2000.

You know what was good about them clubs them days? They used to cook. At night, a certain hour of the night, a pasta marinara, "Anthony, go to D'Anese's bakery and get three, four, five loaves of bread." They used to take the bread, they used to cut, they used to open, take the middle out. If they didn't have the tomatoes—oil, pepper, and garlic—fold it and everybody would eat it and enjoy it. Or you used to put tomatoes, basil, pepper, garlic, oil, you know, and that's what my mother used to do. And I used to say to myself, boy everybody knows this recipe? It must have been a famous dish. That was our pizza, it was pizza bread, actually it was raw tomato with oil, parsley, basil, and Italian bread. See in this neighborhood you had six or seven bakeries—Avitable, Midolo's, Sarno's, Carafola's, Gianpappa's. So it was like in walking distance. On a Saturday afternoon, on Collis and Hamilton, my uncle, he was the guy who did all the cooking. So on a Saturday afternoon, maybe ten or twelve guys, and he make aglio e olio, spaghetti with garlic and oil, and they'd all eat it and he'd charge them like fifty cents apiece to help pay for the expenses of the ingredients. So now he'd be sitting there as a young kid [pointing to Tony] and say, "Anthony, go buy four or five loaves." So he went to Avitable down the street because it was hot stuff and he'd bring it to them. And that was the neighborhood family. At nighttime they'd enjoy themselves. Some families like in Saint Andrews [club] on Sunday afternoon, they would cook for three or four families in the club, they had a big pantry. So like you lived here and I lived and we were all friends and on a Sunday afternoon we'd all eat there. You know, they all pulled together, not like today.

"THE NORTHERN CLUBS IN NEW HAVEN"

Rosemarie Foglia spoke in a conference room at City Hall on June 28, 1999. She spoke of the deep respect her parents felt toward southern Italians and how well they got along.

My mother and father were some of the founders of the Petramicca Club because this was the northern Italian group, there was the Settentrionale for the Marchies, the Marchegiani, then the Marchegiano Club in New Haven was also for the Marchegiani but there was nothing for the Piedmontese. They were allowed [to join] but . . . we were into, I guess, territorial things, so this group of northern Italians started this Petramicca Club and my mother and father were part of the founders of this group. But my mother's philosophy to this was that I would marry the nice northern Italian boy because every Sunday or every other Sunday there was a banquet or a dance and off we'd go. We'd take two buses and off we'd go. And I know that was her thought and at some given point I ended up dating

CIRCOLO AVERSANO
176 Wallace Street,
Wooster Square, 1920s.
Founded in 1914
"La Colonia Italiana"

only one Italian. Most people I dated were Irish. And my mother could not understand the numbers and she wasn't into any kind of census or statistics but she knew there were a lot of Italians in New Haven and why couldn't I find one? But I started dating what was my husband to be. We dated for about three years and became engaged. By that time my mother and father truly liked him and had

SAINT ANDREW SOCIETY

Picnic, 1929

Argento family album

a college degree and he was all the right things and he was a Catholic. Catholicism was not the issue. But my mother deep down was still upset because quote, unquote, Irish have a lot of kids and they always went to the bar and all that other good stuff. But she had gotten some of it. But she wrote to my aunt in Italy that I had become officially engaged and I was to be married within a year and this young man was "Irlandese" [Irishman]. And she couldn't understand why I could not find an Italian in this city. And my aunt wrote back from Italy: "I know you're upset about the fact that Rosemarie is engaged to an Irlandese but better he be Irlandese then southern Italian, Bass Italia, piu meglio Irlandese che Bass Italia."

And that was really their philosophy and I came to meet this aunt and uncle and this aunt was just the most gracious, loving person. She owned this little boutique on the main road leading to the piazza, in the town of Montcalvo, which was really cosmopolitan, compared to some of these other towns. And she would stand in front of this shoe store, this boutique, and say, "Bass Italia, Americana, Bass Italia, Americana, Piemontese, Bass Italia cafone [boor]," you know and I finally said to her in Piedmontese, "Ma perche? Me chet' sai che song men piemontes'?" How do you know they're not Piedmontese? And she replied, "Guarda la vesta, la vesta e fiori, colori!" And she was a very stately woman and she was saying, "Just look at the colors of their clothes—yellow, blue—can't you tell? And they have a camera." That was truly Bass Italia, if they had a camera. That was like, oh, how showy to have a camera. And I would say in Piemontese, "But they're traveling, taking pictures." "No, no, no, they're working at the farm but they have to have a camera—it's their status symbol." She never got over it, never, ever got over it and that was it. But it was their attire or their demeanor. And this was it, and oh, they were very nice [southern Italians], but. This was their philosophy, this was her attitude, "Piu meglio Irlandese che Bass Italia," better Irish than southern Italian, and that was it. My grandparents were not wealthy so it isn't that they came from this very exclusive—they were all farmers. Now my cousins are into the wine business and all but this is almost a hobby now. So it isn't that we're certainly above the masses but their attire and their style is just a little more proper in their words, this is it. "Piu meglio un Irlandese che Bass Italia," yes I could still see her saying that.

“Blackutts and the Firecracker”

Tony Sacco spoke at his Wooster Street restaurant on May 19, 2000.

I lived across the street from the Saint Andrew's Society and every night I used to be in that society, like I used to get a bottle of gassosa, I used watch them play [cards] 'o tre sette, briscola, 'a scopa. And you know we had our own gang. One time I brought a firework in my pocket and the guy, Blackutts, was playin' with a cigarette and he says, uh, "Whadda you got?" I said, "Eh, I gotta a firework." He says, "Damma me, give it to me." I says, "No, no you kiddin' me? You'll give my father a heart attack." He says, "No, no, no, no, damma a me." I said, "Blackutts, you're not serious are you?" He says, "No, no, no." So he took the firework. And I'm watching him. He threw his hand in. The next thing you know he took a puff on his cigarette and he's playing with the wick under the table and he lets it go underneath the table. He says, "Scusata, àggia i' affa nu poc' 'e aqua," Pardon me, I've got to go to the bathroom. Oh my God! I ran, I couldn't get to the door fast enough. As soon as he got to the men's room I heard a ba-boom! My God, my father come runnin' out of that club with his hand in his mouth, "When I get you, when I get you!" "I didn't do nothing, [crying voice] I didn't do it," he took the firework from me! They almost had to call the emergency [ambulance], they had to give them old timers a glass a water. [The men said] "Blackutts, ai fatt' una brutta figura, muore subbeto!" Blackutts you did a rotten thing, drop dead. Because they were so shocked over that explosion. I didn't go home for two days after that.

"Provolone and the Macaroni Plants"

My father was a true Amalfitano. He used to be in that Saint Andrews Society Club seven days a week. My God. My mother must a said, I came from Amalfi here, to see him go to the club? What a life. And I used to hang around in there too, you know. My brothers did too, and we got to know [the old timers], they all knew us. When I was a kid that Provolone, he did a lot of crazy things. They used to call him Provolone. His name was Vincenzo Consiglio. We called him Provolone, he must a liked to eat provolone, you eat a lot of provolone they call you provolone. Me, my last name is Sacco, they call me "'o sacc," [pocket], miett' i soldi in da sacc,' put your money in your pocket. They got names for everybody around here, cirasa, cherries, salsice, sausage. I was a little boy. I said, "Hey Provolone, how they get macaroni? Where they make macaroni? How they make macaronis?" He says [mocking voice], "They don't make macaronis, they plant them!" I said, "Really?" He says, "You want linguini, you plant linguini, you want spaghetti, you plant spaghetti, you want fusilli, you plant the fusilli." We went home, we planted the whole yard. My father came home, he went in the yard—he saw the whole yard full of macaroni. He said, "What's this? What's all that?" I said, Provolone said you plant macaroni, you get macaroni trees. "He said that?" I said, Yeah, Dad, Provolone. What the hell, we were six, seven years old. He said [disgusted voice], "Don't mind him, leva chille cose, Take those things out! You don't plant macaroni—he made a joke!" So he went to the club. My father said to Provolone, "Eh Provolone, che suciesso che i criatùri, aiut a dice a piant i spaghetti in da yard?" What happened with the kids? You told them to plant macaroni in the yard? He said [incredulous voice], "Oh, why?" My father said, "They planted the whole yard!" [Provolone said] "È vero?" Is that right? "Yeah," my father said, "They planted the whole yard." And Provolone was laughing. They were a bunch of characters, but they were good people, they were nice people, hard working people. Maybe that's all they got out of life. They devoted themselves to Saint Andrew.

Team sports and competing in games that required strenuous physical effort were foreign concepts to Italian immigrants. In the old country, sweat and toil was equated with the stamina needed to work long hours in the fields, to take the daily hike back and forth from village to countryside, or the considerable muscle strength required to do the grueling, perilous job of fishing. Some of the greatest Italian baseball players—Yogi Berra, Joe DiMaggio, and Phil Rizzuto—met resistance from immigrant parents who saw little career security in sports like baseball. But as their sons signed minor league contracts and gradually rose to stardom for The New York Yankees, they became cultural icons to New Haven's Italian working class. On Sunday afternoons Italian grandfathers who had never heard of baseball in the old country and barely understood the rules of the game were riveted to black and white television screens as they rooted for the Yankees. Watching Joe DiMaggio gracefully circle the bases after hitting a home run, they smiled and thrust an index finger to announce, "Joe ha fatto uno," or Joe hit a home run.

Sons of New Haven's Italian immigrants quickly overcame the conservative old world attitude their parents had toward team sports and participated in organized leagues as early as the 1900s. The boys who played for the "Sons of Italy" baseball team from the Wooster Square neighborhood were supported by the Saint Andrew's Society and the Mary Maddalena Society. In 1910, "The Sannios," a team sponsored by the society Circolo Sannio on Oak Street, won the New Haven city baseball tournament. In the 1920s and '30s, sandlot baseball and football teams named "The Fair Haven Blues," "The Rattlesnakes," and "The Oakleys" sprouted in neighborhood playgrounds and played before sizable crowds in a small bandbox stadium at Lighthouse Point in the Annex.

Daughters of Italian immigrants who yearned to play sports on sandlots and in the streets like their brothers met stronger resistance from parents. Italians held conservative views of women participating in sports, believing a young girl's first responsibility was working to sustain the family, to eventually have children, and then support a husband. In the 1930s and '40s, Clorinda "Schoolgirl Mongillo" Ruocco, New Haven's famous athlete and pioneer woman began changing traditional old world beliefs. An outstanding athlete who excelled on baseball diamonds and basketball courts, she paved the way for future generations of star athletes like Jennifer Rizzotti, who led the University of Connecticut Women's Basketball team to the 1995 championship. In the 1930s, the International Ladies Garment Workers Union sponsored ladies' basketball teams, offering second generation Italian women the chance to play sports in an otherwise dull life of factory work.

"Take My Meatballs, I Don't Want Them"

Joe Simone spoke in a meeting room at Sterling Memorial Library on July 13, 1999.

You'd get goose bumps watching Joe DiMaggio catch a ball or to see him hit a ball and run. To pile in the station wagon, seven, eight kids and two grownups and just go to Yankee Stadium. And you behaved. You sat there and you cheered, put your hat on and your knickers. My father and his brother Dominic were the greatest Yankee admirers that you have ever seen. And just to drive five hours to go watch a game. And you had to drive five hours back after the game—that's ten hours of driving to watch a ball game with seven kids in the car. What we had we took with us, the food. We didn't have any money to buy anything. We used to bring our sandwiches, sometimes we took dishes of macaroni to the ballpark. We were sitting eating sausages and meatball in the ballpark. My uncle got so mad, he picked up his meatballs and threw them at the Red Sox player because the guy hit a home run. And they came and they were going to throw us out of the park. My father is going, "Dom, we came five hours to watch a ball game—what are you doing?" My uncle said, "Did you see that guy? Where does he get off hitting that home run? That guy was struck out, the guy called the wrong pitch and now he hits a home run. Take my meatballs, I don't want them!"

"You're a Girl—You Gotta Stay Home"

Clorinda "Schoolgirl Mongillo" Ruocco spoke at the kitchen of her Fair Haven home on August 18, 1998.

I got more beatings from my mother because I used to go out and play ball. My mother was born in Italy in the province of Benevento, she came here when she was eighteen years old. My father went to work, minded his business, came home. He went to work for the family. My mother was the boss. In other words, she was there all the time for us so she more or less had her set rules, "You do this and you do that—you're not supposed to do that." So naturally she had ten kids, one died when he was nine months old, then she had four boys and there was five of us girls. So when I used to go out and play she said, "I got four boys and they don't play, you're a girl, you got a stay home." Press clothes, wash clothes and all that. But I didn't mind her, I just went. On the way coming home from school this friend of mine, Al Fezza, he was the only one who had a basketball rim on the garage. He

CLORINDA
"SCHOOLGIRL MONGILLO"
RUOCCO

Mongillo family album

even had a basketball. So when you're playing and playing you don't know what time it is because I never had a wristwatch—the first one I got from my husband—not like today, they got wristwatches but they don't look at it. So got home later than I was supposed to, you get out of school at three, you're supposed to be home within fifteen, twenty minutes. And I didn't because I used to play. So one time I come at five o'clock at night, aye, forget about it, [my mother asked] "Addó si state? Che ste facendo?" Where were you? What were you doing? Ba-beep, ba-bop, and all that. But that was her way, and she couldn't see it no how. Well, in our yard we had to cut the bottom of a basket and have a rubber ball and shoot it. And even for that I got hollered at because I ruined the basket and my mother had to put the tomatoes in it. She never came to see me play, all the other mothers and fathers came, but my mother never came. Neither did my father because he used to work all the time. My brothers came.

All the time of my career when I played basketball, only once she wouldn't let me go. So the one game when I was supposed to go to Branford to play, the neighbors came over, parents of the other girls, "Mrs. Mongillo, you got to let her go otherwise we're gonna lose." I can't say what she said back to them [laughing]. She said, "Va, vatene, va vatene!" [Go! Get out of here!]. And that was it. She said to me, "State a casa!" You stay home! She called me a few names and that was it. So she wouldn't let me go, and when the girls came back, they were yelling, "Mrs. Mongillo, you made us lose the game." But after that game, when we had to play, I used to throw the bag out the window—luckily I was living on the first floor—throw my uniform in the bag out the window, and then I'd close the window, then I'd walk around. We had five rooms in a row, one, two, three, so the kitchen was way in the back, the window I went out was over there. And I'd jump out the window and I'd have somebody close the window, my brother usually. And I went and play. Then when I got home after a game, instead of saying, "How did you make out?" Ba-da-boom, Ba-da-boom, that's the way it was, she really didn't want me to play and she was against it one hundred percent because I was a girl. She used to say, "Tu si fémmena addá sta a casa," [You are a girl, you stay home]. I was supposed to stay home—the boys were supposed to go out. In the '30s, it isn't like now, now it's "non si capisce a niénte," it's all upside down. Today they go here, they go there whether they're girls or boys, they stay overnight. I started playing when I was twelve, thirteen years old. Nobody taught me, I learned by myself. I used to go down to Quinnipiac Park and play with the boys. The boys had a baseball team and I used to play with them. They had summer playgrounds, you know, you go there and play. This was 1933, 34, 35. I got the name "Schoolgirl" from the baseball player during those times, "Schoolboy Rowe" from the boys. One of them called me "Schoolboy." The other kid said, "She's a girl, call her 'Schoolgirl.'" Nobody knows me by my real name. I'm still Schoolgirl to everybody. I used to play intramural basketball with the girls at Fair Haven. Girls' rules in school was that the court was divided in three sections. You couldn't go over the [dividing line]. If you're a forward, this is the line for the forward, you couldn't go into the center or the guards couldn't go over their line. If you did the other team takes the ball off side. They had teams of six, two forwards, two centers, two guards—this is in the '30s. And the only one that shoot were the forwards, which I was one of the forwards. I was always the captain. I was always the leader not only in sports when I worked, whatever, because I worked with kids practically all my life. I also used to play up the YWCA which they had half court and you had three girls on one side and three girls on the other. Which means three forwards could shoot at the basket. The guards get the ball to the forwards—that's how it works—but you can't go over the middle line. That's girls' rules. In those days those were rules in the schools, I don't know who instituted them. Hop Nuzzo who was our first coach—he got a bunch of girls to play together and he called them "The Mickey Mouse Midgets" because we were young. But when we played with him, we played boys' rules. And we used to play all the teams in greater New Haven, we went out of state a few times but we played mainly in Connecticut. These other teams played boys' rules. In school, the YMCA, it was only girls' rules. But wherever we went, they played boys' rules so we played boys' rules. In boys' rules everybody shoots, you pass the ball around, you run back and forth, back and forth. And the rules then were different. Today after every basket, your opponent takes the ball off side and goes down. When we played after every basket we let the center jump. It was a slower game, low scoring game then. Today, it's faster.

"My Greatest Thrill"

In 1949, I didn't play for the Connecticut Beach Heads because I had a back problem. And the coach had me on the roster. They were playing for the state championship

"CONNECTICUT YANKEE GIRLS" BASEBALL TEAM

Mongillo family album

at Raybestos field against the Wallingford Owlettes. I was in the stands with my husband and son and my sister. Wallingford was ahead 2‒0. Last inning, the Beach Heads had two girls on base with two outs. The coach was Huey Gartland and he called me, he said, "Schoolgirl, come on." I said, "What do you want?" He said, "I want you to pinch hit." I said, "I didn't play all year, what am I gonna pinch hit?" He said, "I want you to pinch hit." I really didn't want to because my son was small and he was crying for his mother and she brought him out into right field. My mother should have been there. "Ba da boom," [laughing] and the those words again, "'O figlio tùjo chiàgna, e tu pazzìa a palla! Eh, sí pazza!" Your son is crying and you're playing baseball? You're crazy! I had dungarees and a shirt on. Somebody gave me a shirt and that was it. So I got up, luckily I got a hit to score the two runs and tie the score. So naturally we had to go into extra innings so he said, "Play third base." I said, "Huey!" I was a little leery you know. I hadn't touched a ball all year. So I played third base. We went into extra innings. In the tenth inning naturally I come up again. Still 2‒2. I come and hit a home run and we won 3‒2. The ball is still going, I mean it. I hit it so hard—I usually hit to left field—I hit it so hard that it went out through the gate at Raybestos field, out of the ballpark. We won and we got the trophy. And that was one of the biggest thrills of my life.

"Scandalosa"

Luisa DeLauro spoke with her daughter Congresswoman Rosa DeLauro at the kitchen table of her Wooster Square home on August 9, 1998.

I played basketball. Yeah, I played baseball with guys on the block. We had what they called the women's league. Oh we had girls' rules, we couldn't go over the court, you had a stay on your own side of the court. Those were the girls' rules. And then I said, "I don't want to play girls' rules unless we change and we play like the boys do boys' rules that you could go to any part of the court. You could only stay on your half of the court, yeah. It was wild. The city of New Haven had a league with eight girls' teams. It was mixed, black and white. As a matter of fact the kids from the Dixwell neighborhood, they were mostly black, and we had the league, you know. And the black kids, they were doing a dinner dance for basketball and then dinner. So they had to select their team. So they picked on us, on our team, the Italian team. So I said to one of the black girls, "How come you decided to play with our team?" And you know what she said? "Because your team is the scrappiest team on the floor." We played hard. I wouldn't think anything of saying, Get out a my way. I was fresh, I was so fresh. Now girls' basketball is big, in those days it was unheard of. I was single, in my teens. I was playing in the lot, baseball one day. And I was the pitcher you know. And here I am throwing the ball; I had shorts on. My grandfather goes by, he goes, "Scandalosa!" That's scandalous! I didn't know what to do, I had to pitch, I couldn't pay attention to him [laughing]. My mother knew it but my grandfather thought it was terrible because I had shorts on and playing with the boys and girls.

LUISA DELAURO AND DAUGHTER
CONGRESSWOMAN ROSA DELAURO
1999
A. Riccio

❝GO LEARN A TRADE❞

Rosemarie Foglia spoke in a conference room at City Hall on June 28, 1999.

My brother was a great basketball player but he was really just a natural athlete. And my father thought that this was the bum effect and only kids that were bums played sports. And there was an entire setup that when they would see my father coming down the street there were whistles and signals so that my brother would know my father was coming down the street. My father would really punish, hit my brother, because he didn't want him to be a bum. And being involved in sports

SARGENT FACTORY BASEBALL TEAM, 1938

Calamo family album

was a bum because you should be working, you should be learning a trade. My brother, God bless him, died at seventy-five and became a millionaire after his stint in the service. He was a Seabee and ended up developing a good part of the Bahamas but always felt that it was my father's discipline and the kicks to the behind that did it because he really did fear that my brother would end up a bookie because we had a few in our neighborhood and it was the easiest way out. And my brother was just very good, my brother was co-captain of the Hillhouse basketball team and belonged to a number of teams. My father never saw him play. There was nothing to be very proud of. My brother ended up with a partial athletic scholarship to a school in Rhode Island and my father said, "No, learn a trade."

"IT WAS THE MOST BEAUTIFUL PARK IN THE CITY"

Tom Consiglio spoke at the Saint Andrew's Society on June 19, 1999. Tom's nickname was "The Lord" because of the unique way he could stop his friends from arguing.

Waterside Park [Wooster Square] was on Water Street between Hamilton and Franklin, it was on the water side with the water on the very end of the park. We had three baseball diamonds at the back of the park. In the front of the park we had benches all along the street and a playground for the kids with swings. And we had a cinderblock path that a person could run around the playground, it was a sand track that you could circle all around. We had a building with a shower and toilet facilities. Besides the baseball fields we had a basketball court and we had room for a football field. It was the most beautiful park in the city. For the people. All the people in the area, they used to go down there in the evening and they'd get the fresh air and watch the bocce players. We had bocce players running all around the park, teams of bocce teams, they followed them and watched them play.

21 *Artists and Singers*

Artists and singers ranked high in Italy's social scale. The United States government recognized the skill of Italian sculptors and painters and commissioned them to create important public art projects. At the Capitol, the sculptor Giuseppe Ceracchi carved marble busts of Washington, Jefferson, John Adams, James Madison, Benjamin Franklin, and Alexander Hamilton. Constatino Brumidi painted the entire ceiling of the Capitol in a stunning fresco of epic proportions reminiscent of the Sistine Chapel and was later dubbed "The Michelangelo of the United States Capitol."[41]

Among the mostly poor Italians of the lower classes arriving in New Haven were a small number of talented artists and singers who had received training in Italy. Francis Coiro, who apprenticed as an artist in southern Italy, decorated palatial lobbies of New Haven's movie theatres in gold leaf design and painted murals at local schools under the Works Project Administration. He later began a company in Fair Haven, "The Decorative Art Shop," that built and designed stage sets for operas in New York City. The church of Saint Anthony was painted by Domenico Biondi, a trained artist from the Art Institute of Naples, who covered the ceiling of Saint Anthony's Church in magnificent Renaissance-style scenes of "The Apparition of the Baby Jesus to Saint Anthony," "The Death of Saint Joseph," and "The Apparition of the Sacred Heart to the Blessed Margaret of Loque." In the 1930s, Joseph Simoni decorated ceilings of local churches with figures of angels and saints using black and white photographs and adding colors from his imagination. In 1901, the Cofrancesco brothers—Oscar, Andrea, and Domenico—skilled stonecutters from Cerreto Sannita, began a stonecutting business in the Oak Street neighborhood and sold decorative stones for lawns, granite cornerstones for buildings, and gravestones with busts and figures carved in high and low relief. As in shoemaking, carpentry, and barbering trades that required an apprenticeship period, stonecutting offered young boys like Domenico Rossi work in the Cofrancesco shop. Domenico began his apprenticeship at ten and by age fourteen he had begun using a hammer and chisel to create the highly-skilled work of engraving letters on gravestones.

In 1921, Guiseppina Pane began singing Neapolitan songs at the San Carlino Theatre at the age of eight and won first prize in a regional voice contest at fourteen, singing an aria from "La Boheme." Trained by her mother, Antonette Pastore, who insisted on keeping the musical tradition of "Canzone Napoletane," or Neapolitan songs, alive in America, she gave up singing opera and appeared on stage in New Haven and New York with famous Italian singers Carlo Buti and Gilda Mignonette. She and her husband Luigi produced "The White Sister" at the Shubert Theatre featuring Lillian Gish. In the 1950s, she appeared in shows in the eastern United States and Canada and shared the spotlight with Claudio Villa, Mario Merola, Massimo Ranieri, Paul Anka, Lou Monte, Jimmy Roselli, and Bobby Vinton. Guiseppina Pane's musical legacy has been passed to her daughter Nina who appears at summer feasts singing Neapolitan songs with a passion and feeling that would have made her mother proud.

"PROMISE ME YOU WON'T LET IT DIE"

Nina Pane Sanseverino and her sister Josie Pane Lawrence spoke at the kitchen table of their home in New Haven on July 30, 1999.

My mother Giuseppina's mother was a singer, Antonette Pastore. My mother's parents, Antonette and Tommaso, were from Formicola in Italy. She used to say, "A la venivano tutte fémmene belle," All the women who came from Formicola are beautiful. And she played the guitar and she taught Mom a lot of the songs. And at times they would go out together doing duets in New Haven. Antonette—"Tonette" they used to call her—was very funny, she used to sing what they call "macchiètte," [character sketches] funny songs that made you laugh:

> Aiére, che sucesso in da marchetta,
> Che guaio ha combinato Donna Cuncietta,
> Dinto marchetta, dinto in a marchetta,
> Tutte le spése l' ha caduto,
> E che mòsse ha tenuto.

> Yesterday in the market,
> What trouble befell Lady Concetta,
> In the market, in the market,
> All her groceries fell down,
> And what a face she had.

And she was like the life of the party. Everybody loved her; she used to tell jokes. My grandmother was in charge of two busloads going to San Gennaro feast in New York. The minute she'd get on the bus she would put this big hat on and something around her and with a box of Ritz crackers, she'd go and give everybody

GIUSEPPINA PANE
In concert

Pane family album

like it was communion—she was supposed to be San Gennaro—it was so funny.
She was a typical joker. And everybody would have that and that was to start off
our day. Then we would say a prayer. My mother Giuseppina was on stage at the
San Carlino theatre in New Haven when she was just eight years old; she was studying voice with Maestro Luigi Casillio and she was learning opera. She had a great
voice, quite a range. She was fourteen years old and sang "Mi Chiamano Mimi"
from "La Bohème" in a talent show and she won first prize. She loved opera but
her mother wanted her to sing Neapolitan. My parents loved the opera. God
knows I would sit as a little girl and listen to the radio with them on a Saturday
afternoon and they'd have it live from the Met and I'd listen to all the operas with
them. My mother did all the music for the silent movies at Tubi's Nicolette on
Grand Avenue. There was just a piano and she did the background music; she read

music. She studied her vocal studies in opera with Maestro Francesco Riggio. But then of course at her mother's insistence she just went back to the Neapolitan. She was well known. She was a great artist. If she went through the right channels I'm sure she would have been a big star. She is in the Italian field in Connecticut but she could have made Hollywood. She had facial expressions when she read poetry; she'd make you cry or she'd make you laugh, she had a little bit of everything in her. My mother was good for everybody. She was very charitable, very giving, very loving, very kind, very passionate—she had it all with her. When they called her to sing at the feasts if they said this job will pay so much money she would get entertainment that cost over that. She would come home with nothing for herself. In addition she put money out of her pocket because she made sure all the performers were here before and after the show. After the show an entourage of people would follow and she'd have full course meals at her home. At the end she was very sick and in a home—she was half-paralyzed—and she said, "I want you to promise me that you won't let it die, I want you to continue with the Italian theatre to do the Neapolitan shows. Don't let it die, I lived my whole life for that music." And she said, "Don't let Daddy's name die." The name Pane meant everything to her, they had a wonderful marriage.

"SIGNED J.M.J."

Rose and Larry Gherardi spoke at the kitchen table in their Hamden home on October 12, 1999. Rose enjoyed giving her paintings away as gifts.

They wanted to give me a scholarship from Yale. I said, No, I could be an artist without studying. My father never said, "Go to work." When I went in to that shirt factory—not that I had to work—I just thought my sister is working and she was bringing home money and buying herself some nice clothes and everything so I thought maybe I should. But I didn't have to. My father encouraged me. He was a stonemason and he knew quite a bit about art, singers, and opera. He loved stuff like that; he was well read, a very knowledgeable guy. And he used to tell me stories about the different artists—he told me about Raphael and Michelangelo and all these different stories. He inspired me to become an artist. So that's how I started drawing pictures of him—I was just a little kid when I drew a picture of him. He used to sit in a rocking chair and read the paper and so I used to sketch him. He said, "Lolli," that was my nickname, "I like it only you made me look too old." It doesn't, it looked just like him. And in fact I find out I'm starting to look like him to a tee. I feel that God gave us a talent. And I'm not out to make money on it. In fact if I like a person I'll give them my paintings because I know people that charge a lot of money for paintings and it's an art that God gave me. In fact if you like something here, I'll give it to you. If my wife [Rose] makes a portrait of someone, she'll keep it covered and when the two parents come, she'll watch your face to know that she got it. I can tell how the person feels, that's an artist for you. I like old people because I think they have a lot to express; they live life, wrinkles in their face. I love to paint and I wish I live

ROSE GHERARDI
Artist, at work in her studio,
Hamden, 1999
A. Riccio

long enough to finish all the paintings I've started. I always put J.M.J. on all
paintings—Jesus, Mary, and Joseph.

"AN ARTISAN IN NEW HAVEN"

Ettore and Julia Coiro spoke at the dining room table of their Fair Haven
home on November 30, 1998. Their father Francis left his name and address
with those of other craftsmen in a hidden area of the ceiling of the Starr Reading Room of Sterling Memorial Library in 1930.

My father came from Lauro di Sessa Aurunca. The was nothing to do there. There
was no work. He went to school there and was educated in Caserta. He went to the

PEQUOT THEATRE LOBBY
Grand Avenue,
Fair Haven, 1930s

Coiro family album

art school there. It was a very well known school of art, almost as good as Pratt in Brooklyn but not quite. There was no way to earn a living. When there's nobody there, there's nothing to do, nobody stays there—it's very simple. They go away, they go where they can. My father was an only child, if they didn't have a buck or two, who else had it? My father's stepfather was an interior decorator and he did a lot of churches and that's mainly where the work was, in special buildings and in churches. He was the one who taught my father. He even designed the marriage certificate. It was very beautiful and it looked like the design work that my father eventually did. He tried to get all these different jobs in the art field but at the time it was hard in the '20s. He used to work on homes and doing specialty things in homes but it didn't pay well. He used to make the design and in order for him to transfer those designs onto whatever wall or ceiling he was going to put it on he would perforate them by pin pricking. In the due process he made sketches, small-scale sketches and enlarged them to the scale of whatever the building to be decorated. And he changed his design in scale to the scale of what he had to do. That's when he made the rough pieces and it was our job as kids to do the pin pricking. We would take a thick piece of rug we'd put down and he would spread that out for us and he had a pencil with a little pricker, like a shoemaker's awl. We had to do all those outlines; we used to outline all those things and there was plenty of it to outline. Then they would put them up on the ceilings and wall and he used some kind of a powder to transfer the outline, like a stencil. He did repetitive motifs, circles with a star or a flower in it. He would take a piece of paper with a rough sketch; he would bring it up to the ceiling, rub charcoal on it and then tap it, tap it, repeat it, all the way around the ceiling. Tap it, tap it, tap it. Then he had the scale and he knew it would fit all the way around the way it would go, otherwise he would be lost. And the he would start painting it. They painted by sections. He kept moving it along until he got the whole motif done. He worked on Saint Francis, Saint Michael, and Saint Mary, all the funeral homes on Chapel Street, the Maresca Funeral Home, all this type of designing work, repetitive, stenciling. When you did a funeral home in those days it wasn't just wallpaper it was painted, nicely done. They had gesso, the little patterns they used to make of plaster and then they would glue them to the ceilings and then he would gold leaf them or paint them. They would make the pattern they wanted they would enclose the pattern they wanted and would fill it in. He did gold leafing if they had the money, like Yale had the bucks, he would do the gold leaf but if not he would paint it. He did work at Sterling Library and he was very proud of that. He used hair static on the brushes—rub it in his hair to get the static—and then apply it to the gold leaf, and suck it right up and stick it up there. It he would just brush it off and it would stick to where he had the glue. He always had the flecks of gold in his hair from doing that. Gold leaf used to come in a book, with little thin sheets of tissues in between and you opened up those leaves and there it is and you had to be very careful because it was very delicate. That's why you had to have the very soft brush to pick it up with. Growing up we had beautiful ceilings in the dining and living room in our home on Lombard Street that he designed and oil painted. They laid an artist canvas on the ceiling. You would scaffold the whole area of the living room, then we would take the canvas and unravel it and just tack it up there and he'd come around with the brush and get it up there tight. We kids, when my father couldn't get artisans to do it, he needed people to help hold the stuff up there, particularly with the canvases, and we used to go up on the scaffolds. And finally it would all be there.

FRANCIS COIRO
(far right)
At the studio working on a
stage set for "Aida,"
547 Ferry Street,
Fair Haven, 1920s

Coiro family album

And he would do a section, then do another section. But when it was painted, you
see, there were no cracks in the plaster because it had canvas covering the whole
ceiling. Any cracks, if there were any, were behind the canvas so you couldn't see
them. Just an ordinary piece of canvas taken out of a potato bag. It was in rows of
six foot and unlimited length and he would size it, what we called gluing it. And
little bit by little, two or three guys—it was a lot of work doing this, applying that
canvas to the ceiling. Then he would put the transfer pattern on it and the drawing
was applied later. He used to make his own tools. He made his own planes for carving the trim. You had to because if it was a certain contour you had to cut the blade
to fit that contour, to fit whatever job he was doing. He made his own special
molding for his picture frames. He made the stage sets, the props, and the construction that supported the sets for the "Aida" with the Egyptian motifs.

"Painting Church Ceiling Murals"

Joe Simone spoke in a meeting room in Sterling Library on July 19, 1999.

My father found out he couldn't get work because he was an Italian and he decided to change his name in the '20s from Simoni to Simone so it sounded like it was French. Here in New Haven you couldn't get work unless you were Irish or your name didn't end in a vowel. It was sad. Just to think that people couldn't go to work. And there were jobs. But you couldn't get them. They found it hard. New Haven was a very Irish town. It was ridiculous, really. We all lived together but we couldn't work together. And that's the truth. You couldn't earn money together but you lived together. And it wasn't only in that trade. My father-in-law was a mason and he used to tell me the same thing. He changed his name from DiFabriti and he added s to his name to DiFabritis. And they thought he was Greek so they hired him. My cousin, Marchitto, he changed his name to March, he could off the itto, legally changed his name to March to sound English so he could get work in the business world. And then my father started to get a lot of work as a painter. He went to all the churches here in the local area. He was an artist; he used to do the murals. He was a very knowledgeable painter when it came to murals. He would do the figures and it was his job to paint them and put them up there off of a picture and paint them. They used some sort of gold paint in those days, actually had twenty-four carat gold in the paint. He painted the ceilings at Saint Mary's, Saint Michael's, Saint Stanislaus. He would ask them where they wanted the scenes up there and they were put a certain way. He would sketch whatever he had to do and then figure out the colors, talk it over with the pastor and use his own imagination. I think he took the design from drawings and then put it on to the ceiling. I watched him up there doing it. There was a lot of climbing; he used to be on his back all the time. It was oil paint and eventually after years went by he got sick from it and he died a young man. He died from mostly lead poisoning at thirty-seven, it killed his kidneys, and it turned into cancer of some sort. When I was seven, he used to take me to the churches with him in the '40s. He used to take me to do the jobs with him. I could see him up there painting on his back. I never seen Michelangelo but I can imagine Michelangelo doing something like that on the scaffolding and with the heat up there—it must have been something else. They had to use lead paint up there because lead paint lasted; water paint would never last up there with the heat. My father was something to see, to watch him do his work. He didn't keep track of time or nothing. He would take his lunch up there. He used to give me things to occupy myself with. He used to put drop cloth down and give me little pieces, some wood and some paint and I'd paint it. He used to let me paint while he was painting. He showed me how to paint. He wanted me to learn a trade. When I used to ask him questions, he would go, "You just keep your elbow flowing, and keep your wrist moving and never take your eyes off it—stay close to your work." He meant with your eyes you had to be close so you don't go out of the lines. You would draw the figure first on the ceiling and then paint it. He would have to draw

JOSEPH SIMONE AND SON JOSEPH

1934

Simone family album

them first and then paint them in. This was off of a picture. He would take the pictures and paint from the picture—he was like an artist. He would take pictures
from whatever they wanted—from the priest or whoever he talked to—and would
take the pictures and paint them up there and then fill them in with the colors that
he had copied. Because don't forget there wasn't any colors—his imagination was
great. They only had black and white photographs in those days; there was no
color. And he put the colors in, his own colors. He would mix them and paint
them. And that's how I became a painter—I painted for thirty years. My father had
a partner, Warren, and he was black, a real nice guy. He was a partner with my
father because nobody would hire black people in those days but my father would.
My father never said a bad word about a black person in his life. And he wouldn't
allow it in his house. He knew that he was a good painter and he liked the guy a lot.
They were good friends. Warren used to go to work on a bicycle. He used to carry

his big valise. He had a big suitcase and the painters used to carry all their brushes and everything in a suitcase and put it on the back of the bicycle and you could see him coming down with a black suit, white shirt and tie and even had hats on. Sometimes I used to go with Warren when my father was too busy to watch me. This black fellow was such a nice guy. It was important that you eat when you were with Warren. Warren used to tell me, "You are what you eat." And he used to bring things that I never ate before to the jobs, yeah, and I used to eat what he had. Some black-eyed peas and stuff like that, dishes with rice in it. Lot of fish, Warren loved fish. And he used to go down and catch it and then he'd have it all cooked and everything. He'd bring to the job. Warren was a good fisherman too. See, my father and his partner used to go to work in suits and ties; that's how painters were in those days. They dressed up in a white shirt and tie and dark suits. And when they got to the job they would change. They called themselves "maestro" of some sort; there was a name for a painter in them days. He always told me, "You are a painter only if you went to work with a suit and tie." I used to watch him get dressed in the morning. It was fun to watch him get dressed because I used to say, "Where you going? To a wedding?" He'd say, "No, no, this is what you do when you go to work."

"LIFE AS A PHOTOGRAPHER"

John Mongillo spoke at the kitchen table of his home in Hamden on July 27, 1999.

I started photography when I was a kid. I always took pictures and movies, I'd say I was twelve or thirteen, something like that. I got a job for Harvey and Lewis. They were located on Chapel Street in New Haven. And that meant I got acquainted with Louie Dest, and he was very fond of me and they gave me a bicycle to go to the drug store to pick up the film. Then bring the film back in there and hang around in there. Then he would teach me how to process the roll of film in the lab. This is where I got started. Then they had like the inside of a chimney, you know the square thing that goes down like that. That's what they used for a tank. Then they had some stainless steel wire. Then they would clip the roll on one of the clotheslines to keep it steady. Then we'd shake them maybe five or six minutes and that was it, they would dry up. Then we'd make prints. Then I used to deliver the film to the drug store. That was probably the main thing that really hit me. And then word got around that I was taking pictures and this one friend of mine asked me if I wanted to go partners with this man. And so he set up a meeting so we met and that's how I got started in professional business taking wedding pictures. I also freelanced for the local newspapers, the Associated Press, The United Press, the Register, Journal Courier, The New York Times, freelancing. When I used to get something that was outstanding they used to call up United Press out of New York or AP out of New Haven, and so some of my stuff appeared nationwide. Then I did work for the FBI. That there, they used to have one guy on the fire escape, another guy outside the door of the dark room, a couple of guys downstairs. They wanted to make sure I processed what I had, you can't blame them. So I was making a living on that. For the news work I used to do, like covering accidents, they would pay me two dollars and my name, my credit line. So after a while, like I'd come up to you with my name, they'd give a dollar extra. Then with that dollar extra I'd ask you, "Did you see the photo in the paper? Yeah. Well I took it." They didn't even notice the credit line. So I cut that out, I'd say, Give me the extra buck. So that was something to talk about.

We opened up a studio in the late 1930s—Webber Studio on 1066 Chapel Street. We went up to him and asked him if we could pay rent for every wedding we did. So we paid him three dollars for every wedding I booked to use his studio and to process the film and this and that. We started off with the candids; the photographer would follow the bride all day long. It was extra money. They called them candid shots. You're getting married, right? So you want candid shots instead of studio shots. So now it would start at the house with your girlfriend by the mirror, the mother fixing the veil, the garter shot and the mother, the maid of honor and then the bride alone in the house, and of course, you got her there and you got time, so that's like a portrait. We used to follow them to the railroad station. In those days they used to go on their honeymoon by train. I started off to take pictures of them down the New Haven railroad station, make out they had the picture by the ticket widow office, take that picture, then on the platform of the train. Then if there was time enough I used to get outside and shoot them in the seat of the train. A couple of times I got screwed, I was in there and I had to go to Bridgeport and then come back. Then the other shot was from the window, with her inside waving goodbye. And then, during those days people were kind a broke. They'd send their wife up to pay the balance and then they'd give you an excuse, the groom used to come up, says, "My wife is pregnant." I'd say, give me ten or fifteen dollars, you know. So I was doing photographs, twelve dollars and fifty cents a dozen, studio pictures eight by ten. Oh yeah, we made a few bucks during those days, we weren't too bad. To me actually, as long as a person sees it [the photo] and makes it out, that's it [a good professional photographer] to me. If he's hitting the mark and he's making good money, then he sends in how to take photos and this and that with the light. What the hell, anybody can do that. I had to learn that from the beginning to make my portraits come out, that I used to sell.

22

Meat Markets, Pastry Shops, Bakeries, and Pizzerias

Throughout the small self-contained villages across the Italian south, housewives shopped daily in local "macellerie," or butcher shops, "panifici," or bakeries, "alimentari," or general grocery stores, or "mercati," open markets in the Town Square. "Venditori ambulanti," or peddlers, sold their wares and services in the streets ranging from herbs to scissor sharpening to pot mending.[42] Italian women traditionally demanded the freshest fruits and vegetables inspecting them by look and feel before engaging in ceremonious haggling with vendors for the lowest possible price. Small family-run shops doubled as social centers where familiar clientele exchanged news of the latest happenings in the town: how the young bride walked in the family's procession from her rose-pedal strewn alleyway to the local church, the sad funeral for the beloved parish priest who died suddenly the day before, or the latest political intrigues brewing at the "municipio," or town hall. Italian shopping customs continued in New Haven's neighborhoods where family-run businesses and specialty shops catered to old world tastes. Before freezers and one-stop shopping at big box supermarkets, Italian women were known to make four or five daily stops at local stores in the neighborhood—all within walking distance from their tenement apartments—to buy fresh ingredients for the evening meal. Italian American stores dotted the main streets of New Haven's neighborhoods. Fair Haven's Grand Avenue was strung with fruit and vegetable stores, bakeries, fish markets, and newspaper stands where Italian language newspapers were on sale. Legion Avenue had a sausage market that specialized in selling homemade pickled eggplants; the Hill had a live poultry market where freshly killed chickens were strung together and carried home; and Wooster Street had five bakeries, two pastry shops, and five meat markets that accommodated the special tastes of neighborhood customers. Old world pizza recipes brought to America by the first immigrants were passed on to sons, brothers, and cousins who learned the business and branched out into pizzerias around the city. Family-run establishments employing three generations of men and women who worked full time during the week gathered on Sunday afternoons to break bread at tables in the backrooms of their stores.

"How Pepe's Got Started"

Nick Vitagliano spoke at the kitchen table of his home in Branford on June 2, 2000. He often joked about his advanced age and poor health, saying, "I'm so old I don't even buy green bananas anymore."

The old timers always told me how Frank Pepe became popular and became successful. At the time there was an open air market, that was the big market on Hill Street and Commerce Street. Everybody used to go up there with the "caretti," carts, you'd load up merchandise and bring it to the store back on Wooster Street. Now Frank Pepe saw a need; these people were hungry early in the morning in the cold and everything else, in wintertime. So he used to make pizzas, four or five pizzas in the big pads, he used to put them on his head and walk through the market.

NUZZO FAMILY PORTRAIT
Grand Apizza on Grand Avenue,
Fair Haven, 1994,
Fred Nuzzo, owner, at center

A. Riccio

When got there he used to put them down on a box, the people were "affamata, mangiavano le pizze," they were starving and they used to eat the pizzas. And everybody donated their dollar bill or whatever the cost was. But at least they had a little something to keep their belly warm. That's how he started. Not even a horse and wagon, he used to put it on his head, he used to walk. When he opened up he was in the backyard, where The Spot is now. There were chickens running around. The pizzas then were just tomato, grated cheese, salt and pepper. Plain and "alicia," anchovy. No such a thing as salami and hot sausage or pepperoni. No mozzarella! Never, because they didn't like it anyway because as soon as it got cool it was chewy and they didn't like that. You know what they called mozzarella that's warm and strings? They called it "a mozzarella telefona," because it was like telephone wire.

"It Was a Delicate Coexistence"

Mike and Rose Caprio spoke by their pool of their North Branford home on July 10, 1999.

All the bookies would hang out there. All the cops would go in there and have lunch. Chief McManus used to call up down there, "Are you guys out there doing your work?" And he would go in the meat market all the time. Some people like to gamble; some people don't like to gamble. And there's Italians who like to gamble and Italians who don't like to gamble. It's like everything else and every place else. The only thing: it's more publicized because of the gangsters. There was a Jewish mafia, there was the Irish mafia—they call it mafia and they all think it's Italians but it wasn't just Italians, really wasn't. The bookies all had little tricks. They used to hide their slips. Most of the time they remembered the numbers and how much people played and who played. But when they had a busy day what they used to do, they used to take a little, tiny piece of paper—they always wore long sleeved shirts with cuffs—they'd write the numbers on it, put the initials and very, very tiny. They used to call their pencils "cheater pencils" because they used to grind them down small and put them behind their ears. Some wore a hat with a hatband, collars with the cuffs, pants cuffs inside the belt they'd hide little slips of paper. So they'd keep all this information. One day they raided down on Wooster Street and in the meat market we used to keep sawdust on the floor. So this one bookie, being that he used to be in the store all the time, used to know how to walk on the sawdust because it would make the floors very, very slippery. So when they started chasing him down Wooster Street he ran into the store. He ran into the store and ran into the bathroom in the back of the store, ran behind my uncle and my father. So now the cops come running in and they're screaming and yelling, they're running and slipping all over the place in the store, they're flying grabbing counters, knives are flying all over the place. All right, he's in the bathroom. Now he's so nervous, there's only a hook and eye on the bathroom door to keep it closed. He can't get the hook and eye done so he's holding the hook in his hand. And he's got his hat and he's throwing the stuff in the toilet, he's throwing the stuff from his cuffs in the toilet, flushing

LUCIEN, ANTHONY, AND VINCENT CAPRIO
(left to right) Mike's Meat Market, 127 Wooster Street, 1950s

Caprio family album

everything down the toilet, all the slips. That happened all the time. Because my uncle was a cop and walked a beat on Wooster Street, all his friends used to come down so it would be like shifts. One shift you'd have cops having lunch in the store, the next shift you'd have the bookies having lunch in the store. And the chief would drift in and have lunch. We used to make him the ham pie for Easter. You know how many ham pies I have to make? The doctor, the chief . . . it was a delicate coexistence of two subcultures. But that's the way it was.

❝The Real Pizza❞

John "Johnny Blake" Calamo spoke in his kitchen at the apartment complex for seniors on December 29, 1998. He got his nickname from riding on the back of Blakeslee's trucks.

The pizzas they make today, they don't know how to make them. No way. When they made those pizzas they were this thick. You know Pepe's on Wooster Street?

We used to get pizza from there. Nice. Sizzling hot, oh big ones. What they [now] call large, to us they were medium. Oh we used to get big pizza. On All Saints Day you used to bring the ingredients to the baker and they used to make you two big pizzas. And there was only two kinds of pizza: crushed tomato pizza with oil, sliced garlic, and a little grated cheese—not what the cheese that they put on today. Those pizzas today are no good for you. And they used to make anchovy pizza because the Italian people, a lot of them, they used to get them, they used to like to drink, you know they used to drink, oh. All that stuff that they put on the pizza today—that's ridiculous. It's no good for you. Or they put a lot of cheese, right? Pepperoni. What you need? We used to put pepperoni when we made the sauce, be a different flavor, you know. But not the way they make them. I walked in two pizza places. The girl comes, I said, I want a tomato pizza. They didn't even know what a tomato pizza was! I went to another pizza place. I went in there, I told her. They didn't know. The next time I went there, we went for dinner, the girl said, "I know what a tomato pizza is." I said, It's too late now. They gave me a pizza with sliced tomatoes on it! No! That's cardboard like that—you want a pizza that you can chew. When they used to put the oil on the tomato pizza before the oil used to run off the pizza—they used to put enough. You get a pizza today; it's dry. I would have told them, Aye! Where's the oil over here? Yeah.

❝The Old Bakeries❞

John Nappi spoke in the kitchen of his East Haven home on July 3, 1999.

'A fest' [the feast] was the best. I remember when Frank Pepe used to sell—he used to come around selling the slices of pizza with that big hat, in the crowds selling the pizza, ten cents a piece. What do you think we used to pay for a pie? Twenty-five cents in those days. That's all mozzarella and plain [sauce] with the grated cheese and oregano, nothing else. Now they got everything, with the sausage and garbage and all—who the hell wants all that? I like a plain all the time. When I worked in the D'Anese's bakery the old people, they used come in there. On Sunday night they used to bake Italian bread. Eleven cents a loaf like that. They used to make—they wouldn't use the wood—they used the kindling wood from the woods. They used to get these big bundles of it. And that's how they used to warm up the ovens. Then they used to mop it out. And that's how they used to bake the bread, everything was done by hand, not with machines like they do today. And the eleven cents loaf of bread was beautiful, well cooked and the taste was beautiful. And everybody used to wait because the first helping used to come out at six o'clock—everybody on a Sunday night going to D'Anese's bakery waiting for the bread to come out. And then they used to bake the cigola bread. People used to bring their own lard, then they'd make the cigola, you'd bring it to them, say "Make me a big loaf with it," and they used to mix it the dough for you and make the loaf of bread for you and charge you so much. On the other corner there was another bakery, Avitabile's on Hamilton and Wooster, then across the street was Sarno's bakery, then there was Midolo's. Everything was there, I tell you, it was something on Wooster Street—it looked like Mulberry Street in New York, same thing.

"LIFE IN A PASTRY SHOP**"**

Luisa DeLauro spoke in the kitchen of her Wooster Square home on August 9, 1998.

We used to make our gelati, spumoni, my mother used to make that all from scratch. She knew the mixture from my father's family because his family in Italy had a hotel. And everything was done right there in the hotel. My father died in 1918 during the Spanish Flu epidemic. A lot of stuff my mother didn't know. It's uncanny, it's really eerie, my mother would dream, my father would come in her

CANESTRI'S PASTRY SHOP
Wooster Street,
1940s
DeLauro family album

dreams and tell her what to put, what to do. He worked at Sargent and then he would bake at night, he would prepare the pastries and during the daytime my mother would be in the store to sell the pastry. It was great, the kids used to run around all over the place and my mother would say to us, "Look, I love you, I love the kids, please go home." My mother used to buy the crates of eggs. Oh, my nephew! My mother used to have this little room. We used to call it the cold room, the storage room, a small little room and she would put, like, twenty dozens in the crate. The kid sat down in the middle of the room, cracking all the eggs. And we didn't know he was doing this. But the eggs started oozing out from under the door! And my mother opened the door and there's this little rotten kid cracking the eggs [laughing]. But everybody worked down there, my mother did, her sisters, my sister Rae made the cream, everybody had their jobs. I took care of the customers, I was the fresh one. My sister Mary would clean, wash the windows, my sister Carmel would decorate the wedding cakes, teamwork like. And then the kids would run crazy all over the store, it was a big store, it was like all around the corner, they used to chase each other. They worked on marble, it was taken here from Italy, it was a big piece because the dough was hot. They made Italian cream with big wooden paddles, we made torrone, which was made from honey and it took five or six hours. Then they would throw it on the marble table and then you had to work hard with a rolling pin. My mother would get the almonds and we'd blanch them and then toast them and then with the mortar, smash them and then into the sieve. When she made the almond macaroons it used to be like a powder. This went on every day. We used to put the toasted almonds in it, them then we'd stretch it out and we used make torronecini, cut them in small pieces, wrap them in nice paper with a fringe on the end. It was a lot of work but it was a lot of closeness. But it was fun because we were family oriented, we had Sunday dinners together, the entire family, all our kids, all the grandchildren. We couldn't get a table large enough so my brother made the table, a great big oval table.

"ZUCCHINI AND THE WEDDING CAKES"

Rose Durso spoke at the kitchen table of Joe and Lena Riccio's home in the Annex on February 2, 1998.

Mrs. Canestri would come to my father's farm. You know, i cucuzziélli [little squash]? All the long stems of the zucchini, they would take them, cut them all one size and the small baby leaves and dip them in sugar, treat them in sugar. And then they'd decorate the wedding cakes and birthday cakes. And my father didn't take any money or anything. He'd say, "Go out there and pick what you want." The leaves, the small leaves of the cuccuziélli plants and the long stems were pretty, green. Almost every Sunday they'd come up with their nice clean bushel with paper in it and they'd go there—Luisella, Mrs. Canestri herself, and

Cesare, the husband, they'd go there, they'd bend down and they'd pick all the pretty little small leaves and the stems. And I'd say, I wonder what they do with this? Then my mother told me they crystallize them in sugar and put them on the birthday cakes. But how Luisella used to work! All night long to make the pastries, all night long, her and the kids all hustling to get the pastries ready for the weekend.

"Life at the Meat Market"

John Nappi spoke at the kitchen table of his East Haven home on July 3, 1999.

I learned to cut meat at Stiano's, I was about twelve, thirteen years old, I was going to grammar school. My father brought me there, says, "You got a learn a trade." In those days they were the boss you know. So I used to get out a school and go there, I started from scratch, how cut meat, how to bone, how to skin calves, we had a do all that. Boy we worked—seven days a week you had a work. They used to work all the way to Saturdays till eleven, twelve o'clock, on a Sunday a half day. Well the old people, I got to know them all. As a matter of fact a lot of them used to call me "surucillo," little mouse. And I used to get a kick out of it. So I got along with them good, you know why? I used to treat the old ladies—I used to have respect for them. In those days, all those old women, they used to have petticoats under there, long gowns and dresses all the way down to their ankles and underneath they used to have a tie where they used to have a cloth bag. And in the cloth bag they had those pocketbooks that you used to open. Now when they used to pay, they used to say to me, "Surucillo, turn around, nun guarda!" Little mouse, turn around and don't look at us. You couldn't see anything anyway! [Laughing] So I used to get a kick out of it. I used to sit in between the cash register; I had a chair. Sometimes they used to gossip. Now this one day the old ladies come in, they were talking about somebody. I knew they were talking about this woman. And they were saying about her going out and fooling around with somebody. But I understood here and there because you'd be surprised, like this old lady said, "'O sapone d'America lava tutte le macchie." You know what that meant? The soap in the United States washes away all the sins they had in the old country. That's what they meant. So a lot of them had "horns" [affairs] in the old country, come here and now they thought they were big shots. So they knew, understand? So they had all these sayings and I used to get a kick out of it. I used to sit in between the cash register and the little chair. So they were talking one day about some woman. They thought I didn't understand Italian. So now I get up and they see me after they got through. So one woman says "Tu capisci l'Italiano?" Do you understand Italian? So I said in Italian, "No, i' sóngo Germanese," No, I'm German. Oh, they could have died! They were worried [laughing] because I understood them, I knew what they were talking about too, in those days.

23

Holiday Celebrations

Holidays in Italy celebrated the birth dates of patron saints of towns and the holy days of the Church. In Sicily, there were thirty-seven holidays alone for patron saints. In the drab life of the simple peasant, holidays were a form of recreation and festivity that represented high points of the year, a time to pause and share the company of friends and family with exchanges of goodwill. Holiday celebrations centered on meals where special dishes were prepared with almost sacramental reverence. In the southern tradition of hospitality, there was always room at the table for one more family member or friends of the extended family.

In New Haven, Italian immigrants marked the seasons according to Italian holidays: The Feast of the Epiphany on January 6, the Feast of Saint Anthony on January 17, Saint Joseph's Day on March 19, "Carnevale," or Italian Halloween, during the Season of Lent, Easter, and Easter Monday. In 1892, Columbus Day was celebrated on a massive scale: 125,000 people watched the parade, which included thirty-six bands and eleven drum corps.[43] Non-Italians viewed the observance of Italian holidays and feast days as obstacles to assimilation. In 1893, the Annual Report of the Board of Education reported "a large number of children of foreign parents were absent because they observe as holy days several of the regular school days."[44] Some Italians fasted in observance of holy days. On the birthday of La Madonna d'Assunta, or The Lady of the Assumption, on August 14, Italians of the Campania region fasted on water and watermelon. At Easter the "pastiéra," or Easter pie was flavored with hambone juice, mixed with rice and cheese and baked. One mother who wanted her eight children to observe the Lenten fast by not eating meat in any form warned them not to touch the "pastiéra" until Holy Saturday at noon because of "'o sèrpe," the magical snake that supposedly slithered through the pie, leaving air pockets as proof it was real. Children were instructed that "Cuando sciogliono le campane," or only when the church bells rang at noon on Holy Saturday signifying that Christ had risen from the dead, could the Easter fast be broken, 'o sèrpe, or the snake, would leave, and the pies could then be eaten. Women baked Easter loaves of braided-shaped sweetbreads intertwined with eggs known as "'a pigna." A favorite among Marchegiani at Christmas was "la crescia," a puffy loaf of bread baked with parmigiana cheese and spiced with pepper. People from Amalfi ate a traditional meal of "pasta e ceci," or macaroni and ceci beans, on Palm Sunday and "pasta lenticchie," or lentil soup, on New Year's day. "Pizzelle e baccalà," or codfish wrapped in dough, fried in olive oil, and sweetened with honey or sugar, was a New Year tradition among people from the Sessa Aurunca area of the Campania.

Observations of the holidays were almost sacred rites for Italian American families. Before the age of television, storytelling provided most of the entertainment. Often, older family members recounted life experiences in Italy and old family stories were recited to the young. Family identity was kept alive by the oral tradition; fables and proverbs were often used to remind the young to abide by the foundations of "la via vecchia," or the traditional way of doing things. During holiday gatherings where animated and passionate table conversations took place and everyone participated, Italians practiced their homegrown version of positive reinforcement long before modern psychology invented the term. As second and third generation Italians pursued higher education, entered professional careers, and moved away, they lost contact with the older generation. With the passing of generations, original religious and cultural meanings of Italian holidays faded from family memory.

"The Serenade"

Joseph "Babe" Dogolo spoke at the kitchen table of his East Haven home on September 15, 1999.

My father and his brother-in-law, Jimmy Amore, on New Year's Eve, we used to walk. They used to take us kids from Wooster Street, go over the Tomlinson Bridge to Forbes Avenue and bring "a serenàta," the serenade for New Year, to their friends, this house, that house, [singing] "E mo' vidimmo e 'o capo 'e l'anno, per tric e trac," And now we see the New Year, tric and trac. That was a tradition. [singing] Here comes the New Year's, and we used to bang-a, bang-a, bang-a, bang-a with the sticks, zint-a, zint-a, zint-a. You get three two-by-fours, one, two, three with the tomato cans on the ends—zint-a, zint-a, zint-a—that was the band. My uncle had the mandolin—ding, ding, ding. Then you walk with my father and these old guys. And we were kids. Walk eight steps and stop. And [the men] blah, blah, blah and talk-a, talk-a-talk. Eight more steps and ba, ba, ba, ba. And us kids, in the back, we used to follow them. It took a half, three-quarters of an hour to walk from Wooster Street over the Tomlinson Bridge. Who knows what they talked about? They [the grownups] used to talk in Italian—strong—because we were just coming up, you know what I mean? New Haven was a thing of beauty. I loved New Haven.

JOSEPH "BABE" DOGOLO
At home in East Haven,
1999
A. Riccio

❝ MARCHING ON CHRISTMAS EVE ❞

Antonette and Salvatore Salemme spoke at the kitchen table of their North
Haven home on August 15, 1998.

What I do like to remember is Christmas. My father always used to buy a few
pine cones and we used to have a big black stove with the coal and the week before
Christmas he used to come home with them and we used to put them in the oven
and they used to open up, the pignoli nuts. Then he would take them out and you
could smell the aroma throughout the whole house. And all us kids—my mother
had four children, two boys, two girls, and then we used to pick the pignoli, some
we used to eat them, some we used to put in the meatballs. Then Christmas Eve

PROTO FAMILY CELEBRATION.
Castle Street, Fair Haven, 1948
Rose Sansone, standing second from left.

Proto family album

in my house was a big to-do. My mother had two sisters, well she had more, but these two were her favorites, her older sister and her younger sister. She always invited them and their children for Christmas Eve because my younger aunt really had nothing and my mother used to feel sorry for them. My parents weren't well to do; they both worked very hard. The whole week before Christmas my house was a hustle and bustle. My mother used to work as a dressmaker but when she came home at night we used to do all these things. Christmas Eve would come now and my mother's two sisters and all their kids were coming. And we were very, very close. And I remember at midnight, we had the whole shebang; I don't know how she did it with the little money that they had. She had everything. And of course we spent days cooking. Strictly fish. Crabs and spaghetti, calamari, baccalà, we used to have the baccalà salad—my mother used to make it with the lemon. We used to soak the baccalà, maybe three weeks before. She would put it in the tub in a pan water and then while we were home she would let that water drip day and night so that the water would interchange till this baccalà got soft. Then we would parboil it and shred it into a salad with lemon, olives, salt and pepper, and garlic. Delicious, my father used to love it. Then we used to fry baccalà, we wanted that, we used to dip it in flour and fry it, that was another dish we had. Sometimes she would make baccalà with potatoes in the tomato sauce. They made stuff that was very, very cheap to make because the money wasn't there, very cheap meals when you come right down to it. That's what all the Italians made. Now Christmas Eve came and we'd have all this fish, the broccoli with the lemon, the baccalà, and my father was crazy about eels. We used to go buy them in this fish market. I remember my mother bringing them home and then we would get pliers—they cut off the head—and we'd get a hold of the skin, then we'd pull it and the whole thing would come off. We'd wash that, then dip in flour and fry that because that was one of my father's favorites too. We did everything for my father. My mother did, she was very Italian. We had that and the spaghetti and the broccoli and the eels, the calamari, the baccalà. Then of course we had all the cookies, i struffoli, i guànti. They [aunts] would come with their kids and I don't remember them bringing anything or doing anything either. My house was the central house for everybody. It was great because we used to have a wonderful time. My father would make all kinds of decorations for the tree, he called it "o presèpio," the manger, on the side, he made it with the mirrors, it looked like a waterfall, he was very into that stuff. But he never put baby Jesus in the crib. Came midnight of Christmas Eve, that's something I'll always remember. My father used to put this Italian record on just before midnight, they call it "O Bambino," we'd get up from the dinner table and all of us would march around the table and go all around into the living room and the smallest one of the family, the youngest usually, got the honor of carrying baby Jesus.

"She Sang All the Time"

Rose Sansone spoke at the kitchen table of her Fair Haven home on August 18, 1998.

For Christmas, we never had a Christmas tree put up until Christmas Eve. Christmas Eve they had to put up the Christmas tree. And I was small and I believed in Santa Claus. So they sent me to bed. They were putting up the Christmas tree, all of a sudden I heard them tiptoeing—they came into the bedroom where I was. There was a clothes closet and they went there and took all the toys and put them under the tree. And that's how I found out there was no Santa Claus because we couldn't put up a tree a week before the way they do now. My mother [singing] used to sing all the time, "Tu Scende delle Stelle,"

'O re di cielo, E venne una grotta, A freddo Angelo, Oh Bambino mio divino, lo ti vido, qui a trema, O beato, e cuando dico.

66 MY HUSBAND'S CHRISTMAS AT WORK 99

Rose Savo spoke at the kitchen table of her Annex home on July 28, 2000.

I remember the holiday, when he came home from work when they had the party. And he's trying to explain to us Christmas carols. He worked in Sperry and Barnes for years. So he says, "Today, come hanno fatt' bella in do shop oggi. Prima i mie-zeiuorno ha venuto 'o superintend, tutti cuand' in do dining room. Ama iuta in do dining room. Aye, che bellu mangia!" Today, what a beautiful thing they did in the shop. Right before noon the superintendent came and we all went into the dining room. What a feast we had!

And he mentioned everything they had to eat. E dopo ama cantata eppure 'i canzóne Natale," And after we ate, we even sang Christmas songs.

So we asked him, "Che canzóni?" What songs did you sing? He said, proudly, "Ama cantato ciccio-bella." We sang ciccio bella. My brother-in-law, it was comical, said, "Yeah pop, E come è? Ciccio bella? Come ha cantata pure vùie?" Yeah, Pop, tell us how that song Ciccio bella goes? And did you sing along too? So my father [singing the same melody as Jingle Bells] started singing "Ciccio bella," "Ciccio-bel, ciccio-bel, ciccio-bel-o-bel" The song was jingle bells! He had his own language [smiling]. He never knew English.

66 CHRISTMAS AT LEE'S 99

Rose Durso spoke at the kitchen table at Joe and Lena Riccio's home in the Annex on February 1, 1998. She had known them for over seventy years.

Then I'd go to Lee's [Lena Morrone's] house. And they had the house like us. Bare, bare necessities, and we'd have Christmas and the mother [Antonia] would take out the chocolate pies, with the rice and everything—she had a heart of gold, a heart of gold. Oh, my mother too! The same way. Anything they had, they shared. Now they didn't have much, but they'd share it. You get some people that won't share a crumb now. That's the difference, you see? So those were the good days. Christmas came, all your aunts and uncles, everybody would get together and have dinner together, the kids would play. What do you see, you don't see much of that anymore. And we enjoyed that. We all got together, played on the table, you shoot the marble to me, I shoot it to you—we thought that was fun. It was nothing, it was child's play but we thought it was great. You're innocent, you know, you take everything for granted. We were happy kids and we respected the way it should be. And I don't regret that I lived in that era.

"Waiting for the Factory Whistles on New Year's Eve"

Frank "Mel" DeLieto spoke at the kitchen table in his Annex home on
March 26, 2000.

New Year's Eve was a big deal. Sitting around, waiting for twelve o'clock. Play a
little bingo till twelve o'clock comes. Twelve o'clock comes, this was all at home.
Now you didn't have enough money to go out and celebrate. And what you
think you were waiting for? For the factory whistles to blow. Then go outside,
"Happy New Year!" Everybody was out in the middle of the street. And that's
what it was all about, waiting for the whistles to blow on New Year's Eve, all
right? And for years that's all you did. And everybody got out in the street, con-
gratulate each other, on Warren, Wooster Street. Out in the middle of the
street, you listened to the whistles, you threw out the fireworks, you did everything. Unbelievable. Get salutes and here we are, we're celebrating the New
Year. But as a kid, that's all I remember, just running outside. Everybody comes
out of the house. You waited till twelve o'clock—boom!—and you went out to
listen to the whistles and everybody's hollerin' "Happy New Year," who's out the
window, who's in the street. Unbelievable. That was family related. See, that's
what's missing today. You can't tell people that. I've been here twenty-eight
years, it's amazing they [my neighbors] can look at you and not even say hello.
Me, I say hello to everybody. Who cares? I know he saw me and didn't say hello
to me. I'll say, hello, how ya' doing? Nice day, whatever. What does it cost? Not
a penny. See, everything today, people put in values. Time is money to people.
In those days it was nothing.

"New Year's Eve"

Rose Durso spoke at the dining room table of Lena and Joe Riccio's home
in the Annex on February 1, 1998.

We were always together. And on New Year's Eve she [Lena Morrone] would
sleep at my house, yeah, her, Louise Orefice, Alice Vanacore, me, because I was
the oldest one, my sisters were all smaller than me, and we'd have 'e zéppole and
everything, my uncle Tuttoro with a guitara e 'o mandolino, the guitar and the
mandolin, the one in the jug, when you blow in the jug, like the hillbillys, another one with 'a sfrigatore, the washboard, and they'd all be around the table,
my mother would cook the chicken, the nuts, the fish, the wine and we had great
times. Then one of them would sing "Senza Mamma," Without A Mother and
your mother would cry and I would cry with her, that was a sad song. One my
uncle's friends would sing it and there were five or six.

"New Year's Eve"

Rose Sansone spoke at the kitchen table of her Fair Haven home on August 1, 1998.

We all used to get together New Year's Eve and we used to have a big supper. And then we used to wait for midnight. And at midnight, all the whistles would blow. We used to have the supply house on Grand Avenue, they used to blow the whistles. Saint Francis used to ring the church bells. On Clay Street we used to have a porch. Everybody used to go out there with the covers of the pans and we used to bang and who took the covers, the pans with spoons and we used to bang and we used to sing [singing] "È Venuto L'Anno Nuovo, Cu Tric e Trac e Bott' e Saluta Chesta Notte." This was the song:

È venuto l'anno nuovo, cu trichi trac e botta, e saluta chesta notta, E allegria! E allegria!

Cu trichi trac e botta, E allegria! New Years has come, with tric and trac and bang and health on this night, Joy! Joy! That was it.

"The Smells at Christmas"

John Nappi spoke at the kitchen table of his East Haven home on July 6, 1999.

In those days we had cold stoves. Now during the holidays they used to put, my mother used to put the apples, core em' and put sugar inside and they'd bake em'. And on the stove they used to put chestnuts. Beautiful! And slices of the apples, it used to smell. And the oranges. Just the smell around the house. And they had the pinecones, they used to open up and they used to get "i pignoli" from them. They used to bake em'. They used to buy em' like that, "i pini" they used to call em'. But the smell, that was really Christmas! Not like today, strictly business, you know what I mean? What a difference it is. Then they used to bake from early in the morning. All kinds of pies, bread, she'd make sweet bread, she [my mother] used to make "'i casatielli" those things with the eggs on them and all that. I dunno know how the hell they did it, those old people with all the big families. But come one or two o'clock in the afternoon, everything was ready on the holidays to eat. They used to make the cicorea, dandelion soup—it took them hours to clean them alone. Then they used to put everything in there, prosciutto, everything, oh that was something! But I tell ya, you enjoyed it. Today, now everything in the cans. Forget it. The kids today don't understand this, they don't know what they're missing; it's really memories that'll stay with you forever. The old people, not only that, for the respect that you had for the old people.

"HOLY WEEK"

Joe and Lena Riccio spoke at their kitchen table in their Annex home on
May 23, 1999.

We couldn't jump rope. My mother used to say, "È peccato a zumpà'. Gesù
Crist' è mòrte," It's a sin to jump around because Jesus died. We couldn't sing.
Anything that was enjoyable. We couldn't play records. Holy Week we were
supposed to be in mourning. We couldn't dig dandelions because it was digging
the ground. My mother used to say that God is supposed to be dead and you're
jumping on him. And when you cut the dandelions you put the knife in the
ground, it was the same thing. We couldn't have salad with vinegar because they
took vinegar and wiped Christ's brow and mouth. So they couldn't have vinegar.
We couldn't eat eggs because it came out of the chicken and the chicken was
meat. Cheese, milk, butter you couldn't eat because it came from a cow and it
was a meat product. Fish we used to eat. All the bars used to be closed on Good
Friday, package stores used to be closed. But the almighty dollar won. See, those
things are all gone now. Those are all things that commanded like respect and
faith. It's all gone. And that's the problem. There's no respect for anything—no
respect for authority, no respect for other people's feelings, no respect for anything at all. Guys go through red lights; nobody cares. Nobody is afraid to be
punished.

"LENTEN TRADITIONS"

Rose Sansone spoke at her kitchen table in her Fair Haven home on June
2,1998.

Before Lent starts, for the Mardis Gras, my mother used to make "'o leatine."
She used to buy the pigs feet, the pigs ears, the pigs tail, the pigs snout and she
used to boil that. And you boil it and boil it and as you're boiling it, you take out
all that grease that comes up. After that gets cold, you put a little vinegar in it
and you put salt. And then she used to put them in different bowls and she used
to put them out in the hall. In that it used to get like a gelatin. And that was
something, that was another tradition we had she used to make just before Lent
started.

On Shrove Tuesday, the day before Ash Wednesday, we used to have another big time. We used to have lasagna with the meatballs and the sausage.
And then from Tuesday until Sunday we didn't have no meat again because then
came Ash Wednesday and Good Friday, so we didn't have no meat either. Those
were our traditions that we had.

"Bringing Palm, Bringing Peace"

Anthony Santacroce, Mary Santacroce and Angelina Crisculo spoke at the
kitchen table of Angelina's East Haven home on December 21, 1999.

Well, I know that they [our parents] would say that if have any enemies, you give
them a palm, you kiss them and you're making up. And this what they [the old
people] told us. You used to kiss their hand. They used to go house to house in the
family, they'd go see 'a zi' 'o zi', 'a nonna, the aunt, the uncle, the grandmother.
You'd bring the palm and there would be peace. That's what they used to say. But
we never had no trouble with nobody. But today you need all the palm in the world.
It was like the branch of peace.

"The Meaning of Palm Sunday"

Ralph Marcarelli spoke in the living room of his Wooster Square home on
May 28, 2000.

The fact that you were expected to do certain things and be a certain kind of person was common. It was common not only among the Italians here, it was common among all those of European migration. You were expected to know and you
did know what would disgrace your family so you didn't do it. And when somebody
did do it, it was a disgrace. Obviously, everyone saw it and everyone talked about it.
So a whole multitude of things that you might have been tempted by human weak-
ness to do, you wouldn't do because in the back of your mind it would disgrace your
family. You weren't worried, particularly if you were a guy, about a beating or any
physical consequences. You were worried about the hurt that it would do to your
parents, your family, the name, the pride and all the rest of those things. Moreover,
you were absolutely expected to pay proper respect to relatives, to elders whether it
was the family strictly speaking or whether the broader comparaggine, compari,
comari, godparents, godfathers and godmothers. So that, for example, a day like
Palm Sunday was a day when you roamed all over creation bringing palm to every
conceivable member of your family to whom you could bring the palm. You went
to the cemetery of course. The holidays were like that. It was a coming and going,
in and out of houses. On Palm Sunday, if you were on the outs with someone or
vice versa, and that person came to you bringing palm or you went to that person
bringing palm, that was it. It would be considered blasphemy—blasphemy literally—to turn that person away. And it was a marvelous thing. More so when you
start to think of not really the symbolism but the occasion. This was Christian; it
was the celebration of a triumphal entry into Jerusalem by Our Lord. And this was
sacramental; this blessed palm. There was no way that you turned anybody away.
And consequently a whole host of hard feelings would dissipate willy-nilly whether

you really wanted to or not, you'd have to do it. And that's my point. Having to do things is enormously important in this world. Because it brings us to do the right thing, it's the force of tradition, it's the force of morality, it's the force of religion, it's the force of western civilization. You have to do this. Once we decide that we don't have to do a damn thing the net result is, in fact, we don't do it. Now we may not do it out of malice; we may not do it because we don't bother thinking of it anymore. And of course that is prologue to a very sad story because what we stop thinking about disappears. And our traditions in that manner disappear.

"Palm Sunday"

John Nappi spoke at the kitchen table of his East Haven home on July 28, 2000.

You know what my father used to say? When we'd sit down to eat, [he'd say] "Put 'a lanterna,' the lantern on the table." Know what he meant? Put the gallon of wine on the table. Come the holidays, say Palm Sunday and Easter, the old man sat at the head of the table. Start from my oldest brother, had to go kiss his hand. That was the way they used to do it. I was the youngest, be the last one. Kiss the old man's hand. Nobody moved until—I swear, he was something! You talk about respect. And that's the way it was. So we used to go right around, first my oldest brother, my oldest sister, go right down, I was the last one, had to go kiss the old man's hand. Then he used to bless the table and the food and the palm with holy water. We still do it in the family. We say a prayer to thank the Lord for the food and all that, then they all hold hands and then after the blessing and the prayer, you eat. You don't do that today. That's what the palm was for, for the make up time [to settle feuds], for peace. See, another words according to the Bible, when Jesus went into the town, the palm and the olive branch was for peace. But they turned around and instead of peace, they crucified the man. Of course these kids, they don't understand, they don't do it today. See, there was the difference. That's why respect was the difference.

"I've Got a Lawyer on Easter Sunday"

Rose Savo spoke at the kitchen table of her home in the Annex on July 28, 2000.

On Easter Sunday they used to bless the table and each and every one of us, we had a say grace and we had to kiss my father's hand. Oh yeah. One by one, we used to go around—my father used to sit at the head of the table. We used to kiss my father's hand. I says, "Why can't we kiss Mamma's hand?" [laughing] My mother would say, "Chilla patita campa a casa, patita porta i soldi a casa," Your father is the one who takes care of the house, he's the one who brings the money home. She always referred to me as, "I tenga 'nu avvocato ccà," I've got a lawyer here.

❝Holy Thursday❞

Lou and Rose Marie Guarino spoke at the kitchen table of their home in
Orange on August 2, 2000.

We were lucky we had three churches, because we used to go to Saint Anthony's,
Saint John's, and Sacred Heart. On Holy Thursday we used to visit all three of
them. That was the tradition that you went to three churches on Holy Thursday.
The significance, I don't know, being Holy Thursday, something with the Last
Supper, the churches were all decorated, beautifully decorated with banks of flowers and the tradition was to visit three churches. Thursday was the celebration of
the Last Supper as I remember it, the churches were beautifully decorated with
candles, flowers. And then the next day everything was stripped and then draped
in the purple for Good Friday. They tore down that Saint John's church which they
should have never torn down. That was a beautiful, beautiful church. I could see,
you want to take the school, you want to take the convent, the rectory, fine, but the
church, they never should've taken the church down.

❝Holy Saturday❞

Tony Vitolo, Anthony Santacroce, and Mary Santacroce spoke at the kitchen
table of Angelina Criscuolo's East Haven home on December 21, 1999.

On Palm Sunday you get the palm, bring it home. And then for Holy Saturday you
would get a small bottle of Holy Water and then on Easter Sunday, before we ate,
my father always used to bless the table with the palm and bless the food. My
father used to throw a little extra at me, he said I needed it. But I still do that with
my family. In fact, last past Palm Sunday I had my seven-year-old grandson do it,
he did the blessing. So it's a little something hopefully, it'll continue. The most important thing was the family. Still is. And I just hope that somehow that can come
back for all peoples, really because that's what's killing this country today, the demise of the family. It's killing us. The social programs obviously are not working,
you can pour all the money you want into them; it's not going to work.

❝The Casatiéllo on Easter❞

Anthony Santacroce spoke at his sister Angelina Criscuolo's kitchen on December 21, 1999.

It usually was about eight inches around and it had the same symbol of Christ with
the three prongs and right on the top was always a little white lamb to signify the
Lamb of God. And it was a very popular cake. And we used to get one each, a small
one. And we used to look forward to that. And that was the highlight of Easter.

"We Always Had New Clothes"

Antonette Salemme spoke at the kitchen table of her North Haven home on
August 15, 1998.

My mother used to sew. Every holiday I had new clothes. Even though she was on
a budget, she would take us the month or week before and she would get the newspaper and put it up against us and cut out a pattern. And I always had a new outfit
for Easter, for Christmas, to go to school. My mother always made our clothes.
And I always had—they weren't the best—but they were new clothes.

In 1860, only 2.5 percent of the Italian population spoke the Italian language.[45] By the time of the Unification in the 1870s, almost the entire southern population spoke in different regional dialects. Except for the "prominenti" who were educated in superior northern Italian schools, most of New Haven's immigrants spoke ancestral dialects of their native regions in Italy. In Sicily, the dialect of the lower classes was referred to as "il dialetto della levandaia," or the dialect of the washing women. Walking the streets of the Hill neighborhood in the 1900s, one could have heard dialects of Piedmont, Veneto, Le Marche, Campania, Abruzzi, Tuscany, Emilia-Romagna, Calabria, Puglie, and Sicily. Strains of Neapolitan dialect from the Campania region were heard most frequently, especially in the Wooster Square, the Annex, Forbes Avenue, and Fair Haven neighborhoods. Neapolitan, which had its roots in Latin, as most other dialects, became the official language of the Kingdom of Naples during the reign of King Alfonso I of Aragon in the fifteenth century. Public speeches, official notices, and laws were written in Neapolitan. Neapolitan theatre, poetry, and the famous "Canzone Napoletane," or Neapolitan songs, which were performed in concert halls and at religious festivals in New Haven, originated in the 1600s. Neapolitan dialect spoken in New Haven reflected its Greek, Arabic, and Spanish influences. Italians of the Campania referred to a coffin as "'o taùto" from the Arabic "tābūt," an act of kindness was known as "'a crianza," from its Spanish roots, and "'o purtuallo," or orange, from the Greek "portovallis."

Most of New Haven's immigrants had little identification with Italian nationhood and considered themselves Siciliani, Barese, Marchegiani, Piemontesi, or Veneziani before Italian. Regional allegiances and identities were reinforced by the dialect spoken at home, with friends at social clubs from the same towns and at jobs where Italians in the same trades often worked. The political, geographic, and cultural divide that segregated Italy by region and village continued in New Haven because of the inability to understand each other's language. Southern Italians hearing the Piedmontese dialect of Italy's northwest region for the first time thought it French and the heavily Latinized words of the Venetian dialect must have seemed a foreign language to anyone outside the region. The Italian word for orange is "arancia," but in the Marchegiano dialect it is "melarance," in Neapolitan, "purtuallo."

The Italian word for parsley is "prezzemolo," but in the Marchegiano dialect the word is "erbetta," "petrusino" in Neapolitan. Sicilians refer to a tomato as "puma-doru," Piedmontese "tomatico," and Marchegiani, "pomdor." Regional dialects often identified an individual belonging to a certain social class in Italy, a distinction that continued in New Haven between northerners and southerners.

Educated northerners who spoke model Italian looked down on less educated southerners for speaking "meridionale," or "Bass Italia," southern Italian, which they considered a language of the lower classes. Southerners thought northerners snobs for speaking what they considered the "high-classed" Italian, the same language they associated with educated government officials and wealthy landowners in Italy.

The use of Italian dialects began to erode during World War II when 600,000 unregistered Italians were listed as enemy aliens. Posters were circulated with images of Hitler, Mussolini, and Hirohito with the bold caption, "Don't Speak the Enemy's Language! Speak American!"[46] Fear of being labeled "un-American" by the government caused many Italians to conceal their identities by suppressing the use of their language. Another language loss occurred during the '40s and '50s when many third generation Italian Americans completed the assimilation process after attending public schools. Many American-born children connected the Italian language to the outdated folk culture of their parents and grandparents who they sometimes regarded as "cafonish," or backward, and outside of American main-stream culture. In some families the Italian language was relegated to side conversations between grown ups who wanted to keep sensitive subjects away from children.

In the past decade there has been a resurgence of interest in Italian dialects. For many third and fourth generation Italian Americans, hearing a few words or short phrases of Italian recalled from youth act as memory triggers that conjure up an earlier time when immigrant grandparents spoke in Italian dialect at home and lived with children and grandchildren in New Haven's old neighborhoods. Re-newed interest in New Haven's Neapolitan dialect recently inspired a local news-paper columnist to write a series of editorials to explain the meanings of Neapolitan words still heard around the city. When an Italian American of northern ancestry wrote a letter calling Neapolitan a "gutteral" language, it prompted a flurry of angry letters from Italian Americans of southern heritage, reigniting old cultural tensions between northerners and southerners, which had seemingly been lost to history.

Today, Neapolitan words like "capotuósto" are sometimes used in conversations to refer to a thickheaded person. Some words have morphed into new words in English. Something repugnant or offensive was "schifoso," which has become the half-English, half-Italian adjective, "skeevie," or even the infinitive, "to skeeve." Italians incorporated English words into their own language. In tenement houses, or homes without indoor plumbing, the bathroom was referred to as the backhouse because of its location in the backyard; it became known to Italians as "'o back-hause." Some words that once conveyed deep meaning to Italian Americans have been redefined by the movie industry. The word "compare," or godfather, signified a respected person of high moral values chosen by a family to baptize a child. In case of an unexpected death to a father or mother, the godfather or godmother assumed the role of surrogate parent for the child. In "Il Padrino," or "The Godfather," the traditional Italian American "compare," or godfather, became a made-for-movie godfather with a sinister side as head of a gangster family. After the huge commercial success of "The Godfather," and the string of wise guy movies of the same genre that followed during the '80s and '90s, the word "compare" evolved into the phonetically spelled word, "goombah." "Goombah" has now become the modern catch phrase for the decades-old stereotypical Italian American wise guy starring in the latest generation of gangster movies the public has come to expect, a disparaging name casually injected into conversations referring to anyone of Italian ancestry.

The colorful dialects that represented almost every region of Italy and were spoken in New Haven's ethnic neighborhoods have faded from collective memory and are all but dead languages in Italy. On a recent trip to Italy an elderly Italian American from New Haven tried to converse by speaking the Neapolitan dialect of

EMIDDIO AND SILVIO CAVALIERE
Cavaliere's grocery store
two days before final closing,
Wooster Street, 1998

A. Riccio

WILLIAM ROSSI
At the Legion Avenue
Reunion Outing, 2000

A. Riccio

his Amalfitani grandparents. While shopping at an upscale boutique in Rome's posh commercial district, he struck up a conversation with the sales clerk. Immediately upon hearing him speak in dialect, the clerk politely asked, "Perche parla questa lingua antica?" Why do you speak the old-fashioned language?

❝The Old Dialect❞

Emiddio Cavaliere spoke in the closing days of his Wooster Street grocery store, "Cavaliere's" on May 6, 1998.

When archbishop DePalma came from Amalfi, he was amazed. He said, "There's more culture here over Saint Andrew than there is in Amalfi. But they don't give a damn anymore about religion. Still, another thing that was really odd. When this schoolteacher came from Italy during a student exchange. We had a little gathering at Saint Michael's hall. So everybody's talking Amalfitano, I mean the old Amalfitano. So the woman is listening, now she has a doctorate degree. So she said, "We lost this accent twenty years ago, you guys still have it." I said, "It's not going to change here because we're not in contact with the changing Italian language so we have . . ." She said, "You have what we lost—the real Neapolitan dialect." She said, "It's gone."

"A THIRD DIALECT"

William Rossi spoke at a picnic table during the Oak Street Reunion picnic on August 27, 2000. He chuckled when he talked about the differences between his parents' dialects.

My father came from Cerreto Sannita in 1905, and my mother is from Cusano Mutri. They are both on little mountaintops and they are seven miles about and the people speak two different dialects. So when I was born, a third dialect was created because listening to my mother and my father talk and trying to speak the dialects—they are copies of the language—evidently, I copied a little of both, so it became a third dialect.

"COME ON. GET ON"

Joe Riccio spoke at the kitchen table of his home in the Annex on June 26, 1999.

This had to be 1921 and Savin Rock used to be quite the place to go in them days you know. I was about seven, eight years old and my brother had to be about three or four. On this Sunday she was going to take us to Savin Rock and we lived on Filmore Street and about seven houses to Grand Avenue where the trolleys used to run. So we get up to the trolley car stop, now at that time I was in school and I could read. My mother couldn't read so I thought I was a pretty smart kid. And the trolley car comes up and I'll never forget it to this day. There was a big "A" on it. It said Shelton Avenue and mother said, "Come on, get on." And I said to her "No, that doesn't go to Savin Rock." She says, "Get on!" I said, "Nooo, that doesn't go to Savin Rock." Poom! I got a slap right across my mouth. And I got on and I said to myself, boy she thinks she's smart—she's dumb, she don't know. Wait till she finds out that she's going to the wrong place—I wonder what she's going to do. So we get down to the transfer point and she took a transfer. So we get off on one side, cross the street and we take a trolley marked "Savin Rock." Ooh, I said, my mother knows what it's all about. I had a little more respect for her. In them days [1920s] they didn't speak English at all.

"We Lived in an English Neighborhood"

Anthony Fiondella spoke in the living room of his East Haven home on December 11, 1998.

We were treated like the blacks. You were like a black person in those days if you were Italian. They called you a wop, a guinea. The bully in your class would pick on you. Any of the minorities are treated that way. Now they're picking on the Puerto Ricans—they're part of the United States. But because they are Puerto Ricans, they're treated like the blacks. We were discriminated against when we were kids. I recall being called a guinea and wop. The bullies were the ones if you punched them once they'd be careful the next time. We lived in an English neighborhood [Forbes Avenue at the turn of the century] with people with names like Redding, Morgan, Russell, Carpenter, and Johnson and my mother would talk Italian to us. That's why we could sort of understand it but we never could speak Italian. I didn't live amongst the Italians; we were the only family out there so we'd answer in English. I remember going to my mother and saying that, you know from now on I'm going to try to answer you in Italian so I'll learn. But I ended up not—I could say a few words—but I would be able to carry on a conversation. I think some of the old Italian customers [in the '20s and '30s] used to think: "He can't be a very smart pharmacist, he can't even talk Italian." I don't know if they said it or not—I used to think that they might. My parents would be talking to us. You'd think that if you knew what they were saying you could talk it, wouldn't you? That's why I could say a few words in Italian.

"They Never Learned English"

Frank DePonte spoke at the kitchen table of Joe and Lena Riccio's Annex home on November 21, 1999.

I was born in New Haven as most of us were, along the Wooster Street area. It was like being back in Italy for them. My grandmother never spoke English till the day she died. My grandfather, the same way. The older immigrants never had to learn or had the desire to learn to speak English. When you say Wooster Street, now we were maybe on Collis Street, which is a block over. But the neighborhood was really considered the Wooster Street area, from Olive Street to East Street. East Street used to be Route One and trucks would go by all day and all night because that was the only major route. And when we moved to Morris Cove [Annex] I couldn't sleep because it was so damn quiet, all you heard was crickets, I mean I was used to noise all night. Then I used to have to come in the city because I couldn't sleep, it was just too quiet out there. And that was considered like the boondocks— Townsend Avenue, Morris Cove—that was like going out of town when you went down there because people didn't have cars, everybody lived close to the city and everybody walked. Saturday you couldn't walk downtown, it was wall to wall people.

You had to walk, they didn't have cars. On one side and the other boundary was Water Street. And the northern boundary might have been Grand Avenue and beyond, maybe State Street. I think when you got to State Street it began to mix. They were literally areas, neighborhoods—you had a Jewish neighborhood in one of part of town around the Legion Avenue, for example, the Polish, the Irish had their own neighborhood in the [Fair Haven] Heights.

❝Son, It's a Chamber Pot❞

Joe Riccio spoke at the kitchen table of his home in the Annex on June 26, 1999.

Everybody had a chamber pot in them days. But we didn't call it a chamber pot. In Italian we called it something else, "pisciatura." Ours broke and my mother takes me to one of these stores and she says to me, "Dice che vuoie 'a pisciatura," Tell the man you want a chamber pot. So, and I didn't know how to say pisciatura—there was a Jewish fella—and I didn't know how to say pisciatura in English. So I says to him, "We're looking for a piss pot." So he puts his a hand on my shoulder, he says, "Son, you call this a chamber pot." That was a chamber pot.

❝You Had to Speak Italian❞

Joseph "Pip" Scarpellino spoke in the living room of his Wooster Street home on August 7, 1999. His father was a stonecutter who cut the stones for the famous Poli Theatre in New Haven.

At that time, 1914, going to the stores, if you didn't speak Italian, you were out of luck on Wooster Street. Of course all the storeowners were Italian and the kids were a little too small to take care of the business. And that's how we learned. Well, nobody speaks Italian anymore anyway. In fact I don't know whether I could speak it anymore.

❝Going to Night School❞

Charlie Mascola spoke in the living room of his Annex home on January 5, 1999.

In them days, my father couldn't read or write English, even when he died. My mother went to night school, at Woodward School. And naturally, in them days they had no babysitters and she used to take me with her. And it's comical, I'll tell you. They were reading third grade books. Now we'd go there and somebody would get up and read the book, and till this day I can almost picture them: "John love Mary. John, she's got a dog. His a name is a Spot." Well, in the meantime, we're all giggling and the teacher over there is saying, "Now don't giggle." He says, "Every time that a she's a comin' home, Spot is a waitin' at the door." And finally they threw us out of the room; they wouldn't let us stay anymore. Because it was just hysterical. Because we were big shots and I went to the eighth grade and she's [my mother] reading third grade books and she's thirty-five, forty years old. It was comical but she learned how to read English and she could read the paper and it was amazing. She died at eighty-four years and when she was eighty years old she could read with her glasses off.

"TALK ENGLISH"

Diane and Lou Landino spoke on the back porch of their home in the Annex on August 7, 1999.

My father did not want to speak Italian. He wanted to become an American citizen and he wouldn't allow us to speak Italian in the house. He spoke English every day, mainly because he wanted to get his citizenship papers and he felt if he talked more fluently he would stand a better chance of getting it. And that was his one aim. Above all else, he wanted to be an American citizen. So when they started talking Italian he would say to them in Italian, "Talk English." Pop always wanted to better himself.

"I HAVE TO KNOW WHAT YOU ARE SAYING"

Rose Durso spoke at Joe and Lena Riccio's home in the Annex on February 1, 1998.

Most of the time of my life I spoke Italian because my mother didn't know a word in American. My father, eh, he managed. But my mother used to say [commanding tone], "In da chesta casa, parlatata l'Italian'—Aggia capi' chella che diciette," In this house, you have to speak Italian—I have to know what you're all saying. Ah! All right? [with gusto] Your mother Lena was right with me, her mother Antoniella, God rest her soul! What a beautiful lady. Oh what a beautiful woman she was. And the same thing, they [the Morrone family] had to talk in Italian. We couldn't use one word in English. My father, you know, you could manage to get a few words in but not my mother. And my aunt from New York was just as bad. And all my other aunts were just as bad—strictly Italian, see, strictly Italian all of us. That's why I know so much and I remember, you know. I kept it alive. My sisters, no. My sisters are entirely different from me. They won't talk Italian if they can help it. Once in a while a word, I tell them, "Why don't you talk in Italian, what are you ashamed of your heritage?" [My sisters say] "Oh, Ro, you go with the old-fashioned." Why is that old-fashioned? My sisters don't want me to talk in Italian that much. "Why? Why do you talk? Oh no, no." Well, they got a friend that all she does is talk in Italian—she's owns Lucibello's Pastry Shop. She's a schoolteacher, an intelligent woman and she talks Italian. She said, "I'm proud of my heritage." And that's the way I feel too. Maybe a few words now and then, you know, in between and they [my sisters] don't even like that. They're different from me. I'm the oldest one and I go with the old-fashioned ways and customs, okay? And I love it. That's how I was brought up and that's how I'm gonna die. My sisters don't have that attitude.

25

Life by the Sea

Since ancient times fishermen plied the waters of Italy's 4,100 miles of sea coast and fishing was the most important industry of the south and the islands.[47] Despite the rigors and dangers of the life they faced, fishermen were considered the lowest in the social scale, below even the poorest farmer. Fisherman abided by the custom which forbade them from seeking a wife among the daughters of farmers.[48] Poor Sicilian fishermen emigrated to cities with harbors and coastlines, like Boston, where they eventually owned their fleets and moved to other fishing towns like Gloucester and Rockport. In San Francisco, Genovesi, Tuscans, and Sicilians docked over seven hundred of their fishing vessels at Fisherman's Wharf. Within four years of their arrival in 1870, Sicilian fishermen had been successful enough to return home for their families and to begin a chain migration of three thousand Sicilians from the Isola delle Femmine.[49]

Immigrant fishermen from southern towns along the Amalfitano coast discovered the pristine waters of Long Island Sound and New Haven harbor teeming with flatfish, flounder, mackerel, whiting fish, butterfish, blackfish, eel, oysters, and squid. Lobsters caught in Long Island Sound were plentiful and razor clams and quahogs could be harvested from beaches along the coastline east and west of New Haven. The bluffs at Fort Hale Park overlooking the harbor and the picturesque bay of Morris Cove in the Annex resembled the majestic way Amalfi, Castellammare di Stabia, and Atrani overlooked the Mediterranean. In August and September, bounties of bluefish were caught from the docks at Waterside Park. Prior to its destruction by oil companies in the late 1920s, Waterside Park had a canal near East Street that led to the harbor where fishermen with nets caught eel, flatfish, and sardines. A second canal near Brown Street was a favorite swimming spot for young boys of the neighborhood.

At five a.m., Amalfitani fishermen with nicknames like "Ntuzz" Orso or "'O Blackutts" Consiglio, and the four Gargano brothers left the docks on the waterfront, returning in late afternoon with the catch of the day. Fish were sorted into piles and sold to peddlers with pushcarts and horse and wagon teams nicknamed "Tatore," Salvatore Consiglio, and "Andrea Mio," My Andrew. Owners of local fish markets joined in the bidding with peddlers for choice fish by throwing fingers.

GIUSTINO "A SARD" APPI
Fishing in his rowboat in New Haven Harbor, 1930s

Appi family album

Another fisherman from Amalfi, "'O Parente," ran a commercial fishing boat taking fishermen on excursions to the breakwaters outside the harbor in Long Island Sound. Giustino Appi, known to locals as "'A Sard," or sardine, and his wife Bonaventura rowed their hand-built boat along shorelines to fish for eels, a favorite dish among their Italian customers. At the docks they unloaded the daily catch onto a pushcart to begin his daily route on foot through the streets of the Wooster Square neighborhood. Bonaventura mended the fishing nets and sold fish on ice from her backyard on 61 Wooster Street. Some fishing families—Criscuolo, D'Amato, and Gambardella—began contracting fishing boats and distributing their catch by truck to and from other cities in the northeast. The grandsons of Antonio Gambardella, who began as a simple fish peddler selling from a pushcart, ran the largest wholesale fish business in the area, the Reliable Fish Corporation. Family-run fish markets appeared in all parts of the city, offering fresh fish to their customers, and were heavily patronized at holidays. On the feast of Saint Andrew on July 12th, Amalfi-tani fisherman, like Sicilian fishermen who staged the Madonna of the Porticello Feast at Fisherman's Wharf in San Francisco, paid homage to their patron saint by carrying the statue of Saint Andrew to New Haven's waterfront and out to sea where their vessels and waters were blessed.

❝LIFE AS A LOBSTER FISHERMAN❞

Dominic Randi spoke at the kitchen table of his East Haven home on July 27, 1999. His friendly handshake was as strong as a vise grip.

I lived near the water in Morris Cove, near the sea wall. My father was a merchant seaman; he used to travel. He originally came from Amalfi. So did my mother.

BONAVENTURA AND
GIUSTINO "A SARD" APPI

Appi family album

Near the water, where they do a lot of fishing. So I inherited it from my father. I've been lobstering since 1944. I could raise up the shade and see if it was good weather or bad weather. If it was bad weather I wouldn't go out because I respected that water. You don't respect that water, that water won't respect you. Because the water—God forbid—you're out there, you never know what's going to happen. I used to row out there. I tell you it was nice, especially in the morning when you see that sun come up, nice and quiet. How many times I got caught out there in a squall. Out of nowhere, all of sudden it starts to blow. Rough weather, water. I fished all the way to December. I used to have ice on my face and I never even wore gloves. Always by hand, I pulled. It took about three-quarters of an hour to get to the breakwaters and then you'd be out there all day, pulling the pods. You'd put a string of pods every twenty feet near the breakwaters. I used to make my own

DOMENIC RANDI
On his fishing boat,
late 1950s

Randi family album

wooden pods, buy the lattes for two cents apiece and put bricks in there for ballast, for weight. It's got what they call a parlor and a kitchen. The kitchen is where you put the bait. There's an opening and the lobster crawls in backwards into the pod. When he gets into the pod he starts eating. After he gets a belly full then he goes out the back way, what they call the parlor. He gets caught there and he can't get out because there's a narrow opening with a spring. It catches in there and it stays there and that's how you get them. We got out there, early in the morning, especially on a good day; we start pulling our pods. We start from one end of the breakwaters to the other end. And when we pulled pods then, we used to pull them all by hand. Now they got a winch, they use a winch to pull them, but before then, they never did, all by hand. And you used to pull maybe 100, 125 pods by hand.

They weighed eighty to ninety pounds from under the water. We used to get the lobsters, we had to gauge them and they had to be two and three quarters, from the inside of the back shell to the tail. If it was a hot day you covered them up with seawater. We had openings. The back latte on the pod had to be an inch and three-quarters to let the small lobsters out. And the ones that were in there were legitimate lobsters. You had to check to see if they had any eggs. If they had any eggs in them you throw them back in the water. When you throw them back in the water, you make sure you don't throw them, you just drop them in the water because you could knock all the eggs out, see? And all the eggs they carry—they carry about, oh, twenty-five, thirty thousand eggs, they're little bee-bees, they look like little small bee-bee grapes bunched underneath the shell. When they hatch, out of thirty thousand, maybe a thousand will survive because a lot of them are eaten by the fish.

"I WAS THINKING OF THE FAMILY"

In the middle of the sound, between Long Island and Connecticut. On the boat was low, it didn't have railings up above your knee to support yourself. Now when we were throwing the pods—you usually throw the buoy over first—but this time we threw the pod. Pick up the pod, you throw it over, then the rope, the boat goes slow, but he gunned the motor and when you gun, it whips. He thought everything—all the pods were over. The rope whipped up. But he realized there was still the rope there. When he sped the boat up to go ahead, the rope wrapped, picked up, wrapped around my arm and pulled me overboard because I couldn't support myself against the railing. I couldn't break it because it was pulling me, the pod. And I went over with the pod with the rope around my pod, around my hand. And I went down with the boots on. When I went down, going down, I was thinking of the family. You think, the family, everybody. I turned over, threw the boots off and I'm coming up, coming up, coming up. I swallowed some water. I saw a hole like this [above] started getting wider and wider, the light, and it gets big—ah, you're coming. Finally—ah, the light. It was a small hole like this and you keep coming up, it got bigger and bigger. I was lucky, I tell you. It was in October. And he's out there, he throws me a life preserver! I was lucky, I must have gone fifty feet down because I had the boots on. A good thing I always carry a knife—I cut the rope underwater.

"WORKING AS AN OYSTER MAN"

Alfred Nargi spoke at the kitchen table of his nephew Louis Nargi's Annex home on July 15, 1999.

I worked with my Daddy and my brother Lou, we worked in stone quarries cutting up rocks that were half a ton, you drill them, put the little wedges in there. You'd get a star drill and a three pound sledgehammer and you hit it and the star drill would make it go down about three inches and you make four or five holes in the big rock. Then you get little wedges with half rounds they call them and you put it in there and you tap them with a three pound hammer, nice, then you get the sledgehammer and you hit—domp! And it splits the rock. It was a couple of hours work just making all the holes. After you split the rock, you make small rock from big rock. What they used to do with them, my father used to sell them to the oyster people. And the oyster people used to take these rocks, they called them "buoy stones." My father used to buy them from Blakeslee's, all big rock, and we used to drill them and split them and make them the size that we wanted for the oyster people who grow oysters. By hand, everything was by hand in the old days, in the late '30s. We were only kids, sixteen, seventeen years old. We sold them to Mister E. E. Ball. If you go by Quinnipiac Avenue you see the shells there. And in Branford we had the shells that were thirty-five, forty foot piles. My brother—God rest his soul—come after me, he said, "You want to work?" I said, "Doing what?" He said, "Shoveling oysters." What did I know about shoveling oysters? I was just a scrimpy little kid, 130 pounds. I was only fifteen years old, I was just two days out of school and I went to work shoveling the oysters in a wheel barrel, going up the plank, dropping them on a big scow, like sixty, seventy feet long. At low tide you were going down like this and at high tide you were going up this way. In the old days—now they use water pressure to blow them right off the barge—you had to shovel them until that thing was clean. Now you take a barge that's sixty, sixty-five feet long and load it up—that's a lot of hand shoveling, hand shoveling going on, hand shoveling going off. You'd throw them off and this is what you do all day long. We'd make two trips a day, one in the morning and one at night. Mister Ball would tow the barge out to the Thimble Islands—that's what the buoy stones were for—we'd sink the stone with a pole on it. And that would mark his territory in Thimble Islands where he planted his oyster shells. He had a designated area with the stones that hold all the poles straight up. That's how he knew where his shells were, when he goes back to pick them up. They plant them in the water and whatever happens in the water, they grow to oysters again, they make eggs in the shell and they become oysters. They know when it's time to pick and they go out and they dredge and they come up with the oyster shells. And then they'd come back, sell them to the oyster people, and get all the shells and plant them again, see? When the oysters germinate the shells get together and they form oysters again. That's why they don't throw the shells away. If you go down by Quinnipiac [River] right now you'll see all the piles of oyster shells. And from Branford, we'd go out to Thimble Island and shovel the shells off by hand. And once we unloaded that, we'd go back and made another, two loads a day. And that's what we used to do. Half a dollar an hour. Getting bitten alive by mosquitoes and gnats all day. No wonder why we couldn't put any weight on, you're getting bit! Twenty-one dollars a week, six days a week, nine hours a day. That's what we did for the oyster people. And today if they had to work like that they'd say they were being abused. They had a place where all the women opened them up and they get the oysters and they can them or get them ready to sell them. After they take them out of the shell, they get all shells and they come out on a conveyor and they go up to the lot piling up a little at time. Before you know it, you got a pile twenty, twenty-five foot high.

GARGANO BROTHERS
At fishing pier, Waterside Park, 1940s
Nappi family album

"Sciavechiéllo, 'a Rézza and Merluzzi"

Nick and Mary Vitagliano spoke at the kitchen table of their Branford home
on June 2, 2000.

The people around the neighborhood, that's how I learned it. If you really wanted
a lot of fish, you go with two men with "'a rézza," a net. But if you wanted bait and
a few fishes for your family, you used to go in with "'o sciavechiéllo." That's the net
you throw over here and they catch the shiners to go after bluefish, all right? Now

when you walk in the water there you don't see nothing, there's nothing. But as you're walking like that, the net goes down and drags the bottom and you bring everything in and lay it on top of the beach—bop, bop, bop—everything is jumping, you know, and you open it up, and you open quick, put them in pails otherwise they get away from you fast. I used to enjoy that at Lighthouse, Fort Hale. New Haven was very nautical. In fact there used to be fishermen across the street from where I lived and as kids we used to see them mending the nets. We kids would go there, we'd sit there and gawk at him [Mr. Appi] stringing the nets that broke. He

LIGHTHOUSE PIER
Annex, 1910

Postcard

used to do it for a living. And he had a little stand right near his house near Wooster Street and he used to go down to Sargent's green, there used to be water there. He lived near Hamilton Street and he had a stand there and he used to sell the fish that he would catch. There used to be a dock down at Waterside Park. If you walked down Water Street and walked through the park, you went right to the water and that whole front of that waterside side of the water where it ended was all docks. Places where a boat could tie up and we used to run down there and these boats used to come in. A dollar for a bag of fish like this, the best fish you wan a eat, 'i merluzz' [codfish], bluefish. Whitings, they were most delicious fish, and my mother used to love to cook those fish. She used to poach them, used to boil them and take the skin off very carefully and take that whole fish nice, was still on the bone, she used to fix it with garlic and oil, ma che saporita! Boy it was tasty!

"FISHING WITH MY GRANDFATHER IN 1920"

Louise Orefice spoke with her brother Anthony in the living room of her home in the Annex on October 31, 1998. She recalled that movies starring Rudolf Valentino, Tom Mix, and Gloria Swanson were the only form of entertainment in her day.

My grandfather was a fisherman from Amalfi. There was no work in those days, he used to fish off the waters of Amalfi so they could eat. He came here to see if he could make a living. He didn't know how to read or write, he was illiterate so he didn't get nowhere. To get a job he had to do some writing, he didn't know how to write. He couldn't get a job. All he knew how to do was go fishing. He had his own boat. He took me fishing. He used to have a rowboat, he had a motor on it to get out to the breakwaters. I was a little girl and he took me fishing with him [at Fort Hale in the Annex]. He gave me a drop line and I was fishing. Before you know I got an eel and at the end of eel's tail was a crab. Now in my innocence I was trying to save the crab not to fall in the water again. I went and bent over and I fell in. And my grandfather was at the other end of the boat, and he didn't hear the noise, the splash. So when I called him, I went down in the water and I came up again and I held on the boat and I called grandfather. And when I called grandfather, instead of getting excited that I went in the water, he was swearing, I wouldn't repeat it, it was a bad word. So he took me home and that was it. I couldn't go fishing anymore with him. I was fortunate to have come back up. It wasn't my time yet. And that's how we lived. Poor existence, that's all, very poorly.

"SUMMER AT WATERSIDE PARK"

John Nappi spoke on July 3, 1999 at his East Haven home.

They used to have places where the old people used to go play cards, go play bocce. You ought to have seen every weekend nights at this time in the summer.

What these kids got today, they got nothing. I tell you, even though it was Depression, we had things—it was beautiful. Nice parks. Now today whenever you got to go, it costs you. But down there you could have done anything. There was a beautiful bathhouse, you want to swim, there used to be the dock, go down the stairs and learn how to swim. We all learned how to swim down there at waterside where they had the Starin Lines. You had to learn how to swim because they'd throw you overboard and then they used to watch you, so everybody knew how to swim. That's why I never got sick on ship and I covered over twenty-five thousand miles on water in the Pacific during the war. We were brought up near the water. In those days, you know what we used to do? Off the poles, catch all kinds of fish. There was crabs—blue shelled crabs that big with the soft shell. We used to go with the rowboats, all along the pilings with the net and pick up the soft shell and the hard shell. In an hour you pick up two dozen crabs—that's how beautiful it used to be down there. They used to catch blue fish, flat fish, mackerel, eels, everything. No more. It's dead. In September, the end of August when the blue fish run, the dock used to be full of people. They had everything down there. Today there's nothing, these kids missed. I tell you, I'm not sorry I was born when I was born because it was altogether different, the families and the friends, it was different.

"Wintertime at Waterside Park"

You know what they used to do in the wintertime? They used to go all the ways out to the dock down on Waterside Park, the boats used to come down there with the barges with lumber and potatoes. And they used to unload down there. They worked hard those people, God bless them. They had two baseball fields, a soccer field. We used to have the Irish who used to come down and they used to come and play soccer down the other end. They had the industrial baseball like, like Sargent and Sperry and Barnes and Winchesters, H. B. Ives, C. Cowles. And you know who used to come down there? The Colored Giants. All black, oh they were terrific! They used to travel like the Globetrotters. Waterside Park was one of the best parks. When they had the hurricane in 1938, that's what ruined it. The dock was washed away, trees and all. There was a big bathhouse, one side for the girls, other side for the boys. Now the old women, they used to go, it was for free. Every Wednesday was for the older people, the older women, they used to go down there, they used to take their showers. And we used to play ball and take showers. Then we used to play ball, go down to the dock where the ships used to come in. The tugs used to bring in the big barges, flat barges. They used to have lumber on there and potatoes from Long Island. Then the Starin Lines ships used to come in. They even had Canadian liquor down there. How those tenders worked down there, worked on the Starin Lines, it was tough work, boy. They were stevedores. They had no union then. They used to put on extra people, if they wanted to make extra money, you go down there and the ship came in they'd put on guys. But they had regulars working there for the Starin Lines Company. But if they were behind you'd go down there and they'd say we need so many extra guys. So a boss used to come—Tony Vitolo's father was like a boss there—so he used to come on the corner, "Anybody wants to work, we got extra work." So they used to go to work down there, because they even paid extra money, the stevedores. One day I was a kid, you won't believe this. They brought in liquor. So me and Tony Vallombroso—that's an old family—his father was one of the original charter members of Sant Andrea—so we went down, they said they needed somebody to unload the liquor. We only put in one load, I says, not for me, that's

ITALIAN STEVEDORES
Waterfront, 1900s

Vitolo family album

not for me, I ran out of there. I says how do these people do that? They had cases of liquor and we had to take the hand trucks, they used to put six on top to bring them to the trucks. Once. I left. I couldn't work. It was too tough. I said to myself, how do these old people do this? Had a be an animal, I swear to God, they worked. You wan a talk about the Italian people? They built this country, they can say whatever they want. And they built New Haven too.

"FISHING EXCURSIONS"

They were from Amalfi, they were fishermen the majority of them. All the ones that started the Sant Andrea Club, they were all sailors in the Italian navy, or they were fisherman, all in the fish business. They all worked hard. They used to push the pushcarts from Wooster Street to Legion Avenue, go sell to the Jews. Some of them had horse and wagons. My father-in-law, after his wife died, he married a Jewish woman and had one of the first fish markets up there in the Jewish section. The Criscuolos, the Amendolas, the Gambardellas, the Bonitos, they were all fishermen. Every Sunday, this guy, "O Parent'" they used to call him, Mister Parente, he used to have a boat that used to take all the old timers from the club on excursions to go fishing. Get on there, bring, they used to bring their lunches. And they'd go out to the lighthouse breakers out there. And there was a lighthouse out there too. This day a storm came up. So they weren't coming home. You didn't have like you have today, Fort Hale you got your Coast Guard. They didn't have them then from there. They had to come in from New London around through there. So everybody was worried because it was really rough. We found out the next day they were all drunk, they got the guy—the lighthouse keeper—drunk in the lighthouse, they all brought wine. The old man came home on a Monday, they tied up the boat on the side of the breakers and they stayed up there. Oh that was something. And the old man, he was something, he said "We had a good time, what are you worried about?"

They all had nicknames. One guy they called "Andrea Mio." There was another guy, Blackie, "Blackutts," they used to call him. He used to have a little shed in the back where they would put the ice. And they used to put the fish in there. All the fish, the truck used to come down, then they used to put the fish and make bushels out a them and eight or nine or ten or whatever fishermen used to throw fingers to see which baskets they wanted with all the mixed fish. That's how they used to do it. See, because that little shed that they had there was like an icehouse, keep them it there, it was cold. Then you had the Gambardellas, they were all fisherman, the Acquarulos, one of them was named "Zi Prèvete," Uncle priest, because he was gonna become a priest I understand.

There was an old man, he was a fisherman, his name was Gennaro. Big man, he was a nice man, ruddy complexion, white hair. So one day I come home and my father gave me a backhander, he says, "Hey, you got no respect." I said, "What are you talking about, Pop?" He says, "When Gennaro went by

ANDREW AND JOSEPHINE GAMBARDELLA
Washington Avenue Fish Market,
the Hill, 1940s

DePalma family album

you didn't greet him." I didn't even see the old man, I swear to God! He went and told my father I had no respect for him. That's the way they were years ago. And I had a get a slap in the mouth. And I never even saw him. We were near the Wooster Spa, Wooster and Franklin, we had the club there. Across the street was a poolroom. And we used to hang around there after we used to eat. He said I had no respect because I didn't greet him. Those were the type of people they were.

"Long Wharf"

Along Long Wharf, the railroad used to come down there. There was a big fence where Sperry and Barnes was; the trains used to come in with the hogs and they get em' off a there and run em' in there and slaughter them there. There was a breaker and a lighthouse there. Then further there was a long wharf, very long, you can see the pilings, I don't know if they're still there. When we had the hurricane in 1938 the thing disappeared. Everything was blown away, destroyed the whole thing. It went almost out to the channel. If you look out there there's still maybe—we used to call it the ten poles, some of the ten poles are still over there with a marker where it starts the channel. Every day we were down there as kids swimming all around there. Most of all the guys learned how to swim there. And then Starin Lines was down there, they had the Richard Peck for excursions on Sunday morning and go all the way to Pleasure Beach or Rye Beach, New York. I think it cost a buck, a couple a bucks to go back and forth. People used to bring their lunches, the Italian people the macaroni all cooked, everything in it, you know, it was beautiful. Well down there where Waterside Park was, where the Starin Lines was, the transports used to come in, the boats, big ships. They used to unload there, they had stevedores working there unloading. They used to bring everything in down there, from liquor to cars and everything.

"New Haven Harbor before the Gas Tanks"

Salvatore "Gary" Garibaldi and Tony Sacco spoke at Tony's Wooster Street restaurant on May 19, 2000.

In those days the water in New Haven was clean. The seaport at that time—now it's a seaport—there weren't as many gas and oil tanks in those days. Now there's two or three hundred. Now it's a seaport and this is why we are dirty. All those tanks never were there, on this side of the [Quinnipiac] bridge and the other side of the bridge. Tad Jones owned all that land on the other side of the bridge, all those tanks. It was a big coal industry and a seaport bringing iron and wood, other materials from all over the country, all over the world, were coming here. Then later on they got into the gasoline business and started building tanks and tanks.

The tanks began to sprout up around the late '20s and '30s and '40s and they continued going. Then on the other side of the bridge, as we go out [north] was a boat called the Richard Peck. It was like a cruise ship. And every Sunday if you had a buck or two, they'd go from New Haven to New York and they'd come back at night time. So kids like him and I when they came back or before they left we'd go down the dock. And these people would throw pennies at us. And naturally we would look for the pennies and we'd fight for the pennies.

26

New Haven's Italian Americans in World War II

During World War II, over one million Italian Americans joined the U.S. military force of twelve million men and fought in every major battle where they distinguished themselves as good soldiers and loyal Americans.[50] City welfare officials in New Haven like Huey Gartland, who had earlier criticized Italians for having large families, changed his mind when Italian American parents sent four, five, and as many as seven of their sons to fight in the war. During the Italian campaign, one of the bloodiest of the war where American casualties numbered 114,000, Italian Americans sometimes fought in the same villages and farmlands of their ancestors. At the same time Italian Americans were dying on foreign battlegrounds, the United States government, convinced that threats to national security would come from sympathetic aliens living in the country, enacted a relocation program on the west coast, moving Italian noncitizens considered enemy aliens to safe zones. Law-abiding Italians, some of whom had sons fighting in the war, were required to register at post offices, adhere to curfews, and forced to surrender radios and cameras. Some were taken away to internment camps without warning where they were interrogated without legal representation and interned.

Italians on the east coast fared better than those on the west coast. Some had radios confiscated and incidents of noncitizens having to register with the government were sporadic. But there were some disturbing cases. Pasquale DeCicco, who once headed the Italian Consulate in New Haven, received a visit from government marshals who arrested him and brought him to Hartford and East Boston for questioning. Despite being an American citizen since 1909, DeCicco was interned for over a year for what the government claimed were dangerous actions during World War I when he served in the Italian army as an ally of the United States.

During the war, in New Haven Italian families were proud to have sons and brothers fighting for their country. Some displayed satin American flags in windows of their homes, a blue star representing each son in the armed forces. Gold stars replaced blue ones when a son was killed in action. Children who had to translate the unbearable message from English to Italian read telegrams to parents declaring sons missing in action. When a government telegram arrived at the Morrone family's

Annex home in 1943, the number of blue stars changed from five to four. A lone gold star glistened in the Morrone window, testifying that their son Ugo was missing in the Pacific after a Japanese shore battery opened fire on his disabled PT boat, scoring a direct hit. Mrs. Carbone, an old family friend who lived nearby and had recently lost both of her sons in the war, made frequent "visite" to Antonia Morrone's home where the two women consoled each other behind closed doors.

"They Wanted to Impound Us"

Salvatore "Gary" Garibaldi spoke at Tony and Lucille's restaurant on April 17, 2000. He was one of Connecticut's most decorated veterans and won the Distinguished Service Cross during the Italian campaign.

When Japan attacked the west coast, the very next day our Congress, our administration in power, impounded all the Japanese assets, bank accounts, and homes of the Japanese who were living on the west coast and put them into a camp in Utah, like a concentration camp. They were citizens too, and noncitizens. The next he [Roosevelt] tried to do that with the Italians because Italy declared war on us the next day. Mayor Fiorello La Guardia, mayor of the city of New York, five foot tall, he challenged Roosevelt. He said, "I'll have a revolution in this country—you're not going to do what you did to the Japanese. The Italians of the East Coast will form into a revolutionary army and we'll march on to Washington." And Roosevelt didn't take the challenge. And that's why you think, us Italians, the first sons and daughters of Italian immigrants—our fathers and mothers and me as a son would have been put in a camp in the midwest like you had in Utah. Because our parents came from Italy. And to think of those Italian American kids who volunteered or were drafted into the service of this country became heroes like John Bassolone, the greatest hero, who was awarded the Congressional Medal of Honor, one of the first to receive that. Two highest military honors, he got. And then there were other Italian American kids that were recipients of other medals for their bravery and courage in combat.

"The Landing at Salerno"

They were the most hard fought days of war that I went through. The Italian campaign was the worst campaign you could fight. When I landed in the first wave at Paestum, we had no air power; we got slaughtered by the German planes. Now when we went in there you were lucky to get on the beach. We were in landing crafts. They would drop us in five or six feet of water. They're Navy people and they're a little scared to come in and because they figure there's mines and iron bars underneath the water. Remember that—the Germans had mine fields and irons in the water. High tide would hide them. The Navy guys knew it. So they wouldn't come into the land because they figured they would go—crash [hits table]! And now as we got off the ships, maybe two miles out, before we made the push to come in, we circled around for an hour, hour and a half with all those troops on the ships. We didn't go in individually; they all lined up and then we went. Ninety-nine percent of the men on those landing crafts were victims because a lot of them were never on the water and they got seasick. Throwing up on you, pissing, shitting . . . and you're standing in with them, we were crowded, forty of us. So when we went in you were at the mercy of God. And the Germans are shooting. So just to make the landing on the beach was unbelievable. A lot of the guys got killed, a lot of guys drowned because of being in the five feet of water, with the heavy equipment, you went down. I was able to swim a little; then I was able to touch the ground, as you're coming in, you could feel the land below the water. And you walk and you're crawling—you're not standing up—you're a dead duck you stand up. You got to put your head over the water, put it down, go forward on your hands and knees. And when you get onto the beach you don't stand up, "Hey, I'm here!" You're here all right—you'd got like a sieve with the machine guns the Germans were shooting. So you crawl like a rat, looking. And now you're looking around, [whispering],"Hey, anybody . . . anybody." [Another voice] "Who?" Then you hear a guy say, "I'm here, I'm here." Now we're trying to group. Because we had certain stations where to meet on the beach.

" MONTE CASSINO "

We took highway 8 to go to Cassino—bloody battle. That wasn't supposed to last not more than two, three days. What happened? We find ourselves fighting—stalemated—up in Cassino, in the mountains. Cassino is the town in between; the monastery on the mountain. Well, what happens? We dig in. Foxholes like rats, three feet deep, foxhole all the way the down. We're overlooking on the other side of the mountain—that side of the mountain was higher than ours so they had perfect observation—that's where the monastery was. Winter. Snow, rain, freezing. We didn't shave; no haircuts. I was up there for close to forty-two days. We never took our clothes off. What are you going to do? You think you are going to take a bath or shower? You had all to do to survive. The mule pack would come from Caserta below to the highway to bring us food, ammunition, blankets. They'd bring you up canteens of water, five gallon cans. You got two hundred men spread out on that side of the mountain. You didn't use that water to shave. Where, who you got to shave for? Anybody there is out to kill you. Water was limited because as the mules were coming up through that highway the Germans seemed to have it zeroed in. You think they smelled the mules? And they threw in artillery. And half of the mules would go over the mountains and got killed and the rations didn't come up as much as they started with. Now those of us who got wounded or killed, after the mules came up there they unloaded the mule teams. They would put the wounded people on the mules like [pathetic voice] bags of potatoes. Two soldiers wounded on a mule. Rope them up, hit [claps hands] the mule, hope he goes down to Caserta from down through the mountains. The Germans were throwing artillery. If you didn't die up there, got hit, the mule went over the mountain—you got killed because you were tied to the mule. A lot of men got killed that way. Sometimes you would say to yourself it would be better if I try to walk down than to take the mule. Now you're living like a rat in a hole. Christmas Eve, '43, my birthday. I'm in a hole with another guy. And I'm reminiscing about my days when we had Christmas parties at my house. And I'm saying to him, within another hour, it'll be my birthday. I said, look where I am now. God let me see daylight. We used to pray for daylight. When daylight came we prayed for sunset. We were living like animals. Frozen. Men get trench feet. They would put you on the mule and send you down. And the order was to never take your shoes off because you can't put them on. Frozen feet, your foot would get blue. When they got blue, kid, your feet were going to be amputated. So when you saw blue, tell the guy with the mule train I got . . . my legs froze. I saw men in foxholes, shell-shocked. I would say to the lieutenant, He's shell-shocked. We couldn't take him out of the hole—he'd kill you. He feared. "How do you get him out of the hole? [Voice of the lieutenant] Gary you know? Why don't you jump in the hole with him?" Not only me, but other guys did it too. They give you a syringe. Hit 'em. That'll knock him out. Then we drag him out like a bag of potatoes and put on top of a mule—hope he gets down to the rear. Unbelievable—the atrocity, agony of war. What makes men—men wind up like animals? Men losing their minds; don't know who they are. They got out of the foxholes, they . . . screaming. He's gone—battle fatigue. What a sight. See a guy like you walking around yelling and you don't know where you are. How are we going to get you? We had no medical officer up there. The greatest men on the front lines were the medics—we called them medicos. In our company we only had two of them—imagine two medicos! They are not armed. The only thing that they have for self-preservation so that the Germans wouldn't shoot them—they had a helmet with a Red Cross and a Red Cross band. In all fairness, that German soldier is firing at us—he couldn't make out that Red Cross. At least I had a rifle—I could defend myself. When they came in here they didn't know he was Red Cross man; they would shoot him just like they would try to shoot at me. He was the hero. And when one of us got wounded and we call for Medico! Medico! And when he came to us he tried his best to do as much medical attention as he could. And he also did it for the German. Because a medico's oath was to take care of all soldiers regardless whether foe or not. I saw German medicos treating our men. They took the same oath. I saw them doing it—I could have shot him. What am I shooting him for? He's treating one of my men that is wounded. I may be a casualty five minutes from now. He may be able to come over and take care of me. He was a hero.

❝The End of the Yorktown❞

Anthony Vanacore spoke on the back porch of his North Haven home on November 20, 1998.

We were up in Portland, Maine on Thursday. We were supposed to go to Norfolk, Virginia to get in the dry dock on the Saturday. So we took off for Norfolk and we got there Saturday morning. So we unloaded all the ammunition off the ship and all the perishable food because we were going to be without power because of dry dock for maybe three or four days. So we used to have weekend liberty; cat houses all the ways on both sides of the street. Everybody used to have a time. Sunday morning we get up and all of a sudden the MP's come dashing down the street, "Everybody back to the ships—Pearl Harbor has been bombed!" We all said, "What are you talking about?" The MP's said, "The Japs bombed Pearl Harbor—get back to the ship." So everybody hightails it back to the ship. Already the stuff that we offloaded is coming back on, all the food, the ammunition—boom! Yard workers came welding forty millimeter canons on the catwalks, putting more armament. So, I'll be a son of a gun, Sunday afternoon, cast off, go outside the harbor and wait for orders from Washington. So we waited there maybe a day and we got orders to go to the west coast. So we went down through the Panama Canal. So now before we went there, because the ship had our name in the back and on the sides, they took them down covered the name in the back because they didn't want anybody to know the name of the ship and where we were going. A big ship like that! So we even had the name on the back of our raincoats—the name of the ship—painted off. We're transiting the canal and we stopped in Panama City because the captain had to go into town to get his further orders from Washington. So we're waiting for him to come back. So he finally comes back late that afternoon. Sunday, it's a custom, when the captain leaves his ship, they announce it over the speaker—they don't say the captain—they say U.S.S. Yorktown leaving. Then when he came back, "U.S.S. Yorktown returning." The guy without thinking—we were supposed to be . . . you know what I mean? He gets up there, "U.S.S. Yorktown returning!" Everybody jumped, "What the hell is going on?" The captain stormed aboard, "Who's that guy? Get rid . . ." I don't know what happened to him but he gave [our position] us away. At that time the Japanese subs were on the west coast—they bombed a few places in California, off the coast into the Navy yards. And any ship that left, they would go for it. So they had to send a lot of destroyers. Now we no sooner got out of the Panama Canal—we had destroyers that were assigned to us, two on each side, four destroyers. They get a submarine alert: "Submarines detected." Uurrrhh! Everybody banging, "Man your battle stations!" Don't you know they knew we were coming? From that incident in Panama. They already had the word, "Carrier coming through—the Yorktown coming through." They were waiting for us. The destroyers chased them away and we went up to San Diego to load supplies to bring over somewhere, planes, aerial bombs. So we departed with four destroyers and two cruisers, one on each side of our force. So we're going, "Where we going?" "I don't know." Finally somebody comes down from the top, "We're going to Samoa." Everything is secret; they don't tell you nothing. So we went to Samoa and dropped off all that stuff. So while we're there the Japanese were threatening Australia and New Zealand—they were getting closer and closer. So they ordered us to go down and patrol, to try to get some of the Jap ships that were coming down. Our planes, their mission was to go in and bomb the Japanese enclaves that were already set in the New Guinea. Around January 1941, we were on the other side of New Zealand. These planes attacked us—our planes were off looking for them. So now they attacked us and the Lexington. And the Lexington had just got through fueling some of their planes that had come back; they were low on fuel. And they bombed us and the Lexington. We had some bomb hits on the deck. I ran to the island structure. The Lexington got caught with their gas still in their lines and it started to burn and they couldn't put the fires out and we couldn't get near it because the flames were shooting, the gasoline was burning, the planes were burning, guys are jumping overboard. So the Lexington—the destroyers and the cruisers—picked up as many people as they could. And then they sent a destroyer there to sink it. And they sunk it. That was the Battle of the Coral Sea. We were the only ship in the Navy that had a radar on it. We had a guy there, he was an enlisted warrant officer, was trained how to operate that thing. And he got a blip on the screen that these were planes were coming so everybody took cover. What they done was that they hit the flight deck and they ripped up a couple of cables that we used to catch the planes that landed. That was my division—had to take care of them things. So I had to go out there with another kid and cover up the hole because on the ship we had an island. Up against the island we had big sheets of steel that we were supposed to put over the hole if they punch up the deck so that the planes could still land. We were taking away all the debris—the broken cables and everything. We get another warning blip—"Take cover! Enemy planes!" So he runs. I thought that he was going to run to the island, open the door this way and go in there because it's steel. The door had a step so that if the waves washed over it wouldn't go through into the island. Anyway, he's running, I figured he's going to go open the door, go in. He goes past the door. I said, What the hell, this guy is nuts. So I run over; they don't just open the door. Had a wheel on there. You spin the wheel and it pushed the bars back, then you opened the door. So I opened the door, step over, got one foot out, another foot. I grabbed the door and I put my foot in, I'm closing the door, all of a sudden the door—boom! Bangs shut. I look. There's a hole in the door—a piece of shrapnel must have hit the door, went through the door, I don't know where the hell it landed. I said, "Jesus, man I just made it in time." The other kid got it in the back—I found out later if he had gone in the island and left the door opened he would have been saved. So while in there, in this cubbyhole there, that's where the smoke from the fire rooms, the uptakes up to the funnels. That used to be for them to get rid of the smoke. And I'm leaned up against it. And I could hear something rattling down that thing. It was a bomb! I didn't know where the hell to hide. I go down where the boiler rooms were and it exploded down there and it put out all the [engine] fires. So now the ship runs out of steam and we're dead in the water. So they had to work like hell to get the fires lit again, bring up steam and we were doing about three or four knots, just enough so that you steer the ship to move. We had some damage from a near miss—hits the water and explodes. So we had holes on the hull of the ship and our divers went overboard and covered them up. They used to weld them. We stopped at a place called the "Friendly Islands." We stopped at Tonga and the ship-fitting department tried to fix the holes that we had. They patched us up. We went back to port in San Francisco. We had some guy on the west coast who broke the code so that we could pick up their transmissions and translate them and we knew just exactly what they were going to do.

"The Battle of Midway"

The first thing we got was a bomb attack—they punctured the deck with about four or five bombs. Then we got three torpedo hits on the port side, the left side. Now I was on the flight deck and I ran when they said take cover, to the right hand side. Underneath the flight deck we had workshops—I went there to take cover from all the shrapnel flying around although a bomb could have hit the deck and went into the room I was in for all I know. Anyway now I'm in there and one torpedo hit the ship—the ship rose and it settled down. Half a minute or so—boom! Another one. Up and then down. The boat lifted up. The third one hit—drruumm! And it came down. Now when it came down the third time, it started to list because the water went in. So now the captain thought we were going to capsize. So he ordered everybody to abandon ship. Now we had no boats because they took them off because they were wood and they were afraid that if a bomb hit them the wood would fly and hurt people. They only left one boat, the captain's gig. So that was for him and some of his high-ranking officers; the admiral were going to use that boat. The rest of us—over the side. Now I can't go over this way and jump in the water because the boat might capsize and I'd be caught. I had to come down the other side. So they had ropes that they put down so we could shimmy down. But now I got a lifejacket on and I'm coming down the rope and now I can't hold on the rope—it started slipping through my hands, burning my hands. I said, frigit, and I let go and I—bowpp—I went down and I come up. So now these jackets were cotton that was supposed to keep you afloat for only a two or three hours. Then it would get waterlogged. So I had this thing on. So I'm in the water and I'm swimming, looking for people—a lot of kids in the water—and we're all drifting away. The captain comes by and he's passing me and some other guys. And the chaplain of the boat—he was a Protestant chaplain, used to have services—we used call him "Bum Dope Hamilton." He used to come in our room and drink our coffee. He used to give us all the bad news, scare us, "Gee, you know we just spotted a big Japanese . . ." Anyway, he's up there [fawning voice], "Have patience fellows, we're going to be all picked up." We're in the water and he's going dry, nice and dry. He's nice and dry, "Have patience fellows." He should have jumped overboard with us!

It gets dark early. So I'm in the water, looking. Not a soul in sight. So I start swimming overhand, boong, boong. I had taken my shoes off because they told us if you go overboard take your shoes off, tie them around your neck in case you get washed up on a coral atoll you won't cut your feet up. So that's what I did. They said that; I did it. Reached down, took them off, put them around my neck, start swimming, looking around to see if I could find anything floating I could latch to, because there were no ships in the area as far as I could see. All of a sudden I see a white flash! I said, God, a shark! So I put the speed on, going like a son of a bitch, he's still there. Finally I couldn't swim anymore. So I said, I got to do something. Somewhere I read or heard that if you hit them on the nose, you scare them away. I said, I'll try, so I turned around waiting . . . Where the hell is this shark? No shark; he must have ran away. So anyway I looked down, looking. I see something white.

I go look. I'm barefooted—the socks came off. Honest to God, this is not a lie, I mean I swear on all my . . . I seen the flashing of my feet, flashing back. You kick, you know. I thought it was a shark. And it wasn't. Now it's starting to get dark. So I bomp! I go down and I go up with my arms and I'm looking, I'm looking and the smoke is getting closer. I went overboard around noontime and now it's sunset. I see smoke in the distance. A ship. The life jacket is getting waterlogged. I'll be a son of a gun; somebody must have seen me. To this day I can't figure how the hell they saw me. And this ship comes. So he didn't want to get too close to me because they were afraid I would get washed up under the propeller. So anyway, they stop and I go to the ship. They had a line about this three inches in diameter that they threw over the side. And they told me to grab it, so I did. Grabbed the line. Now here I am covered with oil, my hair and my face. So I grabbed the line and they pulled me up. I'd get about halfway up and with the rope being wet and the floating oil on the water that got on it, they would pull me up, I'd get halfway up and I'd start to slip down. And I would have to let go because my hands were burning, starting to hurt from sliding on the rope. I'd go down and I would open my eyes still looking to see if there were any sharks and I could see the propeller of the destroyer idling. Come up again, grabbed the rope, they pulled me up again. I slipped down again. Now when I came up I heard the captain yelling, "Get that man aboard, we got to get out of here." I said, Jesus, if he decides to take off, that propeller is going to chew me up. So I come the third time, I yelled at them, tie a couple of knots in it, so I can hold on. So they did. And now it was dark. So they made a couple of knots in it, throw it in. I grabbed it and I held and they jerked me out of the water like a fish—pow!—I landed on the deck. The minute I landed on the deck—sssshht—off they went. Now I'm soaking wet covered with oil—I want to get warm. So I went over to the smokestacks and put my hand on it and they were warm from the fires in the boilers. So I'm hugging the smokestack to get some heat. So finally somebody come over to me and said, "How you doing?" I said, "Well I'm a little cold." He said "Well, why don't you go down below, there's some of your shipmates down there in that room." So I went down there and I just plopped myself down on the deck and rested.

"I Fought Against My Own Father"

Antonio Colavolpe spoke in the backyard of his home in Fair Haven on July 18, 1999.

Before the war my father wanted the rest of the family to come to New Haven. Unfortunately, America was in the Depression and my father wrote to us: "I'm afraid to bring my family to America now," and so we stayed in Amalfi. I had started filing emigration papers before the war but I didn't complete them in time because my father had sent me the wrong papers. So I had to stay in Amalfi. I was called into the Italian army in 1940. But if things had gone right I would have become an American soldier. When we got to Tunis, the battle was almost over. I was

ANTONIO COLAVOLPE
In Italian army,
1940
Colavolpe family album

in the office. At one time when I was there they asked if anybody knew how to type. So I raised my hand. That was my job. It was an experience. We didn't get that far into the desert; we never made it to Tobruk or Libya. We were in the mountains fighting but we were bombed heavily. After a month the war was over for us. The Americans passed by where we were camped and they took us prisoner. We started marching a few miles, the Americans left us, and we passed a French camp and were taken in the hands of the French in Tunis. They treated us much differently than the Americans. The French had almost nothing. They took everything from us. The Americans didn't do that; they didn't need anything. I had a watch that was given to me by my best man and I had to sell it to the French for two loaves of bread. They used to give us food in the concentration camp in Algiers. They gave us carrots almost every day and a piece of donkey meat twice a week. My father was still in America and he couldn't send any money. I used to be the head of the family—I was the first one in the family so I supported the family even when I was in the army. They used to pay me and they used to send it to my mother [in Amalfi] because my father couldn't send any money. While I was fighting in Tunis, my father was here in New Haven. I could say I was fighting against my father even though he wasn't in the army because he was too old. He was already an American citizen.

(translated from Italian)

"A Ball Turret Gunner"

Fred Nuzzo spoke in the living room of his Fair Haven Heights home on July 22, 1999. He was awarded The Air Medal, The Good Conduct Medal, The European Medal, and The Peace Medal for his many bombing missions.

I was eighteen and I knew I was going to be draft age so I volunteered for the Air Force. I had to go in anyhow so this way I had my choice. That's why they drafted kids, like eighteen, nineteen, twenty years old because we had no fear. When you're young you have no fear of anything. So when you go in the service you're more like a daredevil, because they go up in the air, you do this, you shoot this. So what? It's nothing. But after a few years go by and you learn these things, become twenty, twenty-five years old, you become a veteran. And you know these things are dangerous, which you didn't know when you were eighteen. So I joined the Air Force instead of going into the regular army or go into the infantry. So I picked out the branch that I wanted; to become a pilot and all that. But then they had too many of them and on our discharge they put down "washed out for the convenience of the government" because they had too many of them. So they sent us to aerial gunnery school. They started you with a bee-bee gun; then you work your way up from a 22 to a 38 to a 45 to a machine gun. And then when you're ready you go in a plane and you shoot targets. They were single engine planes and they're not steady. It was tough. After that we went to the two-engine plane then we went to the four-engine bomber. Then after that they shipped us overseas. We went on a lot of bombing missions. We were based in Cirignola, near Foggia on the Adriatic side of Italy. On a bomber you have a crew of ten. You have two waist gunners, you have a top turret gunner, a ball turret gunner, you have a nose gunner and a tail gunner. And we each had our positions to watch out for fighter planes. I had the back end of the plane—I had to look for planes out that way. I was in a turret; the new ones were bubbles. These here were turrets. You got in them and you controlled them like being in a swivel chair. You pressed the grips for the guns and the turret moved that way with your guns. You had no armor or nothing; it was plastic. Our planes got shot up quite a bit with flak, when the Germans shoot up the 88s, they call it flak, all little pieces of metal. Like when we're flying over the Alps twenty-five, thirty thousand feet, they had artillery up there in the mountains—it's like shooting at something flying at five thousand feet. They had deadly aim, those Germans. You come back and your plane

AIRMAN FRED NUZZO
Eighteen-year-old tail gunner,
Foggia, Italy,
before a bombing mission
over Germany, 1944

Nuzzo family album

looks like cheesecake. They're the ones who invented the radar for the antiaircraft guns. The two waist gunners had aluminum foil. And we used to throw it out a little door in the waist and the two waist gunners used to throw out all this tin foil to distract the radar on the artillery guns on the ground. And the aluminum foil used to screw up their radar—sometimes it worked, sometimes it didn't. Sometimes if you'd get a good tailwind and you drop your bombs. And we all flew in formation; we had a big formation of planes. We had seven, fourteen, twenty-eight bombers in a formation; each squadron consisted of so many planes. Then you could see the gunners were way off because as you're leaving the target you could see all the black flak out in the distance nowhere near us. The tailwind saved us from all that gunning. One day they shot out all our controls on one plane. He [the pilot] gave us a choice, he said, "You can either stay with us, stay with the plane or you can bail out." We could bail out either over Yugoslavia and then he crossed the Adriatic and he said, "Well, we got to Italy, you can bail out now," which was in friendly territory. But we said, "We came this far, we might as well stick with you." We couldn't land manually; the pilot was only nineteen years old and had to land on automatic pilot. As soon as the plane hit the ground, grabbed control of it because there was no manual controls. Thank God he made a good landing. He got the Distinguished Flying Cross; we didn't get anything. Thirty-four missions I made. I needed one more to come home and the war ended. I needed thirty-five and they sent you home.

"Uncle Nino"

Alphonse Di Benedetto spoke at the home of Kim and Mike Rogers on April 14, 2000.

When he got older he came over [from Italy], he was single and he came here in 1937. But he still was of age to be drafted. He got drafted. He can't speak English and he gets drafted into the U.S. Army! He doesn't understand anything they're saying, not a word. But they took him anyway. He only lasted three months. He was up in camp in Massachusetts. When they used to have reveille in the morning and the sergeant would call out the names, he couldn't understand. When he heard his name he was supposed to respond and give his serial number. So the only way he could comply, he wrote it on a piece of cardboard and put it on a stick. He would stand at attention. They'd call his name. He'd pick up [laughing] the sign! Then they put him on guard duty. This guy is coming along and Nino stopped him. The guy was a general. But my uncle didn't know a general from a private. The guy tried to explain to him. Uncle Nino just went on, "Oh no, rrr-rrr-rrr." And he wouldn't let the guy go by! That was one incident. The other time was when something had happened [at the camp]. He was told where the alarms were. So he knew he had to go pull an alarm. But he didn't know which one. What the hell, he pulled them all [laughing]! All the lights came on in the camp, the sirens, the M.P.s—you'd think the place was being bombed! That did it. Discharge!

"What Kind of a Bomb Is That?"

William Rossi spoke at a picnic table during the Oak Street Reunion on August 27, 2000.

We fought a war; we got rid of a s.o.b. I volunteered. I didn't have to go in. I volunteered the night when I heard that four thousand Jewish children had or were having their blood drawn from their bodies for a blood bank for the German army and that the Pope had been asked by Roosevelt to intervene and the Pope said to the effect that he didn't want to intervene politically. Four thousand Jewish children had blood drawn out of their veins to supply the blood banks for the German army. And I turned around—I was working on submarines and I was on my way home to

New Haven—I turned around went back to New London to volunteer my service. I wanted to do something, but I didn't want to kill. I had to go to the New Haven recruiting office and I recruited myself. And I didn't want to kill so I joined the Sea Bees. And I wound up on Tinian Island with the atom bomb. I'm one of the few people you'll ever meet to put his hand on the [atomic] bomb. We were there when the bomb was delivered. We dug the pits for the bomb so that the B-29 would crawl over the bomb. The bomb would be hydraulically lifted onto the plane and then the final component part would be put on route to be dropped. We asked the pilot what kind of a bomb that was. It looked like a cylindrical tank. The pilots were all young guys. We asked him, "What kind of a bomb is this?" He said, "I really don't know," he said, "Except that I understand it has the detonating force of 20,000 blockbusters." Well you know that boggled the mind. You know what a blockbuster is? A blockbuster is a bomb that they used in Germany that when they dropped on various [city] blocks, it blew the roof off, the furniture out, windows out of every building. Now the buildings in Germany are solid stone buildings, very well built. It just blew the roofs and everything off, blew out the buildings and the whole block. Were not talking about one building, we're talking about the block. It was known as a blockbuster. Twenty thousand of those? Can you imagine 20,000? But it turned out to be even greater. Because if those pilots, if that B-29, if they didn't after that bomb, move away fast enough, they would have been caught in the upswing of the bomb. Almost did. I had no idea that this was an atomic bomb; it was known as the "fat boy." Some of us just patted it, but we couldn't write on it or anything like that. We wanted to say, "Here's to you Tojo."

"I Can Still See Them"

John Nappi spoke at the kitchen table of his East Haven home on July 8, 1999. He recalled meeting Marines from the Wooster Square neighborhood—Gargano, Mansi, and Ruggerio—on Guadacanal. After a year and half of combat as a medic, he was hospitalized for malaria. Upon recovery, he volunteered for malaria experiments in New Zealand to help find a cure for his fellow soldiers. On two occasions, his temperature reached 107 degrees, almost ending his life.

I can actually see their faces. I actually [voice cracking, eyes tearing] see their faces, all the guys and friends that died—I don't forget them. A lot of them used to come to my house before they died. Some ate with me. And some of the guys that I saw, even on the islands [in the Pacific] that got killed, a lot of times I see them. Like in the movie Sergeant Ryan. So when the captain told him that his brothers were dead, they were going to take him home, he said, "I'm not going home." Says, "Why?" He says, "My brothers are here now." Know what he meant? The guys that he fought with were his brothers and you'd be surprised, you're just like brothers when you fight shoulder to shoulder. That's what he meant, I knew what he meant. They become closer to you than your own family. Because you depend on that man, he depends on you. He says, "My brothers are here." And that made a big hit,

SARGEANT JOHN NAPPI AND FRANK MONGILLO
(left to right) In the Solomon Islands

Nappi family album

when he said that. Because in combat the guy next to you is better than your brother. Your brother is home. You're with him. He's protecting you. That's what it is in combat—you don't look out for yourself. And I used to tell the older guys to look out for the younger guys, because they're green, you got to show them.

"WE GATHERED"

Rosina Ginnetti Cusick spoke at the Annex home of her niece Antonia on September 25, 1999.

I was in nurse's training at the time. I remember getting a phone call to home that Sonny [my brother] had died [in France]. Came in the house, and there was a doctor tending to my mother. He tried to tend to my mother—he tried to tend to my mother, she wouldn't have him. He was a doctor from Chapel Street, Doctor Saverino. She wanted Doctor Petrelli. And she would not allow this doctor to give her anything—it had to be Doctor Petrelli, they had strong faith in the Italian doctors they knew. And then I got on the phone and tracked down my brother [Serafino] Sam, he was at his girlfriend's house. And so the family gathered.

"THE INVASION OF ITALY"

Carlo Catania spoke at Joe Riccio's office in the Annex on June 16, 1999.

I remember the invasion. They [Americans] came through a place called Gela [in Sicily]. I don't think it took them more than nine or ten days. Patton was already in Rome, a long ways off, through the mountains. I remember when the first tank came through Monreale [a town near Palermo]. Everybody heard them coming, and they yelled, "Hey! Hey! They're coming! They're coming!" And then all of a sudden, the first tank to enter the town, and everyone is yelling. All of a sudden the tank stopped moving [pause]. You know, the turret started to move around, and everybody got very quiet [pause]. They felt, maybe they [the Americans] saw something, maybe there's something around here that we don't know about. But that was just a procedure. When you go in at night, you just don't go rollin' in, you stop and look around. Well, he stopped, rolled around—all of a sudden the gun went up in the air. He opened the hatch. Somebody came out. And they figured it was all right. And the people yelled. "The tanks!" Two and a half weeks, non-stop, down to Palermo, to Messina. In fact, on the plains of Catania there was a famous tank battle, but it didn't last too long and of course we won all the battles.

"I YEARNED TO COME HOME"

I always yearned to come back here, always. I hated the place [Palermo] for Chrissakes! Remember I was born over here [in the U.S.]. I remembered, you know, nice movies, hot dogs, hamburgers, you know, popcorn—stuff over there they never heard of. It didn't exist. Plus the fact it was during the war—you're lucky if you had a piece of bread for Chrissakes. And I used to say I don't think they're that bad over there [America], which they weren't. Over here they had stamps and all that but nobody starved. Everybody ate pretty good. I remember during the war over there. One item you couldn't buy if you traded it with diamonds because it didn't exist. Coffee—real coffee. It was completely gone. And yet, I'm reading an article on Ethiopia and I understand they grow coffee in Ethiopia. E che cazz'? What the heck? We used to own it [Ethiopia]. How come we never got any coffee? They could've given us a few grams of it, un cento grammi, un novecento grammi, a couple hundred grams, you know, just to carry us. Nothing. Bread lines used to be a mile long and believe it or not, you know who had to stay in line? My mother. Even at that time I said, "Ma, I will not stand in that line—I'll starve before I stand over there, I hate it." Stand in line for two hours for a lousy piece of bread I wouldn't feed to my dog? The only good place you could get good flour was if you went in the interior—there were cars and trucks but they were army and if somebody had a car they didn't have gasoline to put in. So guys used to go with knapsacks, with bicycles. You'd travel forty, fifty miles and come back with about twenty pounds of flour to make bread. You call that living? I did it a couple of times and I said, "Ma, we'll have to do with what we got here, I ain't gonna take no long rides like that." Plus the fact they had la polizia stradale, the traffic police, as they called it. They were on the corners and you know what I found out? That if you were young, if you ran the stop sign they wouldn't shoot, I mean they'd shoot but they'd shoot up in the air. And I did it a couple of times and I said I hope they shoot the bag. I heard shoot, boom, boom, boom, "Fermati!" Stop ! Poom! Poom! I was gone. Yeah man, I was gone. They had motorcycles too. But they ain't gonna come after a guy who's got twenty pounds of flour. I mean I could see if I was trying to get through with a couple tons. "Fermati!" Stop at once! "Io, non mi fermo," I'm not stopping, you're gonna have to shoot me. And then I was sayin', what am I talkin' about? I told my mother, I said, "Ma, they're shootin' at me, I can't, I'm too young to die yet. I got a go back to the United States."

"We Feared the Mailman"

Rose Savo and Rose Donaruma spoke in the kitchen of Rose's Annex home on July 26, 1999.

Everybody cared about everybody. It's true. I remember if you didn't get a letter, everybody consoled you. I remember when we used to stay at my grandmother's, everybody waiting for that mail. It was sad. No mail. The mailman would cross over—he didn't want to see the people if they didn't have any mail. It went on for years. I used to write to my uncle [John Nappi] every day. We wouldn't hear from him for months, for months.

"We Saw Him in the Paper"

Rose Savo spoke in the kitchen of her Annex home on July 28, 2000.

We applied to the Red Cross. Then, finally, even the Red Cross couldn't help us. He came in the paper, on the front page. He [my brother John] was administering first aid to a soldier on the ground. Yeah, we got hysterical. I says, there's Johnny! An AP reporter must have taken a picture of that medical unit. My poor mother! Every day she'd cry. Every day she'd pray. She used to light the candle in front of Saint Anthony, yeah. It was sad because everybody in that area—we were all in tenements—had someone in the war. And they all came home. He went through hell, that boy [my brother John]. He was in the medics. He went after some drugs, some medicine, and on his way there, whatever he had to go, he came across one of his buddies from home . . . strapped to a tree, in strips, all bayoneted, oh, I can't talk about it.

27

The Franklin Street Fire

On January 24, 1957, a rookie fireman named Bart Laurello reported for duty on what seemed a normal day at the Grand Avenue firehouse. At 2:56 that afternoon, with temperatures hovering near zero in New Haven, an unidentified woman reported a fire at 62 Franklin Street, where a roaring blaze was already raging out of control in the worst fire in city history. No one on duty that day could have imagined that within twenty short minutes the eighty-six year old factory building on Franklin Street and its ninety-nine employees would be engulfed in a nightmarish holocaust. Firemen arriving at the scene quickly called for more help, which escalated into a call for a general alarm. Off duty and retired firefighters were called in and, with twenty pieces of fire apparatus, battled the blaze that state fire investigators said started in a refuse barrel on the first floor and raced through wooden staircases and hallways of the four-story building with lightning speed. Workers were alerted to the fire when smoke traveled upward through the building, giving those on the third and fourth floors precious little time to make their escape. Women on the third floor found the main stairway engulfed in an inferno of smoke and fire. Having had no fire drill training and unaware of the safer rear stair exit that would have saved them, many tried the fire escape. To their horror, four women who managed to reach the outdoor fire escape on the upper level of the building found the folding staircase locked in place as searing-hot flames exploded from nearby windows.[51] Trembling and frozen with fear, they hesitated from jumping and perished from the flames. Shrieks and cries from women engulfed in flames horrified onlookers at ground level who stood helplessly in the street below. Others who jumped to the concrete pavement shattered limbs. Panicked workers inside the building trying to avoid the smoke and flames found exit doors that opened inward rather than outward with passageways blocked by fallen coworkers overcome by thick, acrid smoke. Grief-stricken employees who managed to escape and had seen many of their fellow workers trapped inside the doomed building wept at the scene. A priest from Saint Michael's gave dying victims the last rites on the pavement. Ambulances rushed to the scene where they transported badly burned victims to the hospital. School children kept away from the disaster looked out from windows to watch smoke from the burning building billowing in the distance, listening anxiously to the radio for word of missing relatives.

There were many acts of courage and heroism in the face of the disaster. The last time Mrs. Josephine Nastri saw her husband Joseph Nastri, a foreman in the Baer shirt shop, he was wrapped in flames after helping her and another woman escape to safety. The owner of the shop, Mr. Louis Baer, was last seen ordering his employees out of the building and remained behind to make sure everyone had been safely evacuated from the building. Mrs. Therese Sullo, known to her fellow workers as hard working and loyal to those around her, was last seen on an upper level of a fire escape at the height of the fire. A relative stated she stayed behind because of her concern for Mr. Baer, who had recently experienced health problems. Tom Dobroski and his cousins Stanley, Walter, and Frank Myjack, who worked in the S. L. Myjack metal shop on the first floor, saved many trapped women on the second floor fire escape. Walter Myjack ran into the burning building to retrieve a ladder and placed it under the fire escape which was suspended in mid-air. He drove his new Buick below the fire escape, pleading with the badly-shaken women to climb down. Family members witnessed his brother and cousin holding Walter from climbing up the fire escape where he would have met instant death. In the midst of the confusion, Walter and Frank found a sledgehammer and smashed the lock bolt, releasing the fire escape that allowed trapped women to tumble to safety. Witnesses described Tom Dobroski, who received extreme burns to his hands from handling the burning clothes of the victims, climbing to the roof of his cousin Walter's car to rescue women who climbed down his shoulders to safety. Carmine Prete, who sustained burns and a fractured ankle after he jumped from the fourth floor, refused to be taken to the hospital until all those who had escaped were taken away by ambulance and continued helping in the rescue work. Peter Aiello, who had just finished his night shift, was roused out of sleep by his wife who heard the sirens. He ran to the scene of the fire where he helped women on the fire escape to safety, wrapping a badly-burned victim in the new winter coat he had bought the week before.

The tragic loss of life at Franklin Street resulted from the same unregulated workplace conditions that caused the New York Shirtwaist Fire in 1911, where 146 women perished because of locked exit doors and fire ladders that were too short to reach the ninth floor. Forty-six years later in New Haven, thousands of men and women worked under the same dangerous conditions in old factory buildings without sprinkler systems, inadequate fire alarm systems, safe exits, workable fire escapes, or fire drill training programs for employees. A few days after the fire, Chief Thomas J. Collins's official statement to the *New Haven Register* revealed only a partial picture of the tragic causes that led to the fire, saying, "Deaths could have been prevented if workers had been shown alternative escape routes in the building and had not panicked when the locked fire escape failed to open."[52] Although the owners of the building later testified that all fire escapes had been checked and cleared of defects that year, passageways were blocked by bales of clothing and a key fire escape where four women perished failed. In all, fifteen people died in the Franklin Street fire, three of whom were African American women:

Morris Baer, Alma Bradley, Sophie Christodoulidou, Angelina DiRienzo, Matilda Di Ruccio, Winifred Freeman, Herbert Horowitz, Anna Jones, Thema Grillo Lynn, Josephine Marotta, Jessie Josephine Mongillo, Joseph Nastri, Grace Pitman, Angelina Romano, and Therese Sullo.

The seeds for the tragedy on Franklin Street had been planted in the '20s when the New Haven Chamber of Commerce invited needle trade businesses to the city, turning a blind eye toward workplace safety. The Connecticut legislature did little to enact labor laws favorable to workers and New Haven's mayors did little but watch from the sidelines. In 1957, the City of New Haven's Citizens Action Committee report published an eerie photograph of the Franklin Street Fire's aftermath showing a fireman walking away from the smoldering burned-out hulk of 62 Franklin Street. The picture's caption, "A tragic fire is not the way to clear out the blighted parts of the city" served as a subtle reminder of Mayor Lee's forward-looking vision of how his administration would deal with slum conditions and antiquated factory buildings. The Franklin Street Fire represented the culmination of the city and state's historic neglect for the safety of thousands of workers, a critical fact overlooked by the Lee administration in its futuristic campaign to promote the benefits of urban renewal. In the wake of the fire that traumatized an entire city, no public official in state or city government stepped forward to take responsibility for the needless loss of life. Forty years later, the New Haven Fireman's Benevolent Association sponsored a commemorative mass at Saint Michael's church where a packed audience of former factory workers, firefighters, family members, and friends who had lost loved ones in the fire, and neighborhood residents who vividly recalled the terrible events of that cold day in January, reunited in honor of the fifteen victims of the Franklin Street Fire.

"A Young Fireman on the Scene"

Bart Laurello spoke in a meeting room at Sterling Library at Yale University on December 3, 1999. He was a star football player at Hillhouse High School in the late 1940s.

I was only on the job for two weeks when that happened. I was at central and when that fire came in it was in the afternoon—I was new. We were actually upstairs watching television, to be honest with you, in the afternoon when the first alarm came in. They just said, "A factory fire and a lot of smoke." They didn't tell us because you couldn't see the fire right away. So we were the first ones out of the door and we all slid the pole and went on the apparatus and we went out in order: engine 2, engine 4, and truck 1 and the deputy chief. We pulled around the corner and we saw the fire coming out the windows. When I first saw it, never going to a big fire, I really got scared just looking at it. I saw them hollering. So the first thing the chief did was call a second alarm so that brought in three more companies and another chief. Then I heard this, a half-hour after they called a third alarm because the fire was jumping from Chapel Street over to Saint Louis's

BART LAURELLO
At the Franklin Street fire

Laurello family album

church and it had a slate roof. And the slate roof started burning downwards and slate never burns right away. So they had to knock the church down right after the fire. We worried about the people there. There were five companies in that building; we had a machine shop in there, two or three dress shops I can remember. That was the worst part of it, the machines made the floors very oily. They didn't take care of it like they do today. And the floors were so oil-soaked so once that started going you can't put that out because the floors were made of hardwood floors. And the oil was soaking for fifty years in there maybe. And the dress shop had a lot of different cloth around, they had stuff all over the place. Not only that, it's the dust that comes off the material that circulates in the corner and it builds and it builds and then once the fire gets underneath it you can't just put it out. They only had fans then; never had air conditioners and that's the worst thing that could happen. If the fan was on—see this happened in January now—but it still could have been hot in there I don't know. If the fans were on that would throw the fire all different places from the wind from the fans. But I didn't know. We don't know how it could have started. Being just like I was a private, didn't know nothing—they wouldn't talk to me about nothing. The captains and the chiefs maybe know a lot. They had to write out the reports. To this day I . . . "Over here Bart, help this guy with this ladder, try to go inside here." We just ran around like chickens with our heads cut off because you got to listen to the lieutenants and the captains and the chiefs. Somebody said there was an electrician or a welder working someplace and he started it. But it's not true, we don't know, they talked about like that but . . . if they ever found out why they never told anybody. You know, years ago, there wasn't that much pressure. Today if you had fire like that they'd be on your back the next day. No sprinkler system. It would have put out half the fire. The biggest fault of it all now was the doors. The doors opened up the other way, so when the bodies came down trying to get through the door, the first woman opened the door the wrong way and she must have been three hundred pounds and nobody could get out the door. That's why we found a line of them over like this, trying to get out. The smoke was so bad. Most of them died from smoke, not fire. They didn't have too many burns on them but the smoke can kill you worse than fire because in a fire sometimes you can breathe a little better than with smoke. And it was a son of a gun; we had to put on our Scott air packs on right away, that helped us a lot. The chief went in first and he said, "There's bodies in inside." But he didn't know if they were alive or not. So he said, "Get them out." And the first thing we tried to make a line to get the hose lines right near them. But it was mostly smoke, it wasn't fire there—it was the outside of the building that was going harder than the inside. It was amazing. That's why the smoke really killed them more than the fire. Working in those dress shops were all older people; you noticed the ages of the ones that died were all older people. And you can't blame them, they all got frightened and when they went to open the doors, instead of any of the doors going outward, they came inward. So when the girl tried to get the door this way—boom! She tripped or somebody hit her from behind, the first one and they made a pileup and they couldn't move. That was on one floor, I think it was the second floor. The fire escape door and even the doors going out the building and downstairs were wrong, they just made the building . . . There were two places they tried to get out, one was near the fire escape there must have been seven, eight, nine bodies. Then there was another part of the building there was more bodies. They told me after it was one of the worst because of the bodies. We had some tough fires, I mean I had a couple of four alarms—that was a general alarm that got every fireman that was working nights, days—they wanted them to report to help out. Picking up those two and a half inch hose lines in the winter was tough. We must have dropped a thousand feet of hose all around. We had a fire truck all the way on Olive and Chapel to pump all the way to the building because sooner or later it was sucking all the water out of the hydrant just so much came out. And it [the fire] was going, it was going good.

I don't even like to think about it to be honest with you. Like I say, we're lucky—it's not nice to say—we only lost that many. Some got out. I'm so happy some of them got out. There were a lot of people working there—those dress shops had two to three hundred people. They used to call them sweatshops—that's the word they used to use. And the old ladies that worked there . . . I felt so sorry . . . Just a heartache. When you see something like that you try to get it out of your mind. I really did, I'm bringing it back after so many years.

"I Couldn't Go to Work for Three Days"

Tony Sacco and Salvatore "Gary" Garibaldi spoke at Tony and Lucille's Restaurant on May 19, 2000.

The Baers—they were Jewish fellas—had a dress shop there. When I used to come from school I used to go through Chestnut Street into that factory yard there under the arch and come out through Franklin Street. They were loaded with them floors, loaded. I thought they treated them with oil. They used to saturate them to keep the wood live; treat them with oil so it wouldn't dry up. Just like the schools in those days. It went up like a torch. When I saw that fire, I ran there. I was sick. I could hear those girls screaming and nobody could do anything. I saw people trapped on the balcony there, the fire escape and my cousin was helping them out with putting towels on them. When I saw that fire I didn't go to work for three days. And unfortunate—in the shirt factories they had big dumpsters. In those hallways they had big bins and they used to throw all the waste in there. Well, now, if you took a cigarette and threw it in there you start a fire. Unfortunately a fire did take place. It started on the second floor in one of those bins. What happened was, as the girls were running out on the side there was a fire escape. Some son of a gun put a pin in the fire escape that the ladder wouldn't go down. Because a lot of these factory owners would seal the door so that the workers wouldn't leave, escape. And what happened when these girls went out to that fire escape, they couldn't go down. Now the flames were attacking them. And that's how six or seven were one on top of the other on that fire escape. Now Joe Nastri who was also a dress shop owner and operator, he went in it to try to save some of the girls. And Joe went up there, and as he was pulling the girls out into the hallway, the door shut on him and he got killed. And Mayor Lee was there at night. I saw him, he must have been sick. He was yelling, "Hurry up, over there!" I saw him, "Get that ladder, help them people over there!" Everything was out of control; they couldn't control it. And that's why they passed a variance—no more double floors in Connecticut. Everything in New Haven is on one floor. These were obsolete buildings. You know what they used to do in these old factory lofts? Say you had the first floor. And someone had the second floor. Well instead of going outside in the hallway to go upstairs, they would rip part of the floor on the second floor and make a chute. Well now if there was a fire on the first floor, there would be a flue up to the second floor.

"I See Smoke"

Rose Cimmino spoke in the living room of her sister Mary Marino's home on Warren Street on September 7, 1999.

I was working next door to the building. It was like almost together, the building that caught on fire and the building I was working in were almost together. And this girl and I were sitting right near that building. I happened to look out the window and I saw all smoke coming out of the exhaust fan. A lot of smoke. I got a little scared you know. When I see smoke I'm taking off. I really didn't know what happened next door. It was around three o'clock. I'll never forget that because it was my niece's birthday. And they were all upstairs and they heard it on the radio, that there was a fire on Franklin Street. So I told the girl, "Oh, I see smoke there, I'm getting out of here." I took my pocketbook and I ran down. Now when I ran down the stairs, I was at the bottom of the stairs just near the entrance to go out of the door. I met her in the stairway. This girl, Louise Arafano—she finished work early and she was downstairs—she's coming up, hysterical, "Oh, oh, the place is on fire! Everybody's trapped!" She went back upstairs in the building to tell all the people in there that next door they were all trapped. That's how they all got out. About five minutes later they all came down the fire escape. Well when I got out the door the building next door, oh, I couldn't believe it. I went out. I couldn't believe it. Every window in that building, smoke and flames were coming out. My mind was calling my mother. Fire engines coming; people all over, on the corner. I said, let me call my family, I'm all right, it's the building next door. The firemen were there—awful. I tell you I was one of the first of the girls that ran down from the building next door to that building. If I ran near that alleyway or something I would have seen all those people on the fire escape trying to get off. But I didn't go there to look. I went on the corner where there was Frankie's Restaurant on the corner. You know what? I didn't want to stay too long there because I knew my mother was going to be worried. That building, those places were fire hazards. The fire escape didn't work. You see, years ago they never had a fire drill, they never . . . I'm glad there isn't any more of those buildings. Then we moved to Strauss-Adler building and over there we had fire drills. We used to go down the fire escape and go out. You know most of these shirt factories and things they used to go into these older buildings. And you worried about . . . I always looked for entrances.

"We Got Caught on the Fire Escape"

Anna Gambardella spoke at the home of Kim and Mike Rogers in New Haven on February 16, 2000.

We made it to the fire escape but we all got stuck on the fire escape. When the firemen came, they had a break the extension—it wouldn't move because it got stuck. The staircase of the fire escape itself, it wasn't locked; it was jammed. Like when

John Mongillo Sr./For the Register

Rescuers approach the fire escape platform where some of the factory workers were trapped by the flames.

FIRE ESCAPE
John Mongillo photo

something rusts and it corrodes and it doesn't pay attention, nobody . . . They should have taken care of that. And even the firemen when they came, "Don't you know that this is hazardous, you have to fix it." But it wasn't. This is why we couldn't get out. We couldn't get down. And the fireman had to break it. When that happened we all tumbled down, one another and we all fell. I remember my boss went back into the factory to get someone out of the elevator and he got caught in the elevator. That was a very sad thing. And we had a mass every year until the bosses died, like his sons, Mr. Nastri died, but we kept the masses going every 24th of January. We really went through a lot. It was a beautiful place to work and Mr. Baer was a wonderful boss. Fifteen people died in that fire. They came from all over to help, it was unbelievable. You got to remember that we were caught upstairs. We didn't know what was going on. The fire alarm never went off so we were still working at our machines. That's the whole thing—we never knew anything. The back doors were all locked, couldn't get out the back, so when somebody opened the door going out to the stairs they smelled the smoke. And that's how we knew the place was on fire. And that's when we left our machines, then we all went to the fire escape because we couldn't get out to the steps because the fire blocked the staircase. The elevators were still running where he was taking some people out by the elevator but that's where my boss got caught. When he went in to get the last person out, that's when he got caught in there. They were beautiful, beautiful people but . . . how it ever started nobody knows. They never, never knew, they never mentioned how it started. Some people think that somebody threw a lit cigarette or a match because there was always barrels full of wet cloths with oil. And most of the people were smoking all the time so they think that . . . but they are still not sure the way it started. We lost a lot of nice people. I don't remember their names now because you know as you get older you forget everything. Joe Nastri, he was the boss on the third floor—he got most of his girls out but he died in the fire. He saved his girls. Most of those girls were all out on the third floor. Most of the girls on the second floor were all out, first floor, second floor, and the fourth floor—they were all out. We were the only ones who were in there and we working at our machines while this was all going on and we never knew anything until like I said, one of the women smelled the smoke and she went toward the door and that's when she saw the fire and that's when the boss started leading us to the fire escape. We couldn't get out; we were jammed on the fire escape because there were so many girls, this one here didn't work. This is why we got caught on the third floor. Opposite the fire escape side, there was another way out that we didn't know about. And it so happened that the boss's son was away at the time—he had gone on business and wasn't there—he knew about the other side but his father didn't. I'll never understand how the father didn't know it too. I mean here you are working in a building for so many years, you don't know? It was not nice; it was a very, very sad day. The first few years [after the fire] were tough, very, very tough, it was hard to talk about it. If I was anywhere and there was somebody said fire, I would go out of my mind—it was . . . it's not easy. Even now it's a little hard to talk about it but it's better than what it was. Even when I'm working and somebody says there's a leak of something I almost panic . . . it's not easy . . . it's very, very hard.

"We Knew Them"

John and Mary Nappi spoke at the kitchen of their East Haven home on September 15, 1999.

That was the time my wife ran all the way from downtown. She thought that the kids were in school and they said there was a fire in Saint Michael's. People running, the girls are running. As a matter of fact, the Argento girl, Anna Argento Villano was burnt, all her legs. What they did, they did wrong. They took her stockings off; it stuck to the skin. Shouldn't have, they should of wet it first, see? Some got caught on the fire escape, they couldn't come down. They died there. The fire escape got stuck, it wasn't working. Whoever inspected it, somebody

ANNA ARGENTO VILLANO
1929 wedding photo,
jumped from fire escape after
being burned in the fire

Spatuzzi family album

made a mistake. They didn't know whether it was working or not. Now, Mr. Baer, and he said to his other people he wanted to get them out. He died in there, he got stuck there. But he got some of them out. But he ran back—he was Jewish I think—went back to try to get them . . . I don't know how many died, but I remember when they were throwing the building down how many bodies they found there. I was there when they were throwing everything down and the firemen were going through the debris to find bodies—they were putting them in the sacks—I got sick, I left, I couldn't stay. I didn't want to stay; I couldn't see them charred and all. It was only a half a block from the house. Sure we knew some of these women because they used to go by the house, going to work there from Wooster Street down Franklin Street, it was only half a block away. See what happened there, down on the first floor was a machine shop. There was oil down. What acted as a flue was the elevator, the shaft. The fire spread right away. I heard somebody was using an acetylene torch—that's what I read about but I don't know—and then, when it picked up they couldn't put it out and it spread through where the elevator shaft was and the flame went right up the elevator shaft. Acted like a flue, you know and that's how it got to the top. It spread so fast that the girls got caught there, they tried to go out through the back, some of them, and the fire escape wasn't working, was stuck—I don't know how many girls got stuck on there. And my wife was coming from downtown and she heard that Saint Michael's school was on fire, so she was running because my kids were going to school there. And that's when I saw some of the girls running through the backyard.

"They Went Back to Get Their Money"

Mary Altieri spoke in the kitchen of her home in Fair Haven on January 13, 1999.

I watched it. I was working across the way and I seen girls coming down the fire escape with their hair standing up in the air and everything. They went back to Mr. Baer upstairs to get their pocketbooks—they went down, they got caught in the fire. I only seen the girls when they were getting on fire and my mother and father got the notice here that it was my place. But it wasn't. It was right across from us. My poor father came with my son—he was so small then—looking for me. I was going to go home at three o'clock—isn't it funny—and I said, Eh, I'll wait a few more minutes. When I got out of there I saw all these people. I ran home to get the bus. It was bad, it was really bad. Screaming. One of my friends—God bless her—she jumped the fire escape and broke her leg and everything. She's like a little crippled now. But it was awful, it was awful. To see them people screaming, their hair up in the air, burning, their hair up. It was awful. Oh, it was terrible! I was working there doing my business and I see them all screaming and fire engines. I said, Oh my God, the building is on fire, look at that woman coming down. She couldn't jump the fire escape, she came down. I don't know what they did at the end, they must have put blankets on her. That son of a gun. She went upstairs to get her pocketbook because there was two hundred dollars in the pocketbook. She had to get material for the curtains. To hell with the goddamn two hundred. She died. Nice girl, really nice girl.

66 A FACE APPEARED 99

John Mongillo spoke at the kitchen table of his Hamden home on July 27, 1999.

Well I'm working in my own studio on 99 Temple Street and I was doing work, doing the prints of weddings. Over the scanner, we got "Bad fire at Chapel and Franklin Street." So right away I jumped in the car and I got down there. I took the movie camera and the 4×5 Speed Graphic. And I'm up on the roof walking around on the garage roof next to the fire. My foot went through the roof about seven or eight inches, it's a good thing when I pulled it out I didn't get hurt. And I kept shooting [pictures] for them. Then all the wire service came down and they wanted pictures. The Franklin Street Fire film that I shot—all the stations used it and they've been using it every time the anniversary shows up. They were yelling and yelling, they couldn't get down. Then they had a couple of guys—heroes—one of them was an off duty fireman come down, told them to jump. Then another guy told them to slide down the drainpipe. One man was sliding down and the thing let go and he hurt his leg. [My photos show] everything was locked and they couldn't get out so they got trampled all over. The derrick up there was scraping and finding bodies—so I was up in the bucket and I'm taking pictures, all of a sudden you'd see a face appear. The photos I got [of the fire], I proved it.

66 LUCKY I WENT HOME EARLY 99

Antonette Sicignano spoke in the kitchen of her home on Wooster Street on August 30, 1999.

I was working there on Franklin Street, across the street from the fire. I went home that day because I had no work on my job so I went home. And when I went home—we had the radio—the girl said, "You know, there's a fire on Franklin Street I think I hear." It was three o'clock in the afternoon. So I said, Gee I don't know. Before you know everybody was looking for me because I wasn't coming out. You see, in the front of the building they used to cut the shirts, all the parts. And then after that they used to have an iron door and in the door you went into the factory. They closed that iron door, everybody got out because the smoke was going all into the factory. But I wasn't working. I had my aunt living around there, she came looking for me. My sister Rae, she said, "No, she went home early, she had no work." Good thing I didn't, I would a maybe . . . My sister, she said the boss made them all go in the back, said, "Go out through the back." He stopped them because they saw so much smoke. I knew one of them. I knew her family. My brother Sal was best man for her sister. They didn't even have the . . . She was burned to a crisp.

"She Stayed Too Long"

Louise Orefice spoke in the living room of her home in the Annex on October 31, 1998.

Something was swept in the trash, maybe a cigarette butt or something and the darn fire started at the beginning of the stairs of the first floor. And then before anybody noticed, it went, they couldn't get out. They were trapped. The stairway that they were supposed to come down, it was burning and they had to jump off windows and off the fire escapes, oh, it was terrible. Poor people, a lot of people got killed in that fire. I knew quite a few people in there. They lost their lives. There was a girl that I knew, instead of running out, she didn't think the fire was that serious. Instead of running out, she had to fix her work and everything. She got caught in the fire. She thought it was just, you know, nothing. And she figured, "Oh, why waste the time running out, I might as well do my work here and then I run out." And she got trapped. She died. They [survivors] were talking about, "How did she get caught?" She stayed too long to fix the work. She thought it wasn't gonna be a serious fire. It was too bad. Poor people.

"He Wanted to Go in the Building"

Rose Savo spoke at the kitchen table of her home in the Annex on July 28, 2000.

I remember the fire. One of my brothers, my brother Henry, he thought I was workin' there, but I wasn't working there at all. He went wild. They had all to do to hold him back. He wanted to go in the building because he thought I was in there, yeah. And all those girls, I knew one of them, Laudano, her and a bunch of girls that worked there they all came to my house — I didn't even know them — they were hysterical the poor girls. I gave them coffee to drink. They were shakin'. One of them had just jumped out of a window. All the girls lived on Wooster Street.

"Mommy, Look at All the Smoke"

Rose Donaruma spoke at the kitchen table of Rose Savo's home on July 26, 1999.

You could smell the burning flesh. My son didn't feel well that day so he woke up from a nap and he went to the window and he said, "Mommy, look at all the smoke!" And I looked over and the flames started shooting out and in ten minutes everything was chaotic. You could not believe what happened. The burning flesh was horrible.

FIRE AFTERMATH
City of New Haven

"They Raised Them Out in Sacks"

Rose Durso spoke at the living room table of Joe and Lena Riccio's home in the Annex on February 1, 1998.

The Franklin Fire. Somebody left a pile of old rags saturated with oil in the corridor as you went in the vestibule. Oil was flammable that it soon catches. The way I was made to understand from a person that was in there that all those rags were all bunched up on the floor and somebody carelessly threw a cigarette and it lit one big [fire] and spread. It was in January. Somebody threw a cigarette onto it and that's what started that fire that killed fifteen people. I knew one—I forgot her name, pretty little girl—she had just married and they had built a house out in North Haven. She died. Small little thing. Pretty. My aunt thought that I was in that factory, she called my mother, she got all upset. My mother said, "I don't know anything about it." And of course I come home and my mother felt good, she said, "What happened? I heard . . ." No, when I got home my mother informed me. When I left there was no fire across the street. After I got home [my mother] said, "Zi' Teresina called, she thought you were in that fire." I said, "What fire?" She said, "There was a fire on Franklin Street." And that's how I found out. It was Baer dress shop. Even the boss, Mr. Baer died. Trying to help the girls. The boss himself, Mr. Baer, he was nice. He went back in and got burnt to death. See, what happened is that they all got, of course—anybody, it's a natural reaction—nervous and they went on the fire escape, everything bunched up. And they got panicky and they remained on there and the walls fell, it [fire escape] got stuck also—they couldn't get down. They panicked. Some jumped. It was a little bit of everything. Sad thing. Because of the swelling of the fire, it distorted all the locks and everything. They couldn't get out. It was an awful thing. It was a tragedy. The next morning that I went to work everything was exposed, all the machines were black and all the icicles hanging from the machines. It was scary. Haunting, it was. Terrible, and just the frame, some little steel frame was left. And then as we were having lunch, unfortunately, we used to stand by the windows, there were the bodies. They were pulling them up like big hams in sacks. And they tied the sacks on top with a crane and they pushed them up to pick them up. We had to go away, I couldn't look at it, I couldn't. I said, My God, look at that! It was a tragedy. And the families didn't even get nothing out of it. See, there was no inspectors who went around in those days, they had no sprinklers, nothing modern to try to prevent anything like that. No modern things. Not at all. And the bosses went along. They didn't care. They wanted work produced in order to make money, you know, and nothing to prevent that from getting worse. It was strictly business, nothing else, strictly. And we were the slaves, right Lee [Lena]? We were in those days, we really were.

Before construction of Interstate 95 and the Quinnipiac Bridge in the '50s, the Annex existed as an area of modest homes near large tracts of open fields and long stretches of wooded groves along its coastline on Long Island Sound. For Italian immigrants who lived in cramped spaces of tenement houses in the inner city, moving to single dwellings in undeveloped sections of the Annex meant returning to the conditions many had known in rural Italy, a rustic community where they found "l'aria cehiù fina," or the fresh air of the country. Established Yankee families lived on estates in the upper Annex on Townsend and Woodward Avenue where their homesteads overlooked Long Island Sound. Townsend and Woodward Avenues, named after the families of early Yankee settlers, began in the lower Annex and ran parallel along the coastline to Morris Cove and Fort Hale Park. The Granniss Corner Pharmacy on Forbes and Woodward Avenue was the demarcation point between the upper and lower Annex, which doubled as a trolley car stop and shook when the trolley approached its storefront to discharge passengers. Trolley men making stops dropped by the pharmacy for "spiritis fermentus," or a shot of whiskey.

Around the turn of the century, the Annex was a melting pot community where the newly-arrived Fiondellas, Acamporas, and Ginnettis lived side by side with old established families of Burwells, Grannisses, and Russells. In 1920, the Apuzzo family from Wooster Street purchased land from Mr. Granniss to build their new home on Woodward Avenue. In an Italian American version of old-fashioned barn raising, the family called upon twelve of their "paesani" to help dig the foundation with a sleigh-like device with handles that scooped out the earth. Together they mixed one hundred bags of concrete by hand. When the job of laying the concrete foundation was finished late that night, Mrs. Apuzzo cooked twenty pounds of macaroni. A barrel of homemade wine was consumed and the men departed with a simple "thank you."

From the early 1900s, the Burwell Street enclave evolved in the lower Annex with many features of a transplanted southern Italian farming village intact, a settlement quietly tucked away behind a thickly-forested ridge that acted as a natural barrier from Townsend Avenue, a place where English was a second language spoken by the children of Italian immigrants when they were old enough to attend the local Woodward School. At the center of this rural neighborhood was the Giannelli family farm, a large tract of farmland that spanned some fifty or sixty acres between Burwell and Oakley Street. During the summer months, one could notice 'Zi Rosa stooped over as she worked her acre-sized vegetable garden next to the farm from sun up to sundown, bonnet and long dress flowing with a bottle of homemade wine constantly at her side. Everyone in the neighborhood knew "Z'ntone," or Uncle Anthony, who converted his small barn on Burwell Street into "Z'ntone's Shack," a social club for locals where he scooped out fresh plates of lupini beans from a barrel and served homemade wine and bottled beer to his "paesani" who played for drinks and nickels in animated old world finger-throwing contests called "mórra." Other locals dropped in to partner off with friends and compete in bocce matches in the outdoor wood-framed court just outside the barn.

The Annex dairy, run by the Logioco family, processed fresh milk transported from the Adinolfi family farm in North Haven. On weekends the nearby Annex theatre handed out Depression-ware plates to moviegoers attending double features for twenty-five cents. Mr. Burrell ran a seed shop on the street bearing his family's name and Italian families survived bitter winters on vegetables grown in the rich virgin soil of family gardens. In autumn, families gathered around backyard fireplaces for "a conserva" where the harvest of tomatoes were washed, peeled, and ground in "a machinetta," or grinder, the puree placed in thick bottles with seals and boiled in large oval-shaped pans with handles on either side known as "a tinna." Some built backyard grape arbors, known as "a prèula," the size of modern car ports framed by two-by-fours and old pipes and held together by wires that produced enough clusters of black grape to make jelly stored in glass jars for the winter. A large picnic table sat under the canopy of grapes where communal meals took place in summer months with cousins, uncles, aunts, and friends of the family who lived nearby, many from the same town in Italy. Everyone on the street turned out for the yearly pig roast that featured a delicacy known as "a sanguinàta," rice fried in pig blood, seasoned with citron and bay leaves, stuffed into pig intestines, and baked. Neighbors borrowed whiskey stills to make special holiday liqueurs—strega, risoria, annisette, and annisone—to share with friends and families during the holidays. Poor families who had never heard of the holiday of Thanksgiving celebrated "La Festa e Gallina," or the Feast of the Chicken, substituting the more affordable "capone," or capon, for turkey. Families in the neighborhood maintained close ties through intermarriage. Young men "kept company" for many years with same girls from the neighborhood and later married. When a mother or father was chosen to baptize a child, the godparent observed the old world practice of being called a "San Giuanne" or a Saint John, with the parents of the baptized child.

On a September night in 1938, five civic-minded young men from the Burrell Street neighborhood—Joseph Riccio, Anthony Ruocco, Anthony Ferraiuolo, and Albert and Salvatore Vanacore—held a meeting in Pasquale Mascola's barn on Granniss Corner. With a heartfelt interest in helping neighborhood youth, they founded the Annex Young Men's Association, a grassroots organization that sponsored sports teams, ran benefit dinners and minstrel shows to pay for uniforms, and later provided college scholarships to young men of the community. In the '30s and '40s, Sunday afternoon football games featuring the home Annex team against their cross-town rivals attracted thousands of spectators at Annex field. At the end of every baseball season, an award ceremony took place at the Annex Little League Park where a little leaguer who demonstrated good sportsmanship on and off the field that year won the highest award, the Anthony J. Ginnetti Memorial Award For Sportsmanship, given by the Annex Young Men's Association in memory of Anthony, who died fighting in the hedgerows of France after landing in Normandy in World War II.

Until 1957, the Annex evolved as an independent borough of the city whose citizens paid modest taxes to its local town government known as the Fairmont Association, which had its own firehouse and police force. In a move to force the Annex to relinquish its independent status, the city threatened to charge its residents exorbitant fees to connect badly-needed public water and sewer lines unless it joined the city and paid tax to New Haven. Political pressure from the Lee administration eventually forced the Annex to abolish its local government and the legislature passed an ordinance to dissolve the Fairmont Association. Once the Annex became part of the city, the community experienced substantial increases in their tax bills.

"They Were Like Owls"

Rose Durso spoke in the living room of her two childhood friends, Joe and Lena Riccio in the Annex on February 1, 1998.

In the summer we'd go outside, play marbles, ball, or jump rope. That was it, there was no excitement. And if you went out with a guy after you reached a certain age your mother watched you like a hawk. You had to be home at a certain hour. All we did was Lena [Morrone] and I and the whole bunch, we'd walk around the neighborhood, go to Oakley Street and back and then down on Main Street, that's all we did. We were, we couldn't. Our mothers were owls, see, and that was our life. You can't say you had a good time, you went here. Shows? Who was gonna take you to the show? The shows were downtown, right? Fifteen cents, double feature. And with the serial, "The Lone Ranger," "The Perils of Pauline," all that I remember. Nineteen-twenties, I was a kid and my older cousin, my mother would say, "Addo iat?" Where are you going?" Then they opened up a show in the Annex and we'd go there. And my mother would be right in front at nine o'clock to see if were in the show or where we were. Suspicious minds. And she'd be there waiting, we'd come out and we'd all go home together. No dancing and stuff like they have now. Or the girls getting cars, going with their boyfriends—that didn't exist. You were clean cut, all the way, you know.

"We Needed the Shoes"

Then one time, my father, we needed the shoes. Came the time, the holes wouldn't fill up at the bottom [of the shoes]. So my father went up to the City Hall—somebody said to him, "Nick, go up to City Hall"—it wasn't the Welfare—Macri was the head, the stocky Italian woman. And my father said, "'I, mi miétt' 'o scuórno," I'm ashamed. So they said, "Go, go, you'll get the shoes for the kids, the rubbers or something." My father took the trolley car and went, gave his name and everything. Three days later a big stocky guy by the name of Angelo and Miss Dunn, a slender, little, Irish—a nice girl—her and this guy, they got out a the car, they came in. My mother said, "Sit down." So the guy, a big, stocky fella, said, "I understand that Mrs. D'Amato, that you need help here." So my mother said to me, "Parla, parla," you do the talking. So as usual, I was the lawyer. So he said, "Little girl, tell me." Well, I said, we need shoes. He said, "Well, do you mind if we look around Mrs. D'Amato?" My mother said, "Go ahead, look this is what I got of the rooms." They looked around, she took notes down with the notebook all dressed up, took notes, sat on the rocking chair. She said, "Mrs. D'Amato, we'll let you know in four or five days you'll get an answer, we're gonna evaluate what's here and we'll let you know."

They were right. Four or five days later they roll in with the car again. That day I dunno why my father happened to be home. They came in. My father said, "Sit down, sit down, okay, you wanna coffee?" "No, no." My father made a mistake, he shouldn't of said [laughing] you want coffee. Keep your mouth shut, you know? They said, "Well, Mister D'Amato, we evaluated your case here. You cannot have the shoes for the children." So my father said, "Why?" He was disappointed, you know. "Well, what shall I do? I got the kids and they need shoes, they need rubbers." He turned around, the man. He said, "Well, Mr. D'Amato, there's one solution to your problem. Sell your house and buy your kids the shoes." And my father got mad. After that he got mad, he said, "Where am I gonna bring the kids? Put em' in the farm, outside?" They both walked out, we never got anything. You see the attitude they had? When they were better than you in those days. So my father said, "What am I gonna do?" So my uncle that was wealthier really had pity for us at that point, Christmas was coming, the shoes. . . . Even the top—at least he fixed the soles—but when the top gives in, how you gonna fix them? So my uncle went and he bought shoes for all of us. As I said, those were hard times.

"Waiting for the Chicken Feed Man"

The dresses I wore. Any ol' way. The American kids with all the nice clothes that fitted them. You should see some of the things we wore. We used to get it from the chicken feed sacks. Feedbags! What do you think? When the chicken feed man came, my mother would say, "Va, va amprèssa a chill' òmmo," Quick! Go follow that man! "Why, ma?" "Diciel' [Ask him] that he gives you the saccatiéllo [chicken

JOSEPH AND LENA RICCIO
On Fairmont Avenue,
Annex, 1986

A. Riccio

feed bags], all one color, all one design [pattern]!" I would say, "Ma, he's only got one of each." She insisted, "Va la!" Go, go there! Oh, I used to cry, I used to cry, I didn't want to go—I had a go up to the man and say, "Do you have five or six of one kind?" The man would say, "Dear little girl, sweetheart," he'd say, nice, gentle, it was the same one year in and year out, "Look for yourself if you find them, and then your mother only takes a sack of chicken feed." How could I give her five or six—every one is a different pattern. My mother was still persistent that she wanted all one pattern. She wanted to make curtains on the window. How could I? One color, one another, okay [laughing]? So I said, Ma, go yourself. So she said, "All right a, All right, ti crede, I believe you," after a struggle with the man. They were pretty prints, though. All different—daisies on one, butterflies on another, checks, flowers, roses. They were pretty—cool looking, nice. But you couldn't get any alike, you couldn't. And we didn't have the money to buy it. So that's how I started to fuss around [sewing], 'nu pòcca a volta, a little at a time, I got to where I am now. And the saccatelli [small bags] that the flour came in, we use to make sheets and pillowcases. They were all white. My mother would bleach them for two days in the bleach, keep em' in the bleach, they'd get nice and white. But I had to rip out all of the strings off—and sit down for hours—and rip, rip, rip, rip—it was thick string! 'O spago, Oh, those strings! So then my mother would say, "Soak em' in da tinna," a tub. So I'd put em', I'd soak em' in da tinna, the tub, and two days later all the marks were all off, all white. We'd rinse them with cold water—in the middle of the night—the kids were all asleep. The next morning, we'd hang them all out and they'd come out all nice and white, blow them in the sun, they'd come out even whiter when it was sunny. Then I'd come home after school, I had my little treadle [foot powered] sewing machine—not electric like now—in the kitchen by the two bay windows my mother would say, "Rosie, pigli tutti i saccatiélli," Get all the little sacks, and make me a couple of sheets. And I'd get all those saccatell's, put them together—three, three, three—three, three, three. And I don't want the seam to be thick, like the end, fold it neatly, and then go over it because it hurts everybody that lays on them, they hurt their butt [laughing], they were delicate, you know. So that's what I did. [Mother] "All right, now you made a the sheets, make the pillowcases." And she had lace from Italy and I would put on the trim and they'd look nice. Nice and white. And I'd make "'i mantesìni," aprons, little blouses for myself, trim with something, that's what I would do with it.

“ BIRD SAUCE ON SUNDAYS ”

Lena Riccio spoke at the kitchen table of her home in the Annex on June 13, 1999.

You know 'a cenetura, the ash sifter? When they burned the coal they used to sift the ashes and they'd find maybe a few black coals that didn't burn. So we had a sifter with a handle on it. All the ashes would come out and the few coals that were left, my mother to burn them again. So on a Sunday morning—she had no meat to cook—we used to put the "cenetura" with a string and pull it all the way into the window of the kitchen with bread or corn or something. And when a little bird would go in we'd pull the string and catch the bird. And we'd go get the bird, my mother would twist the neck, kill it, and when she got about six or seven, she'd clean them all up and she make a sauce. That was our meat sauce on a Sunday.

“ LIFE ON THE FAMILY FARM ”

Rose Durso spoke in the living room of Joe and Lena Riccio's home in the Annex on February 1, 1998.

We had chickens, my father would go down the cellar, wring the necks—us kids, we used to run away—wring the necks, "Te, figlióla" Here, my child, five or six spring chickens, you know. And my mother, "Here he comes again with his spring chickens," and my mother clean them, take the feathers off, bake em' with potatoes and mushrooms in the oven and we were all set. And you ate chicken today, chicken tomorrow, chicken tomorrow. And ducks, the ducks. "Go milk the cow." Down on Main Street, down on the farmhouse, we had our farm, six acres of land. We had pumping water—cold—we had a wash the clothes in the winter, my mother would scrub them on the scrub board and me with the tiny, little hands, take 'i lenzùli, the sheets, and ring it in cold water and the next morning hang em' up. No hot water! Your hands got like icicles, okay? Then we'd go in the bedrooms—ice, almost icicles. We had a little gas stove with a pipe extending on the other side, my father would put the match, light, the flames would come like a fireplace, wait an hour until the room heated. We'd go to bed, my mother was ready with the bricks in the stove, heat the bricks, wrap em' in wool, and put by our feet. And then the little stove would go off. Five o'clock in the morning, the poor thing would get up, light that little stove again, heat the room, watch it, have a cup of strong Italian coffee with anisette, shut the stove and we'd get up. The cocoa skins—it wasn't the regular, nice, powdery kind—the cocoa skins from in the can, my mother would boil with water, put some milk in and 'nu biscuòt', a biscuit, or something and I went to school with broken shoes. How do you like them apples? All right!

"Fixing Up Our Shoes"

My shoes had holes under the sole. Then my father discovered something. Where he worked in Sargent, the old belts that went around the machinery, they were saturated with oil. He would cut those, put it on the form of our shoes—twelve or one o'clock at night the poor guy, by the window or by the light and cut up that leather and bang it in. And sometimes the nails [laughing] were too long and they'd get in our feet, but we had no choice. But at least our feet didn't touch the ground. All right, you see what I mean about the olden days? Milk the cow before you got milk. Feed the little pigs, four pigs every year, then we'd kill em' and make the sausage—the liver out, the ribs and everything. And my mother would share her four pigs every year. My uncle Vicienz' would come, they hang up the pigs—pow, pow, pow, pow—the pigs were dead, with a mallet. Oh, how we would cry, how we'd cry. The pigs' head would go down and the little pigs were dead.

"The Monkey Jacket"

Some rich lady gave us a monkey coat, a fur monkey coat. This was a monkey coat, the fur that long. They thought we were poor, you know. This woman got to know us, she had a beautiful car and everything. So my mother said, "e vist,'" You see now? You got this beautiful, warm coat—you won't suffer from cold anymore.

My brother put in on, when he got outside he said, "I don't wan a wear this coat! All the kids are gonna laugh at me." He took it off and he hung it on the billboard, behind the billboard and he went to school only with his shirt, this is the god's honest truth. I said, "What a ya doin', you're gonna catch pneumonia." [brother] "I don't care, I don't want my pals to see me with this coat." The next my mother said, "È miese 'o coat, figlio mi'?" Did you put your coat on my son? "É stato nice, caldo, caldo," it must have been nice and warm. "Yeah, ma," and he would hang the coat again back on the billboard, then come home, take the coat, put it on—it was stiff and frozen. "Ah, bello, nice figlio mio, con 'o coat," Ah, how nice my son, with that coat. And that went on all winter long! He never wore the coat. Then my mother, "Mo' é fatt' troppo piccirello 'o coat, darla a quaccheduno' that can enjoy it," Now it's too small for you, so give it somebody else who can enjoy it. Black. Like a monkey. When he put it on his body looked like a monkey. And that's how we survived.

CHARLES MASCOLA WITH
SISTER, FATHER PASQUALE,
AND MOTHER VIRGINIA
(left to right)
Granniss Corner
Annex, 1930s

Mascola family album

"LIFE IN THE ANNEX"

Everyone knew Charlie Mascola as "The Mayor of the Annex." He spoke in
the living room of his home in the Annex on January 5, 1999 with his son
Chuck and with Joe Riccio.

I knew everybody's father. And I knew all the Yankees; they all came to my shop. I
knew more parents than anybody being in the barbershop and they all knew me. I
knew the Woodwards, the Townsends, the Grannisses, they all got streets named
after them and they owned most of the land. The Italians rented the land. Most of
them [Italians] were meek guys, just happy to have a couple of drinks, go have a
couple of drinks and beers [at the Fireside] must've been a nickel, the most a dime.
And they'd stay there, spend maybe forty, fifty cents to spend the day. But they
were beautiful people, they'd walk by the barbershop with a pail and a fishing pole
to go down fishing off the bridge. But it was so great. I lived up on Townsend Avenue. I would go home sometimes in the afternoon to eat and it would take me three
quarters of an hour to get up the hill because everybody would be on the porch.
You'd stop and talk to everybody. "Come in, have a drink, have a cup of coffee."
People, when they had a big family, most of them had seven, eight, nine kids.
They'd say, "You stay here and eat." You'd say, "Well I can't." They'd say, "Well go
home and tell your mother you're gonna stay and eat at my house." You'd eat at
everybody's house. What the hell, for eight or nine kids, they made "a pisciatura" [a
big pot] pan of macaroni, they could feed two or three more kids, what's the difference—who didn't show up. But it was funny. When that horn used to blow at
twelve o'clock on a Sunday, no matter what the score was, you ran home. If you
weren't home in five minutes, we were all pretty close [by], you sat at the table, you
didn't get to eat because after five minutes, they give you the five minutes to come
in, five after twelve they'd pour the stuff out and when it's gone there's nothing to
eat. There was nothing else, there was nothing in the refrigerator, no potato chips,
no nothing. You ran; we used to run, boy, I'll tell you.

"RESPECTING YOUR MOTHER AND FATHER"

We lived on Townsend Avenue, upstairs and downstairs and every night I come
home and I'd go to my mother downstairs, give her a kiss, "Hi ya Ma, how you
doin?" She'd say, "Good, tank a you, tank you very much." And I'd go upstairs. So
one night I was going out and I didn't go stop downstairs, I went upstairs. Boom,
out. So the next night I went down to my mother and I go to give a kiss and she
turns her face. I said, "What's the matter Ma?" She says, "Eh, last a night I wasn't
your mother?" One thing I got to tell you but when anybody loses respect for their
mother and father, they're done. I mean you cannot control people that lose respect
for their mother and father. Once you lose respect for your mother and father,
you've got nothing. There's nothing in this world.

"INTERMARRIAGE"

They hated us. But when the Italians after a while, they had fights and whatnot, but so much intermarriage. The Italians were good workers don't forget—they gave a day's pay. The Irish didn't because they were always their bosses. A lot of guys come out of a hole, they were digging cesspools, come out and kick the shit out of an Irishman. And after a while it got so they got rid of that guinea crap stuff. They started to fight them. There were a lot of fights, a lot of gang fights. The Irish were big; the Irish were always bigger than us. They were tall. Italians were all short, stumpy ones. Mostly the Irish married the Italian girls. We got a bunch of them down at the Annex Y. M. A club. The only good thing they ever done is marry an Italian girl. And it's true. Because they eat, they love it, you know? The Irish don't cook. You know what a seven course dinner is? A baked potato and a six pack. That's what they call a seven course dinner.

"THEY WERE PROUD PEOPLE"

My father was a little guy. But he wanted to come to this country and he started a business. And he didn't want to show these old Yankees that he was a "dago" or a "guinea" like they used to call us you know. We were dagos—these were Yankees. He moved from James Street in Fair Haven and came here [Annex neighborhood] because one of my sisters wasn't a well girl and she was supposed to have goat's milk. So he had to come to the farm, this is farmland this side of the water. Come over here and he says, "Well I'm not going to show these guys that I'm [a dago] and you would never believe, he didn't have a trace of any accent or anything. He was a proud guy, very, very proud and that's what he wanted to be. He didn't want to show these guys, these old Yankees, that he was a dago or a guinea or a greenhorn, which we were [to them], in them days. They used to call us greenhorns. So he had this business and he owned four houses. I don't know how he did it. I don't know how the Italians did it, I mean the Italians came over here and they were marvelous. Lot of them made money, big money, Fusco [construction] and all them. They didn't know how to speak the language. They didn't have children that could help them. They went alone. But they were proud, they were proud people.

"THANK GOD YOU GOT A YOUR HEALTH"

My mother never knew she was funny, she never said that she was funny. We went to a wedding one time and we're sitting at the table and the fella that had married my niece, a fella named Jim, and he came up and he saw my mother at the table and he came over and kissed her. He says to my mother, "Aunt Virgie, how do you feel?" My mother was kind of a proud woman and she says, "You know, Jim, I feel a pretty good." That's the way she talked, very frank. She says, "How a you feel?"

He said, "Well, you know Aunt Virgie, I have a little heart trouble and I had a cataract operation, I went to the doctors and I got high blood pressure and I got arthritis, you know." So my mother looks up at him and says to him, "Jim, thank God you got a your health." Well, I tell you, I thought we'd fall off the chairs! It was amazing, you couldn't believe it. And she says after, "What I make, a joke?"

"We Were Ashamed"

Rose Durso spoke in the living room of Joe and Lena Riccio's home in the Annex on February 1, 1998.

There were richer kids in our neighborhood, the Annex. There were two classes [of people]. They were mostly American, "My father got a job here, my father is this, my father . . ." What could we say? My father works in a lumberyard? We were ashamed, you know. They really embarrassed us. Could Lena say "My father is a boss or a foreman," could she say that? Oh, don't worry, they mimicked us but good. Kids are like that, spiteful. And in those days they were really cruel. The Italians—Ralph Finocchi—all the poor ones. They made fun of that poor kid. Oh, I felt so bad. He was dark and everything, they made fun, "Here comes the nigger." The American kids had the habit that they would make it obvious that you were poor and they were rich. And that hurt most. Edna Mae Collier used to go in front of the class, toe dance, and Virginia Brown toe dance with those fluffy dresses. "Isn't she wonderful?" The teacher said, "Everybody clap their hands." Us, nobody clapped. We had nothing.

"If You Want That Boy You Better Move to the Country"

Anthony Fiondella, 98 years old, spoke in the living room of his East Haven home on December 5, 1998.

I was a very sickly baby. My mother had twenty children; five were stillborn. In those days kids died because they didn't have all these shots; they died from diphtheria, they died from scarlet fever. My mother used to wheel me along Long Wharf when I was kid every day if the weather was good. The doctor said, "If you want to keep that boy you better move up to the country." Across the bay was the country, imagine that. That's how we happen to move to Granniss Corner. I think we were the first Italian family out there. Because they were all Yankees over there, the Grannisses, the Woodwards and the Townsends—they bought their land from the Indians with a bunch of beads so they owned the whole neighborhood between those three families. That's why they call it the Annex. It used to be part of East Haven. Before we were taken into the city of New Haven, we had what they called the "Fairmont Association." We had our own little government. We paid some taxes to New Haven for hydrants and schooling but otherwise our taxes were not as high as people who lived in New Haven. We paid the association a small tax every

GRANNISS CORNER PHARMACY

1934

Fiondella family album

year and in the long run it was a lot cheaper so every time they had a referendum vote the people voted not to go into the city. But when Mayor Lee took over he forced us into the city through the legislature—he didn't allow us the privilege of having a referendum vote. So we got taken into the city but before that we had our own tax collector, fire chief, and police force of four or five. They had a vote and they voted to annex themselves to the city of New Haven. Just across the Tomlinson Bridge from New Haven was the country. When I was a kid I drove forty cows through the streets there, to pasture. There were trolley cars; the cows would split and go each side. My brother had the job; the farmer was paying my brother three dollars a week to drive the cows to pasture. The farmer took fifty cents out of his three dollars and gave it me [chuckling] every week. The farmyard was right where the bridge goes over I-95 on Woodward Avenue. The Granniss family owned the farm but they leased it and the cows out to a man named Perry. Our job while we were driving them to where they were going to pasture was to keep them off people's lawns, they'd go up on the lawns. That's how I happened to become a pharmacist, I sold peanuts and popcorn on the trolleys outside the drug store. The drug store was the transfer point; you transferred to go to Lighthouse, Stony Creek in Branford. So all the trolleys stopped there. And there was eastern league baseball at Lighthouse Park so the trolleys were crowded and there would be a bunch of us kids on each side of the trolley hollering, "Peanuts, popcorn and crackerjacks." That's how I happened to go to work in the drug store, became a pharmacist. Because they owned the concessions, they were our boss, they're the ones that sent us

ANTONIA, ANTONIO, AND
ALBERT "SONNY" MORRONE,
12 Milton St., Annex
Early 1930s

Morrone family album

out there to sell the peanuts and popcorn. There was no pharmacy college in Connecticut then. I got my assistant pharmacist license when I was eighteen years old in 1918. In those days it wasn't as tough as it is today. And drugs are much better today then they were then. We made everything ourselves right from the crude drug.

"BURWELL STREET IN THE '20s"

Joseph Riccio spoke at the kitchen table of his home in the Annex on August 2, 1998.

Burwell was a street that ran north and south. At the southern end there was one house. And between the beginning of the street, which ran about a mile and a quarter there was eight houses on the east side. The one house on the west side belonged to an old-timer who was called Mr. Burwell—the street was named after him. And he was selling seeds. And he used to keep kids really interested in the history of the local area. There's Peat Meadow; it was started by a group of financiers including a senator supposedly. In the 1800s a rumor was spread that the coal mines were running out of coal and they formed a company to make peat. And to this day that is still all swamp because of where they cut the peat out. Of course the coal mines never finished. On the east side were all Italians except Mr. Burwell who had his house on the west side. There was a barn where this man from downtown had a little land up on the hill and he used to come and plow and stay in the barn. During the summer months he opened the barn up to his friends and he used to sell beer, ten cents a bottle, three bottles for a quarter. And everybody in the neighborhood, on a Sunday when the package stores were closed used to go down and buy three bottles of beer. And all the fellas used to go in and play cards; the elderly people played Italian game called "tre-sette" and the younger element played pinochle. The loser would pay for beer. In those days the street was sparsely traveled by cars. We used to play bocce in the street; we used to play softball in the street. And after a couple of innings we would go in and have a beer and come out and play again, bocce we would play for beer. And this old man made his living selling the beer and he slept. We called him "Zi' 'Ntone" [Uncle Anthony]—his last name was Gambardella. And during the years these Italians made each other "cumpari" [godparents], intermarriage, confirmation, baptisms and it was like one family. Everybody plowed their own land. They used to make their own wine; they tended their chickens and pigs. The parents all spoke Italian; there was no English spoken except the children who had started going to school. We spoke Italian before we spoke English.

Life in the Wooster Square Neighborhood

At the beginning of the twentieth century, the Wooster Square neighborhood was home to an aristocratic class of wealthy merchants and manufacturers, and Irish, Lithuanian, Polish, and French woodworkers and blacksmiths who worked in the carriage industry.[53] As Italians from small towns around Benevento of the Campania moved to the area the 1880s and '90s to work on the railroad and at the nearby L. Candee Rubber Company, Sargent Manufacturing Company, and The New Haven Clock Factory, the Irish moved out to Fair Haven, City Point, and near Edgewood Park, the wealthy Yankee factory owners to Prospect and Orange Streets. The large influx of new immigrants to newly-built tenement houses on Wooster Street and its intersecting side streets dramatically changed the patrician character of the neighborhood. The wealthy residential section of palatial homes in Wooster Square area coexisted with multistory apartment houses with street-level storefronts on Wooster Street a few blocks away. By the early 1900s, the Wooster Square neighborhood was known as "Little Naples," a vibrant community of transplanted southern Italian villagers from the Gioia Sannitica area of the Campania. In the next wave that followed, Italians from the towns of Amalfi, Atrani, Minori, Scafati, and Ravello along the Amalfitano coast brought the animated street life and the language of Naples to its streets.

Wooster Square was the largest of New Haven's Italian neighborhoods, a self-contained urban ghetto teeming with families in multistoried tenement houses where English was a second language and residents stayed within the boundaries of familiar blocks, walking back and forth to work at shirt shops and factories within the embrace of its tree-lined streets. In warm months, residents left their apartment windows open where the sounds of Italian music and delicious aromas from their kitchens drifted down to the street below. Wooster Street had its own macaroni factory, five bakeries, pastry shops, and specialty meat markets. Sicilian families—Cedro, Guiglielmo, Mascari, and Corso—ran wholesale banana businesses on Fair Street and lived on Collis Street. Shopkeepers with nicknames like "Papòcchia," or corn meal, and "O Lataro," or the milkman, catered to the cultural preferences of their customers. Carrano's Market not only sold fancy fruits and newspapers to locals on their way to work, but doubled as a neighborhood employment agency. Matteo, who had been an earlier settler to New Haven in the 1880s, placed young Italian men looking for work at Sargent with a single call to "the Sargent boys." His wife, Antoinette, found jobs for newly arrived girls over lunches of escarole and beans with the owner of the nearby Ideal Shirt factory, Salvatore DeBenedetto, in the backroom kitchen of the store. Street vendors known as "Chi Da Mòrte," or the dead one, and "Carbone," or coal, sold fruit and vegetables from horse-drawn wagons. As he delivered bread to the tenement houses along Wooster Street at five o'clock every morning, Carmelo Midolo, a Sicilian baker, sang Italian arias to his sleeping customers. The local community bank made personal loans based on family name and a handshake. Many who distrusted doctors and turned to healers for their ills and to "mammare," who delivered babies at home for a few dollars. Those afflicted with the "maluocchio," or the evil eye, summoned a "guaritrice," a local woman practiced in the art of "doing the eyes," using oil, water, and secret prayers to exorcise the evil spell. Some Italians marked time by feast days rather than the calendar and children were taught to kneel and kiss the floor when the bells rang out during the Consecration of the Host at nearby Saint Michael's Church in Wooster Square.

Prior to construction of Interstate 91 and the Oak Street Connector in the late '50s, Wooster Street ran to the waterfront where local men played bocce and sandlot baseball at Waterside Park in the shadows of the Sargent factory. Before Standard Oil built huge storage tanks on the waterfront near the Tomlinson Bridge, barges and ships delivered potatoes from Long Island and Canadian liquor to the Starin Lines pier where Italian stevedores unloaded tons of goods and produce. In summer months young boys jumped from piers and people fished from banks of long-destroyed channels leading to the harbor.

Today, Wooster Street draws suburban diners and tourists who stand in long waiting lines in all types of weather to eat at one of its famous pizzerias or landmark restaurants. Walking down Wooster Street, one can still catch glimpses of the old neighborhood and imagine it in its heyday; some of the original brick tenement houses have survived the destruction of the Lee administration's urban redevelopment project of the 1950s, and the Saint Andrew's and Santa Maria Maddalena Societies' buildings are open to society members who still return from the suburbs to be reunited with old childhood friends.

"EAT CARMELO'S BREAD AND YOU'LL NEVER DIE"

Nick and Mary Vitagliano spoke at the kitchen table of their Branford home on June 2, 2000.

There used to be a bakery called Midolo's. He's the one who used to sing. I used to go in there to buy bread or something he used always used to throw the extra biscotti and fresélles and not charge me for it. He knew everybody had a big family you know. And you blessed him in your heart, you'd say, "What a guy, what a nice man." He used to deliver the bread early in the morning because he used to make

CARMELO MIDOLO AND HELPER
Midolo Bakery, 154 Wooster Street, freshly baked "casatielli" or Easter bread, 1940s
(now a parking lot)

Midolo family album

lunches for the husbands and sons and daughters, make lunches out of fresh bread and he used to sing all the way through the whole [Wooster] Street, up and down the street. And then he used to have a saying, "Chi mangia 'o pane 'e Carmelo, non muore mai," Whoever eats Carmelo's bread never dies. He used to sing that, he used to holler it too, Carmelo! 'O pane e Carmelo, non muore mai! Aye, his voice had a carry up three floors, the voice had a carry through windows and they used to hear him. But what a voice he had, he used to sing songs nice, Italian songs.

❝THE STREET VENDORS❞

Lou Landino spoke on the back porch of his Annex home with his wife
Diane on August 6, 1999.

On Hamilton and Chapel you had the rag man come by, you had the fishmonger come by, you had the vegetable man come by, and then you had the guy come by with the—Williams [changed from Guglielmo] I think it was—with the banana cart, all the stale bananas, rotten bananas, you know, worn out bananas, he'd come down the street, five cents you'd grab a half a dozen bananas. You went to the wagon, he was on the street, you'd go, "Hey, how much, how much?" "Take em' for five cents." He'd fill up a bag of bananas for you and they'd be brown, green, whatever. And the fishmonger would come by and he'd skin the fish right there for you. Yeah. You'd buy eel, black, dark and he'd take the head and cut it and take the head in his mouth like this and rip the skin right off the eel. I don't wan a eat em' when they're cooked, this guy's stickin' that dirty, raw eel in his mouth! Everybody just seemed to be a lot happier, that's basically what it was. You knew your next door neighbor and the one over there and the one over there and everybody knew you. Today you're lucky if you know your next door neighbor, you're lucky if they talk to you. We had more comradery between us then, even though our grandparents came from Italy and couldn't talk English but we got along a helluva a lot better than we do today, you know. Where I lived on Hamilton and Chapel we had Carrano—her grandfather was a fishmonger and he used to park his wagon right in the backyard and then every night he'd hose it down and get it ready for the next day's haul. All the fishmongers used to keep their horses and buggies and the pushcarts on a garage on Collis Street. And they'd go out from there, out into the harbor and pull in the lobster pots and the eel pots and then sell that fish on the street that same day so it was fresh. You weren't worried about pollutants or sewage or garbage or anything else. It was right there. Those are the things that you don't have today; you don't have any of that. We had this guy that come down, the iceman and oilman, they used to call him "Pappóne." He'd come down the street and be yellin' out the wagon, "Ice, ice." The next time he'd come down he had coal and oil in the wintertime, selling coal and oil. We had a guy that would come down, "Hey, kid, you wanna make some money?" And you had to carry the two-gallon cans of oil down the alley and dump them in the funnel to go down the cellar to fill oil tanks. And carry the coal bag down, for a nickel or a dime, you know. In the fall when it was wine making season we'd follow the trucks with all the grapes on it, boxes of grape, you know we'd follow it, see where he was gonna stop. Oh he stopped here, say, "Hey mister you need a hand?" "Yeah, sure." So what did we get? We'd throw in a few bunches of grape in our shirt and we'd sit on the curb—prrrt—with the skins out and eat the grape.

❝The Peddlers❞

Mary Santacroce, ninety-eight years old, her son Anthony Santacroce, and Tony Vitolo spoke at the kitchen table of her East Haven home on December 21, 1999. Mary said her husband worked "vascio 'o dock," which meant working at Sargent.

They had the horse and wagon. This was in the '20s. They used to come and sell the ice, they used to peddle groceries, food, a minestra [greens] on the wagon. Remember "Chi Da Mòrte?" [The Dead One], I don't know his name, he used to peddle, he used to have a horse and wagon and he used to peddle minestra, toma-

ANTHONY RUSSO, 19
Fruit and vegetable peddler,
August 13, 1927,
selling "soup bunches,"
to start soups —
celery hearts, parsnip,
parsley, and carrots

Russo family album

toes. I think he used to swear if the wagon wouldn't work, he used to have a horse, he used to beat him up. We used to yell to him when I was kid, "Chi Da Mòrte." and he used to yell back, "Chi da stramòrte." Then there used to be another pushcart man, "Farm A Me," he used to have a push wagon and used have fresh vegetables, he used to come around every morning to sell it. When he used to come by everybody used to go outside and buy. Then there was "'o pappóne," he was the oilman. He always had a dog with him in the truck. They used to come and pick up the garbage—oh, the stink, in the backyard with a horse and wagon, they used to put on their back, drag it out.

"Born at Home"

Tony Sacco and Salvatore "Gary"' Garibaldi spoke over a specially prepared lunch by his old friend Tony Sacco at Tony and Lucille's Restaurant on
May 19, 2000. Sal said that he and his sister were delivered by a midwife
who charged his father four dollars who then tipped her a dollar.

Today you're born in a hospital in a room. We were born in a house. And the lady that helped my mother is still alive—Antonette D'Amato, she's ninety-five years old. I was born on 93 Wooster Street and she lived in the building and she helped Dr. Bovi. And then there was that other woman, Louise, "a mammara" [the mid-wife] that was Dr. LaFemina's sister. You thought she was a registered nurse, she went around. I mean today, you're born in a hospital, it costs three, four thousand dollars. Two dollars in those days. You see the midwives in these areas—practically every city and town at the early stages of the century, every neighborhood had a number of midwives. And childbirth was actually in most homes. Very few people went to a hospital. Because, number one, they feared going to a hospital. The only time you talked about a hospital was when you were dying. So your midwives were—like a guy like Dr. Conte, he did a lot of bringing children into the world because he lived on Wooster Place—say like one hundred kids were born in this area, guaranteed he delivered eighty of them. Then the rest were done by mid-wives. So every little section had a midwife, "a mammara Rosa," "Luisella," and all that. So it all depended on your parents, who they were friends with. See, now in the morning he went to school. When he came home, unknown to him, his mother gave childbirth. By the midwife. They gave you ten cents to go the show. Come back, you find my brother Andrew. That's how they lived in those days. A far cry to what it is today. But we're all—nothing wrong with it, though, we all sur-vived, survived all the sicknesses and came up healthy too. Maybe some people aren't healthy now but we were healthy those days. We had rosy cheeks. "Bev' a 'nu poco 'e vino, Anthony, drink a little wine!"

"Birth Dates"

Tom Consiglio spoke at the Saint Andrew's Society on June 30, 1999.

The women don't remember, they only remember the holiday. It was the feast of Colombo. So I winded up with October 12th, 1914, when Columbus discovered America [laughing]. It happened to be close to the holiday. I may have been born a couple of days before but my mother only remembered the holiday, they don't remember the day actually. Today is different, everybody goes to the hospital; they all get the date, the correct hour and day. In those days the people were born and they gave birth in the houses, the homes. And they remembered the holidays that were close to your birth.

❝I Had Two Birthdays❞

Nick Vitagliano spoke at the kitchen table of his Branford home on June 2, 2000.

April 19th, I was born 1916. When I went into the service, in the army, I had to go get a birth certificate. I go over there, "You were born May 1st." I said, "May 1st? No, no April 19th. Oh no, you made a mistake, there's something wrong here, somebody gave you the wrong date." I said, "No you got the wrong date." My mother, my biological birthdate is April 19th. Then he started reciting, "Your father Tommaso?" "Si." "Your mother Concetta?" "Yes." "You got a sister named Jenny?" "Yes." "You got a brother named Salvatore?" "Yes." He went all the way down the line, named the whole family. He said, "You were born May 1st." Now why was I born May 1st? Because we're all born by "a mammara" [a midwife], Virgilia a mammara. Ma chella teneva le còscie! She had strong legs! She worked under Dr. Conte. He was such a beautiful man, he was such a nice guy. He was always busy. Why shouldn't he be busy, he was always for free. That's what he felt. He felt, where are these poor people gonna run to, they can't even speak the language, what are they gonna say, where does it hurt, probably the poor guy couldn't even say where it hurt. At least in Italian he could express himself. But she used to work all night. She was too tired to go down to City Hall bring these birthdays in there. "Una volta a settimana," once a week, she would bring it down, the whole thing used to accumulate. "When were these babies born? Yesterday. May 1st." So we were all born on the same day. Everyone born on April 19th was registered May 1st. So I celebrate both birthdays. Two times, I have two cakes. That's the way it was.

❝And This Is the Boy❞

Annette Ruocco spoke at the kitchen table of her Annex home on November 17, 1998.

In those days, in the '20s, you had your children in the house. A midwife would come in and deliver the babies. And that poor midwife, she was scared. And I remember coming home from school and she was standing near the door. She said, "Va, viene chiù tarde, viene chùi tarde," Go away and come back later. And then when we came back there's my mother with the twins. From 10 Hamilton, that was near Waterside Park and he had to go down to get Dr. Amatruda. And by the time the doctor came, they were born. When I came back there were twins in the house.

And my little aunt there—because I didn't have a sister, I was looking for a sister—and there was a little girl. And the aunt, with the little boy that was named after her husband, she said, [laughing] "E chist' è 'o [singing voice] maschio, chist' è 'o maschio!" And this is the boy, this is the boy!

"She Died With the Doors Opened"

John Nappi spoke at the kitchen table of his East Haven home on June 6, 1999.

She never closed the doors. Everybody went to her house to eat. Every day she had to feed the animals, the birds. Get bread and get stuff for them. She said, "They got to eat too." My mother said, "Chille che fanno buone alle animali," whoever takes care of the animals, the Lord looks after them too. I went there in the afternoons; there was always somebody in the house. She used to say, "When I go [die] all the doors and all the lights are gonna be opened." This is the truth. 1964. My sister had just taken her [my mother] home. So it was in October. My brother-in-law called me, says, "Mom is in bad shape, better come down." I couldn't get out it was so foggy, there were no lights, no nothing. When I went down there, she was dead. I went in. All the lights, all the doors and the windows, everything was open. She knew, she called my sister, she said, "Come down, I don't feel good." She went and lay down on the bed and that's where she died. All the lights and the doors were open. She said, "That's the way I want to die. My doors, I never closed them to anybody, I'll never close them." You know why? The people knew one another on Wooster Street. Any stranger in the neighborhood, forget it. You never had no robberies in the neighborhood, no trouble. Everybody knew the families. No trouble. If you had a fight, it ain't like today—you have to watch your back. You had a fight, you used to go down the park, you used your hands. That's why you had a learn how to fight. Then you get through, you shake hands and go to the diner, used to have coffee. That's the way it was in those days, I swear to God.

"Everyone Had A Nickname"

When I went to school, there's a guy, his name was Whitehead. In Italian, it was Capobianco. He changed it to Whitehead. They used to call my grandmother "A Zi' Paola" [Aunt Paula]. They didn't know her name. But everybody knew who she was, never knew her name was Anna. They used to her "A Zi' Paola," from the old country. They never used their real name. Now the name was Marseca and they had a grocery store. Know what they used to call him? "Papòcchia!" They called him Papòcchia cuz' that's the names they brought from the old country too. Then I got to know them, know who they were. Like the grandfather, "Papòcchia," corn meal, now who ever knew him? But if you mentioned "Papòcchia" you knew who they were, if you mentioned Marseca you didn't know who they were. You wanna know something? Like with me, they used to call me "Young Nap," they didn't know my name was Johnny. My brother Jimmy, they used to say "he's the older Nap," they called him "Kid Nap." And my brother Henry, they called him "Nanil.'" "Tic Toc" was the best [laughing]. You know how it started with Tic Toc? They had a football team in the '20s and '30s. In those days there was a Ben Tickner, from Harvard, he was an All-American center, so Frank Amendola was a center. So he used to go, "I'm Ben Tickner." They used to kid him. So from there, they cut it down to Tickner. Before you know, Tic Toc! Like Amendola, they called him "capa ianc," "white head," he was a blond. His name is Amendola. It comes to show ya. Now the only way we knew the other Amendola, remember the barber, we used to call him, "Rafaelle 'O Barbiere." And he used to be the treasurer of the Saint Andrea's Club. Then the other Savo man, what do you think they used to call him? " 'O Mòrte," the dead one! I swear to God. I don't know what he was. They used to call him " 'O Mòrte." And the other guy, the Acquarulo, "Zi' Prevete," Uncle the Priest, he was gonna become a priest once I understand. What a priest he would a made! He was a pip that old man. Frank Dioaiuto, his father used to be the president of the Sant Andrea club years ago, and we used to call him "T-Rod." Carrano, they used to call him "Soapie." A lot a them today, still I don't know their real names.

You see, the old people, if you said they were from the Gambardellas, the fish people, but to describe the Gambardella family, they'd say, "Chella songa 'e nipote o 'i figli di a Zi' Paola," that's the nephew or the son of Aunt Paula. So they knew who it was, you know what I mean? My people, they remember my father. They wouldn't say [my last name] Nappi, they used to say "'O figlio di Masta Gaetano," he's Maestro Gaetano's son, he was a cooper, he used to make barrels and stuff like that. So when they had to find one of us, they'd say "O figlio di Masta Gaetano." Someone would say, "'O piccerillo?" The little one? "No, 'O gruosso," No the older one. Now they knew who it was. The Di Crescenzos, the other one was "Matrazzone" they used to call him, I dunno why, they used to make matresses I guess. Like Dr. LaFemina, all the doctors, they were from the beans family—the Colassos—'e fasule, "Beans," they used to call them. There's a lot of names like that, they all had nicknames you know. And that's how they used to recognize these people. See now, truthfully, you get like your name. And the Carranos. There was Tranese, from Atrani, and there was Amalfitans, from Amalfi in the Carranos. Amendola the same way, there was Tranese and Amalfitans. A lot of them, the Gambardellas, Tranese, and Amalfitani because they were together all the time, "Chello è 'o figlio di Zi' Paola, chillo è 'o figlio 'e Masta Gaetano." They called my grandfather, "'O Ferro," Iron, I dunno why, he was a big man. But yet his name was Gambardella, yet they used to go, "Chillo è 'O Ferro," there's Iron. I dunno why. You get the Midolo family, that's a big family, they were bakers. "Chilli songa 'o sicilian', 'o panatiere, 'o sicilian," they are the Sicilian bakers. So you knew who it was. Because there was also the Sarnos over there, they were bakers too. So that's how they used to distinguish between the two. On the corner, the Ippolitos owned the grocery market. They used to call them "'A Cavallaro," I dunno why. Why they called them "Cavallaro," I dunno why, I swear. Their name wasn't Cavallaro. That's how we used to distinguish. If you went to the store, you'd say, "Vag' in da Cavallaro," I'm going to the store. And their name was Ippolito!

"THEY CHANGED THEIR NAMES"

They had trouble with the Irish. Now they had to learn how to fight. And every one of them, the majority, a lot of guys on Wooster Street and that area became fighters all had Irish names. Would you believe this? All Irish names, like Joe Curry, Georgie Day, I can go and on, they changed their names. My wife's uncle Pat Longobardi was one of the first men, he was the only Italian to have trucks for the city. So you know what he told my brothers? "You want a job with city, with the snow? Give an Irish name." This is the honest truth, you gotta ask my brother, one was named O'Sullivan, the other was O'Brien, otherwise you couldn't get put on. Then you picked up your check and you sign whatever names you gave them. And he told them to do that.

"INTERMARRIAGE CHANGED US"

Salvatore "Gary" Garibaldi spoke at the Santa Maria Maddalena Society on April 12, 2000. He was the president of the Wooster Street Business Professional Association beginning in 1995.

Let's be honest about it. There was that difference of respect between nationals. I'm not a racist, but the Irish and Italians didn't love each other. I mean in those days [prior to WW II]. Well, if I went out with an Irish girl indirectly my father and mother would look and say, "There's no other girl?" And likewise with the Irish girl. And that prevailed up until World War II. When you married outside of your nationality you were looked at differently. Lawyers and doctors in those days—they were talked about within the community, "Eh, he married an Irish, he married a Polish girl," like Bill Celentano marrying Piasek, beautiful couple but the Italian and the Polish, they didn't think it was a good thing. In those days, yeah. So, you see, there was that feeling. Which prevailed. And some of those nationals were outspoken. And they abused either the Italian, the Polish, or the Jewish. And likewise in return, the retaliation. In those days the insulting Italian words that they used, a wop, a guinea, a dago. Well you didn't like to hear that. But our parents were subject to that abuse. We were kids. But as we grew older, they [parents] would retaliate, "You Irish bum," you see now, which was disrespectful one to another. Which I'm glad that more or less stopped with World War II. Men and women who went into the armed forces, we traveled not only throughout the country but now we're going overseas. Now we're mixing in with all nationalities. I seen a lot of my friends from Wooster Street and from Chestnut Street, when they went down to Florida, they met a southern girl. Love is love. Or they went to Maine and met a girl from Maine and got married later on. So now it was an accepted thing.

"WE'RE ALL CHILDREN OF GOD"

> Joe and Pat Amarone spoke at the Santa Maria Maddalena Society on October 9, 1999. They recounted their mother telling her ten sons to treat women as if they were their sisters, "Because what you do to other girls, people are gonna do to them."

My mother was the first Italian woman in this neighborhood—this was strictly an Italian neighborhood—which rented to a black family. Because she felt she was discriminated so much when they were here with children. She rented to the first black family, I think the name was Alphonse Brito—his mother was black Portuguese and his father was Italian. But she said she didn't care. They say people are prejudiced, the Italians are prejudiced—not my mother, not my father. They believed if you needed a place to live and you had children, she gave them the rent. There was a lot of resentment. A lot of people didn't like it at the time. To me that wasn't bad, to me that was good. She did something that she believed in, that discrimination— whether you're black, blue, yellow, or brown—didn't matter to her. When she got married she had five children within the period of five and a half years, one right after the other. Now she lived in a rent, she tried to get a rent, and no one would rent with kids because [they thought] we would destroy their property. The majority of the owners then weren't Italians; they were Irish or old Yankee. She was discriminated against because of kids she couldn't get rents. And she made a vow to herself: she would save enough money and buy a home. And the first home she bought was in 1917 at 180 Wooster Street. She accumulated enough money, saved enough money, and she bought that home. And she made a vow to herself, no matter how many children she would have that they would never have to go in to somebody else's rent. That's the story of how we never went to a rent—always had her house to go into. And she felt for other people in our position, like that colored family came in and they needed the rent, she gave them the rent because she said, "You can't discriminate against a family with children whether they're black, green, or yellow." She was not a prejudiced woman—she was Italian, she was proud of being an American here. I'm not saying she wasn't proud of her Italian heritage. She felt she left the old country to come to the new country where the opportunity was. Over there she didn't have that opportunity. To her, the old country was a bad life for her; she came here for a better life. What she always instilled in all of us was not to be prejudiced, definitely not to hurt anybody because of their color, their national origin. She always used to say, "We're all children of God."

"I Saw My Family Every Day"

Tony Vitolo and Anthony Santacroce spoke at the kitchen table of Angelina Criscuolo's home in East Haven on December 21, 1999.

We used to live in the same building, the same tenement building. My sisters got married and they lived downstairs. My aunt lived downstairs. My cousins lived downstairs. Sixteen-family house, twelve of them were my relatives. Whole families were my relatives. And I saw them every day. Now I don't see them for months at a time because they broke up that neighborhood. There was an aunt on one side, a brother; everybody stayed in the area. And there was never any arguments among cousins, family. You saw your grandmother every day; that was a must. That was a big thing, every day. And that's why I tell my children how fortunate they are to have your grandparents, that you could remember [them]. We cared for our parents. Who the hell is gonna take care of us? Nobody. The next generation? It's not instilled in them. We don't have the time. They go away, get their degrees. Not only that, but they're in different states, you don't get to see them, maybe once a year.

"Bank Loans in the Neighborhood"

Anthony Santacroce and Tony Vitolo spoke at the kitchen table of Angelina Criscuolo's home in East Haven on December 21, 1999.

The Pallotti Bank, after years and years, was taken over by the Community Bank. Now I used to work for the Second National Bank, which eventually became Bank of Boston. When we took over that bank, going through their records [the Community Bank] was unbelievable. There were loans made out to Giuseppe for fifty dollars and payments were, well, you know, talking with some of them, well they could only pay fifty cents this month or this week, "Well, don't worry about it, whatever you can pay." Everything was hand written in there, and if you couldn't make a payment don't worry about it. Trying to take that and computerize it, we tried to put onto our system. You couldn't do it because there was no really effective [system]. The loan would be made and then, "Well what kind of a schedule you want to make with payment? Well, whatever, you can get. Well, you know, when you get time you stop in, you make a payment." That's all. There was no rigid monthly payment, whatever you could do. I remember the president of the bank, his name was Rossi. Because I went in there and borrowed money as a kid, like twenty-four years old once, I borrowed four hundred bucks. And Angelo, I knew Angelo Carbone, the vice president, he knew my family. And the old man was sitting at his desk. He had nothing on his desk, not a one paper. He just would sit there. And Angelo goes over there and says, "Chisto è 'o figlio di . . ." This is the son of . . . Mister Rossi said, "Okay." In other words, the old man was passing judgment, he knew who you were. A coupon book, [you paid] two dollars a week. I think that bank helped out a lot of those old timers, a lot of them. It was a very informal kind of thing. I remember talking with the vice president of the bank. He says, "This is impossible, how the hell can you make heads or tails, who made payments or did they make the payments, how much did they give?" And if they made an original loan and they wanted a little more, just tack a little more on it. It wasn't that you renewed the loan, just add another twenty dollars to it or whatever. There was no audit trail. On Wooster Street, every barber shop was a little bank, too. They all loaned money. They had groups, the barber shop was like the focal point where you get six or eight people get together and they'd say, "We're gonna loan money" so everybody puts in money and then people go [and get loans]. Like Ralph the barber. "Ralph, I wanna borrow two hundred." He'd say all right. He would discount the interest off the top, up front, and give you the net amount of the loan. And you paid back the full amount. So if I'd be in there as a kid getting a haircut and people come knock on the window and go, "Ralph," and hold up two fingers, they want two hundred and he'd just nod okay. Nobody got stiffed. There was honor; there was honor among them all. All they did was a handshake. That was it, nothing else. It was all the neighborhood people they knew and trusted. Of course if you didn't pay your name was mud, you wouldn't get a dime anyway.

"He Got the Vig"

Nick Vitagliano spoke at the kitchen table of his home in Branford on June 2, 2000.

Paul Russo was very charitable for the immigrants but still he was a selfish man. He had the bank, so he used to wait for Sargent to pay off [weekly pay] in checks. He was an agent and an investor. They couldn't cash checks no place else because nobody had the money. He used to open up the bank purposely because these immigrants, where would they go cash these checks? No one would cash their checks. He opened up La Banca di Paolo Russo. He would open up only after the paychecks were already issued to these poor immigrants. They used to go house to house looking for some money. But nobody had money to cash checks. They used to have to run to Paul Russo. But he used to take a little vig, he'd take a little vig, it means a little gift, a couple of bucks for himself. He used to charge them to cash their checks. But they were compelled to go to him, nobody else had money. He used to be on the corner of Chestnut and Chapel.

"We Were Happy, We Had Nothing"

Mary Santacroce was 99 years old at the time of her interview at her home on December 21, 1999.

I was born in 1899, I don't remember where in New Haven. I was married in 1918 at Saint Michael's. We went no place. We got married, we went home, my husband's

FRANK LEE
In his Wooster Street garden
DePalma family album

family came over the house. We ate and then they went away, we stayed. That was interesting, huh? Today they go all over. Well, everybody was happy. Because they had nothing. Today everybody's rich. And they think they're somebody, you know. I think they do. Our neighborhood, we used to help one another. If somebody died, they used to go in and see them, bring something. We used to visit one another. Just talk, you know. Very friendly. Today, I lived here for about thirty years, I don't know my neighbors who they are.

"Street Life on Wooster Street"

John Nappi spoke at the kitchen table of his East Haven home on September 15, 1999.

On Wooster and Franklin, there was the DeFelice brothers. They used to make pastry and they had ice cream and lemonade, they used to make all that. And, the brothers used to come out with the ukulele and they used to sing. One brother went to New York; they're all dead now. They were, oh, sing all night on the corner of Wooster and Franklin. Right across the street where they built the highway there was a big sixteen-family house. Downstairs was a big store and they used to have the pastry shop and ice cream parlor. But he made all his own cream, the old man, Francesco. They used to get outside all night, the warm weather, you couldn't sleep anyway. There was no air conditioning. They used to sit out till two in the morning. And they used to play the ukulele, all the old songs, "That Ol' Gang Of Mine," and all those American songs they used to sing. They were English just like us. And the Italians, the old men, when they had a time down the block, all Italian music, forget it, that's all you heard was Italian music. The old man used to come down Wooster Street, the Midolo guy used to deliver fresélles and bread; he used to come down the street, the Sicilian, singing Italian songs. Then on a Sunday morning, they used call him "Carbone," coal, but it wasn't his name. He used to sell i lupini beans. He used to yell from down the block, he used to be so loud, he goes, [shouting] "È venuto Carbone!" Carbone is here! Meant to say he got the lupini on a Sunday morning. You bring out your dish, everybody, they used to come down with the dish. In those days, you don't even see them anymore, everybody made them. They were good. Now you buy them in the jar. We used to buy em' dry. We used to do it yourself. He had em' already done, already cooked, see you boil em' and let em' stay for so many days, you change the water. Oh, he was a pip. You bring out your dish, he used to put in the dish, ten, fifteen cents worth.

"We Put On Our Own Feasts"

Joe and Pat Amarone spoke at the Santa Maria Maddalena Society on October 9, 1999.

People used to want to play with us in the yard because we used to have our own little clique—our family was so big with eighteen kids—next door neighbors, the other ones. Sometimes you know like the feast they have on the street? We used to see the feasts and in the summertime we had nothing to do so we used to have our own miniature feasts, sing. Run streamers in the yard, with the orange papers, bang with the pots and pans, have our own little feasts. Honest to God, it was amazing, growing up. People would want to play with us because there were so many of us. Everybody came to our yard. Sunday afternoons in the summer my mother used to put the big long table and we'd eat outside. She'd cook with the pot and everybody from the back tenement house looking down to see. It was a big crew. Sometimes she'd have some of her sisters, the aunts over, would eat with eighteen of us. In fact we used to have one or two cousins every morning used to come and have breakfast with us. Every morning you'd get half an orange—everything was bought in bulk. Down the market, they knew who she was, knew how many kids because there was always six or seven of us with her, used to walk from Wooster Street down to the Hill section where the market was. She had "a carretta," an old carriage from the kids and she'd load it, sometimes with chickens, sometimes with fruits. It was comical because everybody knew us and my mother was small, just about five feet, she was a beautiful woman. She had jet-black hair where she used keep it up in a bun and then at nighttime she used to let it out and it used to be down to her back. She was a beautiful, well-built woman and she was very vibrant. She had a pure olive oil complexion and all her teeth; I always remember her being beautiful, even in her later years. She had knuckles like a man. Now where do you think that came from? The scrub board with the clothes. Had the old washing machine, you just agitate it by hand and that's how she got the clothes clean. Every Tuesday was wash day in our house. My father used to come home from the shop [Sargent's], all that powder all over his face, just wipe his face down. My mother—the meal was all ready for us to eat—and from 4 o'clock to 5:30 my father would help my mother with the washing machine. She'd send the clothes through the wringer by hand; he'd get them.

"IT WAS ONE BIG FAMILY"

Frank DePonte spoke at the kitchen table of Joe and Lena Riccio's home on November 21, 1999.

We had much, much fewer material things but there was safety. I used to walk around New Haven at three o'clock in the morning. If you tell anybody you walk around New Haven at three o'clock in the morning they think you're crazy. But the place was wide open. Walk around town, meet friends, the restaurants and stores were open and walk home. They had the Candee bowling alley, and I was about thirteen, fourteen and they were allowing me a little bit more freedom and I could stay out late. And I came home—it had to be one o'clock in the morning and a policeman stopped me and he said, "What are you doing here, you crazy?" I said, "What's the matter?" He said, "It's one o'clock in the morning." I said, "Well, I know that, what's the problem, I didn't do anything wrong." He said, "No, but you could be hurt." I was stunned. Who the hell was going to hurt me? I'm related to everybody in the whole area. Who was going to hurt me? You could tell a stranger on Wooster Street in two minutes. They were "forestiere," outsiders, you knew they didn't belong, you could pick them up in a minute. One time, when I was even younger, if you walk two or three blocks away from home base you were almost out of town—that was a no-no, especially when you were young. Some guy kicked me in the ass and told me, "You get back home where you belong." He knew who I was. I don't know that guy from a hole in the wall. But he knew me, "DePonte, you get back home where you belong, you're going to get lost." He gave me a kick in the ass and he sent me home. It was like one big family down there.

"WE WERE WINDOW TO WINDOW"

Emiddio Cavaliere and Mary Giangregorio spoke at Cavaliere's grocery store on Wooster Street on May 6, 1998.

If you go the end of the street here, there's a list of all the guys who got killed. There's a little monument. There's only one name—Dortch—they were black. He was the only non-Italian. All the rest were all Italians. Next door to us in this tenement house on Fair Street, a big building with I don't know how many families and they were black. But we weren't concerned. This was 1945 – 1950. There was a lot of respect among the . . . and there was no problem. You should see how they respected my father, "Hi Mister Anastasio, how are you? What's new, what's going on?" And we had party lines. The only incident I remember that as a little, you know . . . we were a little—I wouldn't say afraid—but there was a little problem. We had a party line with a black family and you know we wanted to use it, they wanted to use it so there were verbal arguments. But that was it, it was nothing else. Never, never, "Oh we got to watch out, we're going by that building." They lived right next door to us. We were window to window, when I say window to window you looked out this window and you saw—if you wanted to be nosy-you could see the people walking by next door—but of course our shades were always down. But it was no problem. In fact, they'd invite to let's say they were having demonstration for household gadgets and things. And they'd call my mother and say, "Mrs. Anastasio, would you like to come?" And my mother used to say, "We should, we don't want to offend them, so let's go." So we went up there. In fact we even went to one of the black wakes. They were so nice, so nice.

"WAKES AT HOME"

Antonette Sicignano spoke in the kitchen of her Wooster Street home on August 30, 1998.

The wakes were in the house. My father's was in the house. He died in bed. The undertaker came took him away and then they brought him back the next day with the casket and all. We had him in our parlor, yeah. Even my fourteen year old sister in 1918. They did everything in the house. They cleaned the body. Then they used to take the casket over and then they used to put a bow on your door. My grandmother and grandfather, too, in the house. People would come and visit. We didn't stay in the room where my sister was; we used to stay in another room. She was alone. We stayed in the kitchen. And the younger ones, they used to send us to the aunts and grandmother. They used to send us away for a while. In fact we lived on the corner of Collis Street and Wallace and the block after was the Wooster Street school. She was going to graduate that year. And they carried her from the house with a horse and wagon, the horse all white with the fringe on it. The people walked on the sides of it. We used to call that the hearse but it was a horse and wagon. And inside it had all fringes. They used to go slow. They had a special little band to follow but not all the way to the cemetery. Just as far as the church. They played sad music, very sad.

"THE NEIGHBORHOOD DOCTOR"

Salvatore "Gary" Garibaldi spoke at the Santa Maria Maddalena Society on April 12, 2000.

In those days the average person—not only in this area but throughout the city— had childbirth at home by a midwife. Very few were able to call upon a doctor and if you did there was only one outstanding doctor in this community and his name was Dr. Harry A. Conte who lived next to Saint Michael's. Dr. Conte was a neighborhood doctor—I'd say he must have delivered ninety-nine percent of the kids in this community. What the midwives couldn't do, he did. In those days they used to charge only two dollars to deliver a child. At that time two dollars [1920s] was a lot of money. And there were other doctors who did likewise like Dr. LaFemina, Dr. Casolino. These men were all born and raised in this neighborhood by their parents who came from southern Italy. So it was great progress to think that you had a son—you came from Italy, from Amalfi or Atrani or Naples or Sorrento—and you were blessed to send a kid to become a medical officer. Just that alone; the mother and father were very proud. Like they would say, "Chillo 'o figlio mio—dottore," That's my son, the doctor. See, that was a great achievement to them. And these men took it upon themselves not only to serve those neighbors but they were very compassionate and never charged half of the times. If they had to receive monetary value for their services they would have been rich fellas. They understood the conditions of the home. And they would say [to the woman in childbirth] "Grazie a Dio, Giuseppina mia, tu tiene 'o figlio . . ." Thank God, my Josephine, you have a son. They even made her feel that they were happy she gave birth to a child.

"THEY ALL COME BACK"

John and Mary Nappi spoke at their kitchen table of their East Haven home on September 15, 1999.

They told us they were taking the house for redevelopment so I live here [in East Haven] but I always worship Wooster Street. Like some people, once they move away, they talk about this section—I still love it. I never talk bad about Wooster Street. My wife was born there, my two kids were born there, my mother and father died over there on Wooster Street, I was baptized and confirmed and everything and married on Wooster Street—how could you forget it? I'm going to go there and get buried on Wooster Street, I guess. That's the only way, I did everything else there. Best street in the world, just like Mulberry Street in New York. I don't care, anything happens today; they come from all over and run to Wooster Street. Even now, that's how close they are. Some of the guys that moved away and bought homes away from Wooster Street, as soon as some of these new condominiums opened, they moved back to Wooster Street. As soon as there was an opening they went back. Because they knew one another, they're still close together. Years ago it really was different, it was beautiful. You got along with everybody, you know what I mean? You knew everybody. Over here, who do we really know? We say hello, maybe how are you, like that, but we don't go in each other's houses or anything. We've been here thirty-six years.

The Hill took its name from the upward slope of streets radiating in all directions from its lowest point, the New Haven railroad station, where rail lines and track beds flooded in heavy rains before the building of Interstate 95. It was a melting pot community, not only of Italians from northern, central, and southern regions who lived side by side on its main arteries and side streets, but also with Russian Jews and the Irish who lived in gracious Victorian homes at City Point and upper Howard Avenue. Northern Italians—Piedmontesi, Veneziani, Toscani and Modenesi—settled on the same streets as Marchegiani and Abruzzese from central Italy and southern Italians from Cerreto Sannita, Cusano Mutri, Caiazzo, Faicchio, and San Lorenzello of the Campania.[54] In the early days of migration at the turn of the century, historical antagonisms between north and south in Italy were transported to the Hill. Skilled northerners, who usually arrived with twice the amount of money as southerners, found work in the trades as skilled masons, tile setters, and carpenters. Some northerners who owned homes sometimes looked down on southerners as "uneducated" and too willing to accept low wages in exchange for steady work as laborers on the railroad or unskilled factory hands at Sargent Manufacturing Company and L. Candee Rubber. Northern Italian homeowners found southern acceptance of substandard housing conditions in neighborhoods like Wooster Square contrary to their higher standard of living. Much like the "prominenti" class of northern Italy, northerners found southern customs and superstitious beliefs puzzling, their cuisine foreign, and their dialects impenetrable. Marriage to southerners was sometimes considered taboo in some northern families and membership to local clubs and societies was segregated according to region.

The Hill neighborhood's open air farmer's market on Minor and Silver Streets attracted shoppers, fruit and vegetable peddlers, and farmers from all over the city and outlying towns as well. Many from the area converged at Trowbridge Square Park behind Sacred Heart church, affectionately renamed by locals "The Guinea Green," where elderly men played bocce and card games of ziganette and young women brought their children in baby carriages. Jewish store owners along Washington and Columbus Avenue, some of whom spoke fluent Italian, ran pharmacies, dry goods stores, and mattress and bedding stores that catered to the needs of their Italian customers. In the '30s, young boys winged precursors of the modern frisbee across neighborhood streets, using empty pie tins from Frisbee Pie outlet on Salem Street.

The Regional Marchegiano Club began in 1909 and later merged with "The Honest Brother's Club." In 1923, the founding members built the Marchegiano Club on Minor Street which served as a central gathering place for generations of Marchegiano families who settled on surrounding streets nearby. During its heyday, from the late '40s to the early '60s, the club featured weekend dances and gala evening events with dinners prepared "Marche style" in the large basement kitchen and sent up on dumbwaiters to the upper kitchen. Many Marchegiani held wedding receptions for their children where the main hall accommodated hundreds of family and friends. The first generation of Marchegiani immigrants, who had been poor shepherds and farmers in Le Marche, joined the ranks of building trades in the '20s and '30s as bricklayers, masons, and construction workers, which made the Hill the largest community of homeowners and skilled workers in the city.[55] Giuliano Giuletti who had been a poor shepherd in the hills of Le Marche until his late teens, found work at a "pick and shovel" job with DeFelice Construction. Surviving on hard bread, onions, and rainwater while tending his flock, he advised his American-born sons Dominic and Concezio, "Guarda l'uccelli, come fanno loro, pure fai tú," or "Watch the birds, if the birds eat it, so can you."

❝Brothers Were Like the Fathers❞

Antonette Salemme spoke at the kitchen table of her North Haven home on August 15, 1998.

We were very, very close even though I was afraid of my older brother, like my father, cuz' if he'd ever seen me—I'd go up the corner where his boyfriends were and he'd say, "Go on home!" He used to smoke and hang out on the corner and we were growin' up and he's smoking, you know, so he didn't want me to see that. I never squealed on him but he used to, "Get out a here, go home!" The big boss. The brothers. That's how it was in those days, the brothers were like fathers. Oh yeah! Definitely. And God forbid if a father should die in a family, the oldest son took over like the big boss. That's the way—it was a custom. We all respected. But it was a lot a fear too. Lot a fear, I think. I was sixty-five years old, I was smoking, and I used to go take care of my father. I wouldn't let my father see me smoking. We used to say, "Pa, I'm going downstairs to wash clothes." And we [my sister] used to go down and have a cigarette, make believe you were washing clothes and then go back upstairs. I mean I was sixty-five.

❝Mom Got a Headache. We All Had a Headache❞

Now when I got the telegram [in Florida] I panicked because you know we were very close as I said. My mother was sick. You know in my house if my mother had a headache, we all had a have a headache, if my brother broke his leg, we all broke a leg. "Oh, your mother got a headache? You can't go out." That's the way it was. Because you know, "your brother got a broken leg, you can't go out." I had a go to a school picnic, my brother was comin' home from the hospital. He was comin' home! But my father wouldn't let me go, he says, "No, your brother is comin' home from the hospital, you can't go to no picnic." I couldn't go.

"The Weekends"

On a Friday night this is what went on at my house. We used to make our own bread, root beer, beer. My father, even though he was a proud man, used to cut our hair on a Friday night when it [had to be cut]. We couldn't buy shoes with four kids. So he had a foot thing. And he used to put it between his legs and get rubber that he used to buy, and he'd cut pattern out of paper, make a pattern the size of our foot, and he had the glue, the nails. My father ended up being a shoemaker. He used to fix all our shoes, every weekend, one week he'd do the shoes, one weekend we'd be gettin' friggin' haircuts, he was very rough almost knock you out. He'd cut over here and say, "Oh, it's too short," and this side shorter and this shorter. Oh, Jesus, I used to hate it, how I used to hate it. And he had a brother-in-law who was a barber and still he used to do it. That's the truth. But he needed the money.

"The Sun Is in the Sky, You Gotta Get Up"

The root beer. We start washing all these friggin' bottles! We'd have root beer and my mother would put them behind the stove, it had to be warm to ferment. And beer. My mother and father used to make it for my father. I remember him buying malt and putting in this big crock, and in there he used to make the beer, then we'd pour it into the bottles, then cap it and then we used to put that in back of the stove so that he had beer for the whole week. My father smoked cigarettes. He had a machine that was iron, it came up and was round. And he used to buy tobacco, the papers and one of us, me or my sister, we'd roll em' up and we'd lick it and make his cigarettes for the week. And then my mother used to let the bread raise and on Saturday—you know how the kids say, "I worked all week, I want to sleep today?" My poor mother! I feel so sorry for her but . . . she used to come in and she used to say, "Aye, the sun is in the sky, ya got a get up." Because now Saturday was not a day of rest, Saturday was now a day of work after working all week on the sewing machine. Oh! But, we'd get up, we'd have to knead the bread, and my mother would make the loaves, we'd let it raise. We'd have bread for the week, okay. That was a typical weekend.

"Chickens and My Irish Friend"

I had an Irish girlfriend. They didn't know anything of what we did, you know? She used to love to come to my house because of all these crazy things she'd see.

To her, it was crazy. Every Saturday morning we'd get up, my mother would drag me to the market on Minor and Meadow Street, across from where the Coliseum is today. I hated it. The farmers from the area had a big open area and they had your own space—it was mostly a food market. So every Saturday she'd drag me down there, I used to be so embarrassed because all my friends on the way down there I'd see. But most of them had to go too. And we'd go down there and my mother would buy live chickens. The Irish girl would come about twelve or one on a Saturday. My mother would take these friggin' chickens home, my father had a beautiful grapevine that he made over a trellis, and we had grapes all hanging you know. And all on the side we had these wires, and underneath we had a big picnic table, we use to eat out there a lot. And my father would tie the chickens feet and wings together and he used to call me "figlióla," young girl, and I hated it, "You got a go kill 'e galline," the chickens. So my girlfriend would come and we'd go downstairs under the grapevine. At first, you know, I didn't like it but then it got to be funny because she used to come and we used to laugh like hell. I slit their throat, I know I'm not that kind, but what do you want me to do? And then the damned chickens would spatter all over them; there'd be blood all over the place until they drained out. And then I would take the hose, we used to wash every-thing down because he had a lovely garden on the side—you could get anything out a there, from celery to parsley—and then these freakin' chickens. We'd take them upstairs—that was the bad part. My mother used to make boiling water. And stink! Oh! She used to dunk them in there, then we had to pull all their feathers off and we had to make sure we got every one of them feathers off. We used to clean em' and Sunday we used to have them for dinner. My girlfriend thought that was terrible. But she used to come every Saturday just see these chickens shake [laughing].

"Life on Spring Street"

The dress shop was across the street, it was in a little store. We had another store on the corner that was Jewish, her name was Levinson. We used to go buy milk in there. But we didn't buy a quart of milk, we used to buy a half a quart, so we would bring our bottle and the Jewish lady would take her quart out and she would pour half in my bottle and then she'd measure it, make sure it was even. She always had a little more than we had. And then we'd bring that home, right, that was how we bought milk. We had Irish people living next door. They used to go play bingo all the time and we were fascinated with her [Mrs. Egan] be-cause she would use her gas bill money to go play bingo and we could never understand it. She'd stay all night playin' with I dunno who. And then we'd meet her comin' home in the morning. She used to tip a little. We got along very well. And the houses were so close that my bedroom window and their bedroom win-dow—you could just about get a person in between—if you had anybody in there, you'd hear them.

〝The Oldest Daughter〟

My mother was a dressmaker and we had a dress shop across the street from my house on Spring Street. And my mother worked there. I never was a kid. I always was treated like an old lady. Number one, I was very tall. And my father used to say, "Let her do it, she's big." Always. I remember eight years old cooking; I used to cook when I came home from school. It wasn't like when I came home from school I could go out, go downtown. No, when I came home from school I used to start the supper, my mother was only across the street. I had a younger sister that tortured me, that little . . . She's alive, that's the one I'm goin' to meet today. My mother use to leave us, we had a do work. I had a cook, she had a clean. She would never—I could never get her to do what she was supposed to do. And then [laughing] she'd wait until my mother was coming home from work—we lived on the second floor—and she'd be coming up the stairs and she'd hang over the banister, crying, and she'd say, "Antonette hit me, Antonette hit me." And before my mother even got in the house I'd get a crack because I was the bad guy. But I couldn't make them understand she wouldn't do what she was supposed to do, you know. But I always had to cook, I was the oldest daughter. The boys in my house, they were treated like, well they didn't have to do much. That was the Italian way. The girls had a hang up their pants, the girls had a wash their clothes in my house. I was the oldest girl and that was it.

〝The Old Market in New Haven〟

Bill Zampa, Joe Panicali, and Ron Mortali spoke at the Marchegiano Club in the Hill section on August 3, 2000.

Come Fall, all the freight cars from California would come in to the spur [line] down to the market with grapes for wine. And all the big vendors—Carbonella, DiSorbo—they would set up the grapes on the sidewalks so that you could go down, open the crates, inspect the grapes to see whether or not they suited your particular taste and the quality that you were looking for. But it would be like a circus down there. Cars and trucks all over the place. There were bidding wars, you'd try to reduce the price of a crate of grapes and they'd look at them and say "Zinfandel, this and that, white, Muscatel." Everybody made wine. We all made wine. All the produce that came into New Haven used to all come in by that spur, the majority of it. It must have been a half a mile long, along Meadow Street, it went from Commerce all the way up to Hill Street. Every Saturday morning they had all the chickens, they had cheese stores, like Quincy Market in Boston, exactly the same concept, trucks would come in and unload. All the local farmers would come in. One of the traits of the Italian people was that it had to be fresh, in other words, if you were buying chicken it had to be walking around. And they had to view that

THE MARKET
Silver and Commerce Streets,
the Hill, 1930s

Saint Anthony Church Archives

particular chicken to make sure it was healthy and it was appealing to the eye. The women would choose the product, whether it would be chicken or rabbits, they'd bring it home live, walk home with the chickens in their hands, take the wings and cross the wings so they wouldn't fly. Always two chickens in their hands walking up Columbus Avenue, a four block walk to the market. Take them home, break the neck, kill them, put them in boiling water, pluck them, gut them, and eat them. Save the feathers for the pillows.

"THE BOARDERS"

Josie DeBenedet spoke at the kitchen table of her North Haven home on
June 10, 1999.

My mother had four or five boarders, their wives would be in Italy and she knew
them—my father knew them—and they would eat and sleep in our home, maybe
for seven, eight dollars a week. They would sleep two in a bed. And then some of
them played the accordion; most of the Italians did. And there was one man, he
played the clarinet and we used to get together and sing all the songs the Marchegians sing, "I Mastroline di Fiore," "Come Pioveva," all those old songs. Carlo Buti
at that time used to sing. At night, where you gonna go? It was cold. At nighttime
what did we do? We stayed around the table and there was always somebody who
would come. We'd have the big coal stove and we'd get these dried beans, fava
beans, green, you could cook it like beans, the chestnuts, i lupini or you wait when
they're dry, you roast them on top of the stove, the black stove. They [the immi-
grants] would talk about the different things [that happened in Italy]. They'd say
[in Italian] my father always used to say near the cemetery nobody wanted to go
because there were spirits or ghosts. Said one day the man was going with his donkey and wagon and little cart and every time he'd get near the cemetery the donkey
would stop. And he would go wild as if to say he saw something there. I don't think
we have ghosts in America. [They would talk] until the stove stayed lit. We had a
lot of friends, we had neighbors with the little victrola and we'd play all the records
by hand. We'd push the table—we had a big table—and our neighbors would come.

"BOCCE AND THE PADRONE"

Sam Troiano spoke at the dining room table of his North Branford home
with his wife Giovannina "Jennie" and his son Gino on May 27, 2000.

My father used to talk real Italian. My father could talk three, four dialects. My
father never went to school, but he could read anything. He couldn't write or spell.
My father was very smart, he knew the Bible from the beginning to the end, he
knew all about the history of Italy. Him and his brother's godfather, they used to get
into heated arguments over parts of Italy, like different towns. They'd say, "This
river was runnin' through this certain town," and he'd say, "No, it was runnin' in a
different town," and they'd argue and argue. But they were very good friends. And
they'd have a few glasses of wine. My father and my grandfather, my mother's
father, they used play cards and argue—they wouldn't talk to each other for months,
maybe for years sometimes over a card game. Yeah. They'd play "padrone" [the
boss]. Even when they played bocce. Even fingers. Did you ever play fingers
[mórra]? No? That's an Italian game, you throw fingers and you try to guess what
number is gonna come out and then say if you get ten points, okay, then you find
out who's the boss. And then the boss, he'd say, "You want to give her a glass of

wine?" And you'd say, "No, I don't wan a give him the glass of wine, I'll drink it." You know? And boy, sometimes you get a guy who likes to drink, he'd get pie-eyed because he would give nobody a drink, he'd drink it all himself. They called it "mórra." Then bocce is the same way. They win a game of bocce, then the closest ball to the pill [small ball] would be the boss, then they got the under boss. The two closest. Now the boss, he tells who he wants to give a drink to. If I don't want the wine, I'd say to the under boss, no I don't want this one, I wan a give it to him. Now the under boss would say, "No," he says, "I won't give it to him—I'll drink it." And he'd drink it. They used to do that, even down the market. On Saturdays, when they'd get through selling, they'd play bocce down there at the market because most of the farmers used to go home and it'd be wide open. Then they used to go into the bar and buy beer and say eight guys were playing, they'd get eight glasses of beer, put it on the counter. Then they'd start that. And then the boss would be—he's the boss—so he could drink as many as he wants but if he drank enough and wants to give a glass to him and the under boss says no, he's drinking it. Arguments. Not only that. Fights. Fist fights down the market over a bocce game.

"Trouble with the Irish"

Eugene Clini spoke in the living room of his home in Hamden with his wife Viola, son Dennis, and daughter Millie on June 23, 1999. He was president of the Marchegiano Club from 1960 to 1979.

The Irish were further up on Howard Avenue. Down below, on Columbus Avenue, Cedar Street where most of the Marchegianos lived. We got along fine—we used to fight all the time. We used to have some real bad fights with the Irish. It was bad; it was no fun. They used call us guinea bastards and everything else. All kinds of names. Up on Washington Avenue there was a club. And one year the Italians owned it, the next year they'd have a fight and then the Irish would take it over. They used to have gang fights between the Italians and the Irish years back, oh yeah. Yeah, we had a lot trouble years ago. My father bought a gun because he had trouble with them. Then they all married the Italians. You know what we used to say? They married Italian because they wanted something good to eat.

"Olive Oil"

Renee Vanacore spoke on the back porch of her North Haven home on November 20, 1999.

My mother used to make like a pizza dough; she used to fry it like a pancake, very thin like a Mexican taco. Then from there she used to sauté the dandelions with onions and oil and garlic, put the dandelions in the middle make like a sandwich in this dough, in this pancake. Then we used to have the wine in the winter. And when she used to make that I used to say, Oh, I'm in heaven. It was so good with a glass of red wine. Who wants steak? That's what we used to live on. We used to make that a lot. She used to make the homemade noodles, thin ones like spaghetti, thinner than that. I used to have a Jewish girlfriend. She used to come to my house so she could have my mother's homemade chicken. She used to get a chicken and cook it all day. I said, "Ma, why are you doing that?" She said, "Because the more you cook it the better soup you get out of it. She used to make wide noodles, the thin, thin noodles by hand. And the square ones. She made bread. My mother used to go to Rossners on Congress Avenue—my mother used to go there years ago— she used to get the best olive oil. We didn't buy the cheap oil; my mother didn't believe in that. I said, Ma, gee. She said, "Olive oil is better for you." She used to bake with olive oil. So when they came out with a sponge cake that you bake with olive oil, my mother said, "Eh! I did that before they were even born." We were brought up with olive oil—not with peanut oil—she didn't believe in that. My mother knew olive oil before they even knew what the hell olive oil was. They used to say years ago "Don't eat olive oil, it's no good for you." My mother said, "It's no good? I've eaten it all my life." My father wouldn't think of getting any other oil because he was fussy. He had to have his wine and the best of food.

Life in the Forbes Avenue Neighborhood

The Forbes Avenue neighborhood and its main thoroughfare, Forbes Avenue, took its name from the Forbes family of eighteenth century shipbuilders. Its side streets led to open grasslands stretching to the coastline of Long Island Sound and New Haven harbor. The Forbes Avenue neighborhood began on the east side of the Tomlinson Bridge where a jitney transported passengers past the bluffs of Kendall's castle overlooking the Sound to the Granniss Corner transfer point at the top of the hill. Prior to the commercial development of its coastline area in the '20s and '30s into an industrialized section of waterfront oil refineries and storage tanks, a sewage disposal plant, and a truck terminal, the neighborhood resembled a transplanted Italian farming village within a melting pot of other ethnicities. Portuguese families lived on Stiles and Kendall Street, Irish on Wheeler, and Polish on Fulton Terrace. Neighborhood oral tradition recalled that Alabama and Connecticut Avenues may have been part of the Underground Railroad, where slaves from Alabama, on their way to their families in other states, took refuge in the homes along Connecticut Avenue near the harbor. Forbes Avenue was a territory of open pastures where cows grazed and young boys walked cattle herds along its trolley car tracks. In open fields of grassy lowlands near Long Island Sound, the Parente family planted alfalfa on their farm with a team of horses and plow, which were later dried, cut down, formed into bales of hay, and fed to livestock. Flaviano Parente and his wife sold cheese, butter, ricotta, and basket cheese from fresh cow milk and often bartered for homemade wine. Once a year they filled two foot tall crocks with lard and meat from butchered pigs and stored them in cabinets of long cellars that extended under passing traffic on Forbes Avenue. When their grandchildren came home from school, they made a snack of lard spread out on bread with sausage. A Jewish vendor from the market on Silver Street in the Hill, known as "O Jude," or the Jew, Mr. Heime, brought chicks, ducklings, and young geese to Mr. Parente, who raised them to a weight of a pound and half on his farm. When Mr. Heime returned for his fattened poultry, he brought a new batch. Paying Mr. Parente for his services, he handed the children a quarter to buy ice cream sodas at Cacace's bakery near Granniss corner. DiGennaro's turkey farm sold fresh chicken, turkey, and eggs to locals. Mr. Perry, a

Yankee fruit and vegetable peddler, sold produce by horse and wagon. Ernie Parente and his nephew Gene Calzetta built their own wagon and sold potatoes, garlic, onions, tomatoes, "sarchiapóne," or long squash, lettuce, and eggplants from the Parente family's five-acre truck farm, which stretched from Fulton Terrace to Stiles Street. The Acabbo family had a cider mill where families brought crates of grapes on wagons that were bought for seventy-five cents at the market to be squeezed into wine. Children swam and fished in pristine waters along the nearby Sound and named the area "Newport." On balmy Sunday afternoons in the summer, an Italian woman named "Cuncietta" held neighborhood get-togethers in her backyard garden where Italian songs were played on mandolins and people sang and drank homemade wine and danced the tarantella. Animated games of bocce took place between men from the neighborhood who shouted and urged teammates to knock opponents' balls out of scoring position, yelling, "Spara!" or shoot.

In the mid-1950s, plans were drawn up to connect Interstate 95 to New Haven, including the building of the Quinnipiac Bridge to ease the growing traffic problem on Route 1. Italians who had purchased land from the city in the 1920s were forced to vacate when the state declared the land by eminent domain to build the new highway. Italian landowners were not paid the fair value of the land but were refunded the amount of taxes paid over the years of ownership. In 1948, Forbes Avenue was deemed an "industrial area" by the city, which attracted many small businesses to open shop with few building regulations or zoning laws. In 1957, the city forced the neighborhood to dissolve its independent governing body, the Fairmont Association, and taxes were raised threefold by the city, some said to help fund the "Model City" project of Mayor Richard Lee.

"WE CALLED IT 'OUR NEWPORT'"

Eugene Calzetta spoke in the living room of his home on Forbes Avenue, on October 10, 1998, where he had lived since 1922.

Then Forbes Avenue was nice and quiet at the time—nothing like it is today. All this land [pointing toward the highway from Forbes Avenue] was farmland down there; everybody had a farm, there were no houses. All gardens—everybody a piece of land down there and they all gardened. There was nothing there but you saw a shack now and then where the ones that farmed kept their tools. Some come down here and plant on Sundays. Trees. We called it "Newport" in the '30s. That [Newport] was the playground of the rich; that was our playground down there. It was a lot; it had a nice grape arbor and a shack with a stove in it. They'd cook the macaroni in the summertime. They'd run a wire from across the street for the electricity for the radios and victrolas—we'd have music and they'd be dancing. They had tarantellas, all the Italian stuff. Cuncietta, Filomèna . . . all Italian names, they used to come there. They're all dancing and drinking. Drinking, dancing, and eating all day like a party. Old man Longobardi—got no funeral—he'd be down there, too, because he liked his oil [wine] the old man, the undertaker [chuckling].

CALZETTA FAMILY
CELESTE PARENTE CALZETTA AND CARMINE CALZETTA,
LUCILLE, EUGENE, AND RITA
At grape arbor on Kendall Street, 1927

Calzetta family album

I never saw my grandfather drunk, but I mean he was always . . . you didn't get a glass of wine with him. He used to get us bombed because when he gave a glass to drink—you know the pint jars that you can with? He'd fill the pint and give it to you. You drink one of them, you're on your fanny. Oh boy, oof! Sometimes a couple of them would come down and they had mandolins, dancing tarantellas. My grandfather's sisters used to come with her kids. There was no highway [I-95] then—it was just green grass. We called it Newport because it was our summer vacation. That was every Sunday. On a Sunday it was a riot down there in Newport. They'd all come down with their wives, their kids. Everything here was all farmland. You could look out here [looks out back window at the highway] and you could see nothing but green. Even where the New Haven terminal is—that's Alabama Street—there used to be DeGennaro's turkey farm. He had a nice piece of land back there and he used to raise turkeys. We had to do our chores. We had to make sure the chickens were fed. The milk—we had to help my grandmother bring the milk in because she was small. And the wine, that was beauty. Had to turn and turn to cut up the grapes. After the wine was made all "'a vernaccia," left-over ground grapes. And then he used to make vinegar, twenty-five gallons I don't know for what. He sold some—if he got a dime, fifteen cents, or a quarter you got a lot of money. My grandfather—everybody that come down for anything nobody ever got refused of anything, whether they had money or not. They all knew each other. He had a good heart my grandfather; he loved the children. I'll never forget—he had two fig trees, my grandfather down there. And we used to dread that in the wintertime because we had to bring it over [bend it] down almost into the ground and if you dare broke a twig on it, oh, you never heard the end of it. "But gramp, you know; you do it." Noo! "M' aggiu fatto viècchio," No, I'm too old to do it. We had to do it. We had to put the trees down, put them down—that was the tough part—and cover them [bury] all up for the winter. He supervised the wrapping of it; then he'd tie it, maybe five or six places. Then you bring it down nice and slow because you couldn't . . . you put into the grave for the winter. Because we had winters then. Now today, they ain't got no winters. Then we had winters, what you call winters. In the springtime when it was ready, you just un-buried it—sshhht—right up there. And he kept them trimmed nice. On Stiles Street, there were all houses and they were all Italian families there; some were even Irish families. They had their kids—they come down they had no money for milk and my grandfather never refused them, gave them the quart, two quarts, whatever it was. My grandmother, she made plenty of butter, cheese, ricotta, basket cheese. They used to cure the sausage and the pork chops and the ribs. Put them in big crock with the grease [pig fat] and store it. We used to go there and we used to steal a pork chop or a piece of sausage, put it on the bread, grease and all, and eat it. We never got no . . . worrying about cholesterol! You're going to die with cholesterol, you kidding? In the summertime we used to do more gosh darn weeding and not like now. He had the hoes and he'd check you. He might assign me to go through the tomatoes, go clean them. And what he meant by that you had to around each plant with the hand claw and make sure to take out the weeds.

My uncle probably had the string beans or the corn. But you had to do it. We could fool around but your work had to be done. He used to say, "Eh, you want to eat? That's it, over there. That's it. You got to eat. Got to make it grow to eat it; you can't eat otherwise." He used to say, "'O mangia nun ci sta," The food isn't there unless you work. He talked mostly Italian; my grandmother never spoke a word of English. My grandfather spoke some English, all broken English. When he was angry it was always in Italian. But if he was telling you something he might say a few words of English, mix it up with the Italian. But when he started in Italian, you didn't say not a word—quiet. Because he was one who believed that the stick counted. The only thing we ever got from him was the snaps—as far as getting whacked, he never hit us, never. He was good. We used to cut the grass with the sickle—dry—then we used to go down there, rake it all up. We had a big barn there. We'd bring the hay back and put the hay in for the wintertime for the cows. And we had to take the cows—my Uncle Ernie and I—we were the two youngest—when we came home from school we had to go and get the cows when they were ready to come home. They'd be grazing down there—at one time we had five—and we'd bring them back so they go back into the barn. And then he taught us how to milk. My Uncle Larry was the best milker—that was his job, milking. I used to try it but I wasn't too good. And then my grandfather wouldn't let us do it because we'd play. My uncle and I, we would squirt each other with the milk and get him mad. He'd take his strap off. Did you ever see those guys in the cowboy movies just crack the whips? He was pretty wide. The belt probably was four feet you know. And he could snap that thing and get four feet; he'd get you on the hand, on the arm. And when you ate—the first thing he done when we sat down at the supper table, he'd take his belt off and used to put his belt beside it over there. Because when you're eating there was no talking allowed at the table. And no fooling around. And naturally, you get guys twelve, thirteen years old, you know what it is, you would do something and before you know it you had a whack on—ccrrr—boom! "Jeezus, gramp, what are you doing?" "Zitt," Keep quiet.

" FARMING ON THE LOTS "

Amelia Buonocore spoke in the living room of her seniors' apartment complex on September 11, 1999. She lived to be 101 years old.

Many years ago on Forbes Avenue, when you pass the Tomlinson Bridge, where the oil tanks are now, near Stiles Street, that place was all empty. Some rich man owned all that land, it was all empty. And he let anybody who wanted to use it, they could go over there and plant. My father—mercy on his soul—went over there two years and planted tomatoes and things like that. So nobody touched it. But after that they got smarter or what, he needed the money, the man was selling the lots and he had lots all the way down to the water. So my father bought seven lots, my brother bought five lots; my other brother bought three lots. My father used to go first, come out of work, stop at the house, maybe had a drink of wine and he used to go down there. He didn't eat. My father was thin, skinny. He used to go down there without eating; then he'd come home seven, eight, o'clock to eat. We used to walk from Brown Street all the way down there. Everything was fenced. And my father used to go down there after work and we used to go down there and dig and the stones and everything and we made a nice farm. I had to push the pushcart. What do you think? Kids had no fun. I worked every day of my life. I come from school, I learned how to cook with my mother — if she went to the lots I had to cook, if she cooked I had to go to the lots so I had to push the cart, push the stuff that was on, push the stuff back [home]. My mother used to grow dandelions. She used to get the seeds from the old country. She used to put squares of these dandelions; they used to grow fast, used to get this high. She used to cut them and make little bunches she used to sell them. The people around there used to come for them because they had no flowers [on them], no bad leaves or anything. You only had to wash them and cook them. They used to say, "Oh, I like to make soup, I'd like to have some dandelions, for the chicken soup." They used to come over there on Saturday [for Sunday's meal].

By the 1920s, Italians from arrival neighborhoods—Oak Street, the Hill, and Wooster Square—began moving into Fair Haven, an Irish and Yankee community of two story clapboard houses, tree-lined streets and boulevards, and a main commercial artery, Grand Avenue, that connected it to the city. The Quinnipiac River divided lower Fair Haven from the Heights, formally named Fair Haven East, a part of East Haven until 1881 when it joined the city of New Haven[55]. Italians found labor-intensive work in Fair Haven at the A. C. Gilbert factory where toys and home goods were manufactured and exported all over the world, at the mammoth New Haven Folding Box plant, and in the oyster industry along the Quinnipiac where river families joined the production lines as shuckers in canning plants along with Poles, Lithuanians, and Portuguese, who were paid by the pint to process fresh oysters. On their way to school young boys stopped on Farren Avenue to watch women shuckers in small plants, three or four grouped at benches, using knives to open "easy" oysters and hammers to tap and small chisels to scoop out "hard" ones. Piles of oyster shells were carried in wheel barrels to nearby docks and barges brought them to sea hatcheries in Long Island Sound where they reproduced for the next harvest season[56].

Grand Avenue became the commercial center of the area with fish markets offering fresh catches of the day, newsstands featuring Italian newspapers, Italian pastry shops, bakeries, social clubs, saloons, dry goods stores, furniture stores, a wholesale candy store, and Jewish-owned clothing stores. Rascati's bakery made loaves of bread with a special chord of dough running across the top that baked into a breadstick. Street peddlers sold fish from their trucks yelling "O pisce!" out their windows as they drove by. Non-English speaking Italians who could not decipher the Jewish ragman's thickly accented, chant-like call "Kesh paid f'rags," or "Cash paid for rags!" as he drove through the streets buying used rags from local housewives, referred to him as "Spebarrecchia" because of the way it sounded to Italian ears. In the Saltonstall Avenue area, locals were referred to by their physical attributes or character traits rather than first names. Someone who had undergone a hernia operation was called "A palla vàscia," or low balls; a person held in low esteem was given the name "'o saràco" after a small fish of little value; a hunch back, "scarteliato"; and a woman of low regard "a culachione," or fatass. Young men in search of wives abided by the old world custom of "'a 'mmasciàta," asking an intermediary to approach a young woman's family for permission to court and marry her. Italian immigrant mothers sometimes hung blood-stained towels out of their apartment windows to prove their daughters had been virgins on the night of their wedding.

Salvatore Russo, an enterprising man from the neighborhood, invented his own bleach for local housewives, a concoction he mixed in a metal vat in his cellar called "star water." As he drove up the street delivering bleach in gallon-sized glass jugs for twenty-five cents, singing "Vicin' 'O Mare" and "Wey Marie," Italian women in Fair Haven and Annex used to say "Oh, here comes Salvatore, the star water man." Italian boys honed their fighting skills in street fights with the Irish, later becoming amateur boxers who fought in the New Haven Arena with anglicized surnames.

On Sunday afternoons, Grand Avenue provided a main cultural attraction to Italian families who walked to Fair Haven Junior High where the "Impressario Teatrale Pane," founded by Giuseppina and Luigi Pane, sponsored Italian recitals and plays in Italian on stage in the school's auditorium. Famous Italian singers made live appearances during the first hour, then returned as actors in three-act plays in Italian written by Don Gaetano D'Aniello. Many of Italy's greatest singers—Aurelio Fierro, Carlo Buti, and Gilda Minionetta—made tour stops on Grand Avenue for Sunday afternoon musical extravaganzas. Circuses performed live stage acts with lions, tigers, and monkeys. After the shows, Clemente DeLucia, a local actor and singer, invited everyone for parties at his "Palm Beach" pizzeria on Grand Avenue. In 1951, the shows were moved to the Dreamland Theatre where movies like "Mala Fémmena" starring Nunzio Gallo were shown. After the movie ended, the actor made a personal appearance and sang on stage. In appreciation for the many shows Giuseppina Pane sponsored in Fair Haven for the large Italian-speaking community, she received the name, "La Mamma della Comunità Italiana," The Mother of the Italian Community.

"THEY THOUGHT WE CAME FROM THE JUNGLE"

Mary Altieri spoke in the kitchen on the second floor of her Fair Haven home on January 13, 1999. She continued sewing into her nineties.

We moved up here on Woolsey Street on July 22, 1928. It was beautiful. My mother cried for a whole month and a half. Because Collis Street [Wooster Square] was beautiful, we used to sing, go out. She didn't want to live here because we thought we were in a cemetery. My mother said, "Mi ha portato in do camposanto," You brought me out here to a cemetery. There were no kids. It was so quiet. No lights out the street. Everything was dark, we couldn't go outside, we couldn't even see the people across the street, it was so dark. The man used to come with pole to light the little lanterns. Sometimes the wind would blow out the light. All Yankee.

PAPPACODA FAMILY.
124 Woolsey Street, Fair Haven, 1930s

Altieri family album

Must have been maybe three or four people, they were Italian, the rest were all Yankee. The only thing, my father used to throw us in the yard—we never could sit out the front. We never went out and said hello, good bye, or were friendly; we were always in the house. My father worked. We always sat in the backyard—we never went outside. My father would never let us go out the front. We had to stay in the yard and play ball. A couple of times my brother threw the ball there, the Yankee people took it and so he punished us to stay in the yard. But they never bothered us. Only she used to get out and she used to go, "If that ball comes over here you're not get it back anymore." Because the American people—we didn't want to make noise, we had to be in bed at seven o'clock at night. My brother couldn't throw the ball out the street. They'd [Yankees] would take it and they'd put it away they wouldn't give it to us. The Yankee people, they were all Yankees, there were four families. Two old ladies never got married, they were real old; they were Yankees. That's the life our kids grew up. Today they go out at one o'clock.

They were wonderful to us. They couldn't get over how nice we were with the kids—how quiet we were. You know, when they heard we had ten kids, they thought we came from the jungle. The woman next door when we bought the house—she was an Irish lady and her name was Anderson, I'll never forgot. She put out a sfaccìma [damned] sign outside for sale. She heard we had ten kids and we were all going to come here and live. She had the sign up two days. She called me, "Miss Pappacoda, come to the fence." She said, "You tell you mother I am not selling the house—you people are wonderful, I don't even hear a squeak out of you." And they were wonderful to us.

"FAITH IN THE NOVENA"

Rose Sansone spoke at her kitchen table at her Fair Haven home on August 18, 1998. A month after her hernia operation at age eighty-four, she mowed her lawn.

When I was young, down in Saint Louis's Church, they used to have the Saint Anne and Saint Theresa's novena—that was in the 1920s. Ever since I could remember that they started that novena that I was old enough, every Tuesday we used to walk from Clay Street down to Saint Louis on Chestnut and Chapel Street and back. There used to be a novena and the place was packed. The novena was a nine day prayer to Saint Anne and Saint Theresa. In order to make this novena you have to go nine consecutive days in July, from the 17th to the 26th, and you have your [special] prayers to say. And I've been making the novena since 1926, and as far as this morning I still say the Saint Theresa and Saint Anne's prayer. We used to have three services over here for Saint Anne's novena, three of them there used to be, that's how many people used to come. That was during the war. Now you're lucky if you get half a church full for a novena for one service. And years ago, the 25th of July was Saint Christopher and if you came to this [Saint Donato's] church with your car, the priest would be standing outside, he'd bless your car, and there would be somebody with the basket, you had to put a donation in the basket. Now there's no more Saint Christopher—they threw him out, now it's Saint James, no more Saint Christopher. I don't know why they threw him out. Last week my daughter-in-law called me that her daughter-in-law is expecting a baby anytime these next two weeks and she was worried because the baby wasn't in position and she may have to go for a cesarean. I said, "Okay, Nancy, I'll light the candle." She said, "Well she's going tonight to the doctor to see if the baby turned." I said, Okay. I went in there, I said, "My Saint Anne," I lit the candle, I said "Saint Anne, Give me my wish." At night I called her up, I said, "Nancy, how did Lisa make out?" She said, "Everything is great." I said, "Thank you, Saint Anne!" You got to have your faith.

"MA, ALL THE CRABS!"

One time my husband and two kids went crabbing. My daughter-in-law, well she wasn't my daughter-in-law yet, she came over and they had so many crabs they had to throw them in the bathtub. The whole bathtub was full of crabs. She went home and she said, "Oh, Ma, I went over Chris's house, you should see all the crabs in the bathroom." Her mother said, "Oooh, Carol, don't go in the bathroom if they have crabs. You may get them!"

"You're Buying That Guinea Stuff?"

Ettore and Julia Coiro spoke in the dining room of the family Fair Haven home on November 30, 1999. Their father proposed to their mother on the Water Street bridge, saying, "If you don't say you'll marry me, I'll jump off this bridge."

In those days being Italian was not easy because you were poked fun at so much. It made people feel inferior. Discrimination against Italian-speaking people. It seemed as though if they weren't Italian and you were Italian they would say things that were derogatory that made you feel inferior. I was never ashamed of the fact that I was Italian. People knew it and we had a few gangs of kids, some of us Italian, some of us, other than. But the people that we fought all the way were the Irish and it's a known fact we had to fight Irish all the way through the '20s and '30s. And we did. I couldn't walk home without being intercepted by the Saint Francis kids and they were all Irish. If I was alone I'd come home bloody sometimes. Mom would ask and I would say nothing. But the next day when I was walking down the street I always made sure I had some company with me and they beat it every time. It's a known fact: the Irish fought the Italians all the time. But that's mostly the kids and to a certain extent it's dead. The Irish at that time saw the Italians as a threat to taking away their jobs, which they were here first and that was the reason there was that animosity. Did you ever read the book, when the Italian came over here, they were looking for work around the turn of the century and they had laborers twenty-five cents and hour, Italians fifteen? Where we lived on Lombard Street, either side was Irish. And that's the funny part of it, it seems like so many of my friends were Irish. I remember when one of our neighbors used to send over to my mother for garlic and olive oil. Now they could well afford to buy their own but they used to send over to mom for it because they didn't want to go into an Italian store to buy it. They would be embarrassed to go into an Italian store and buy it. I suppose if any of their friends saw them going in there, they'd say, "Oh, you're buying guinea stuff." That's probably what they'd say.

"Grand Avenue"

Rose Sansone spoke at her kitchen table at her Fair Haven home on August 18, 1998.

There were a lot of stores. There was the five and ten on Blatchley and Grand, then there was a hardware store, there was a pastry shop, there was McCarthy's bakery

THE DREAMLAND THEATRE

Grand Avenue, Fair Haven, 1950s

New Haven Jewish Historical Society Archives

over here. Every Saturday we used to go over there as we got older, we used to buy a coffeecake for Sunday. That was our treat on Sunday—we only had cake once a week. And next to McCarthy's there was a china man store that they used to press the shirts. And every time we'd go by there, we would run, "China man! China man!" And we would run by the china man's store because we were afraid he was going to come out after us. We had Canon's [theatre], for five cents we used to go the show every Saturday. We used to see the news first, "The Ears and the Eyes of the World," then we used to see the coming attractions, then two big pictures—Charlie Chaplin pictures—all those old pictures for five cents. We used to have two big pictures and then we used to have a serial. Every Saturday they showed you a part and then it would be continued the next week. Further up was Pequot [Theatre], it was ten cents. We used to go from two to five, we used to see all them pictures. And while you were in there, Mister Canon would walk down with a cane because a lot of the boys used to pee on the floor [laughing] because they didn't have toilets in the show. And if you talked—because they weren't talking pictures you know—so if you talked he would come and tap you with the cane to tell you to shut up. He would walk up and down all during the whole show. And for a penny we'd buy a penny's worth of candy or something.

"You Want To Make Lemonade?"

We used to have the Hygenic Ice House in Poplar Street because we used to have the iceboxes. They used to make the ice on State Street. And they used to bring it to the Hygenic Ice. And the ice trucks used to come down Blatchley Avenue come down Clay Street go into Poplar Street. My mother used to say, "You want to make the lemonade? Well go get the ice." And we used to get the ice. We used to wait for the ice truck to go by. Me and my brother Ralph, we used to grab hold of the wagon—and we used to run to the ice house because we used to pick up all the scrap ice that used to fall. Because they used to sweep out the icehouse to get out all the broken pieces of ice and we used to get the ice and bring it home. And we used to make lemonade. We had a lemonade machine and we used to make lemonade. Then we used to put a stand outside. We used to sell the lemonade for a penny. And then we had the icebox, my mother would say, "Go buy ten cents worth of ice." We used to take the wagon, we used to go around the corner and for ten cents you got a big piece of ice and then you had to take and put the towel around and carry it upstairs and put it in the ice box. When the trucks used to come down with the ice, they used to have the platform in the back. And what they used to do, all the kids, the trucks when they go by, they used to run, they used to get in the back of the truck and hold on and ride to the icehouse in the back of the truck. Just to get ice; that's how we used to get our ice.

"Fair Haven Street Vendors"

Then we used to have the sheenie, we used to call him. We used to get all the old rags, anybody had old rags, we used to get all the old rags and we used to put them in a bag and when the sheenie go by, we'd say, "Hey, sheenie, we got rags!" He used to come with the scale and used to weigh the rags and he used to give you so much a pound for the rags that you have. A lot of people used to put stones in the bottom of the bag to make it heavier [laughs]. Then there used to be the man who used to come down, like once a week. You had old bones, you used to save all the old bones and they used to come down with the truck. You bring the old bones there, they give you a bucket of soap. And that's what we used to use to wash the clothes, the brown soap, it was like a jello. The trucks used to come down with the gel—we used to keep all the old bones—you bring it there and they gave you that to wash clothes. They'd come once a week, once every two weeks. We would run down Poplar Street to bring the bones. When the guy used to come walking with a little cart. He used to bring the scissors and knives downstairs and he used to sharpen them for us. We used to have DeFeo's bakery on Filmore Street; he lived right around the corner from us. He used to bring us bread every morning. Hot bread every morning for three cents a loaf. We used to find it near the door. My father used to go downstairs every morning, pick up the loaf of bread for the day, for three cents a loaf.

"Street Games in Fair Haven"

There was no cars then. We used to go out in the street and play "piggy." Did you ever play piggy? You get the old broom, you cut a piece off of the broom and you shave a point on it like a pencil. And then you used to make the piggy, used to point one end of it and get another piece of stick. And then with another stick you had to hit that piggy, with the other part of the broomstick, to let it go. And you'd hit it and if you hit it far, then you run to the corners. Then we used to get the four corners on Clay Street and Poplar Street. We used to get over there and play the kitty corner. It was like playing baseball. You had to run from one corner to the other, from base to base just like they play baseball now.

"You Italians Don't Belong Here"

I used to have to get up every Sunday morning and go to six o'clock mass at Saint Francis because I had to come home and wash the shirts for my three brothers. So I had to iron them the afternoon and I used to go to the six o'clock mass. Father Fitzmorris, the pastor, would get on the altar and he used to make the sermon at the pulpit and he used to say, "You Italian people don't belong here. Go to your own church, you don't belong here." I was there. I heard it myself, if I didn't hear it I'd say, well, I don't believe it. Six o'clock mass! He had the nerve to tell us we that don't belong there. Go to your own church? Yeah, they didn't want the Italian people there, so that's how they built Saint Donato church here. And we had an Irish priest here, Father Kelly. He was the first priest over here. And that's how the Italian people start coming here. So I've been going to Saint Donato since 1920—a long time. This church was built the same year I was born, see? If you weren't Irish you couldn't go to the Saint Francis School. He wouldn't take you. And then when it came over—Saint Donato—you had to be Italian to come to this church. And if you were getting married you had to marry an Italian or if you were Irish you had to marry an Italian to go there. Just like Saint Michael's, it was

BOCCE PLAYERS
Castle Street,
Fair Haven

Sansone family album

the same way, an Italian parish. Well, at Saint Donato there was no six o'clock mass so I had to go to a six o'clock [mass] so I could come home and start washing clothes. And a lot of times, when I'd come home my father would have the dough—he used to mix the dough—to make the macaroni. And my mother and me, we used to make the "macheroncielli," you know, the home made macaroni. My father used to make the dough and her and I, we used to sit down and make the macheronciellis on the Sundays when I didn't have to wash the clothes. But he had to mix the dough on Sundays. Oh yeah, they didn't want us in Saint Francis church. Every Sunday, he used to tell us that, "You Italian people don't belong here, go to your own church." Every Sunday. The only kids that could go there had to be Irish kids and I don't how my nephews Sally and Chris ever got to go there. They didn't want no Italian kids there—they had to be all Irish.

33

Life in the Legion Avenue Neighborhood

The Legion Avenue neighborhood was one of the poorest in the city of New Haven. It was a gritty working class area with rows of dilapidated tenement houses that ran along Oak Street, a main artery that connected to Legion Avenue, a retail strip of Italian and Jewish bakeries, delicatessens, luncheonettes, hardware stores, and kosher butcher shops. Legion Avenue was the first point of entry for many European immigrants—Irish, Jews, Italians, Greeks, Ukrainians, and Poles—eager to establish a foothold into the American way of life. It was a neighborhood where young boys working in their fathers' scrap metal businesses knew the difference between copper and brass before they knew the difference between boys and girls. It was the place where giant corporations like Perri Sausage started in a small butcher shop and where Lenders, a multimillion dollar business, began blanching bagels in a converted two-car garage. Despite the visible poverty of its timeworn storefronts and broken-down buildings, it was a proud place whose multiethnic inhabitants were described by lifelong resident William Rossi in these words: "Legion Avenue was the most democratic neighborhood in the United States."

Traditions and culture were shared across nationalities in the Legion Avenue melting pot. Jewish women sent kosher dishes to Italian neighbors and Polish women cooked kielbasa dinners for the Irish families next door. Italians attended funeral services in synagogues of their Jewish friends and African Americans were welcomed in the homes of their Caucasian neighbors. The Jewish Community Center was opened to everyone for weekly dances. In kosher delicatessens and meat markets, store clerks waited on Italian-speaking customers in Italian with Yiddish accents. Hardware stores doubled as informal social centers where neighbors buying goods compared the size of the tomatoes and eggplants from their backyard gardens.

The demise of Legion Avenue began on a night in 1953 when Richard Lee, campaigning door to door, was overcome by the stench and filth from inside one of the tenement buildings. He vowed to do something to upgrade the slum conditions, a promise he kept as mayor in 1957, when the city embarked on the Oak

Street Connector Project. With skillful organizing, the mayor won overwhelming citizen support by assembling the CAC, the Citizens Action Committee, which acted as a rubber stamp for the plan. Few voices opposing the project were heard. 881 families were moved to other neighborhoods where, instead of walking to the corner store and visiting a neighbor along the way, they now needed to travel by car. Small merchants were relocated to new areas where their old clients seldom traded; they went out of business soon after.

Today, buildings like the Knights of Columbus headquarters, the out-of-business Malley's and Macy's stores with an empty and crumbling parking garage adjacent, and the rusting Coliseum, stand as the Lee administration's solution to rid Oak Street of slum conditions. The Oak Street Connector Project, designed to speed highway traffic into the modernized downtown area of the 1960s, abruptly ends at Legion Avenue. An empty corridor of vacant land that once was home to many families on Legion Avenue is a ghostly reminder of the failure of a city administration whose highway and neighborhood redevelopment plan fell short.

"Why Can't We Just Be People?"

William Rossi spoke at a picnic table during the Oak Street Reunion picnic on August 27, 2000. Tanned and fit, he continued swimming at the beach into his nineties.

I would say that there was more democracy on Legion Avenue in those days than can ever be accredited to any community anywhere in the world right now. Because we didn't know each other as a Jew, or Italian, or a black. There was, "How are you? How you doing? Haven't seen you in a while." Or, "How's your son doing? Oh by the way, I need some work done in my house," and so forth and so on. We never knew the nationality of these people—it didn't matter. Nationality was not a catchphrase or a key word in those days. When you wanted something you went to whatever store you wanted to get anything. It was a nice, easy relationship you had with people. Nobody was tight about anything. No hang-ups. This is why people were freer in their mind because you didn't have these damned hang-ups. So a lot of us are bound, we're tied, we're untied by the hang-ups—whether it's a religious hang-up or a nationality hang-up or a color hang-up, whatever the hang-up is—a lot of people are living it. And I see more of it today than I saw in my youth. And I don't know what's happening or who's fomenting it. I know that the media plays a big part in that. When they use terms like "the first black steps up to a certain position" or "the first Italian does this" or "the first Jew . . ." like they're doing with Joe Lieberman. Joe Lieberman was a neighbor of mine—a nice guy. And as an Attorney General in Connecticut he was a helluva nice guy. Now to point him out as—it's almost like pointing out a freak—it's not right. Why can't we just be people?

"It Was a Melting Pot"

Lou Guarino spoke at the kitchen table of his home in Orange on August 24, 2000.

It was a melting pot. It really was literally, exactly that. Everyone knew everyone and everyone cared about everyone—that was the important thing, they cared about each other. If someone had a problem, everyone helped in any way they could. It didn't bother them though because this is how they lived. I mean this is what they did. Just because the guy's Polish or Jewish or black, they didn't care, he's a person, he's a human being. Like we lived on Scranton Street, was like a twelve-family apartment house, what they call condos today. You would have Italians, Jewish, and Polish in the same unit. And everybody on Sunday, everybody cooking different things, a pot of sauce on the stove. On Saturdays, with the Jewish, because we had a lot of Jewish people around, on Saturdays they'd say, "Little boy, I'll give you a nickel please turn our lights off or on," because on Saturdays they couldn't touch the lights, you had to put the light on for them or turn the stove on because in their religion they couldn't touch that.

Everybody knew everybody. We used to go to the Jewish Center to play basketball or C.Y.O at Saint John's or we'd go to the YMCA for swimming and basketball, they used to play the industrial league and everything else. That was all our entertainment, we didn't have to go to Boston, Hartford, or New York or anything like that. Not even go into New Haven, we had everything you could possibly have. We had shoemakers, we had laundromats, we had sandlot ball fields. We played sandlot ball right in the middle of Legion Avenue; there was Blakeslee's lot where they used to keep their heavy equipment right next to the grammar school that we used to go. And there's where we played softball and football. And we used our own imagination. That's how we entertained ourselves. Scranton school on Scranton Street, we'd go there in the summertime, we spent all summer, we played softball, we played horseshoes, we played paddle tennis, and that was how we entertained ourselves. Italians and the Jewish people. We got along perfect. It was a beautiful neighborhood and we all got along perfect because we used to go to the Jewish Center—we were allowed to play basketball, ping-pong, they would have dances and we'd go to the Jewish dances. It was a community where there was no segregation, put it that way. Everybody did everything together. In today's world we've lost that value. Our kids, when they were going to school, it wasn't like us. We lived within a block of everybody. Here [in Orange] they live within miles and really they have no communication other than in school. See, we had communications after school all the time. We never lost that value and we always respected the family and other people.

"LA COOPERATIVA"
Francesco Maturo, owner, at center
with son Charles and granddaughter Lucille,
Legion Avenue, 1927

Rossi family album

"La Cooperativa Italiana"

William Rossi spoke at a picnic table during the Oak Street Reunion picnic
on August 27, 2000.

My grandfather, Francesco Maturo, set up shop there on Legion Avenue. He
opened up a confectionery store, America's first cooperative food market. He
opened up a grocery store—"La Cooperativa Italiana," the Italian cooperative—
and when people wanted certain goods and things, what they did, he had them pay
up front so he could buy these particular goods because he knew now that he was
going sell them. And he used to give them a piece of paper. Now nothing pre-
printed, nothing authoritative, authenticated or anything like that. A piece of
paper because in those days everybody lived on the honor system. The honor
system was prevalent. The honor system was widespread. You gave your word on
the handshake and it meant a great deal. A handshake on a contract was better
than any written legal thing they could write up in Philadelphia or anywhere. It
meant something. You know why? That person's character was in that hand at that
time. It meant a lot. And he sold them at discount. Who came in there? Just the
Italians. If I remember correctly there were three or four Jewish people that came
in there who understood what a cooperative was—whether they were Italian Jews
or Jewish Jews, or whatever it was, but they were friendly people and they saw a
chance to save a dollar. And it worked very well.

"It Was Like Italy"

Lou Guarino spoke at the kitchen table of his home in Orange on August
24, 2000.

The neighborhood where we grew up was Legion Avenue, where I was born, me
and my twin brother, we got five brothers, and we all lived there, and my mother
and father. We had everything there; you didn't have to go to New York, Boston, or
Hartford for entertainment or for shopping. We had bakeries, we had grocery
stores—not like Stop and Shop—but we had grocery stores, we had dry goods
stores, Kliggers, and everybody would go to Kliggers and buy their one suit a year,
their first communion suit and shoes. We had pizza there, we had delis, the Jewish
deli, the Italian deli, we had Gallucci's Market, we had the best sausage in town, was
Perri's Sausage. He was the king of sausage. We had Lender's Bagels, everything
was there, we had movies, we had the Victory Theatre. We had everything. We even
had the hardware store, we didn't have Home Depot but Alpert's Hardware Store
where they could buy things to fix the house up. Because it was walking distance and
that's the way they lived. That's the way it is in Italy, these small towns, exactly the
same way. They got everything there what they make out of it. And that's the way
they live. They [my parents] were comfortable, they were in heaven. Because they

ITALIAN WAKE AT HOME
Upstate New York

Mongillo family album

knew so and so and that so and so. We didn't have to go downtown for anything. The only time we went downtown was the big treat at Christmas time. You'd go to Shartenbergs and all that for Santa Claus and that was it.

"FUNERAL PROCESSIONS AND WAKES AT HOME"

Pat Barone spoke in the living room of his West Haven home on May 5, 1999.

I could remember sitting on Oak Street in front of my father's store and Saint Anthony's church is where it is today and the funerals would come up Oak Street. And they had the horse and wagons; they used to call them "the hacks." All black, you see them sometimes in the movies. The guys that owned them, it's just like ordering a car for a funeral. They used to order a hack to go to the funeral. They had pieces over the horse's ears and they would put roses in there. They would really wash them and polish them and everything. The people that were poor, they walked in back of the hacks to the cemetery. In front they had the hearse wagon first with the body. They had a band that used to play. The band used to play all the way up Oak Street, cross Legion Avenue, cross all that swamp and meadows where the boulevard is today and there was a little wooden bridge going over the river there and they used to bring the bodies up into Saint Lawrence Cemetery. They played like church music going all the way up there; you could hear a lot of the noise, the trombones and the heavy music. In them days, you died in the house—you were three days in the house. The wakes were twenty-four hours a day. You had a black ribbon on the front door and the front door was open and people came and went. If you were lucky enough to have a parlor they took all the furniture out and they laid the body in the parlor and everybody came. And people would congregate in the kitchen, here or there, have a cup of coffee or something and then go if you didn't have a parlor. And somebody was on watch twenty-four hours a day. There was somebody in the room with the casket twenty-four hours a day. They used to have them in the house three days, they used to wake them for three days and three nights. And today they got to go for two hours, they think ... see, all that is all lost, and that's the thing that bothers me, all that is lost. All that there closeness of the people, all that beautiful love of the people. Everybody tried to help everybody.

"Cumpari and Cummare"

My mother and father made a lot of friends and of course because my father was in business, which doesn't happen today, they always looked for somebody better. When the kids got confirmation or when they had to baptize somebody, they'd go pick out a cream of the crop someplace, like a businessman or a lawyer or a professional person. My father I don't know how many—I think it's twenty-five or thirty kids he baptized and confirmed. They would go and buy him a little watch, a little ring—that was the gift for the confirmation. And God forbid—we used to call him the godfather, "'o cumpare"—God forbid you met him on the street or he came in the house and you didn't shake hands and hug him and kiss him like he was a brother. Sometime you got the whack in front of him or you got it afterward, see? When we went to see one of my father's "cumpares" or "cummares," a godmother or godfather, like they would come to our house for dinner, or we'd go there. On the way my father would give us the schooling, both in English and Italian. "That's all I want to do is look at you." And when the people came [to our house], the guests got served first and the guests ate. We ate afterwards. Unless there was only maybe one or two then we all sat at the table. But if they had a few people we ate afterward and my mother would put a little table—she would call it "'o bancone," she put a little "bancone" over there, and we'd eat on it, all right? That was a great thing in our life, though. We loved it. We respected our people. When these people came over the thing was they never brought meats or stuff like that because my father had the store. But my father, when we went someplace, he always took a bag, he put fruits and some nuts and stuff and he used to bring it. Or bring a gallon of wine. That was the big thing, you know? You never went no place without bringing something. And you were greeted and everybody loved you. You loved everybody. You respected everybody. Everybody was "'o zi'," "'a zi,'" uncle or aunt. You didn't call them "Hey John." "'O zi',' "'a zi'," even though they weren't related to you, that was the respect. And God forbid somebody came to your house and said to your parents that you went by them and didn't even say hello to them or didn't respect them. You'd get it, but you'd get it good. So that punishment that they gave you educated you—educated you that this is what life is all about, this is what you have to do. They were humble, they didn't have anything and they didn't have any education and they didn't have a lot of money. All that there, I don't know where it went. And I keep saying this with my wife all the time, I don't know where all that stuff went, how it disappeared from this world.

"The Black Families"

Lou Guarino spoke at the kitchen table of his home in Orange on August 24, 2000.

I'll tell you about the blacks. We had a family of blacks living right across the street from us on Auburn Street. I'm talking about the '30s and we had a couple of black families and they were wonderful people. They respected us, we respected them, no problem. Went to school with them, no problem whatsoever. Like today, I mean today it's different. In those days we didn't think of black and white. They were people. Just people they were. We didn't say he was black or African or anything like that. He was his name.

"We Never Left the Neighborhood"

Here's what the people did when they first came over [from Italy]. Everybody would go down to Oak Street, Spruce and Oak Street, right near the bathhouse. That's when they first came over on the boat; that's where they would congregate and live for a while. Then from there, they'd move. They'd move maybe five, six blocks up the road, right? And they always moved, like my parents. We moved at least four, five times, from Spruce Street to Davenport Avenue, to Scranton Street, to Auburn Street, back to Legion Avenue. I was born on Legion Avenue. And everybody seemed to do the same thing. We never moved out of the neighborhood because the neighborhood was so beautiful, you had everything right there and everybody loved everybody and cared about everybody. It was just great. And fortunately, when I got married I became a milkman in 1957 and fortunately my route was in the neighborhood, which I was lucky. And you go through the neighborhood early morning, especially Sunday morning, you'd smell that sauce, that spaghetti and everything, cooking. Oh Madonna! And the same thing with the Jewish bagels, the bagels and rolls at Ticosky's and Lender's and you could smell that aroma. Now today everything is manufactured, God knows where and you don't get that feeling anymore.

Our parents, the same way. When all the Italians and the Jewish, they would sit on their porch, we had a porch in our two family house. And they would sit on their porch and just watch the traffic, whatever traffic there was in those days. There was no cars [laughing], I mean you had how many cars? Half dozen cars. We used to see the black and white car, which was the police car, you know. Everybody would be on the porch and they'd be talking to one another, "Hey, Josephine," across the street from one another. And that was the neighborhood. In fact there was a woman across the street, the Civitello girl, I remember she used to make her own coffee beans and brew them and when she cooked em', oh you could smell that thing! You thought Dunkin Donut had coffee? The smell of that was beautiful, yeah.

❝The Jewish Women Helped Her❞

William Rossi spoke at a picnic table during the Oak Street Reunion picnic on August 27, 2000.

My mother was eight years old when her mother died. And so her father married the maid of the house. They usually did that; the maid was there for so many years and took care of the children and so forth. Usually they were next in line for marriage. It was very easy, you didn't have to go looking, you know? And then she died. So my mother, at twelve years old, became the matron mother of two young boys. There were things she had to buy downtown, she had to learn to go downtown because where all the supply houses were. And she used to have to go through Sylvan Avenue and one time she got lost a little bit. Sylvan Avenue at that time was a Jewish neighborhood. There were a lot of little Jewish stores, supply houses. And the women there usually sat in front of the stores waiting for the customers to come. They noticed that my mother in some sort of trouble. So they took her in—she could barely speak English. Well to make a long story short, they became my mother's mentors after long and she in turn learned the Jewish alphabet, the Jewish numerical system, and we used to have fun at home. We used to ask my mother to repeat the numerical system or the alphabet in Yiddish. This is part of what New Haven was like. Now here was a little immigrant girl, couldn't even speak English too well and these Jewish women helped her. And they gave her all kinds of advice and things and helped her out. One of them even walked down the supply store with her that first time. And this is all real. It's the real real. And I have seen so many changes, I have seen it change from A to Z, that it hurts me to think that we of a certain generation have produced this change by our production of people.

In Italian we have a word, "'o supiérchio," that means it's superfluous—too many things. Too many toys. Which toy do I play with next? In those days you made your toys.

"You Had To Speak Yiddish and Italian"

Raniero "Rene" Pantani spoke at a picnic table during the Oak Street Reunion picnic on August 27, 2000. He was a standup comic under the name "Rene Carle."

My father was from Le Marche, my mother was from Cerreto Sannita, near Benevento and I was in born in "L.A.," Legion Avenue. On Oak Street, you couldn't get a job if you didn't speak Italian or Yiddish. I went to work for Max Wax Kosher Baloney, an old man. He told me how to sprachen Yiddish [to speak Yiddish]. I would help in the fruit department, a woman would come in and she'd say, "a half funt of tzipolla," she wanted a half-pound of onions. And I'd say, Mister Max, a half funt a baloney! He'd answer, "Aieee! You think I'm deaf? She wants tzepollas, [yelling] tzepollas!"

Posso parlare l'italiano anche, napoletano, terra siciliano, I can speak Italian too, even Neapolitan and Sicilian. Languages are the best communication you can have. In those days we used to beat each other up, who had a gang on the corner. We could walk from the boulevard all the way up Oak Street to Congress Avenue and nobody would bother you. It was civilized, a girl could walk the street any hour of the night—nobody would touch her. And if it was late, a neighbor would see to it, "Maryanne, come on, I'll give you a quick lift home."

"Weddings on Legion Avenue"

Jenny Fazzone spoke in the kitchen of Kim and Mike Rogers's home on Febraury 11, 2000. She recalled walking home from work during the 1938 hurricane as trees fell around her.

My father had a horse and buggy. He used to have the horses right in the back where we lived because we had a big yard. My sister Anna got married with horse and buggy. He used to go to weddings. At that time they used to have weddings and people used to go from house to house, they used to throw a tray of confetti with money. The horses were all decorated clean and nice. We used to decorate the horses with red and white ribbons and we used to put sheets in the buggy for the brides. That was nice, the carriage in the summertime, getting married in the summertime, everything was open, nothing was closed. It was just a buggy, really. When my father used to come back from the wedding, he had a lot of candy and money in the carriage there. And he had a chest there and we used to put everything in that chest and the kids used to have a ball getting the candy out of the chest and the money. At that time they used to get married, they used to go from house to people would say, "Stop at the house," and throw confetti at you. They used to make a tray and they'd come out and throw it all over you.

"She Screamed. I Screamed"

Josie DeBenedet spoke at the kitchen table of her North Haven home on June 10, 1999.

We didn't even have a bathtub. On a Sunday we used to have the big washtubs in the kitchen. After we finished eating then my mother would put me in the tub there to take a bath. In the summer we'd go to the bathhouse on Oak Street. It was a nickel. They'd give a little bar of soap and a towel. And one day I went in. I don't remember if I forgot the towel or the soap bar. So I went to get it. There was a woman there where she collected money. I said I forgot whatever it was. Then when I went back I went in the wrong stall. There was a colored woman—I had never seen a naked colored woman—I screamed. It looked like a bear. Even her, she screamed. And I screamed, I said, "Oooh, excuse me." I was a kid.

"The Fruit Wrappers"

Pat Barone spoke in the living room of his West Haven home on May 5, 1999.

We had the meat store and in order to preserve the fruit, when it came in, every orange, every apple was wrapped in tissue paper. You see that sometimes today. We used to have a sheet that we used to mark down. Twenty for Mr. Barone, twenty for Mr. Capone, twenty for them—till we ran out. Everybody came there. That's what they used for toilet paper. The storekeepers, they'd go to the store-keepers and ask for it. And of course you try to satisfy everybody so you put every-body on a quota. And we used to count them out and hand them to the people. All right? Things were really rough. And when you went to the bathroom, you think it's like today? You got toilet paper, you got this, you got that. The reason we moved from Oak Street, there were families, two stores on the ground level, two families on the second level and two families on the third level. The whole four families used one bathroom in the hall, one toilet, not a bathroom. There was no sink, there was no nothing. It was like a little closet. No light in there, nothing. Before they put that in, we used to get up at night, down the hall and out the back and go to the outhouse to go to the bathroom. I can vaguely remember going out-side with the snow on the ground. Before you could go to the bathroom you had to dress up. We had the wooden floors in them days; they used to scrub the wooden floors, scrub the whole hall, the stairs. And everybody in the building did it, didn't say, "Today's your turn." Everybody did it, they started on the top and they came all the way down.

"Saturday Night on Oak Street"

On a Saturday night my mother had a copper kettle—heat the water on the stove. Put the copper kettle on the table and put the three of us in there one at a time. That was our bath. That was how we grew up. Then after a while across the street from us they put the city-run bathhouse on the corner of Oak Street and Spruce Street. And they used to have a special every Saturday, five cents towel and a bar of soap. And you went in to take a shower not a bath. You didn't have a tub or anything like that. They didn't worry about putting anything on the floor for your feet, they didn't worry about you're going to get sick, everybody is there or everybody is around you. Everybody went in, they took a shower. And it was all open, you didn't have a special stall that you went into, all the things that they got today. That's why I say they got too much today. And we were happy.

"We Shared Each Other's Dishes"

Lou and Rose Marie Guarino spoke at the kitchen table of their home in Orange on August 24, 2000.

We were exposed to all kinds of [ethnic] foods, we tried everything. My mother used to cook eel and send it across the street and the next day, the lady would say, "What was that?" My mother would say, "Eel! Ahhh, you made me eat eel!" Or she'd make artichokes and she'd send artichokes to somebody, whoever it was, a non-Italian and they'd say, "What are you supposed to do with this thing?" They didn't even know what to do with it. On Fridays, it was meatless, and so every Friday night you had the standard, you know, it was either filet of fish of some kind, pasta fasule, pasta and beans, or pizza. That was nice because if my mother made pizza, my Jewish neighbors across the street ate pizza that night, she sent some over. She made matza ball soup, she'd send the bowl over to our house. The Polish lady made kielbasa or whatever, they shared, they'd send a little taste, you know, just a little taste—a big bowl like this! They were very generous, they were very compatible. All of them. It didn't make any difference. Like we had Rositani's bakery, which was Rositani's pizza and we would go there, order pizza, take it home. And the Jewish people would do the same thing, they'd go to Rositani. And vice versa, we would go to the Jewish deli and get a corned beef and cabbage sandwich or something or lox or cream cheese and bagels. I tell you, it's just something that the politicians ruin on us. It's so valuable that a neighborhood like that [existed]. I think Mayor Lee destroyed the city itself because he sold the two schools in New Haven to Yale. He sold Commercial High and he sold Hillhouse High, which was well known throughout the country at that time. There's a lot of people in New Haven—hate him because he destroyed. Well, the feeling was, things are old, knock it down, build new. But today they're looking at it differently. Restore. Preserve.

34

Highways and Urban Renewal: New Haven Forever Changed

After two unsuccessful mayoral campaigns, Richard C. Lee defeated the Republican incumbent William Celantano in 1953, setting the stage for one of the most sweeping and controversial urban renewal projects of any city in the country. The youngest mayor in the city's history brought considerable talents to City Hall: strong organizing skills, a winner-take-all management style, and a knack for attracting the most talented men and women in the country to his administration. As mayor, Lee made urban renewal his first priority, hiring top-notch grant writers who placed New Haven first in line for the five hundred million dollars available under the Federal Housing Act of 1954. Under the bold and assertive Lee administration, which received the highest percentage of federal funding for redevelopment of any city in the country, New Haven's renewal project became the nation's blueprint for eradicating slums.

Richard Lee's political master stroke for selling his renewal plan for the city came in the creation of the CAC, the Citizens Action Committee, which included Republican businessmen, the President of Yale, Whitney Griswold, representatives from the New Haven railroad, the president of a local bank, and a chairman of the board of a local utility.58 The committee's four hundred members lent credibility to the mayor's ambitious plans, removing any suspicion of partisan politics or criticism aimed at a headstrong leader who would win at all costs. Conspicuously absent from the committee were any social service agencies or representatives of the poor and working class who stood in the path of the administration's wrecking ball and would be most affected by the negative aspects of urban renewal. At the time, many evicted from their homes had little recourse but to move on, and their internalized protest and deep resentment over the loss of their neighborhoods reverberates through the city to this day.

New Haven's dilapidated and neglected neighborhoods slated for renewal were referred to by city planners as "slum areas." Lee's planning consultant, Maurice Rotival, redesigned New Haven as a gateway city, as an open door where highway traffic from Interstate 91 north and 95 south could conveniently enter by the newly constructed Oak Street Connector. At the mayor's insistence, the Connector was designed to cut a wide swath through the heart of the city to attract suburban shoppers to its modern downtown stores where a parking garage adjacent to the new Malley's, designed by Paul Rudolph, would handle the anticipated high volume of incoming traffic.

By the mid-1950s, Richard Lee had become a spokesman for urban renewal, inviting officials from other cities to watch bulldozers demolish slum areas and level three blocks of the prime downtown commercial properties. The mayor appeared in magazine articles that praised his political skill and courage, portraying him as a man who was bringing an old dying city back to life. The first Head Start and Legal Assistance programs in the nation were launched in New Haven. During the heady days of urban renewal, New Haven was looked upon as a centerpiece of the program's success and was given the title "Model City."

To construct a wide corridor for the Oak Street Connector, heavily populated sidestreets extending on Wooster Street's south side were demolished, destroying houses that stood in the way of the Connector's path. The farmers market and homes close to the railroad station in the Hill were cleared; the commercial heart of the Legion Avenue neighborhood was bulldozed and with it many residential homes. The Church Street project cleared three city blocks of established businesses at the city's core, replacing them with Malley's, Macy's, and later The Omni hotel and the Chapel Square Mall.

Mayor Lee's ambitious plan to revitalize New Haven destroyed the rhythms of life in the quotidian worlds of its working class neighborhoods and transformed the city's intricate human mosaic into heaps of rubble. Busy city streets and well-worn sidewalks where people walked back and forth to work turned into empty boulevards or disappeared from city maps. Local mom and pop stores—neighborhood landmarks where proprietors and customers had forged old bonds of friendships— were closed and knocked down. Vibrant multi-ethnic neighborhoods teeming with large families who prayed at nearby churches and synagogues and whose children attended the same schools and played together in its streets, where neighbors called to each other from tenement house windows, and where friends and families sat on front porches and stoops or gathered around backyard picnic tables beneath grape arbors, were razed for highways and cleared for modern high rises. Automobiles replaced sidewalks as a means of getting to work; elevators replaced walk-ups. Many residents forced to leave found the new private spaces and single dwellings of the suburbs the kind of place where neighbors hardly knew each other, replacing forever the familiar sounds and lively shared spaces of the old city. In *City: Urbanism and Its End*, Douglas Rae noted that 2,216 businesses in the city were lost and 4,752 families in Wooster Square, the Hill, Fair Haven, and Oak Street (Legion Avenue) were displaced during urban renewal.[59] In his pamphlet "Relocating Families: The New Haven Experience 1956-1966," Alvin A. Mermin, who served as director of the Family Relocation Office for the Lee administration during urban renewal, described the chaotic and often improvisational process of relocating hundreds of displaced families because of poor planning strategies or clear guidelines from city or federal government.[60] As the trend to live in suburbs accelerated in the late 1960s and '70s, the Oak Street Connector, which had been heralded as the gateway for attracting shoppers to the city, became the highway for the exodus out of New Haven.

What New Haven's housing experts and city planners considered substandard housing at the time of urban renewal during the 1950s—poor plumbing facilities, worn finishes on exteriors and unfinished cellars—was an accepted way of life for many of New Haven's Italians who kept their modest homes and cold water apartments meticulously clean. Substandard housing conditions and street addresses were not as important as the assurance of familiar surroundings and the embrace of security one found in New Haven's old ethnic neighborhoods. One Redevelopment Agency housing director epitomized the arrogance of the Lee administration's plan, stating that eliminating slums meant a chance to "upgrade not only a family's housing but also its mode of life."[61] But for Italians who had worked long and hard hours living frugally to save money to buy homes or operated small family stores in New Haven's old neighborhoods, owning a home or business meant attainment of the American dream. Some looked forward to moving out of old run-down neighborhoods to better areas, a trend that started in the 1920s. But for many who did not want to leave their homes and streets and were displaced by urban renewal, the loss of neighborhood meant the loss of identity, of culture, of lifestyle, and of self.[62]

"It Was a Political Highway"

Eugene and Frances Calzetta spoke on October 10, 1998 in the living room of the Forbes Avenue family home their father built in 1922.

During the depression my grandfather bought the land from Fulton Terrace to Stiles Street, where the highway is today. When the state took the land—I remember in the auctions he paid thirty-five, forty dollars. The highest he ever paid was seventy-five dollars for a piece of property. The state [in the late '50s] gave only the Depression price—they gave him what he paid for it plus all the taxes he paid for twenty years, whatever it was. They said, "Take this or go to court." But if you didn't take that and you went to court you weren't going to get . . . because they condemned for eminent domain. They stole that—how much you think that land was worth? That thing is probably worth eight or ten million dollars. It was a political highway. The highway was going through the [areas] of cronies and people of power. The only reason why you have the screwy design is because a lot of political strings pulled, power versus nonpower and the reason it ended up in the awfulness of what the highway has been and continues is because it was all politically controlled and who would get what. And that's why the configuration is all wrong and they could go through and steal from and essentially were much quieter here with the farms. It was the same Italian people—only higher density—on the Wooster Street side [of the Quinnipiac Bridge]. Mayor Lee and Ribicoff, the mayor's buddy up at the state, held the power over a powerless group of people. The guy who headed the DOT at the time had glory on his mind and nothing on hell's earth would have made him change his mind on that highway. So the people had absolutely nothing to say despite the fact that there was outcry from downtown—the

INTERCHANGE AND OAK STREET CONNECTOR PLAN, 1956

City of New Haven Archives

Wooster Square area—because they were knocking it all down and rumbling over here because we didn't have the numbers and they were just coming through and taking the farmland for next to nothing. It was raw political power. They at that time did not listen to the people. Joe Mariani was the construction company and he told them when they were building this thing. You know when you come off I-91 into here? Joe Mariani told them, "It's [the connector] going to be a death trap. It's wrong, it should never be." And the dip where you come down from downtown, that interchange to London and Hartford, Mariani said, "That's the worst possible thing is going to happen—you're going to get people killed. That's the biggest mistake they'll ever make in their life, having the traffic come and cut across into a highway." No truer words were said. But they rammed it through. As a matter of fact, Joe got killed himself. He had a heart attack under the bridge coming up that way—the same place he told them was the most dangerous. And the reason they done that was because of C. Cowles—see, C. Cowles is powerful. Ever notice there, the C. Cowles building is about six inches from the highway. That's the reason; C. Cowles had enough power; he wouldn't cut a deal. According to legend, Sargent wanted a new building but did not want to pay for it so if they could reconfigure it so that it would take up the old Sargent building, they could get a new building without paying a penny. But you can't prove this—it's the common knowledge of the territory but who you going to tell? No one is going to believe you anyway. Nine tenths of the people know it. A lot of people hate Mayor Lee; that's the truth. Because they know what he was. They know that he was a thief. As a driver for Chief Collins and Mayor Lee you couldn't help but hear this because, what the hell, you're driving and you're not that far and they're in the back seat. And it was understood that you'd keep your mouth closed. I can talk now—they're all dead except Lee. They didn't have ten cents in their pocket. His [Lee's] brother was a salesman for Bethlehem steel; all the work was given to him for the Coliseum. He made a fortune with it. They're all millionaires. They didn't have ten cents in their pocket. How do you get this all of a sudden?

"Mayor Lee and New Haven"

Ralph Marcarelli spoke at Cavaliere's grocery store May 6, 1998.

Bill Celantano finally was elected mayor after many years of Irish Democratic rule in the city. Now when I was a small kid I can remember even the first election and the fervor of the Italians—it was very much a pro-Italian as far as the Italians were concerned—battle. The ranks of the Republican Party being filled by Italians because of the discrimination of the Irish Democrats—the Irish period—and they were all Democrats. That's what drew the line; I don't think there were any particularly philosophic reasons. Colonel Ullman who was the state party chairman was wise enough to understand that the Italians would be fertile field for enrollment in the Republican Party since the Irish in fact were all Democrats. And he got the Italians interested and into the party. Bill Celantano had started the redevelopment plan but hadn't done much about it. Richard Lee seized on—I think always to aggrandize himself because he had huge draconian ambitions to go way beyond the mayoralty of the city. He might have had he not been as diabolically proud as he was—he might well have gotten to the U.S. Senate. He found something to launch himself into the national spotlight and he did that largely in conjunction with Yale University, with a group of young Turks of that day, all archliberals, all imbued with what government could or couldn't do. And by and large, there was no couldn't. It was all could do, should do. And he began to expand on this theme of redevelopment, which of course is an irony because he didn't redevelop anything. My notion of redevelopment is that you do exactly that: you take something and then you change it from what it was to something different while maintaining its identity. I was a young Republican and I was absolutely incensed to see the city begin to fall to pieces under the wrecker's ball. And that's precisely what was happening there with these grandiose, utopian schemes, which of course never really took effect. We had a thriving city, pretty much self-contained. Perfection? No, of course not. But we didn't have any slums in any real sense at all—there were no slums in this city. There were some poor neighborhoods but they were not slums, as we understand them today. And even those poorer neighborhoods were very colorful, very active, very human, just thriving with business and activities. One only has to think of Grand Avenue from its start downtown all the way up to the [Fair Haven] Heights—it was a beehive of activity, store after store. Downtown was wonderful. I don't think you had to go outside of a few square blocks to get anything you really wanted in terms of trade and commerce and products. And that went from buttons and pins and needles through yard goods, through furniture to luxurious fur coats and diamond rings—it was all very readily available downtown. Dick Lee in essence destroyed all that. Now did he do it on purpose? I don't think so. I think he was misguided to put it mildly, I think he was deliberately devious—he was doing that to further his own political career. And he did indeed get national publicity for the "Model City." I used to get up and give speeches and say: This is the very model of what a city should not be. But it was the Model City, it was the city in which the federal government spent more per capita on the so-called redevelopment than in any other city in the country, and of course ultimately we had and have a gross failure. There is no downtown. The origins of the no downtown were in Richard Lee. To this very day he still manages to get himself honors and medals and so forth—that's all he ever did. And people still fall for it. I think it was interesting when Ed Logue [Redevelopment Agency Director] died some months back, *The New York Times* article about him stated that New Haven was his great failure. Apart from its lasting economic impact, it had a terrible social impact. From the standpoint of the Italians it had the effect—some would say and I would be one of them—that it had the deliberate effect of driving many Italians out of the city. There's no proof; no one is going to say it. Lee was a megalomaniac. The one ward that he could not take was the tenth ward, center of which was Wooster Street. And that had been of course the symbolic and maybe real center of the Italian population in terms of sheer numbers. And that used to enrage him to no end that many people have said and I quite believe that it is no coincidence that I-95 and I-91 both went right through that area. It's true that he kept Wooster Square largely however due to the efforts of the owners of the property. Wooster Square was kept sort of as the Hollywood stage setting when guests would come in to view his great successes; they would bring them down here for redevelopment. He sent people packing to East Haven, Hamden, Woodbridge, and Branford, Orange—wherever they could afford to go, heartbroken very often. You know the

Italians of course had the so-called village mentality. They settled among their own—they wouldn't have moved. Perfectly comfortable to be there; they did aspire by and large . . . their children often did, to get to the lawns and the dream houses. But those who were here had everything here and had no reason to leave. You don't leave a place when you're perfectly happy there. Well, they were forced to, because there was no two ways about it. Lee was smart enough to buy virtually everybody off; there were a handful of us who would make a public outcry and sometimes the papers would pick it up because they had to print something. But you battled hope and against hope but you were pretty certain that given the politics of the day—he was a master politician—there was no question about it. He in conjunction with Arthur Barbieri, in a certain sense, bought up the city and turned it into a city where it was no longer possible to elect a Republican mayor. The population itself did that and so their bait by dint of jobs and patronage and so forth. So you had an element in the city which was the political army that was turned out on Election Day that was obviously feeding from the troughs so to speak. They weren't interested in seeing these people thrown out. Slowly but surely you were getting people who might vote Republican leaving the city so they weren't here to vote against those people at all. And the irony was that this wasn't any grassroots kind of thing. Grassroots were certainly involved with all kinds of skullduggery and shenanigans—Lee voted the cemeteries and admitted to it. I was at a public dinner where he admitted to that—ha, ha, ha. They'd do all kinds of things. And actually they co-opted the entire city. But again it wasn't a grassroots thing; it was something led by the elite. And among the liberals, that's always the way it happens—the elite lead. Ostensibly for the good of the public but that doesn't really happen. It certainly didn't happen here. Yale University, the ruling WASP element centered in Wiggin and Dana and Tyler and Cooper Law firms—they made a lot of money on this; that was the whole point. Tons of people were making lots of money. There was no viable alternative because he would buy off the opposition and bought off much of the opposition in jobs or patronage of one kind or another. The [CAC] Citizens Action Committee was no more than a front group for Richard Lee; they would rubber stamp whatever he wanted. They were people with prestige around the community. If they were aware of what they were doing they should be ashamed if they're still living that they made themselves party to any of that. If they weren't, they were totally duped. Of course and he really knew how to flatter people all over the place—he was an ingenious politician, I won't take that away from him.

They can say anything they want; I say take a look at New Haven. Wooster Street is a ghost of the past now; it isn't the thriving hub it used to be. The human mosaic that I knew growing up in New Haven has been shattered. It's painful for me to leave Wooster Square to go in any direction to see the changes wrought. And this can be laid at the doorstep of Richard C. Lee and company, no question. Would it have been different had he not. . . ? I think so. Exactly how different, I have no way of knowing. But when you stop to think that millions and countless millions were poured into this city to achieve the effect we have, it's a travesty, absolute travesty, virtually criminal as far as I'm concerned. There are little pieces of it extant, which is a sort of a sadness. It's like looking at the ruins of Pompeii, you'll have a glimpse of the glory that was the mosaic and the decorations and so forth and so on but of course you see ruin all around you. That's New Haven.

"Everything a Model City Should Not Be"

Emiddio Cavaliere and Ralph Marcarelli spoke at Cavaliere's Wooster Street grocery store on May 6, 1998.

They were driven out of the city—they went to wherever they could find and they had to get mortgages on their houses, which they never had. Most of these architects that were from Yale. Look what they did for Libby's [Italian Pastry Shop]. It had to be a French style. Look at the damned thing across the street! It looks like a bridge. The guy had no choice—that's what's got to go up; it had to be a French style. To me it looks like the side of a bridge, that whole architectural thing. They had to go along with it. But there are any number of people who will never be convinced otherwise than this: that the tenth and eleventh wards were strongly Republican wards. They had backed Celantano. They were the Italian wards. They had rebelled against many years of the Irish Democratic rule of the town and the subsequent persecution of the Italians. And finally they managed to elect Bill Celantano as mayor. So this ward in particular—Tony Paolillo was the ward chairman—remained staunchly Republican. This in the face of Lee's ever-increasing influence in the city. He could not break this ward, simply could not take this ward. Coincidental? Of course anybody can make the argument. Was it coincidental that you had the conjunction of I-95 and I-91 right in this ward wiping everything out? We don't think it was coincidental under any circumstances. I say it was a mini-Kosovo, a form of ethnic cleansing. They'll deny it but I'll assert it. What they did was use the square as a Hollywood stage setting so that when people came in to see the marvels wrought by this great mayor, they would be brought down to Wooster Square—gorgeous homes anyway of course—that was preserved by the Italians who had been there all those years and fundamentally the undertakers. You see the funeral directors were down here in abundance and they had a large part really in stabilizing the neighborhood. Obviously the presence of the Italian national church there, Saint Michael's, did as well. I said it more than once and I said it publicly: that redevelopment was going to be the cause of the fall of our parish churches. And it has been. Saint Patrick's went; Saint John's went near Yale. Saint Michael's, which had 10,000 parishioners up till the '40s, is truly in jeopardy. It doesn't seem to be at the moment but I assure you it is. We had our first holy communion on Sunday. Do you know how many first holy communicants there were? One. Do you have any idea how many funerals we've had in the past year? About 140. Now if that doesn't tell a tale. There's no more families. They closed the schools and there's nobody else; they closed Saint Michael's school and they closed the Polish school, Saint Stan's. But the ills of the city have their root in

Lee's redevelopment plan—I will say that until the day I die. What we are today is a direct result of what they did. I said way back then it was the very model of what a city should not be. They took down brownstone houses next door. They could have repaired that. Brownstone you take down? My God. I said it aloud then: if you're going to redevelop neighborhoods, then redevelop the neighborhood. What does that mean? That means you erect some type of temporary housing someplace—the city had massive properties everywhere if they wanted to do it— go into the rehabilitation of a neighborhood, rehabilitate the homes in whatever manner you do so, move those people temporarily and then put them back where they came from.

"IT WAS DONE ON PURPOSE"

Andrea Colavolpe spoke at the Saint Andrew's Society on June 14, 1999.

They wanted to renovate the city. Mayor Lee couldn't beat our alderman De-Palma. How could he defeat this person? I have to demolish it and defeat the Republicans. It was done on purpose—he destroyed an Italian neighborhood here in New Haven—an unforgettable thing—because he couldn't defeat Michael DePalma, a Republican he never could beat. He knocked everything down. The only way I can beat him I got to knock down this place and maybe I can get the Democrats in. And that's the way he got them in—by knocking everything down. And that's the way it is. But in one way it was good he knocked it down because there were houses without bathrooms—everything was outside. They didn't have bathtubs—everything was outside. All these homes he destroyed, few had bathtubs and bathrooms in the house. Then came the big supermarkets that replaced all the small stores my mother used to still like. She used to go out in the morning and did her shopping; everyone did their little shopping at the butchers, the vegetable stores.

(translated from Italian)

"THE MONEY RAN OUT"

Nick Aiello spoke at the union office on January 27, 1999.

It was politically motivated. That was a Republican stronghold from what I gather, see? And so redevelopment came through, so what would you do normally? If you're looking to get rid of opposition . . . I'm not saying that's what happened but that's the rumor. That Wooster Square ward, that tenth ward was a Republican stronghold for quite some time, all the time. Politically it's a Democratic city. The only Republican mayor we've ever had since Murphy was Celentano. Since Celentano there hasn't been a Republican mayor. They took a chance at redevelopment. Good idea. But then the money ran out. Like with Long Wharf, they got all kinds of money. Then when the money runs out, you wind up with empty buildings like you have in New Haven. Beautiful city, all kinds of pastry stores, all kinds of Italian import stores, all kinds of grocery stores. Then came the supermarkets. We used to have a grocery store on every corner.

❝IT WAS THE ONLY LIFE THEY KNEW❞

Terese Gabucci spoke at her daughter's North Branford deli on July 28, 2000.

It was really a neighborhood. Most of them were wooden, two family houses. The only one family houses were on the small side streets. Legion Avenue was mostly all two and three family homes. You didn't lock your doors; if you were sick your neighbors ran over. Everybody knew everybody else. No one ever moved away. When I got married I lived right around the corner. All of us, we didn't leave the neighborhood. The Jews and the Italians really struggled to get ahead because they were all just working people. It wasn't an affluent area—all working people. The only reason my parents moved was because the state came through. None of them wanted to move. A lot of the old neighbors, they moved up to Hamden. It's funny how they all migrated together. Mayor Lee was going to make it—was it a highway or a connector? Well, they developed Frontage Road but they never did anything with Legion Avenue, not on our end. Half of it is just barren. It's nothing. He did nothing with it. Those people would have never left there, my mother, none of them would have left there. You know, it was the only life they knew. Now there's just a parking lot—those were all little family-owned stores, Radin's chicken market, you used to go in, pick out the chicken walking around, he'd kill it, and next to him was Joe Mondillo's garage, Rositani's Bakery, the Victory Theatre. In those days it isn't like today; there was no organized protest. Some of the houses they didn't touch. There are still houses on Legion Avenue; there were still a few families left there and they're probably the same old families that were there anyway, unless they're all dead. My father died six months after they moved. And we always say, "They missed it, all their lives just revolved around that little neighborhood. We walked to Saint Anthony's church, we walked to the football games at Yale Bowl; you walked to everything. My mother and father never owned a car. Mister Mazzacane owned a little store there on Legion Avenue for years and years and everybody in the neighborhood shopped at Mazzacane's. It was a little fresh fruit, vegetables, meats—the typical little Italian grocery store. He sold the store to his cousin. And he was living up in Hamden, but he was driving to New Haven to go the store and he was in a big accident. He wasn't accustomed to driving around like that. Here's a little old Italian man—you uprooted him, moved him out to Hamden to a beautiful home—but he had to drive all the way from there to Legion Avenue to run the store. I don't know if the car skidded and went under the bus or a truck—he was killed.

NEW HAVEN BEFORE THE HIGHWAY
Looking east, 1956

City of New Haven Archives

"THEY TOOK AWAY OUR DIGNITY"

Theresa Argento spoke at the kitchen table of her home in the Annex on
May 23, 1999. In 1984, she founded The South Italy Religious Society of
Wooster Street, an organization of seven societies under one umbrella.

Shall I tell you my feelings about Dick Lee? I don't respect him. They can give him
all kinds of honors. To me I don't think he deserves it because he ruined not only the
Italian neighborhood, he ruined the Polish neighborhood; he went all the way

down. He ruined the Hill section. What is there now? Parking lots? That's all there is. We were notified by letter, "eminent domain" that the state was coming through and that we had to move out. In our building my mother had her market, on the other side my husband his dry cleaning plant. He got knocked right out of business. Then upstairs my mother had her apartment and my sister Vinnie lived on the other side and upstairs Lucille and we had our apartment. They notified us we had to get out. Now the whole neighborhood was in an uproar. I remember Lucille who lived on the second floor of our house. She said to me, "I heard in the shop that they're going to take the building." "Lucille," I said, "They won't take the building." Are you kidding? They came right smack through our bedroom! [Years later] Mayor Lee was on a lot of boards with my brother Frank. So he said to my brother one day, "Frank, where did you come from, what neighborhood?" He said, "Wooster Square." The Mayor said, "Yeah, whereabouts on Wooster Square?" So my brother told him. He said, "Oh for Chrissakes, you don't mean to tell me I chased you out?" My brother said, "You certainly did, you came right through our bedroom." There was nothing you could do—it was eminent domain. That's it. It's the government. They come in and say I want this property and you have to give it to me. That's it. I grant you, they call them tenement houses. But one thing I know—that those Italians kept those so-called tenement houses spanking clean. You could have eaten off those floors in the hallways—in the hallways. They would scrub—no linoleum, nothing, no floor covering—they had wood. They would bleach those floors, wash the outside stairs and they helped one another those people there. They get a letter from the state—we have to look. We looked for one whole year. My mother wasn't ready to close [the store]. And my mother enjoyed it—she loved it. She had all her friends that came in—people from the shirt shops, they shopped and in the afternoon she changed her front apron and you came in and had a cup of demitasse with my mother. My mother had friends every day; when I came home from the office I didn't know if there was going to be just us for dinner or she had friends of hers coming. For one year we looked all over the city of New Haven. Now we had a problem. We could have gone to Branford. That would have killed my mother because she wanted to be close to church. We were still going to Saint Michael's. One whole year we had the realtor look. The straw that broke the camel's back was that they took us to a house on Ferry Street; the stench was just disgusting. I was so upset with him, I said, "You're coming up to my apartment—if you can't duplicate what I have, I don't need you—I'll get somebody else." That's how he took us here. And still when we took my mother here, my mother was so despondent that she cried every day. One day I heard the front door close because we had an apartment for my mother in the new house. But I didn't think anything of it. So later I went to get my mother to get up; she's not there. Couldn't find her all day long. We hunted high and low for her; we couldn't find her. We thought she did something to herself, she was so despondent. We called the police department. She evidently was at one of her friends' house but still today we don't know what house she was at, but she came home late at night and wouldn't tell us where she was. She was just unhappy. She was tired of being here. She was so used to seeing people. It's one thing to say I'm going to move out of this neighborhood because I want to go downtown but when you

NEW HAVEN AFTER THE HIGHWAY
Looking east, September, 1957

City of New Haven Archives

come in and say, Well, listen now you have to move whether you like it or not, you have to move. That changes your whole perspective, you don't like it. I don't like what you're telling me. This is a free country? It's not a free country—you're dictating to me. Eminent domain—you can't stop progress. Was that fair to my mother, in her so-called golden years, to be despondent and unhappy? I don't think that was fair to my mother and a lot of those elderly people. They didn't want to move. I grant you some of them probably had a dollar, they could have moved. But a lot of them didn't. Everybody was upset—that's why they still wanted to be together. A lot of them moved to East Haven, to Townsend Avenue, to Morris Cove. My mother got a pittance—not only my mother, but also all those people that owned property be-cause it was the state of Connecticut. And then it was, "Hurry up, hurry up, hurry up, you have to leave," and you had to follow the crowd. They demolished the buildings and then it stayed dormant for a couple of years. What was the reason for letting us get out so quickly? And nobody was against anything. It was just a letter. We didn't even bother to sell. Who was going to buy it? Everybody had to move. And our priest, Father Francis, warned those people; he begged them, "Don't sell your homes." Be-cause all Wooster Street moved out and all Chapel Street, a lot of them were staying with their family members and they felt, "What good are we here? Let's sell our property." So they sold it for a pittance. What upsets me most of all is that nobody ever asked the people that were displaced, "We have property available, would you like to come back to Wooster Square?" We were never given that opportunity. Then they had the redevelopment agency. They had meetings to tell us what they were going to do. Now they're proud of Wooster Square. But Wooster Square was always pretty; they're proud of Wooster Square, they're talking about the perimeter of the park. You know what redevelopment was? If you had a business they would try to es-tablish you and maybe even compensate you for your problems. You know what? We got a pittance even from redevelopment. It was like taking your dignity away from you. We lost our dignity; they didn't respect us at all. You're killing them; you're chas-ing them out of their homes. That's the bottom line, chasing them out of their homes. That's why at the feasts it's one big reunion. When we have dinners we have to tell them, "Would you please sit down, we want to start the program—would you k-i-n-d-l-y sit down?" They're still socializing they're so happy to see one another.

"A SINGLE PURPOSE PROPERTY"

Alphonse Di Benedetto spoke at the home of Kim and Mike Rogers on March 14, 2000. At the time of urban renewal, he was a staunch critic of the "The Model City."

Redevelopment was going to take the property [Planet Shirt Factory]. As an owner where property was going to be taken by redevelopment, you had the first right to rebuy the property and put up a new building of some type. The old had to come down so that whole area on east Chapel and Hamilton and East Street and all that—the redevelopment people had all that property torn down and had it re-designed as "single purpose property," and that's why you have a building with a lot of lawn around it and so forth. So I approached the people at the redevelopment agency and I said, Yeah, we're interested in repurchasing the property and we'd like to build a new building so that our employees can continue to stay in New Haven and work for us. They said, "Well, what kind of a building you want to build?" I said, I want to build a two-story building and we'll have our shirt factory on the second floor and we'll have stores on the first floor. They said, "Oh, no, no, no, you can't do that, we don't want that. It has to be a one-purpose property." I said, "Why don't you want stores?" They said, "Well, we just don't want it." I said, "So what you're telling me is that I got two hundred employees upstairs, comes lunch time there's no place for them to eat lunch or buy lunch, comes the end of the day, there's no place for them to do any shopping." So these are all people that are going to come from East Haven or North Haven—come to work in New Haven—and then leave without spending a dime. What kind of business logic is that? Because in those days before redevelopment, you had all kinds of stores in that area—drug stores, barber shops, restaurants and so forth. So I said, "No, we don't want to build that kind of a building." So we let it go. And because of this they had to find jobs elsewhere. Some of the redevelopment involved where they lived and they moved.

"Lee Was Very Clever"

William Rossi spoke at the Oak Street Reunion on August 27, 2000.

In redevelopment what you do is you shake people up. And you put people that you want to put in particular areas. I don't care if the politicians say it's not so. It is absolutely so. They design and they place. And the people have very, very little to say about that. They may go to the polls and vote but they vote after the deed. And if they do vote before the deed, the deed is already worked out on paper. They still vote after the deed. Because politics doesn't work on today and tomorrow. Politics works five, ten, fifteen, twenty years ahead. Lee was very clever; he was one of the most clever politicians I've ever met. Celentano was the mayor in October, 1954, when Eisenhower declared all the renovations of the cities going on—that's when they put the money into the communities. Broadway, by Yale University, was demolished. Buildings came down, streets were repaved. It wasn't Celantano who went out there and had his picture taken. It was Lee who was going to run against Celantano. Very clever. So every time under the redevelopment plan of Eisenhower—this is 1954 now—under that plan every time a building came down, Lee's picture was there, every time a building went up, Lee's was there. So what has happened? We sort of hold him responsible for it. We think that it was poor planning. Well what has happened? You devastated whole areas of housing—neighbors, neighborhoods—where people were neighbors. Never would you see policemen on Legion Avenue. Never. And if policemen went through there it was because he was probably told that he had to cover so much territory. I don't remember squad cars roaming around like we have now. The only time we ever saw a squad car was if something bad happened. The foot patrolman was very visible and he was usually accepted by the neighborhood.

"Che Gazz è Cheste Eminent Domain?"

Frank DePonte spoke in the living room of Joe and Lena Riccio's Annex home on November 21, 1999.

My mother was from Atrani, she was Atranese, my father was from Minori, he was Minorese. The state said we need this property. There was newspaper stories about what they planned on doing and somebody came down from the state and said, "We need this property." They made an offer and of course these people didn't want to move. It was totally comfortable to them. It was like being back home [in Italy]. But there was no resisting. I think the only resisting was they dickered a little bit over the price. I think that maybe the original offer was like ten thousand. My parents went crazy because, "Where am I going to live? It's my whole life—my roots are here, where am I going to go? I have no place to go!" I'll never forget when we went to look for another house and the guy wanted fourteen thousand five hundred. We had to pick my mother up off the floor. She didn't think there was that much money in the world. She said, "How am I going to buy this? How can I do this?" We had a friend of ours, a liaison with the city, you could go to him, he was in politics, he understood and he told us, "If they want this there's nothing you can do. That's their right and their power." I told my mother, they're going to take the house, it is eminent domain. My mother didn't know what the hell eminent domain was, she said, "Che gazz è cheste eminent domain," What the hell is this eminent domain? She said [in Italian], "What are they saying? It's my house. I paid for it. What do you mean somebody can come and take it? This is America. They can't do that here." So I tried to explain it to her, Mom, you know, this is what he said, they have the power because if it's for the good of many, they can take something even though you don't want to sell because it has a larger benefit. But she didn't want to hear anything of that. You know we lived there, that was our home. We kept a little grocery store for a little while because they bought it but they let us live in it for a while until they decided to knock it down. They had plans to build but there was a lag time, so they let us stay there for a while. But that didn't satisfy her. She would come on the trolley from Pope Street in Morris Cove down to the store again. I'd say, What are you doing? You can't do this—sooner or later we got to leave. But it was hard for her to change. That was eminent domain. We had to give up everything, the store.

66 WE WORKED ALL OUR LIVES FOR IT 99

Josie DeBenedet spoke in the kitchen of her North Haven home on June 6, 1999. She worked with her mother in a shirt factory.

They were giving him a banquet or something this week. I saw his picture in the paper. Mayor Lee. They're honoring him because of the work he did. What work? He ruined New Haven. New Haven was such a beautiful city. He tore all the houses down. We lived on Carlisle Street [in the Hill] near the railroad station. There were all trees on the street along the road there. Beautiful, everybody kept their own home. We had a beautiful three family house. We had five rooms; we had heat, everything, a store. But everybody who owned a house lived in the house. And we all took care of it. We had tile in the kitchen, in the bathroom, tile in the vestibule, tile in the pantry. That was my husband's trade. And we kept our home nice. At nighttime, after supper, we'd all meet downstairs in the driveway and sit down. The ice cream man would come by and we'd buy an ice cream and it was nice. We didn't have to worry about anything. Now you get afraid. Mayor Lee, he's the one that started everything. When redevelopment came in 1959 they offered us twelve thousand dollars. We had a furnace for each family—we had everything and my husband said, "No, what am I gonna do with twelve thousand, I can't go buy another house." Every time the man who Lee sent, Mr. Kemp, the realtor, he came to represent the city and said that the house is got to go down because they were going to build the highway and this and that and you have to. Then they said they were going to send someone to appraise the house. He would sit down and bring papers and they said, "Well you know if the house is not worth it, after all we're going to knock it down and this and that." So my husband said, "All right, you want to take it but we worked all our lives for it and now that we're settled you want to take it away on us. For what? What are you going to do?" They [the city] were going to do so much and it's still all . . . did you see it? Oh, it's terrible down there. So we fought it, fought it, and we finally got fifteen. If not, they would have condemned it, they would have taken it from us. We were the first ones. See, the other people after, because they kept going higher and higher, then they saw what we were getting—and we didn't get nothing. Then they started to fight over . . . and things changed and they were getting more money [for their houses] but we didn't get nothing because we were the first ones and if we didn't accept that there, they were going to condemn the house. They had the Bertolini brothers with the big ball to knock down the houses. One of the brothers happened to know my husband because they're Veneziani, Venetians. He called up my husband over here because he belonged to the same club and he said, "Hey Rico, today we were crying, we were knocking your house down. It took us about two hours more than we should have taken because we couldn't knock the tile down."

"At Least Wooster Street Got a Highway through It"

Pat Barone spoke in the living room of his West Haven home on May 5, 1999.

That was Mayor Lee. Mayor Lee was in progress [Wooster Square] at that time. And he told all the people again—that was all Italian, Collis Street and all those streets in there—they were all Italians. They had little homes. But they were proud—they owned the home, they used to wash them, they used to clean them. He used to say, "Aw, you get out of here, you get a better neighborhood and then we're gonna put through here . . . we're gonna do this, we're gonna do that." People didn't want it, but they were forced out. Because of the highway. They came along, said they were going to put a highway in, and they did it. In them days the state came along, the city came along and they did it. The mayor was the boss. He was the boss; it isn't like today. If they want to take my house today—yeah they can condemn and take it—but it's gonna take them two years maybe before it goes

New Haven Neighborhoods Before the Highways

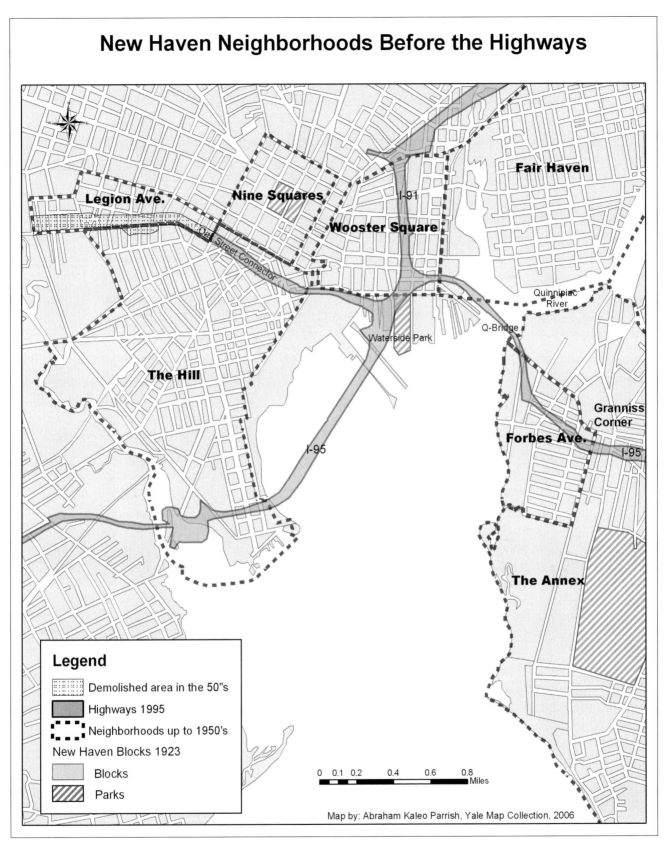

Legend

Demolished area in the 50"s

Highways 1995

Neighborhoods up to 1950's

New Haven Blocks 1923

Blocks

Parks

0   0.1 0.2   0.4   0.6   0.8
                                        Miles

Map by: Abraham Kaleo Parrish, Yale Map Collection, 2006

Map of New Haven in 1923 with 1950s highway overlay. The 1923 map was titled "The Price and Lee's Map of the City of New Haven," and was prepared by A. B. Hill, a civil engineer. It was geo-referenced with neighborhood blocks digitized and overlaid with a geo-referenced 1995 air photo of I-95, I-91 and the Oak Street Connector digitized by the Connecticut Department of Environmental Protection. The highway overlay was derived from 1995 Digital Ortho Quarter Quads (SE, SW, and NE) by the Connecticut DEP.

Yale Map Collection

through. They condemned them and took it right away. They gave you a few days to move out. That's how fast it was. And it cost them poor people—didn't have anything—half of them didn't have an education, half of them didn't know what it was all about. So they abide by the law, the law says they're going to take your property, they just let them take it. Some people fought them but it wasn't enough, it wasn't enough. You understand what I'm saying? They took part of Sargent's too. It wasn't enough of people squawking. They divided people up, they bought their houses and everything and people had to go so people were moving to the suburbs. A lot of people hocked themselves right up to go buy another house because what they got for that wasn't half enough to go buy a house. See, Wooster Street got hurt, but Legion Avenue got hurt more than Wooster Street. Route 34. Do you know how many hundreds of houses they knocked down there and did nothing with it? At least Wooster Street they put a highway, they did something over there. What did they do with 34 all the way up? Legion Avenue was a home on Sunday morning for all the Jewish and Italian people. Everybody met on Legion Avenue on a Sunday morning. You couldn't find a parking space, you maybe parked two blocks away because you knew you were going to be socializing. You went there to buy hard rolls or cake—you went to Ticotsky's or you went to Olmers or you went to Mister Brown's or you went to White's, the hardware store, the butcher market, the fruit stores. They were all open on Sunday morning because there was a law [The Blue Law] that if you were closed on Saturday you could open on Sunday. The Jewish people, that was their Sabbath Day, they were closed on Saturday, and they opened on Sunday. And everybody met everybody on Legion Avenue. They came from Hamden, from North Haven, from West Haven—everybody went to Legion Avenue. And when you got to Legion Avenue, the aroma from the bakeries that were going full blast, the beautiful smell of the bread and the cake. It was just unreal, unreal. It was a great place. They knocked everything down. Everything went.

"THEY CRIED"

Luisa DeLauro spoke in the kitchen of her Wooster Square home on August 9, 1998.

It was such a disaster when they threw down Wooster Street. I tell you, there were tons of people that were displaced. And they cried, they didn't want to leave Wooster Street because everything was there. The doctors were here, the midwives were here, the grocery stores, the butcher, the shoemakers, the chicken man, the dry goods store, the baker, everything was down here. We never had to leave the Wooster Square community. We never had to leave the community, we never had to go downtown, I didn't know what downtown was like because we had everything right there in Wooster Square, right on the street. It was a delightful neighborhood. We had the pharmacist. When somebody was sick we'd go to the drug

store. We had two drug stores and somebody had this or that and they would pre-
scribe. We wouldn't get the doctor right away. It was very close, everybody walked
in everybody's house any time of the day. And then they'd holler out the window, to
my mother "Luisella, did you see this?" And people cried. When Dick Lee became
mayor the highway came through so they cut off Wooster Street, which went all
the way up to East Street. Now it's only up to Franklin, so we lost Hamilton, Wallace and East, three full blocks heavily populated by the Italian people. This is
where all the Italians, when they came from Italy, they all migrated down here. You
know they didn't go outside this neighborhood. I tell you a lot of those people cried
and cried. They didn't pay attention to the people, they just did what they had to
do. It was the law of eminent domain. They took houses, people lost their houses.
And they cried, they didn't want to move out of the neighborhood. Most of them
went to live on the east shore. You know, Dick Lee at the time was running for
mayor and the Italian people were very upset with him, they said he did it deliberately, to get rid of the Italian vote. I don't know if that's true or not but the people
felt that way. He was afraid to come down here because people would razz him.
There was one guy on Saint John Street, he would get out the window and he'd say,
"Get the hell out a this neighborhood, Dick Lee, you go to hell." They still curse
him up and down. It was a culture of better living conditions for people but it disrupted a community of neighborhoods.

"I Saw Them Every Day"

Tony Vitolo spoke in the kitchen of Angelina Criscuolo's East Haven home
on December 21, 1999.

We used to live in the same building, the same tenement building. My sisters got
married and they lived downstairs. My aunt lived downstairs. My cousins lived
downstairs. Sixteen family house, twelve were my relatives. Whole families were
my relatives. And I saw them every day. Now I don't see them for months at a time
because they broke up that neighborhood.

"It Killed Them"

Lou and Rose Marie Guarino spoke at the kitchen table of their home in
Orange on August 24, 2000. Rose Marie's mother cooked with "recipes
by eye."

We they [the state] took the house, I think that's what killed them to tell you the
truth. When they took their house on Legion Avenue, because their dream was to
own a house, I think they bought the house in maybe 1948. And that was their
dream. All their lives, they wanted to buy a house. That was their American
dream. You come to America, you get a job, you own your own house and have a

garden in back, a vegetable garden and all that and that was their dream. They finally got it, you know. Because we had been moving all over the neighborhood. And they thought they were settled. And then wham! The state came along and said they were going take their property in "eminent domain." They were heartbroken, they said, "What do you mean?" Everybody got upset, here they had a two family house, they fixed it and everything, and they were proud of it, they had their own garden in the back because a lot of Italians grew their own vegetables in those days. And they were upset. They took the house, which they got peanuts for, and they moved to East Haven on Charter Oak Avenue. It killed them, you know why? They used to walk to church, walk down the avenue, go shopping, right? Now they moved over to Charter Oak Avenue, they had to walk a mile to get the bus if they wanted to go somewhere, there wasn't any shops close, any grocery stores or anything else. During that kind of living in their lifetime it destroyed them. And both of them died. But they were sad because they lost their friends, friends they had been with since they came over to this country and the politicians never realized what they did. All they worried about was the highway, which didn't materialize. But they ruined a lot of families and they killed a lot of families. It was their microcosm, that was their world. They sat on the front porches, they could walk to church, they could walk to the drug store, they walked to the doctor who was around the corner. And they knew everybody. It was a mixed ethnic neighborhood—there were Jews, Italians, Poles, Irish, Greeks, Portuguese, blacks, everyone. There was no discrimination or racial differences, they were all sort of like family. And these people were happy there. And then they bought the house in East Haven, in the "burbs," in the suburbs. They both died. They didn't know anyone there. They couldn't go anywhere on their own if their sons didn't come and pick them up. It was a sad thing. It was a waste. They were happy. This was their dream, they bought their house and they thought they'd be there forever until their last days and it didn't work out that way. If the highway materialized, well, they needed to do it. But it never came to pass. And up to the day they died [my parents] they even saw that the neighborhood wasn't being developed and all that.

"I Can't Show My Grandchildren Where I Was Born"

Tom Consiglio spoke at the Saint Andrew Society on June 30, 1999.

I was born on Collis Street. There's hardly anything left to it, they knocked it all down, all the houses. Like where I was born, the house went down. I can't show my grandchildren where I was born, this is the house where I was born. It went down through the highway construction and redevelopment. But we lost a lot of houses in this neighborhood and the people who had to move, they moved in with their children who had married and moved out of the area. The people that owned the houses they were paid for by the redevelopment. Some maybe didn't agree with the price, they could always go to court and get a little more. But before, everybody remained on the same block. Your aunts and uncles, your grandparents lived across the street, everybody lived in the area. When you got married you didn't go out of this neighborhood. You got a room someplace, right in the area. Now the kids move to California, they move all over. But those days they were all together. But redevelopment was a good thing because the house I was born in, even in the house I moved to with my family was three stories high. The restrooms were in the hallway. And the family in the front and in the back shared the same bathroom. And on the other side of the hall there was another bathroom and two families on each side shared the bathroom. But we had no bathtubs. We had no facilities to take a bath at all. I used to go to the bathhouse on St. John Street, you paid a nickel and they'd give you a towel and everybody went there. And they had a pool there and you could a jumped in the water. That's the only facility we had. Or you washed in the sinks, you know.

We had a redevelopment committee, renewal committee that worked with the Renewal Agency. We had a committee and we were told all about what was going to happen and we listened and voted on a lot of things. I was on the Wooster Square Renewal Committee. I wasn't a paid member. I never was a paid member of the city so many times I was called upon to bring up a project in front of the Board of Aldermen saying how I agreed, I thought it would be a good thing to do and they used me a lot of times when we ever had to bring up a new project with redevelopment. They put schools, you know and I agreed with everything they did. But I thought it was a good thing, I think it was. A very good thing. It [redevelopment] was like a test thing to see how it works out with the people, if it caused any problems. Of course there were plenty of houses left. The redevelopment took a lot of houses, the state took a lot of houses. But people still found places, they moved to East Haven, Branford, not too far away.

❝The Highway❞

John Nappi spoke in the kitchen of his home in East Haven on June 28, 2000.

You know, the politicians have to make money, you know that. They didn't have to do that. The way I understand, when they built that road, that road [the highway] was supposed to go straight over the sound, from Woodward Avenue right into West Haven. Instead they made the curve, even the engineer made the remark, "This was the worst planning ever," because it makes a curve like this, it almost runs into C. Cowles building, from C. Cowles building you can step right out to the highway, ever see that? It shouldn't be like that. Now all those lands, they took all those homes were taken. Somebody made money in the deal. Where they says if it went over the Sound, from Woodward Avenue to West Haven, they would a only taken about a half dozen homes—it would been straight across. All the homes on Wooster Street, Hamilton Street, Franklin Street, they took a lot of homes. He [Lee] never won in that ward. I tell ya, I met the guy, I knew him good. Lee was a good guy. You wouldn't believe this with Mayor Lee. I worked for the school system. You know when he was mayor we never had a union. Or we had it, but we never had a contract. Handshake and he kept his word.

"They Took Away a Lot of History"

Frank "Mel" DeLieto spoke at the kitchen table in his Annex home on March 26, 2000. He fought in The Battle of the Bulge.

Frankly speaking, the neighborhood was really broken up, and I tell ya, Mayor Lee is the guy who really did it. Alderman Mike DePalma was alderman of the tenth ward for years. He was the only Republican that used to get elected. So what do you do? You try to break down the neighborhood, and that's what he did. And people thought it was for the betterment of the neighborhood. No, see, that's what killed people. All the old people had to go the suburbs, East Haven, Guilford, most of them moved to East Haven, then you had the Annex. And they took away a lot of history, really a lot of history. There was no open meetings that I could remember. Of course when I got home after the war—a lot of guys were just anxious to get home—and then a lot of these things started to take place. Then they put the highway right through Franklin Street. They should have never destroyed that in my opinion. And the reasons why you have trouble today, the Quinnipiac Bridge alone. You see where coming north, why they have no room? Because Sargent refused to move at that time. So they went around it. That's why they don't have enough lanes. Now what happens. Sargent finally moves. And the bridge is all screwed up because of the fact they don't have enough room. They ended up moving where they are now on Long Wharf but they stayed [during construction of I-95]. When that I-95 came in, it was obsolete when they got through building it, they just don't have enough room for the amount of cars going through, you just don't have enough room. That's a fact. In fact, the guy that designed the damn highway got killed on it. It was dangerous, very dangerous. You see, you can go upstate to Massachusetts, the highways are altogether different. If you have an accident on the Quinnipiac Bridge forget about it. You tie up. Any part of I-95, you're gonna have trouble. They don't have an off shoulder to take the wreck and put it aside. The highway took everything away.

"We Had Beautiful Brownstone Houses"

Tony Sacco spoke at his Wooster Street restaurant on May 19, 2000.

We were all Republicans. That's why Mister Lee didn't like us. You know, they didn't have to knock all these houses down. They spent three, four hundred million to make this [highway] ramp [end of Wooster Street] and now they want to spend another five, six hundred million to take it down. So who's who? They don't know what they're doing anymore. They had brownstone houses on this street, they had all kind a beautiful houses, all they needed was a little bit of hot water, heat in them, you know. We had to move to the [Columbus] mall from 109 Wooster Street—gee, I was paying eighteen dollars a month, I went to 105, I had a go see a doctor [laughing]. But we had hardwood floors, our own shower, bathroom. I didn't like the mall.

❝THE HOUSES WERE OBSOLETE❞

Salvatore "Gary" Garibaldi spoke at Tony and Lucille's restaurant on May 19, 2000.

You have to remember, very few people took part in it [Citizens Action Committee]. One of Mayor Richard C. Lee's projects was the implementation of the state highway, I-91, I-95. And instead of putting it through like in a place that wouldn't affect people in the community, he put it right in the middle of the area. So in that movement a lot of brownstone houses and beautiful homes he could have restored, were bulldozed. Yes he did have community meetings, but community meetings were made up of men and women that were more or less in favor of what he was doing. And if you or I went down there and objected, our own neighbors would say, "Hey, look at what he's gonna do for us. He's gonna restore Wooster Street, he's gonna put a school here, this here and all that." And they swallowed it. Here's the reason for it. Many of those men and women of our age inherited the mother or father's property. Without no question the property at that time—due to the Depression years and during wartime—much was needed to restore and rehabilitate these buildings and they didn't do it. So now as the parents are getting older and dying, the younger people were getting married and were moving out of the community, to the suburbs. Well, when mother and dad died the house was left to the sons and daughters. Well, now with this here program that Dick Lee put forward, they became like rich overnight because the house that they had, say like on Collis and Hamilton, they couldn't sell it for five thousand dollars. But because of the highway going through and the new redevelopment plans, much money was there in grants from Washington D.C. So now when they purchased your property they just didn't purchase by the house, they purchased by the land. So all these homes had big yards in the back, you had plenty of land, so when they got the price in those days, they were getting like thirty-five, forty thousand dollars to sell their homes. The houses were already obsolete; you didn't like to hear that. Rat infested, and all that, cockroaches. These people at that time don't like to hear that. I lived it, I lived it. So now what happens? This being a strong Republican area, he [Mayor Lee] was very happy to destroy the area because he was gonna receive relief himself in getting hit by votes in the election time. All these people went for it they couldn't sell their houses. Big properties, club room downstairs, three stories, in the alleyway, a soda shop—they couldn't sell that property—who would buy that for five thousand dollars? But along comes Dick Lee. When they measured the land they might have sold it for maybe for twenty, twenty-five thousand dollars. So it was a welcome thing to do.

"REFLECTIONS ON WOOSTER STREET"

Frank Carrano spoke at the union office on June 28, 1999.

I lived right here on Chapel Street until I was twenty-two years old. We moved out when they tore the place down. You know, we had a store [Carrano's Market] and we lived upstairs and it was perfectly fine. We were happy there. But I think what happens when you think back on it is you have a tendency to idealize that whole part of your life. Because it was a wonderful neighborhood with respect to the people who lived there, the family values, the caring environment where people knew people and, you know, they cared about people. You knew everybody on your block. You could walk around one, two, three blocks and just about everybody knew who you were and you knew them; you knew their families. And that's very nice. That's something that is no longer true in most cases today. People live in a very isolated type of environment. But when you think about some of the conditions that people lived in—they weren't all that terrific. I mean most of them were cold water flats, walk-up apartments, three rooms, maybe four rooms. Now whether over time those properties would have been upgraded remains to be seen. You'll never know that. So I think when we talk about the wonderful neighborhood we're talking in many cases about a neighborhood filled with caring people, people who shared the same values and I mean, everyone was Italian. I don't think I met a non-Italian person until I went to high school. I went to grammar school in the neighborhood. Everybody I knew was Italian, everybody came from the same background I came from. Some were first generation as I was, some were second generation, but everybody was Italian. And so that's what I think we hold on to. That's what we really think of when we think of that old neighborhood. But it would have been interesting to see how time would have treated that whole area [Wooster Street] because most of the buildings were turn of the century buildings and most of them didn't have too many amenities. But the buildings that remain are the kind of flagship buildings like around Wooster Park, those were the homes that were where the original residents of Wooster Square lived. And what's left of Wooster Street is pretty much a shadow of what was there originally. But for me, the neighborhood is not so much the physical aspect of it but the human aspect of it, the emotional aspect of living in a place where you felt comfortable, where you felt a spirit of family togetherness and in sync with everybody else. People pretty much shared the same family values. And that was terrific.

I don't think there was any grand plan to devastate the Italian enclave of Wooster Square for political purposes. I think it was expedient. Of course there's a type of double whammy here because you also had the highway coming through. You know, for instance the place I lived in was the victim of the highway. And that was separate from what was going on with the other redevelopment in the city. So they were concurrently happening. The state project was to build I-91 and I-95 because until then all you had was Route 1, very slow moving Route 1. So all of that was happening almost at the same time the city was getting involved in this massive redevelopment plan. So some of what happened in Wooster Square was the highway, some of what happened in Wooster Square was redevelopment. I think what happened with redevelopment was people really didn't know how to do redevelopment. So what they did was tear everything down thinking that building everything new was the best way to go. Unfortunately they found out a generation later that it's not the best way to go because when they moved all those people out they never came back. And so it destroyed large portions of New Haven with respect to their livability. But at the time I think they just didn't know any better. I think they just did what they thought was the modern thing to do, you know, to kind a break through, let's get rid of these old places, let's put something new and a lot got lost in the process.

I used to kid with him [Mayor Lee] later. You know I still keep in touch with him from time to time and I went to this event they had where they named a courthouse after him. He wasn't there, he couldn't make it but his wife was there and his children. And I used to kid him when I worked pretty closely with him when he was at the United Way because the president of the New Haven Labor Council. I used to tell him that when I was living in Wooster Square and they started all this stuff [redevelopment] the people used to talk about you buy this doll, this Dick Lee doll, you wind it up and tears your house down. He always got a kick out of that, when I would remind him of that. You know, that's the reputation you have on Wooster Square, watch out for the Dick Lee, he'll come in and tear your house down. But he realized I think that some of what he did didn't work and some of what he did was probably the first step in a process that was going to happen anyway.

I try to explain to my kids—because you grow up in suburbia—it's different. I don't think they can even understand what you mean we you talk about a feeling of community, a feeling of neighborhood because that's something foreign to people nowadays. You know, you live on a street, you don't really live . . . I mean maybe it's true in some places. It's not true where I live. We've lived there for thirty years, I know the people across the street, I know the people behind us, next door, you know, it's different. I mean we have no real contact or connection with each other just because we live on the same street whereas over here [Wooster Street] you lived in an area that was like, hey, we're connected in some way, we share all these common things that makes us somehow—connects us to each other. It's no longer true. I don't think it'll probably ever be true again. Maybe to the same degree with these people who live in these planned communities where everybody lives and you all go to the same community center and all this stuff. To some degree, maybe it's a little like that, but not really.

When it was happening [redevelopment] here it was happening in other places. There was the federal government saying, you know, here's the money, renew yourselves, and reinvent yourselves. So that's what they did. They came in and plowed everything down and got rid of everybody. And then when they were ready people were supposed to come back. Trouble is, they never came back. That's what they were saying, this was temporary, you move out. But once people moved, they moved. They went to East Haven. Some people made the move to Fair Haven, which was supposed to be kind of moving away from that kind of inner city and then out to East Haven, Morris Cove, which was the next way to go. But they never came back after that. They put up that mall on Wooster Street, which was supposed to generate a lot of other, the Columbus Mall, the housing complex they have there. But the few people who stayed, stayed there but they never really generated any additional building or they never put up any other—there were never any opportunities for people to come back. And most people didn't want to come back to a three-room flat. They wanted to improve their lot in life a little bit.

That [the late '50s] was a period of time that was on the brink, before the mass media, communication and television were just beginning to emerge. So newspapers were very important for people to get information. And we sold all the newspapers, you know, and not just the New Haven newspapers but the New York newspapers, we sold the Italian newspaper and those newspapers were very important. The men in particular in the morning on the way to work would stop and buy the newspaper, pick up some cigars, cigarettes, whatever. And then later in the day the women would come and shop for the meal. And the women who worked across the street from us because there were shirt and dress factories all around the perimeter of our store. They would shop after work, stop by, do their shopping, bring it home and that was their meal for the night. It wasn't this freezing things and buying once a month. This was pretty much on a daily basis. And of course we put all the produce outside so they didn't have to come into the store, they could shop right on the street. We had this wooden—we called it the stand—but it was essentially a platform which was on a forty-five degree angle and every morning we'd bring out all the stuff and displayed it and brought back in the store it at night. From spring through fall that stuff came out every day because you wanted to make it as convenient as possible for the women to shop and not to have to even come inside. Sometimes they'd come in on their lunch hour and we would hold the stuff in the store and they'd pick up the bag on the way home from the shirt factories. There was the Ideal [shirt factory] across the street, The Sunbeam, The Planet. We relied on them. They were the mainstays of our business.

We opened at six in the morning to get all the early shift workers. We stayed until well into the evening to get the last minute customers. But we lived—the store was part of our home—we lived right there. It wasn't like we had to close the store and then go home, we were still in the back of the store. That's where the big kitchen was, that was where my mother cooked, we ate our meals over there. So if anybody came in you just walked through and you took care of them. So it was very much a part of your life and the store was very much a part of the community. The women would come in the morning and my mother would be in there and they'd talk—a little gossip—in Italian. In the afternoon around two o'clock my mother always made a pot of Italian coffee and someone who was in the store would come and sit down, take her little coffee break. She made the coffee and used the same pot and I remember that she always sweetened the coffee to her taste, so she would put whatever two spoons or three spoons of sugar in the coffeepot. And then when she poured it, it was already sweetened, you didn't need to bother sweetening it, it was [laughing] sweetened to the right degree of sweetness. And that was part of the ritual. So it was a very social environment. That was the social environment for people. The women didn't go anywhere. The women who didn't work, what they did in the morning was to go out and shop and took that stuff home and made the meal for the day. Shopping was an everyday thing much as it is in Europe still, you go out every day and buy what you're going to have for dinner that day. So, a lot of socializing around that. Going to the drugstore, whatever, that was all part of the fabric of the neighborhood but also the way you kept in touch with people. People very rarely visited each other. It wasn't the kind of neighborhood where you went to visit so and so. Very little of that. People pretty much stayed in their own apartment with your own family but you socialized in these other environments—at the store, in church, the drugstore, the pastry shop, the fish market—all of these places where you met people and that's how you knew them. And of course, because we had the business, we knew a lot of people because they came into the store and so we had a wider, broader spectrum of acquaintances through the business.

I can remember taking back my sons when they were ten, eleven years old, taking them to a store. And this particular store had a salesperson. And they had never seen a salesperson, someone who actually came to you and asked, may I help you? And I can remember having to explain to them who this person was—this is a person, you know, who helps you shop because they had never seen—because when you go shopping you're on your own. And that's what's happened now, it's an impersonal, you shop in a large market. I think that's one of the reasons why some of these specialty stores have become popular. I live in Branford and there's a book shop in the center of town run by the Esposito family and the thing about them is that when you walk into that store they make you feel as though they're happy to see you, they know who you are, they know everybody's name, and you want to go back because you feel as though it matters to them that you have come in. Whereas I take clothes to a cleaner every week. I have all my shirts laundered. I mean every single week. And every time I walk in the woman has to ask my name. She has to look at the slip from last week, you know, to be able to write my name in spite of the fact that I go every week, every single week. And I usually spend about twenty-five bucks and yet I could be walking in for the first time. I mean they kind a recognize me but you would think, whereas twenty-five or thirty years ago I would consider it to be my responsibility to know you, to make you feel welcome, you know, you're my customer, this kind of thing. So it's very different, very different. None of that happens anymore.

Things change. But things change the way they do but you always ask the question—I always do—is that part of the natural process of change or could it have been different? And I'd like to think it could have been different if there had been more thought given and if you were able to reflect more on what the reaction to the action you're taking will be. But unfortunately, usually that doesn't happen. Urban planners. Redevelopers. I remember that became a word everybody hated. Redevelopment. What does it mean? What are you redeveloping? I know for me it took on a very negative context because everything that happened was in the name of redevelopment and no one understood what it was, what it was supposed to do or what the purpose of it was other than to improve things, get rid of the old and bring in the new. Got rid of the old but it never quite brought in the new and a lot of it remained uncompleted, even to this day. They ran out of money, they ran out of plans. Everything stopped. But at the time I guess people thought it was going to reinvent New Haven.

When all this [redevelopment] started I was only fourteen, fifteen years old and not that interested in and sort of on the periphery of being aware of what was going on. But I do remember in the neighborhood a great concern about whose property would go, who would have to move. And of course there were a lot of people who were renting. Most of the neighborhood was made up of tenants, not property owners and so for them it was a big dilemma because they had to find another place to live. Most people lived in multifamily houses. I can remember one of the large buildings behind our property on Wooster had, maybe, twelve families living in it. It was not uncommon to see buildings with six families, four families. I don't remember a one family house anywhere in the neighborhood, really. I mean there might have been a handful of them—throwbacks—but most of the properties were multifamily and most of the people rented. So when all this started the big concern was, where am I gonna go, where am I gonna find an apartment? For some people it was the impetus to buy a small house somewhere, you know, move to Fair Haven, move to somewhere else and buy a small house. For others and because of the uncertainty of what was going to happen the majority of people just left. They didn't wait around to wait and see what was going to happen. I remember all that confusion at that time. Even with us, where we lived there were four families in the house we lived in and what was going to happen to everybody?

My mother never adjusted, really, to leaving the neighborhood. Because that was the center of their life was just being able to walk outside and be there. Not like you get in a car and drive somewhere. So I think for those people it was a very serious adjustment. Some of them never really adjusted. I know my mother never adjusted to moving out of the neighborhood and living somewhere else. It was just never the same for her. I guess it depends on the time of your life when it happens. Midlife or beyond I think the adjustment is always harder. It certainly was for her.

What I realize now is that their experiences [my older sisters] were much different from mine and they grew up at the most intense period of time when I think the neighborhood was at its height with respect to the number of people living there and the sheer volume of activity that was going on. My recollection from age eight until the time I moved out of there—even though as people got married very often they stayed in the neighborhood. The daughters found an apartment not too far from where their mothers were. But some people had already started to move. Whereas with their experience not only were there more people living there but the neighborhood had more of everything. There were more grocery stores, there were more of everything you know up and down Wooster Street so that, even as I recall, you could find five pastry shops—it was the golden age of the neighborhood. It must have been from the stories I hear from them [older sisters] from the mid-'20s, early '30s, probably right up to the war, because the war—across the country—

DEGREGORIO FAMILY
On Cain Street between
Wallace and East Street,
1940s, destroyed by the highway

DeGregorio family album

changed things in that neighborhood, too. When people came back things were different. Service men came back, they got married and a lot of them moved away. But through that period, through the start of the war, I think really was the golden age of the neighborhood. I think it was a time when the interpersonal relationships that people had really cemented their feelings about the neighborhood. I can hear my sisters talking now about families as though they were still living there, you know, even now. So it's a very strong, deeply rooted kind of personal experience they feel about that. And I'm always interested to hear the stories they have to tell because these are not, these things were no longer happening when I was growing up. They were already getting married and leaving our family.

My oldest sister is eighteen years older than I am so there's quite a spread there. But in spite of that I think we've managed to keep, we have very similar feelings about our experience growing up. And of course my entire family lived in that neighborhood, my aunts, my uncles, cousins, everybody was there. And that was true of most people. On a holiday you could visit every member of your family by simply walking around the corner, down the block, you know. Because the tradition was to visit on every holiday, to visit your family, your aunts, uncles, whatever. You could do that. The tradition for Italians, like on Palm Sunday for instance, you would visit, exchange palm and the kids would always get a half dollar or dollar, whatever. And you could just walk through the neighborhood. I could go visit all my uncles and aunts just by walking and in a three block radius—they all lived there. That's no longer the case. The car was not necessary for your day to day existence. Most people walked to work. Everybody who worked in that neighborhood—if you worked in Sargent or Shellhorn down the street here, all the dress shops, the shirt factories, all of those places, you walked to work. All the movie theaters were within three blocks of the neighborhood. I would not change my experience growing up there for anything. I'm kind of a throwback because I was the last in my family. So I've got one foot in one generation and another foot in another generation and my contemporaries that I come into contact with, and through my work now, have very different experiences. Most of them—their families would have already moved away, they would be the second generation, whereas I'm still the first generation even though I'm a part of the second generation. But I wouldn't change any of that. It was a wonderful place to grow up and I value and cherish all of that and it was wonderful. Terrific.

"WOOSTER STREET WILL REMAIN FOREVER"

Andrea Colavolpe spoke at the Saint Andrew Society on June 14, 1999. He recalled how much Wooster Street reminded him of Amalfi when he arrived in 1947.

This area of Wooster Street would not have made it this far if it wasn't for the two societies, people should always thank the mutual aid societies—Saint Andrews and Santa Maria Maddalena—that Wooster Street still exists. The feast has been revived. The tradition of Wooster Street will remain forever; even though it has been destroyed they haven't destroyed the traditions. People come from all over back here—when they hear Wooster Street, that's like the famous street in New York, that's Fifth Avenue in New Haven, Connecticut. We've got the most beautiful restaurants in New Haven on Wooster Street. You have the best pizzas on Wooster Street.

Afterword: New Haven Today

By Philip Langdon

New Haven today is a much different city than when Italian immigration was running strong. Certainly it is a less populous place. For three decades, from 1920 to the century's midpoint, the city's population hovered just above 160,000. But after reaching a peak of 164,443 in 1950, when highway construction and urban renewal had not yet leveled swaths of the city and uprooted thousands of people, the number began slipping—to 152,048 in 1960, to 137,707 in 1970, and to 123,626 in 2000. In half a century the city's population fell by nearly 25 percent, even while New Haven County as a whole grew by 51 percent, to 824,008. Today just over one in seven residents of New Haven County lives within the Elm City's boundaries.

The dispersal followed every path that geography allowed. It marched eastward, northward, and westward; it went in every direction except south into the briny waters of Long Island Sound. Italian Americans did not, however, spread out uniformly. Most of them went in directions they had already been heading, but now in larger leaps—moving a few miles rather than a few blocks. Thousands of Italian Americans relocated to East Haven, which remains substantially Italian to this day. Large numbers migrated to Branford, North Haven, Hamden, and West Haven. Some of the most well-heeled settled in Orange.

A relatively small portion moved to the wooded suburbs of Woodbridge and Bethany, some of them establishing small farms. The number of Italians remained fairly low in Westville, a section of the city full of handsome houses built in the first half of the twentieth century. Westville was known for its Jewish character. In New Haven, people still clustered, to some extent, among those of their own race or ethnic background, until intermarriage, anti-discrimination statutes, and the appeal of mainstream culture gradually eroded old differences. Just as the rising Italian Americans ignored the pleasant early twentieth-century houses and tree-lined streets of Westville, they largely passed by the imposing (and costly to maintain) early twentieth-century houses of the East Rock neighborhood. In the postwar period, fewer and fewer of New Haven's Italian Americans were interested in a style of living that involved old houses on city streets. As the second, third, and later generations moved into the middle class, they preferred newer houses, closer to the ground, in neighborhoods served by automobiles and roadside shopping centers rather than by a walk to a corner store. The preferences of New Haven's Italian Americans meshed well with the postwar era's suburban aspirations. From the end of World War II through most of the remainder of the century, the prevailing American aspiration was for a ranch house with lawn on all sides, or a cape, a split-level, a "Colonial," or some other kind of single-family dwelling, removed from the hurly-burly of old urban neighborhoods. Italians left behind the two- and three-family houses, apartment buildings, and tenements of the city and embraced lower-density settings—environments that, according to the thinking of the era, were better suited for raising families. The days of large numbers of immigrants from the south of Italy living close together, one family on top of another, were at an end.

From the 1920s to the mid-1960s, federal immigration policy prevented massive migrations from abroad. Consequently, no flood of newcomers from other countries washed across New Haven. There was, to be sure, migration from other sections of the United States Poor African Americans, many of them forced off the farms of the South as machinery made their toil superfluous, arrived in the Elm City in sizable numbers. There was also a large exodus from the U.S.-controlled island of Puerto Rico to mainland cities such as New York, Philadelphia, and New Haven. Many of the new arrivals had little experience with urban living; they were especially ill-prepared for a city whose demand for unskilled labor and manual trades was sharply contracting. Business in the last half of the twentieth century had far less need for strong backs and nimble fingers than it did when boatloads of Italians were arriving for jobs at Sargent hardware and other factories. Inevitably, friction arose between the remaining Italian Americans and the incoming blacks and Puerto Ricans. The worsening crime rate and the race riots of the 1960s made New Haven—at least large sections of it—a terrain that many Italian-Americans were happy to bid farewell to.

But because the influx of African Americans and Puerto Ricans was smaller than the earlier flows of immigration from abroad, the remaining Italians nonetheless stood to inherit and govern New Haven for quite a while. As the last large ethnic group from Europe, they exerted extensive influence over government and politics in the city and over the affairs of nearby communities. According to the 2000 Census, Italian Americans comprised New Haven County's largest ethnic group.

Each November's election returns affirm their prominence; Italian Americans hold major offices in the towns of New Haven County. Since 1991 the New Haven area has been represented in Congress by Rosa DeLauro, a Democrat whose parents, both aldermen, lived in the Wooster Square neighborhood. (An exception to the prevailing Italian American pattern, DeLauro settled in the East Rock neighborhood.) Italians have remained a force in city politics. Of the five mayors since Richard Lee's long tenure ended in 1970, three have been Italian American: Bart Guida, who served from 1970 to 1976; former police chief Biagio

DiLieto, who served as mayor from 1980 to 1990; and John DeStefano Jr., who has presided over City Hall since 1994.

The preeminence of Italians in local politics is destined to come to an end, perhaps soon. Because so much of the Italian population has migrated to the suburbs, the city is now only 10.5 percent Italian American. In fact, far fewer of the city's residents have Italian ancestry than do residents of the rest of the county. In the county as a whole, 24.4 percent of the population is Italian American. New Haven has had one black mayor, John Daniels, who served two terms during the financially difficult and crime-besieged early 1990s. People speculate how long it will be before the city elects its first Hispanic mayor. As the Italian proportion of New Haven's population ages and diminishes, the newer ethnic groups, especially those from Puerto Rico and Latin America, are steadily gaining political power. The Census Bureau reported that 21.4 percent of New Haven's residents in 2000 were Hispanic (two-thirds of them of Puerto Rican heritage), 36.1 percent were African American, and 35.6 percent were nonHispanic whites.

Political power is, in any event, less critical to the advancement of the region's Italian Americans than it once was. Not a large number depend on patronage work or assistance from City Hall; they have advanced from mostly humble jobs into a broad mix of occupations and professions. Many men in earlier generations worked as bricklayers and stonemasons. Now, Italian Americans are in charge of most of New Haven's construction firms; they have become the organizers and owners. Italians early displayed a talent for gardening and food preparation; today they operate many restaurants as well as the Orange Street gourmet produce stores that give the East Rock neighborhood some of its urban appeal. With their theatricality, Italians such as Ernest Borgnine (born Ermes Effron Borgnino to Italian immigrants in Hamden, later schooled in New Haven) became popular performers. The outspoken, fiercely intelligent Joel Schiavone, whose family was in the scrap business, emerged in the 1990s as the developer most responsible for rehabilitating buildings on Chapel Street and filling them with retailers and residents. A sizable number of Italians went into medicine and other professions. The Italian impact on higher education has been less noticeable, but a son of New Haven, Renaissance scholar A. Bartlett Giamatti, became president of that old elite institution, Yale University, serving from 1978 to 1986 before he left to become commissioner of baseball. Hundreds of Italian Americans have established or headed small businesses in New Haven.

For all the Italian prominence today, it is not hard to detect the passing of the old ways. Restaurants and eating places indicate what's happening. When out-of-town journalists visit New Haven, customarily they pay homage to Wooster Street, long celebrated for its Italian restaurants, including the two stars of the pizza firmament, Sally's and Pepe's. A trip to New Haven is viewed as incomplete without a white pizza at Sally's or Pepe's. This is New Haven culinary tradition, passed down for generations. Yet, in truth, Wooster Street doesn't matter as much as it used to. Eating places with white pizzas or red sauces go on serving customers, but they no longer represent what is most exciting in contemporary New Haven. What generates more interest is the flowering of newer restaurants, many of them downtown.

The newer places serve Malaysian food, Japanese food, Ethiopian, nouvelle cuisine, Latin American, Thai, Chinese, and other varieties. New Haven has become a well-regarded restaurant town, and although Italian food is part of the mix, it is now just one specialty among many. It is not critical to good dining in New Haven. There is a sense that the Italian era is fading.

Perhaps if fewer of the Italian Americans had gone to the suburbs, it would be different. But maybe not. Ethnicity dissipates, even without the stark disruptions that Mayor Lee forced upon New Haven during the radical urban surgery of the 1950s and 1960s. In any event, the city has never fully recovered from Lee's ill-conceived urban renewal and his destructive but partly necessary highway construction. (Long-distance traffic sorely needed the Connecticut Turnpike, later known as Interstate 95; the Route 34 Connector, on the other hand, gouged a path of demolition that did more harm than good.)

During urban renewal's heyday, Lee and his top administrators won national praise for knocking down the old and obsolete and raising the new and modern. New Haven was "the greatest success story in the history of the world," U.S. Labor Secretary Willard Wirtz declared in 1964.[1] From a financial perspective, it seemed for a while that the city had won a gigantic jackpot. By 1965, New Haven had received $745 per capita for urban renewal, nearly three times the ratio of grants awarded to the second-highest-funded city (Newark, New Jersey) and more than twenty times the per capita funding of New York.[2] In retrospect, it is clear that much of this money was spent in ways that interrupted and ultimately damaged local life. Urban renewal displaced 2,216 businesses—a horrendous loss for a city of New Haven's size.[3] Yale Professor Douglas W. Rae estimates that urban renewal forced 7,704 households—22,496 individuals, or fully one-fifth of the city's inhabitants—to move.[4] The relocations led to the construction of additional public housing projects, some of which became the sites of festering problems. As the interviews in this book's final chapter reveal, emotions continue to run strong more than a generation after the end of widespread government-sponsored demolition. When the New Haven Colony Historical Society sponsored a symposium in late 2002 on the legacy of urban renewal, the most emotional point was a discussion in which old-timers from Legion Avenue lamented the government-sponsored destruction of their neighborhood. These wounds will not heal. As long as there are people living who remember the old places first-hand, a sense of a tragic loss will remain.

What is also troubling is that in significant ways, City Hall hasn't changed as much as it should. When money is available from higher levels of government, the temptation is to pursue it even if it means once again disrupting neighborhoods. New Haven is currently carrying out a multiyear $1.5 billion program of school construction and renovation, by the end of which the city will have primary and secondary education facilities equal in many ways to those of the much wealthier suburbs. In the Hill, the replacement of the Prince-Welch School led to demolition of two-and-one-half blocks of houses in a state-designated historic district, more than twenty of the houses owner-occupied. Some of the houses were in poor condition, and there had been problems with drug peddling and other crime. But residents were upset at the prospect of losing their homes, some of which were in good condition, and they pointed out that crime was declining; conditions were improving. Nonetheless, the city's School Construction Program, following the wishes of Mayor DeStefano, leveled the houses on Ward, Asylum, and Baldwin Streets. The city's procedures were less democratic than they should have been. People often learned what was happening only after the important decisions had been made.

The biggest single construction project under way today in the New Haven area is replacement of the Interstate 95 bridge across New Haven Harbor. Where there were six lanes of traffic, clogged from a combination of New Haven area commuter traffic and long-distance travel between New York and Boston, the replacement bridge will have ten lanes. Before that project received the go-ahead from the state Department of Transportation, hundreds of people voiced their opinions about what should be done about congestion during a long, well-attended series of public meetings. The consensus among participating city-dwellers was that a gargantuan bridge was not the answer; instead, a combination of remedies should be attempted, including additional commuter rail service. When all was said and done, though, the state DOT went right ahead and launched its bridge and highway project rather than pursuing a multifaceted transportation project. It is difficult to get governments, whether city or state, to see the old patterns and the existing fabric of development as consistently worth repairing and restoring rather than replacing.

Are there new stories unfolding today that parallel the stories of the Italian immigrants? To some degree there are. Since the early 1990s, New Haven has begun receiving Spanish-speaking newcomers, not just from its traditional source, Puerto Rico, but also from Mexico, El Salvador, Ecuador, Colombia, Chile, and other countries of Central and South America. According to the 2000 Census, of New Haven residents claiming Hispanic lineage, 67 percent are Puerto Rican. The second-largest group is of Mexican heritage: 13 percent. Those figures do not indicate how many are immigrants, rather than descendants of immigrants. Because many Latin Americans have come here illegally and avoid government agencies such as the Census Bureau, it's impossible to know the true number. John Lugo, who works with immigrant families at Community Mediation Services, estimates there are at least two thousand recent immigrants from Latin American countries—"over five thousand if you count West Haven and East Haven." Even that may be an underestimate. Illegal aliens keep their status a secret.

The recent immigrants from Latin American countries work in restaurants, landscaping businesses, cleaning, and other enterprises—predominantly service businesses, since manufacturing has ceased to be a major employer. Many of them are paid under the table and receive less than the minimum wage. "Or," says Lugo, "they may get a salary of $300 but have to work seventy hours a week." As with earlier migrations, the recent arrivals tend to come from particular towns or regions where first a few and then a large number of people departed for Connecticut. Lugo says a considerable number have come from the Mexican state of Tlaxcala, near Mexico City. Most are men, though some have since brought their wives. "The number from Guatemala has also been growing," he observes. "Most of them come from the countryside, where they used to be peasants. There are people from a few Mayan communities. They speak their own language in addition to Spanish.

There are a fair percentage of people from Chile. There are people from Venezuela and Colombia also because of the political situation."

In the city, most of the recent arrivals have found housing in the poorer sections, such as the Hill and Fair Haven. As was true of the early Italians, some intend to return home after they've saved money. Many send money home to their families. Since illegal immigrants are not securely established and are at risk of deportation, it is impossible to predict how many will put down permanent roots. In 1997, the New Haven *Advocate* reported on Guatemalans and Mexicans who lived crammed together—thirty-five workers and family members were stuffed into one broken-down, legally uninhabitable two-family house in Fair Haven—while struggling to support themselves with farm work.[5] Exploitation is not uncommon. At the same time, there is striving and hope. In a few locations, such as Grand Avenue in Fair Haven, businesses run mainly by Mexicans and catering to Latin American needs and tastes have gained a following. There are also a few Argentinean businesses in Fair Haven. If the immigrants stay, they will undoubtedly start more enterprises. One of the things that sets twenty-first-century New Haven apart from New Haven during the peak period of Italian immigration is that the native middle-class population is receptive to the foods of other lands. Local people will support immigrant-run restaurants and perhaps other immigrant enterprises.

Although the new immigrants may repeat some of the patterns of the Italians, it's important to keep in mind how much has changed in employment and in the nature of social life. The New Haven of fifty to one hundred years ago was an intensely personal, close-knit place, comprised of small neighborhoods where people lived close to work and where residents and shopkeepers knew one another. In the 1910s, an estimated three thousand retailers conducted business in working-class neighborhoods and downtown.[6] Just prior to World War I, New Haven boasted 608 grocery stores—the great majority of them tiny neighborhood establishments where the proprietor knew the customers.[7] It was a city in which people walked because they had to live close to the sources of their daily needs and because automobile ownership was not as commonplace as it is today. Boundaries were small and sharp. Today, neighborhood-based retailers are far fewer. Neighborhood ties are weaker. Employers are farther away from the homes of their workers.

The Italian American experience captured in this book is not about to be repeated. New Haven has undergone a transformation, which is composed, as most things are, of both good and bad. There is no going back.

NOTES

1. Jerre Mangione and Ben Morreale, *La Storia: Five Centuries of the Italian American Experience* (New York: Harper-Collins Publishers, 1992), 96.

2. Richard Gambino, *Blood of My Blood (New* York: Doubleday & Company, 1974), 88.

3. Harold Hornstein, *New Haven Celebrates the Bicentennial* (New Haven Bicentennial Commission, 1976).

4. Antonio Cannelli, *La Colonia Italiana di New Haven, Connecticut* (Stabilimento Tipografico A. Cannelli Co., 1921), 77.

5. Ibid. Cannelli's estimate of 60,000 Italians living in New Haven's neighborhoods in 1920 includes a large number who refused to be counted in the census or to become citizens for fear of reprisals or physical harm, 274–275. Jerome K. Myers, *The Differential Time Factor in Assimilation: A Study of Aspects and Processes of Assimilation Among the Italians of New Haven,* Ph.D diss., Yale University, 1950, reported 34,558 Italians in the city in 1920. See 26–27. By 1960, New Haven had the largest percentage of Italians of any city in the United States, See *The Italian Experience in the United States,* Silvano M. Tomasi and Madeline H. Engel (Center for Migration Studies, 1970), 35. By 1930, Italians had formed one-fifth of the state's population and approximately one-third of the population of New Haven, the second largest city in the state. See Samuel Koenig, *Immigrant Settlements in Connecticut: Their Growth and Characteristics* (Works Progress Administration Federal Writers' Project For The State Of Connecticut, Connecticut State Department Of Education, Hartford, 1938), 24–27.

6. Antonio Cannelli reported the potential for violence in New Haven when Italian railroad laborers who were digging track beds for the West Cut were attacked by a mob of over three hundred who threw rocks and beat them with clubs. The Italians were forced to leave and later returned to work under police protection. See *La Colonia Italiana di New Haven, Connecticut* (Stabilimento Tipografico A. Cannelli Co., 1921), 72. Cannelli also described the discrimination Italian workers faced in spite of their strong work ethic, their ability to handle difficult jobs in the factories, and the danger they faced while working to complete the Shoreline East rail line, where ten lost their lives. He described the atmosphere in the city where verbal outbursts of prejudice against Italians were commonplace, 72. Italians in the trades at the turn of the century were also paid less than their native counterparts: the native machinist earned $16.00 for a fifty hour week compared to $12.50 for Italians, native carpenters $19.75, the Italian carpenter $11.50, the native stone cutter earned $4.00 a day, the Italian $2.85. The greatest disparity was stone masons. The native earned $22.05 compared to $11.85, see *United States Dept. of Labor Bulletin, Vol. 15. No's 71–73,* Washington, 1907. Also see Michael J. Petriccione, *The Immigrant City of New Haven: A Study in Italian*

Social Mobility 1890–1930, senior honors thesis, University of New Haven, 1979, 53–54.

7. Thelma A. Dreis, *A Handbook of Social Statistics of New Haven, Connecticut* (New Haven: Yale University Press, 1936), 78. There were four Italian American bankers listed in 1901: Angelo Porto, Antonio Pepe, Pasquale Fusco, and Frank DeLucia. By the '30s, neighborhood banks sprang up around the city: the Pallotti-Andretti Bank on Chapel and Olive Street, the Sons of Italy Industrial Bank, and the Gennaro Franco Bank at Columbus and Water Street, see *New Haven Register,* March 2, 1930.

8. Phyllis H. Williams, *South Italian Folkways in Europe and America* (New Haven: Institute of Human Relations and Yale University Press, 1938), 127.

9. Lassonde, Stephen, *Learning to Forget* (New Haven: Yale University Press, 2005), 53–80.

10. Alfred W. Crosby Jr., *Epidemic and Peace, 1918* (Berkeley: Greenwood Press, 1976), 207.

11. Ibid., 228

12. Ibid., 228.

13. Ibid. For a breakdown of the percentage of deaths in the city of New Haven on the basis of the total population of approximately 162,000, see 207 "Mortality Figures," Table II.

14. Eugene Lyons, *The Life and Death of Sacco and Vanzetti* (New York: DaCapo Press, 1970), 193–194. Nicola Sacco and Bartolomeo Vanzetti composed letters from their jail cells to Sacco's son Dante shortly before their execution (193–195). They offer a look into the states of mind of two condemned men who still wrote with eloquence and humility. On August 18, 1927, Nicola Sacco wrote to his fourteen-year-old son, "Remember always, Dante, in the play of happiness, don't you use all for yourself only, but down yourself just one step, at your side and help the weak ones that cry for help, help the persecuted and the victim because they are your better friends, they are the comrades that fight and fall as your father and Bartolo (Vanzetti) fought and fell yesterday for the conquest and freedom for all poor workers. In this struggle of life you will find more love and you will be loved," After Dante was taunted in school as the son of a murderer, Vanzetti wrote him the day before his execution, on August 21, 1927, "I tell you all this now, for I know well your father, he is not a criminal, but one of the bravest men I ever knew. Someday you will understand what I am about to tell you, that your father has sacrificed everything dear and sacred to the human heart and soul for his faith in liberty and justice for all. That day you will be proud of your father, and if you become brave enough, you will take his place in the struggle between tyranny and liberty and you will vindicate our name and our blood. Remember, and also know, Dante, that if your father and I had been cowards and hypocrites and rinnegators [renegades] of our faith, we would not have been put to death. They would not even have convicted a leprous dog; not even executed a deadly poisonous scorpion on such evidence as they have framed against us. They would have given a new trial to a matricide and habitual felon on the evidence we presented for a new trial" (194).

15. Phyllis H. Williams, *South Italian Folkways in Europe and America* (New Haven: Institute of Human Relations and Yale University Press, New Haven, 1938), 22.

16. Rollin G. Osterwies, *Three Centuries of New Haven* (New Haven: Yale University Press, 1953), 329.

17. Nathan Glazer and Daniel Moynihan, *Beyond the Melting Pot* (Cambridge: M.I.T. Press, 1963), 184. For a greater discussion of the unskilled in Italy, see Leonard Covello, "The Social Background of the Italo-American Schoolchild," 78–102.

18. Bilevitz, "The Connecticut Needle Trades," *The Nation,* November 1932, 477.

19. *New York Times,* May 2, 1886.

20. Frank R. Annunziato, *Made in New Haven,* Labor's Heritage, Vol. 4, No. 4, 26. For a greater discussion of comparative wages in the needle trades in the '30s, see Frank R. Annunziato, *The Corset Industry and its Employees in New Haven During the Gilded Age*; Douglas M. Reynolds and Katheryn Viens, *New England's Disharmony: The Consequences of the Industrial Revolution,* 54. The average weekly wage for corset workers in 1932 was $13.90, women in tailored garments ($13.20), children's apparel ($11.15), women's underwear ($9.75), men's shirts ($9.65) and the average wage of all women in the apparel industry, $12.35. The average wage for one New Haven dress shop was $2.13. In a "contract" shop where sewers finished products from materials sent from New York, the average wage for a fifty hour week was $8.11, and $5.51 for a forty-eight hour week. See William Bilevitz, "The Connecticut Needle Trades," *The Nation,* November 1932, 477.

21. Ibid., Frank R. Annunziato, *Made in New Haven,* Labor's Heritage, Vol. 4, No. 4, 32.

22. Phyllis H. Williams, *South Italian Folkways in Europe and America* (New Haven: Institute of Human Relations and Yale University Press, 1938), 1.

23. Robert Lemley and Jonathan Morris. *The New History of the Italian South: The Mezzogiorno Revisited* (Devon, U.K.: University of Exeter Press, 1997), 95.

24. Ibid., 97.

25. Nathan Glazer and Daniel Moynihan, *Beyond the Melting Pot* (Cambridge: M.I.T. Press, 1963), 184.

26. Jerre Mangione and Ben Morreale, *La Storia: Five Centuries of the Italian American Experience* (New York: Harper-Collins Publishers, 1992), 74.

27. Richard Gambino, *Blood of My Blood* (New York: Doubleday & Company, 1974), 107.

28. Jerome K. Myers, *The Differential Time Factor in Assimilation,* Ph.D. diss., Yale University, 1950, 25.

29. Jerre Mangione and Ben Morreale, *La Storia: Five Centuries of the Italian American Experience* (New York: Harper-Collins Publishers, 1992), 97.

30. Ibid., 89. Elderly storytellers in Boston and New Haven told the author of similar experiences, traveling back and forth to Italy more than ten times.

31. Wyman, Mark, *Round-Trip to America* (Cornell University Press, 1993), 134.

32. Jerome K. Myers, *The Differential Time Factor in Assimilation,* Ph.D. diss., Yale University, 1950. For a full discussion of Italians in unskilled, semiskilled ranks and clerical positions in New Haven, see 109–113. For a breakdown of skilled and unskilled workers during the Depression, see Leo S. Role, *Ethnic Groups in American Society: The Dynamics of Social Assimilation,* Ph.D. diss., Yale University, 1940, 180.

33. Mark J. Minninberg, *Saving New Haven* (New Haven: Fine Arts Publications, 1988), 70. For a full discussion of bank closures, see 65–71.

34. William H. Johnston, *On the Outside Looking In: Irish, Italian and Black Ethnic Politics in an American City,* Ph.D. diss., Yale University, 1977, 9.

35. John B. Whitelaw, *The Administration of the Elementary School as the Coordinating Social Factor in the Community,* Ph.D. diss., Yale University, 1935, 125. While New Haven was in the throes of the Depression, Yale University experienced a building boom of magnificent libraries and school buildings from the fortunes of Standard Oil founders John W. Sterling and Howard S. Harkness. Yale increased their buying of property by 20% while

paying no taxes to the city's depleted grand list, prompting Mayor Murphy to appeal for help. He received a stern reply from President Angel, labelling the city as "a threat not only to liberal education and learning, but to truth itself." See Mark Minneberg, *Saving New Haven* (New Haven: Fine Arts Publications, 1988), 62 – 63.

36. Antonio Cannelli, *La Colonia Italiana di New Haven, Connecticut* (Stabilimento Tipografico A Cannelli Co., 1921), 126. For a full discussion of Italian feasts see *Italian Folkways*, 138.

37. Bolton King and Thomas Okey, *Italy Today* (New York: Charles Scribner's Sons, 1913), 138.

38. Ibid., 380.

39. Morty Miller, *New Haven: The Italian Community*, undergraduate senior thesis, Department of History, Yale University, 1969, 30.

40. William M. Johnston, *On the Outside Looking In: Irish, Italian and Black Ethnic Politics in an American City*, Yale University, Ph.D. diss., 1978, 183. The Marchegiano Club of New Haven listed four thousand members at its high point. See Robert M. Lattanzi, *Oyster Village to Melting Pot: The Hill Section of New Haven* (Chester, Conn.: Pattaconk Book Publications, 2000), 131.

41. Jerre Mangione and Ben Morreale, *La Storia: Five Centuries of the Italian American Experience* (New York: Harper-Collins Publishers, 1992), 22.

42. Phyllis H. Williams, *South Italian Folkways in Europe and America* (New Haven: Yale University Press, 1938), 28.

43. Morty Miller, *New Haven: The Italian Community*, undergraduate senior thesis, Department of History, Yale University, 1969, 34.

44. Ibid., 46. Also in *Annual Report of the Board of Education of the New Haven City School District for the Year Ending 1890*.

45. Jerre Mangione and Ben Morreale, *La Storia: Five Centuries of the Italian American Experience* (New York: Harper-Collins Publishers, 1992), 34.

46. Lawrence DiStasi, *Una Storia Segreta* (Berkeley: Heyday Books, 2001), 306.

47. Phyllis H. Williams, *South Italian Folkways in Europe and America* (New Haven: Yale University Press, 1938), 24.

48. Ibid., 25.

49. Jerre Mangione and Ben Morreale, *La Storia: Five Centuries of the Italian American Experience* (New York: Harper-Collins Publishers, 1992), 197.

50. The National Foundation of Italian Americans estimates that 1.5 million Italian Americans served in World War II. Enlisted men were counted by religion and race rather than ethnicity.

51. Fire Marshall Eugene Milligan's Report of Fire stated that the fire escape failed to operate properly because the women could not push the heavy release bar that would have allowed the fire escape's stairway to swing open and down to ground level. He stated that people pushing behind the first group forced them to duck under the release bar, causing the stairway to remain locked in place. The fire escape apparatus was removed after the fire and tested by the fire department which deemed it operative. Storytellers gave other reasons why the fire escape was locked and failed to open. The first was to keep schoolchildren from playing with it as they walked along the street: the other was to keep workers from leaving the building, a well-known practice by owners.

52. *The New Haven Register,* January 28, 1957.

53. John B. Whitelaw, *The Administration of the Elementary School as the Coordinating Social Factor in the Community,* Ph.D. diss., Yale University, 1935, 111–112.

54. Antonio Cannelli, *La Colonia Italiana di New Haven, Connecticut* (Stabilimento Tipografico A. Cannelli Co., 1921), mentions the actual streets where southern Italians lived, 80. Modenesi from Cavezzo and others from Tuscany are noted living in the Hill. See Robert, M. Lattanzi, *Oyster Village to Melting Pot: The Hill Section of New Haven* (Chester, Conn.: Pattaconk Book Publications, 2000), 129. Storytellers interviewed for this book noted Pugliesi from Bari, Calabrian, and Sicilian families living in the Hill.

55. Samuel Koenig, *Immigrant Settlements in Connecticut: Their Growth and Characteristics* (Works Progress Administration Federal Writers' Project For The State Of Connecticut, Connecticut State Department Of Education, Hartford, 1938), 27–28. Also William M. Johnston, *On the Outside Looking In: Irish, Italian and Black Ethnic Politics in an American City,* Yale University, Ph.D. diss., 1978, 180.

56. Virginia M. Galpin, *New Haven Oyster Industry 1638–1987* (The New Haven Colony Historical Society, 1989), 7. Oysters were the main fishery product in the U.S. in 1900 and eaten three times a week by New Haveners. The author describes the area in earlier times: When a person sailed into New Haven harbor in the middle of the nineteenth century, he saw farmlands, a few houses on the eastern shore, wharves in Morris Cove, settlements of Indians up toward the mouth of the Quinnipiac River, and more farmland behind the oystermen's community in Fair Haven. Oyster farms and shipyards lined the river, Ibid.,17.

57. Mayor Lee's idea of forming the Citizens Action Commission initially met resistance from community and business leaders. After convincing his good friend Whitney Griswold, president of Yale, to sign on as vice chairman, others soon followed. See Allan R. Talbot, *The Mayor's Game* (New York: Harper & Row, 1967), 64. For the composition of the Citizens Action Committee, see Fred Powledge, *Model City* (New York: Simon and Schuster, 1970), 30–31.

58. Douglas W. Rae, *City: Urbanism and Its End* (New Haven: Yale University Press, 2003). For a breakdown of households by neighborhood that were displaced by urban renewal, see 339. For the purposes of this book, the number of households displaced were: Wooster Square, 2710, the Hill, 1049; Oak Street, 886, and Fair Haven, 107 families. For a breakdown in business dislocations by neighborhood, see 343. Wooster Square, 450, Oak Street (Legion Avenue), 250; the Hill, 81; and Fair Haven, 8.

59. Alvin Merman inscribed a personal note to his family on the first page of his pamphlet "Relocating Families; The New Haven Experience 1956–1966," which expressed concern that his original manuscript was "condensed, re-arranged, and emasculated by the feds." He ended the note with a cryptic sentence, "I feel much essential material and warmth has been eliminated," hinting perhaps that the information he recorded about his experiences with poor dislocated families and the unreported shortcomings of relocation planning would have embarrassed HUD and the Lee administration.

60. Fred Powledge, *Model City* (New York: Simon and Schuster, 1970), 79.

61. Herbert J. Gans, *The Urban Villagers* (The Free Press, New York, 1962). The West Enders of Boston, whose neighborhood was bulldozed from 1958 to 1960, did not regard their community as a slum, as professional city planners did, and they shared the same

view of their homes and streets as the residents of New Haven's Wooster Square, Hill, and Legion Avenue neighborhoods prior to their destruction in the 1950s. Boston's caretakers and New Haven's city planners imposed a misguided public policy based on upwardly mobile, suburban middle class values, failing to take into consideration the accepted lifestyle of the working class and their self-contained, independent neighborhoods of the city with their uniquely intricate networks of social interaction. See 315–316.

NOTES TO AFTERWORD: NEW HAVEN TODAY

1. Douglas W. Rae, *City: Urbanism and Its End* (New Haven: Yale University Press, 2003), 351.
2. Rae, 324.
3. Rae, 343.
4. Rae, 338–39.
5. The July 31, 1997 New Haven *Advocate* published a package of articles by Paul Bass and others exposing the deplorable living conditions of migrant workers in Fair Haven and in the Cedar Hill neighborhood. The lead article was "Harvest of Squalor" by Paul Bass with Joshua Westlund. A house at 371 Ferry Street in Fair Haven that was inhabited by thirty-five people was reported on in "The Migrant: In a Living Hell, Still Hopeful" by Bass.
6. Rae, 203.
7. Rae, 236.

BIBLIOGRAPHY

Bakke, Wight E. *After the Shutdown.* New Haven: Institute of Human Relations, Yale University, 1934.

Barberio, G. Chiodi. *Il Progresso degli Italiani nel Connecticut.* New Haven: Maturo's Printing and Publishing Co., 1933.

Cannelli, Antonio. *La Colonia Italiana di New Haven, Connecticut.* Stabilimento Tipografico A. Cannelli Co., New Haven: privately printed, 1921.

Carnevale, Joseph W. *Who's Who Among Americans of Italian Descent in Connecticut.* New Haven, Carnevale Publishing Co., 1942.

Covello, Leonard. *The Social Background of the Italo-American Schoolchild,* Totowa: Rowman and Littlefield, 1972.

Crosby, Alfred W. Jr. *Epidemic and Peace, 1918.* Berkeley: Greenwood Press, 1976.

Chubb, Judith. *Patronage, Power and Poverty.* Cambridge and New York: Cambridge University Press, 1982.

Cupelli, Alberto. *The Italian of Old New Haven.* Privately printed, 1972.

Dahl, Robert A. *Who Governs?* New Haven: Yale University Press, 1961.

D'Ascoli, Francesco. *Nuovo Vocabolario Dialettale Napoletano.* S.A.S., 1993.

DiStasi, Lawrence. *Una Storia Segreta.* Berkeley: Heyday Books, 2001.

Dries, Thelma A. *A Handbook of Social Statistics of New Haven, Connecticut.* New Haven: Yale University Press, 1936.

Foerster, Robert F. *The Italian Emigration of Our Times.* Cambridge: Harvard University Press, 1924.

Galpin, Virginia M. *New Haven Oyster Industry 1638–1987.* The New Haven Colony Historical Society, 1989.

Gambino, Richard. *Blood of My Blood.* New York: Doubleday, 1974.

Gambino, Richard. *Vendetta.* Garden City, New York: Doubleday & Company, Inc., 1977.

Gans, Herbert J. *The Urban Villagers.* New York: The Free Press, 1962.

Glazer, Nathan, and Daniel Moynihan. *Beyond the Melting Pot.* Cambridge: M.I.T. Press, 1963.

Graves, Pierre B. *The Malevolent Eye.* New York: Peter Long Publishing, 1995.

Harney, Robert F., and Scarpaci, Vincenza J. (editors). *Little Italies in North America.* Toronto: The Multicultural History Society of Ontario, 1981.

Hill, Everett G. *A Modern History of New Haven and Eastern New Haven County.* New York: S. J. Clarke Publishing Company, 1918.

Hingham, John. *Strangers in the Land: Patterns of American Nativism 1860–1925.* New Brunswick: Rutgers University Press, 1955.

Hornstein, Harold. *New Haven Celebrates the Bicentennial.* New Haven: New Haven Bicentennial Commission, 1976.

Jacobs, Jane. *The Life and Death of American Cities.* New York: Random House, 1961.

King, Bolton, and Thomas Okey. *Italy Today.* New York: Charles Scribner's Sons, 1913.

Koenig, Samuel. *Immigrant Settlements in Connecticut: Their Growth and Characteristics.* Works Progress Administration Federal Writers' Project for the State of Connecticut, Connecticut State Department of Education, Hartford, 1938.

Krase, Jerome, and Frank M. Sorrentino, eds. *The Review of Italian American Studies.* Lanham, Md.: Lexington Books, 2000.

Lassonde, Stephen. *Learning to Forget: School and Family Life in New Haven's Working Class, 1870–1940.* New Haven: Yale University Press, 2005.

Lattanzi, Robert M. *Oyster Village to Melting Pot: The Hill Section of New Haven.* Chester, Conn.: Pattaconk Book Publications, 2000.

Lemley, Robert, and Jonathan Morris. *The New History of the Italian South: The Mezzogiorno Revisited.* Devon, U.K.: University of Exeter Press, 1997.

Levi, Carlo. *Christ Stopped at Eboli.* New York: Farrar, Straus and Company, 1947.

LoPreato, Joseph. *Italian Americans.* New York: Random House, 1970.

Lyons, Eugene. *The Life and Death of Sacco and Vanzetti.* New York: DaCapo Press, 1970.

Malden, Martin, and Mair Parry. *The Dialects of Italy.* London and New York: Routledge, 1997.

Mangione, Jerre, and Ben Morreale. *La Storia: Five Centuries of the Italian American Experience.* New York: HarperCollins, 1992.

Maynard, Preston, and Marjorie B. Noyes. *Carriages and Clocks, Corsets and Locks: The Rise and Fall of an Industrial City—New Haven, Connecticut.* Hanover, N.H.: University Press of New England, 2004.

Miller, Helen H. *Sicily and the Western Colonies of Greece.* New York: Charles Scribner's Sons, 1965.

Mininberg, Mark J. *Saving New Haven.* New Haven: Fine Arts Publications, 1988.

Nelli, Hubert S. *From Immigrants to Ethnics: The Italian Americans.* Oxford and New York: Oxford University Press, 1983.

New Haven City Directories, 1905–1935. New Haven: Price and Less Co., 1905–1935.

Nugent, Walter. *Crossings: The Great Transatlantic Migration 1870–1914.* Bloomington: Indiana University Press, 1992.

Osterwies, Rollin G. *Three Centuries of New Haven.* New Haven: Yale University Press, 1953.

Powledge, Fred. *Model City.* New York: Simon and Schuster, 1970.

Rae, Douglas W. *City: Urbanism and Its End.* New Haven: Yale University Press, 2003.

Rossi, Adolfo. *Un Italiano in America.* Milan: Treves Brothers, 1894.

Salzano, Antonio. *Vocabolario Napoletano-Italiano.* S.E.N., Napoli, 1980.

Sinclair, Upton. *Boston.* Long Beach: Upton Sinclair, 1928.

Smith, Denis M. *Italy, A Modern History.* Ann Arbor: The University of Michigan Press, 1959.

Sterba, Christopher M. *Good Americans: Italian and Jewish Immigrants during the First World War.* New York: Oxford Universithy Press, 2003.

Strati, Saverio. *Miti, Racconti E Leggende.* Rome: Gangemi Press, 1985.

Talbot, Allan R. *The Mayor's Game.* New York: Harper & Row, 1967.

Tomasi, Silvano M., and Madeline H. Engel. *The Italian American Experience in the United States.* Staten Island, N.Y.: Center for Migration Studies, 1970.

Verga, Giovanni, *I Malavoglia.* Milan, Italy: Oscar Mondadori Press, 1939.

Verga, Giovanni, *The House by the Medlor Tree.* Berkeley: University of California Press, 1983.

Washington, Booker T. *The Man Farthest Down.* Garden City, New York: Doubleday, Page and Company, 1912.

Williams, Phyllis H. *South Italian Folkways in Europe and America.* New Haven: Institute of Human Relations and Yale University Press, 1938.

Wyman, Mark. *Round-Trip to America.* Ithaca and London: Cornell University Press, 1993.

ESSAYS AND THESES

Johnston, William M. *On the Outside Looking In: Irish, Italian and Black Ethnic Politics in an American City.* Ph.D. diss., Yale University, 1977.

Miller, Morty. *New Haven: The Italian Community.* Undergraduate senior thesis, Department of History, Yale University, 1969.

Myers, Jerome K. *The Differential Time Factor in Assimilation: A Study of Aspects and Processes of Assimilation Among the Italians of New Haven.* Ph.D. diss., Yale University, 1950.

Petriccione, Michael J. *The Immigrant City of New Haven: A Study in Italian Social Mobility 1890–1930.* Senior honors thesis, University of New Haven, 1979.

Srole, Leo. *The Ethnic Communal System.* Ph.D. diss., Chicago University, 1940.

Whitelaw, John B. *The Administration of the Elementary School as the Coordinating Social Factor in the Community.* Ph.D. diss., Yale University, 1935.

ARTICLES AND PAMPHLETS

Annunziato, Frank R. "Made in New Haven," *Labor's Heritage,* Vol. 4, No. 4, 26.

———. "The Corset Industry and Its Employees in New Haven during the Gilded Age. In *New England's Disharmony: The Consequences of the Industrial Revolution,* ed. Douglas M. Reynolds and Katheryn Viens.

Bilevitz, William. "The Connecticut Needle Trades," *The Nation,* November 16, 1932.

D'Agostino Mautner, Raeleen. "American Attitudes Towards Italian Americans," *American Italian Defense Association,* October, 2004.

Gurwitt, Rob. "Death of a Neighborhood, New Haven's Oak Street," *Mother Jones,* September/October, 2000.

Lowe, Jeanne R. "Lee of New Haven and His Political Jackpot," *Harper's,* October, 1957.

Merwin, Alvin A. "Relocating Families: The New Haven Experience 1956 to 1966," National Association of Housing and Redevelopment Officials, 1970.

Mulligan, Richard E. Connecticut State Police Investigation Report, February 25, 1957.

New Haven Citizens Action Commission. "New Haven CAC Third Annual Report, 1957."

New Haven Citizens Action Commission. "New Haven CAC Second Annual Report, 1956."

Proto, Neil T. "Sacco and Vanzetti, An Unfinished American Injustice," Italian America, September, 1996.

INDEX OF PHOTOGRAPHS